ECONOMICS AND HUMAN WELFARE

Essays in Honor of Tibor Scitovsky

This is a volume in
ECONOMIC THEORY, ECONOMETRICS,
AND MATHEMATICAL ECONOMICS

A Series of Monographs and Textbooks

Consulting Editor: KARL SHELL

A complete list of titles in this series appears at the end of this volume.

ECONOMICS
AND
HUMAN WELFARE

Essays in Honor of Tibor Scitovsky

Edited by   *MICHAEL J. BOSKIN*
Department of Economics
Stanford University
Stanford, California

 1979

ACADEMIC PRESS
A Subsidiary of Harcourt Brace Jovanovich, Publishers

New York   London   Toronto   Sydney   San Francisco

ACADEMIC PRESS, INC.
111 Fifth Avenue, New York, New York 10003

United Kingdom Edition published by
ACADEMIC PRESS, INC. (LONDON) LTD.
24/28 Oval Road, London NW1 7DX

Library of Congress Cataloging in Publication Data

Main entry under title:

Economics and human welfare.

    1. Economics--Addresses, essays, lectures. 2. Wel-
fare economics--Addresses, essays, lectures. 3. Scitovsky, Tibor. I. Boskin, Michael J.

HB34.E2727   330   78-22519
ISBN 0-12-118850-7

PRINTED IN THE UNITED STATES OF AMERICA

79 80 81 82   9 8 7 6 5 4 3 2 1

Contents

PART I   WELFARE ECONOMICS AND MICROECONOMIC THEORY

Economic Growth and Its Discontents

MOSES ABRAMOVITZ

The Property Rights Doctrine and Demand Revelation under Incomplete Information

KENNETH J. ARROW

On Two Experiments in the Pricing of Theater Tickets

WILLIAM J. BAUMOL

From Growth to the Millenium: Economics and the Transformation of the Idea of Progress

PAUL A. DAVID

Appraisal of Project Appraisal

JÁNOS KORNAI

The Size Distribution of Income: How Has It Changed?

MORDECAI KURZ

PART III MACROECONOMICS

Equilibrium Theory and Growth Theory
NICHOLAS KALDOR

Dynamic Competition and Economic Stability
BURTON H. KLEIN

The Economics of Keynes
JOHN H. POWER

The Aggregate Supply Function in Keynes's General Theory
LORIE TARSHIS

Money and the Money Wage Rate
PAUL WELLS

List of Contributors

Numbers in parentheses indicate the pages on which the authors' contributions begin.

MOSES ABRAMOVITZ (3), Department of Economics, Stanford University, Stanford, California 94305

KENNETH J. ARROW* (23), Project on Efficiency on Decision Making in Economic Systems, Harvard University, Cambridge, Massachusetts 02138

WILLIAM J. BAUMOL (41), Department of Economics, Princeton University, Princeton, New Jersey 08540, and New York University, New York, New York 10003

MICHAEL J. BOSKIN (219), Department of Economics, Stanford University, Stanford, California 94305

PAUL A. DAVID (59), Department of Economics, Stanford University, Stanford, California 94305

PHILIPPE R. DE VILLE (219), Department of Economics, Catholic University of Louvain, 1348 Louvain-Neuve, Belgium

H. ROBERT HELLER (233), Financial Studies Division, Research Department, International Monetary Fund, Washington, D.C. 20431

* Present address: Department of Economics, Stanford University, Stanford, California 94305.

NICHOLAS KALDOR (273), Kings College, Cambridge University, Cambridge, United Kingdom

BURTON H. KLEIN (293), Division of Humanities and Social Sciences, California Institute of Technology, Pasadena, California 91109

JÁNOS KORNAI (75), Institute of Economics, Hungarian Academy of Sciences, Budapest V, Hungary

MORDECAI KURZ (101), Department of Economics, Stanford University, Stanford, California 94305

I. M. D. LITTLE (125), Nuffield College, Oxford OX1 1NF, United Kingdom

RONALD I. MCKINNON (249), Department of Economics, Stanford University, Stanford, California 94305

JOHN H. POWER (321), Department of Economics, University of Hawaii at Monoa, Honolulu, Hawaii 96822

M. W. REDER (133), Graduate School of Business, University of Chicago, Chicago, Illinois 60637

WALTER S. SALANT (147), The Brookings Institution, Washington, D.C. 20036

M. FG. SCOTT (163), Nuffield College, Oxford OX1 1NF, United Kingdom

AMARTYA SEN (183), Oxford University, Oxford OX1 1NF, United Kingdom

J. E. STIGLITZ* (203), Department of Economics, Stanford University, Stanford, California 94305

LORIE TARSHIS (361), Scarborough College, West Hill, Ontario, Canada

PAUL WELLS (393), Department of Economics, University of Illinois, Urbana, Illinois 61801

* Present address: Department of Economics, Princeton University, Princeton, New Jersey 08540.

Preface

Tibor Scitovsky's scholarly work has spanned virtually all of economics. Tibor himself has influenced economists of several generations and many nations. From his earliest papers on welfare economics and the Pigou effect through numerous articles and books on international trade, economic development, and welfare economics to his recent research on the very boundaries of economics and its sister social sciences, his work combines the highest professional standards with a rare originality. The essays that follow, by some of his colleagues, students, and friends, were presented to Tibor in honor of his sixty-fifth birthday. We hope that they not only display that very special affection we all feel for him but live up to the high standards he himself has set.

Acknowledgments

Permission to include previously published material in this work is gratefully acknowledged:

Excerpts on pp. 6 and 9 from Hadley Cantril (1965), *The Pattern of Human Concerns.* Copyright © 1965 by Rutgers, The State University. Reprinted by permission of Rutgers University Press.

Excerpt on p. 60 from J. B. Bury (1932), *The Idea of Progress,* by permission of Macmillan, London and Basingstoke.

Excerpts on pp. 80 and 88 from I. M. D. Little and J. A. Mirrlees (1974), *Project Appraisal and Planning for Developing Countries,* by permission of Heinemann Educational Books Ltd., London, and Basic Books Inc., New York.

Excerpts on pp. 143 and 344 from A. Marshall (1920, 1948), *Principles of Economics,* 8th ed. Published by Macmillan, London and Basingstoke.

Excerpt on p. 152 condensed from *Newsweek.* Copyright 1973, by Newsweek, Inc. All rights reserved. Reprinted by permission.

Excerpt on p. 168 from E. F. Denison (1957), Theoretical aspects of quality change, capital consumption and net capital formation, in *Problems of Capital Formation* (Studies in Income and Wealth, **19**)*,* by permission of the National Bureau of Economic Research.

Excerpt on p. 176 from G. Stuvel (1959), Asset revaluation and terms of trade effects in the framework of the national accounts, *Economic Journal* (June), by permission of Cambridge University Press.

Excerpt on p. 185 from I. M. D. Little (1957), *A Critique of Welfare Economics,* 2nd ed. Copyright © 1957 by Oxford University Press, Inc. Used by permission.

Portions of Ronald S. McKinnon's article are adapted from his book *Money in International*

Exchange: The Convertible Currency System. Copyright © 1979 by Oxford University Press, Inc. Used by permission.

Excerpt on p. 284 from A. A. Young (1928), Increasing returns and economic progress, *Economic Journal* (December), by permission of Cambridge University Press.

Burton H. Klein's article has been expanded into a book-length treatment, *Dynamic Economics,* published by Harvard University Press, Cambridge, Massachusetts, 1977.

Excerpt on p. 322 from A. Leijonhufvud, *On Keynesian Economics and the Economics of Keynes,* by permission of Oxford University Press.

Excerpts on pp. 323 and 324 from Sir John Hicks, *The Crisis in Keynesian Economics.* © 1974 by Sir John Hicks. Basic Books Inc., Publishers, New York.

Excerpts on pp. 327, 336, 337, 338, 346, 350, 352, 353, 354, 355, 362, 363, 364, and 379 from John Maynard Keynes (1936), *The General Theory of Employment, Interest and Money,* used by permission of Macmillan, London and Basingstoke, and Harcourt Brace Jovanovich, New York.

Excerpt on pp. 333 and 334 from R. Solow (1970), *Growth Theory: An Exposition.* Copyright © 1970 by Oxford University Press, Inc. Used by permission.

Excerpt on p. 398 from P. Davidson (1969), A Keynesian view of the relationship between accumulation, money, and the money wage rate, *Economic Journal* **79,** by permission of Cambridge University Press.

PART I

WELFARE ECONOMICS AND MICROECONOMIC THEORY

Economic Growth and Its Discontents

*Moses Abramovitz**

1. The Growing Disenchantment with Economic Growth

Economic growth, whether called by that name or not, has been the prime goal of economic policy for a long time, and it has also been the prime criterion for judging the success of the economic performance of a country. The economists' rationale for this fact is, at least in rough terms, easily understood and briefly stated. National product per head is held to be the objective, measurable counterpart of economic welfare, which

* This paper was originally prepared as a public lecture at the University of Edinburgh and read there on 11 May 1975. It may be particularly appropriate for inclusion in the present volume because it is in good part an elaboration of a question raised and briefly answered by Scitovsky in the course of his important Kinley Lecture (1973) as well as in his later book, *The Joyless Economy* (1976). The present paper also returns to themes taken up in an earlier paper (Abramovitz, 1959). See also footnote 1.

means that part of our total state of satisfaction or happiness which depends on economic activity. Barring changes in income distribution, therefore, an increase in national product per head is supposed to mean an increase in economic welfare. According to the standard doctrine, it does not necessarily mean an increase in people's total welfare. Changes in technology and the modes of production may so alter the character of life as to offset the benefits of greater flows of material things. Economists have relied, however, on a practical judgment, namely, that a change in economic welfare implies a change in total welfare in the same direction, if not in the same degree. Pigou, the founder of welfare economics, said it, and certainly it has been widely believed that having more goods ought to do us *some* good. In addition, it was plausible to think that growing command over goods would also lead people to a more cultivated existence and that that would be conducive to happiness. Not only that, growth of total output seemed to be the most dependable and acceptable means of lifting people out of gross poverty. For poor countries, it is clearly the only way. For rich countries, it seemed the only way that also would avoid political tension and social conflict.

In the years since the World War II, the especially intense interest in growth rested on that basic outlook, but it was strengthened by other, rather special considerations. In many European countries, there had been a serious check to growth since 1913, that is, for over 30 years. Since in those countries it was widely realized that the gap between their incomes and that in the United States was far wider than could be justified by any difference in technological capability or in the skills of the population or in experience with commercial, industrial, or government organization and practice, there was a natural determination to reduce the income gap rapidly. In the Soviet Union, besides the spur of great poverty, there was also the reigning social doctrine which held that the advance to a true communist regime was dependent on the achievement of much higher levels of output. In the former colonial territories, power passed to nationalist governments who regarded industrial and agricultural development as conditions for establishing their new states on stable foundations. Between the Soviet Union and the United States, there were the rivalries of the cold war. In all private enterprise and mixed economies, the experience of the Great Depression had made the avoidance of unemployment a minimum aim. Everyone could see, or thought they could see, the connections between output growth and the provision of jobs. In the United States, finally, there was the special problem of the Blacks. The dominant opinion was that it would be far easier to overcome discrimination and so to promote social harmony in an atmosphere of growth and full employment than in a more nearly stationary economy.

Now, a quarter-century later, two things are abundantly clear. First, by all the usual measures, the growth that was sought was, in fact, achieved—indeed achieved in unexpected, unprecedented, and overflowing degree. It appears in broad measures of real national product per head, and it appears in the narrowest measures of consumption per head. In the developed countries, at least, the growth was widely shared by all income classes. So we have had it, and had it in great measure. But, second, the expected sense of heightened satisfaction, reflecting an appreciation of social gains and of bettered individual lives, is much less clear. Instead, the talk is all of "disenchantment" with growth. In saying this, I am not speaking of the collectivist societies or of the less-developed countries. I know little about them. I am talking of the more affluent industrialized societies of the West, and particularly of the United States. In America and, I believe, in Western Europe, I think one can sense a mood of disappointment in the achievement and, indeed, of increasing opposition to rapid growth in the future. Needless to say, the opposition is not official. It is not public policy, and the ordinary person is still eager for national growth as a source of higher income. But such opposition is the common currency of intellectual, academic, and much political discussion, and it shows itself in ways which suggest that at least an ambivalent attitude has become fairly widespread in America and also in Europe.

Let me give just one rather revealing illustration. At Stanford University, we arrange a gathering each year for our graduates. They spend several days at the University listening to lectures and taking part in seminars. For some years now one of the most popular seminars has been entitled "The Rat Race." Here, in the company of psychologists, sociologists, psychiatrists, etc., the graduates, young and old, conduct an inquest into their lives, and, as the title of the seminar suggests, the central question is why they find existence so frustrating, why they feel themselves on a treadmill.

Now, certain fairly substantial reasons for disappointment, disenchantment, and opposition are, of course, prominent and widely understood. There is the impact of growth on the environment—congestion, pollution, and noise in the cities, the spoiling of the wilderness and of wild life. In more recent years, there is the concern over the future of the race—over our ability to sustain growing populations in the face of declining sources of primary products and of mounting wastes. In the United States, and I believe elsewhere in the West, poverty, as we *measure* it, is just as widespread and the social problems associated with it, crime, drug addiction, and the rest, at least as intense as they were. These considerations raise immensely important questions, and they have been widely debated. I should like to suggest, however, that there has been another, perhaps more subtle, certainly a more personal and intimate source of disenchantment or discontent, and I can express that by saying simply that many people do not feel much better about their lives now than they did a generation ago. They do not seem to feel much happier than they did when, on the average, they were poorer. That, of course, is an assertion about which—to say the least—one cannot be utterly confident. In any event, I am going to cite some systematic evidence in support of it, and I am then going to proceed as if a sense of personal, individual disappointment in the fruits of growth is widespread and go on to talk about the reasons for it.

2. Surveys of Happiness

The evidence of personal disappointment in the fruits of growth comes from the results of successive surveys of their apparent levels of happiness as reported by fairly sizable samples of people.

These surveys are of two types. One is of the type of the Gallup Polls. They were, indeed, made by the Gallup organization and by the National Opinion Research Center in the United States and in certain other countries. In these surveys, intermingled with a variety of other questions, some of which established the income level of the respondents, people were asked to say whether they were "very happy," "pretty happy" (or "fairly happy"), or "not so happy." The other type of survey was made by a sociologist, Hadley Cantril (1965), in a pioneering study of the hopes, fears, and happiness of people in 14 countries. Cantril's technique involves a so-called self-anchoring striving scale. In this procedure, the respondent first describes [Cantril (1965), as quoted by Easterlin (1974, p. 91)],

> as the top anchoring point, his wishes and hopes as he personally conceives them and the realization of which would constitute for him the best possible life. At the other extreme he describes the worries and fears, the preoccupations and frustrations, embodied in his conception of the worst possible life he could imagine. Then, utilizing a non-verbal ladder device [showing a scale from 0 to 10] . . . he is asked where he stands on the ladder today. . . .

Surveys of the Gallup type were made in 9 countries, covering a wide spectrum of income levels, in 1965. Cantril's own surveys were conducted in 14 countries in 1960. Finally, there were 10 Gallup-type surveys conducted at fairly regular intervals in the United States between April 1946 and December 1970.

The results of these surveys were brought together by Easterlin (1974) in a fascinating article called "Does Economic Growth Improve the

Human Lot?'' Easterlin not only arranged the data so as to bring out the association between income and self-rated happiness, he considered carefully the possible biases in the procedure, as identified by the authors of the surveys, by their subsequent critics and by himself. Easterlin takes up such questions as these:

(1)   Could the surrounding questions in the survey have influenced people's responses to the happiness question?

(2)   Were the inquiries in the various surveys comparable over time and across countries?

(3)   Is the concept of happiness relevant in all cultures?

(4)   Were people's reported feelings sufficiently stable as a group in relation to the ups and downs of daily life?

(5)   Will a person report his true feelings and, even if not, is there any evidence of a bias associated with income?

(6)   Do the pooled opinions of outside judges support the answers of the respondents?

(7)   Could the apparent association of happiness with income be biased because of a correlation between income and other factors bearing on happiness?

The answers Easterlin gave to these questions are by no means a complete whitewash of the data, but they are dominantly favorable, and they persuade him that the surveys do, in fact, reveal something significant about the relations between income and people's perceptions of their own states of satisfaction. I rely on his appraisal.

The outcome of Easterlin's review of the surveys is striking. He reveals a contradiction in the reported association between income and happiness, and I propose to call this contradiction the *Easterlin paradox*. The paradox is this. If one considers people in a given country at a given time, one finds what an economist would expect, a strong, consistent, positive association between income and happiness. A much larger fraction of people in the upper income groups report themselves ''very happy'' than in lower income groups. This positive association runs right through all the individual surveys in different countries and in the same country at different times. On the other hand, if one compares countries with widely different income levels at about the same time, differences in reported happiness are small. That is, the percentage reporting themselves ''very happy'' is about the same in countries with high, medium, and low average income. If one compares the happiness reports from a given country, that is, from the United States, over a period of time during which incomes have risen markedly, there is no associated rise in reported happiness. How can these apparently contradictory results be reconciled? What can be frustrating the increase in satisfaction or welfare one would normally expect to accompany increases in average income over time or between countries? There are, in fact, a number of plausible influences. They are not necessarily rival explanations. They can be, and I believe they are, mutually supporting and work together to explain why economic growth seems to yield such disappointing results.

3.   What Can Explain the Easterlin Paradox?[1]

3.1   The Income-Relativity of Aspirations

To economists the Easterlin paradox has a familiar ring. Economists have already met something, which is at least its close cousin, and that is the different association between income, spending, and saving yielded by cross section and time-series data, respectively. The relative income hypothesis developed to explain that puzzle is transferable directly to the present conundrum. We assume that the satisfaction a person obtains from his income depends not on its absolute level but on its relation to those of others in the same community at the same time. If a person stands higher on the income ladder, he is the happier for it. But if there is an increase in the level of income with no change in people's relative positions, then nobody feels better off.

The idea behind the relative income hypothesis is commonplace, homely, and plausible. It gains credence from its apparent usefulness in other applications, not only to explanations of the spending–saving data, but also, as Easterlin has pointed out, to fertility behavior, to labor force participation, and, in the form of theories of "relative deprivation," to the understanding of political protest and popular uprisings.

That attitudes, tastes, and aspirations are governed by the experience of an individual, by his "socialization experience," and, therefore, by the relation of his income to the aspirations of others in his own income class is a cliché among sociologists, and it is only illustrated by the statements which Cantril reports and Easterlin quotes about the material demands of people in different countries. Here are two examples (Easterlin, 1974).

First a well-to-do 45-year-old housewife in India, family income about $80.00 a month:

---

[1] Of the four explanations offered in this section, the first was proposed by Easterlin himself (1974, p. 11 *et seq.*). The first, second, and fourth are suggested in Scitovsky's Kinley lecture (1973). The first and second explanations rest on ideas that have a long history in the writings of those who have been skeptical about the supposed relations between the growth of national wealth and that of individual welfare. They were used earlier by the present writer (1959). The origins of the third explanation are indicated in the text.

> I should like to have a water tap and a water supply in my house. It would also be nice to have electricity. My husband's wages must be increased if our children are to get an education and our daughter is to be married [p. 115].

Now a 28-year-old lawyer in the United States:

> Materially speaking, I would like to provide my family with an income to allow them to live well—to have the proper recreation, to go camping, to have music and dancing lessons for the children, and to have family trips. I wish we could belong to a country club and do more entertaining. We just bought a new home and expect to be satisfied with it—for a number of years [p. 115].

The relative income hypothesis also tells us why our hope that economic growth would eliminate poverty has been frustrated. By any absolute standard, of course, the progress has been enormous. In the mid-1930s, President Roosevelt declared that one-third of the American nation was "ill-housed, ill-clad, ill-nourished." At that time, the family income level below which one-third of United States families fell was $2000 (in 1970 prices). In 1970, less than one-twentieth of families had an income of $2000 or less.

By contemporary standards, however, little, if anything has happened. As incomes rose, the level which the community regards as tolerable also rose, and the rising standard has been embodied in administrative practice, for example, in the income levels used by state and private welfare agencies to fix eligibility for income subsidies. The result is that welfare rolls in the United States have *not* declined as a proportion of the population. Several studies both in the United States over time and across countries suggest that countries tend to set the poverty threshold at approximately one-half the median income in the country, whatever that happens to be (cf. Fuchs, 1967).

The intuitive appeal of the relative income hypothesis and the variety of supporting evidence will, I think, incline many people to believe that it carries some part of an explanation of the Easterlin paradox. And some of them, including some economists, will also agree that it casts some real doubt on the contribution that growth can make to welfare. In fact, such judgments have been made by many economists including some of the fathers of our discipline. Mill wrote [quoted by Pigou (1932)]:

> Men do not desire to be rich but to be richer than other men. The avaricious or covetous man would find little or no satisfaction in the possession of any amount of wealth, if he were the poorest amongst all his neighbors or fellow-countrymen [p. 89].

But, as economists, let us take note of just where we are. The foundation of our discipline admits of no such relativity principles. Our discipline rests on one simple idea: more is better. Once we admit a relative income hypothesis, we are having truck with psychology or sociology or both. And once we do that, we are driven to consider other such noneconomic theories.

3.2. Habituation

I can begin by quoting authority (Pigou, 1951):

> consider two undergraduates precisely alike in temperament and constitution. One is poor and goes on a cheap Continental holiday, stopping the night in youth hostels: the other does an exactly similar tour at much greater expense and stopping at luxury hotels. Each of them is conditioned by habit and experience to his circumstances. Is there any reason to suppose that the rich undergraduate has a better time . . . ? Yet again in prewar days well-to-do people had elaborate meals and had a number of servants to work for them. Now they have simpler meals and do their own work. After they have become accustomed to the new conditions, are they less happy than before? It is very doubtful whether a moderately well-to-do man is appreciably happier now than he would be if transplanted back to the pre-railway wage and attuned to the conditions of that age . . . [p. 294].

This suggests a second hypothesis with which we are also familiar from the spending–saving literature, in which the distinction between permanent and transitory income has been important. Suppose that people's feeling of satisfaction or pleasure depends not on the level of their incomes but on the novelty and stimulation of experiencing a higher level of income than they are used to—and the reverse with feelings of dissatisfaction. How can this help explain the Easterlin paradox? The answer is that the higher income groups are likely to contain a relatively large proportion of people whose incomes have recently risen, while low income groups will contain a relatively high proportion of those whose incomes have recently fallen. That difference will produce a positive association between income level and reported happiness in comparisons across income levels at any given time and place. But if the proportions of recent arrivals in the various income groups remained fairly constant, then in comparisons over time or across countries, there would be no change in the proportions who declare themselves happy.

This hypothesis corresponds to the findings of current psychological theory—in regard to which I am no expert. What I am about to report is based on Scitovsky's Kinley lecture (1973) and on his book, *The Joyless*

Economy (1976). My version is, I fear, a somewhat corrupt simplification of the matter. In the older psychology, and in the view of standard economics, needs and desires, if unfulfilled, cause tension, anxiety, and alertness, what psychologists would call a raised level of *arousal,* which is uncomfortable. Action is taken to reduce the level of arousal by satisfying the need or desire which gave rise to it so far as possible. The lower the level to which arousal can be brought, the greater the feeling of comfort or satisfaction.

Modern psychological theory, backed by a mass of experiment, however, holds that this is only half the story. Arousal can fall to too low a level. When it is too low, animals and humans take pleasure in action and in experience which raises the arousal level. The key to all such action and experience is novelty and change. *Action* which affords such stimulus satisfaction includes challenging work, artistic creation, exploration, and discovery. *Experience* which is a source of stimulation includes the arts, literature, travel, and also apparently the *process* of satisfying a previously unfulfilled need; it includes, therefore, the experience of exploring the novel possibilities of a higher level of income, but not its routine use.

If one can accept these doctrines, then the permanent–transitory distinction and the bias it lends to the population of the various income groups provides at least a partial explanation of the Easterlin paradox, one which is grounded in modern psychology. This view has a further and somewhat disturbing implication. It says that the level of satisfaction depends not—or at least not only—on the level of income but on its growth rate. Other things being equal, we should have to grow *faster* in order to be happier, and we should have to keep on growing just to stay in the same place. Is it any wonder that people feel caught in a rat race? Luckily, the novel experience of higher incomes is not the only source of stimulus satisfaction. There are other ways of finding the pleasures of stimulation than to run faster, though many people find them hard to discover or to cultivate.

3.3 The Rising Prices of Space and Time

The central ideas in the relative income hypothesis are social competition and the frustration of chasing rising aspirations. Actually, however, there is something more substantial in such disappointment than the built-in incapacity of the pursuing greyhound to catch the fleeing rabbit. When an average family thinks about the concrete things it lacks, the presence of which would be just enough to make it happy, it would seem natural that it should envisage them in terms of the particular goods and services, and the style of life of the families they observe who enjoy a larger income. Now surely one of the most important differences between the styles of life of the relatively poor and the relatively rich—at least in the past—was that the rich enjoyed larger living quarters, had more grounds about their houses, enjoyed a location giving easier access to the countryside or could afford comfortable transportation, and, both at home and on holiday, could, if they wanted it, have quiet, privacy, and seclusion. Surely another important difference was that the rich could afford servants and, more generally, command over "services." Now, if a family can raise its level of income relative to that of other families, it can, indeed, afford the life style of the richer families to which it had aspired. But it is well-nigh obvious that if the rise in a family's income occurs together with everyone else's, that will not be the case. The general rise of income is accompanied by a rise in the prices of space and of personal service, so that the average family cannot command more than it had before, certainly not as much as it had hoped for, and many people who used to command a great deal cannot afford as much. This, then is a third explanation of the Easterlin paradox, and I should like to develop the point just a little.

So far as space and matters closely related to space are concerned, the picture is somewhat mixed. Higher income has meant better housing for the average family. People can afford more transport, and automobiles have given ordinary people a wider choice of location, much more freedom of movement, and easier access to the mountains, the lakes, and the seashore than they used to have. On the other hand, a large part of the rise in incomes with which people try to buy spaciousness, ease, privacy, seclusion, an occasional romantic taste of an unspoilt wilderness is dissipated because the competition of more people for the same limited space has, in effect, raised the price of what we want.

As regards servants and "services," the problem is also not quite straightforward. It is not clearly true that the price of all kinds of service has become relatively high. There has been technological progress and productivity growth in the output of some services. With more knowledge, better diagnostic equipment, antibiotics, and so forth, a visit to a physician can now, in many instances, do some good. The price per hour is very high, but the price per cure has probably declined. But it is not easy to think of many equally clear-cut instances of productivity growth in the production of services. The cost of a television performance can be spread over thousands of viewers, but television is not theater. Symphony recordings are cheap per repetition, but listening to a recording is not the same as attending a live concert. Our general sense of the matter is, indeed, that productivity in the production of services has lagged behind that in goods production, and that the relative prices of services have risen steeply with the general rise of incomes. At given absolute levels of income, therefore, one cannot afford to consume as much service as used to be the case. Indeed, in the pure form of the problem, in which we assume that the productivity of an hour's service remains constant, there is a neat paradox which, I believe, Harrod (1958) was the first to define. The average man, no matter how rich he becomes, can never command the service of more than one other average man—even if he spends his entire income to buy it. This means, on the constant productivity assumption, that there is an absolute fixed maximum amount of "services" which average men can command, no matter how rich they become.

Schumpeter (1942, p. 67) expressed the same idea when he pointed out that it was not the things which mattered to Louis XIV which were cheapened by the Industrial Revolution. This statement actually has two implications, and they are both important. First, the poor benefit more than the rich from equal proportional increments of income—in their ability to enlarge the size of their previous market baskets. But, second, as the general average rises to the levels previously occupied by the rich, the new arrivals at each income level are frustrated. They cannot afford the new and different market basket to which they thought their higher incomes would give them access. It is an index-number problem. The initial-year price weights hold out a tantalizing vision of the uses to which we can put more income. But when the future arrives, the price weights have changed. Viewed in the light of the initial-year weights, our position is greatly improved, but who cares for that? Those things which we actually consume in larger quantity now have lower weights; those things which we must still deny ourselves have higher weights. Of course, the upwardly mobile are disappointed. This is only compounded by the annoyance of the older rich who are unable to live even as they used to do and want to do.

The rise in the price of services is the form which the rising price of time takes in the market place. There is, however, also the rising price of time at home, the price of time available for productive activities around the house or for so-called "leisure-time" activities. This is the question that Linder (1970) has dramatized in *The Harried Leisure Class*. Linder, of course, is building on the work of Becker, Muth, Mincer, and others who have been developing a general theory of the allocation of time and claiming that we can understand just about anything by using it, like age at marriage, and who marries whom, and fertility and contraception, labor-force participation, health care, mortality, and now, I understand, the afterlife. So why not a simple thing such as leisure and its uses!

A central proposition of the new theory—it is not, of course, a new proposition—is that consumption consists not in the purchase of consumer goods and services but rather in combining such purchased materials with the consumer's own time and effort to produce final utilities and satisfaction. That, of course, is why some of the newer national income accountants, such as Nordhaus and Tobin (1972), include the value of leisure and other nonmarket activity in their augmented national product account. As with ordinary production, a consumer may combine materials and labor (i.e., leisure) time in varying proportions to produce the largest output of utility with the resources available. Now, in the production of consumption, the consumer has a finite amount of time at his disposal, and this he must divide to best advantage between "work," which provides purchased raw materials, and "leisure," which is the source of value-added in consumption.

What happens to this division? Year by year, in the course of economic growth, people have access to more goods. If these extra goods were manna from heaven, people would certainly reduce working time. The larger flow of goods would have raised the marginal product of leisure time by making such hours more goods-intensive. But the marginal product of working time would not have changed. A shift to leisure would be indicated. In fact, however, the extra goods are generated precisely by a rise in the marginal productivity of work. So the opportunity price of leisure also rises, and there is no clear presumption that work will be cut to afford more time to consume more goods. Of course, in the big picture of industrialization and growth, working hours have fallen, though this was conspicuously not the case in the United States or in some other affluent countries in the postwar period. But even if working time is cut, there is a clear presumption that the division of time will be made such that consumption becomes more goods-intensive per unit of time. So we have Linder's (1970, p. 79) charming picture of the typical prosperous Scandinavian householder desperately "drinking Brazilian coffee, smoking a Dutch cigar, sipping a French cognac, reading *The New York Times,* listening to a Brandenburg Concerto and entertaining his Swedish wife— all at the same time, with varying degrees of success."

All this, of course, means that increments of ordinary net national product yield diminishing increments of utility, since the leisure time– goods ratio has declined—always provided that there has been no autonomous rise in leisure-time productivity, that is, in our ability to convert goods into satisfaction per unit of time. This source of diminishing marginal utility is, of course, over and above the source we usually have in mind, namely, that incremental goods serve to satisfy less and less urgent needs and desires. The scarcity of leisure time is not in itself an explanation of the Easterlin paradox, because it does not itself offer a reconciliation of the cross-section and time-series data on happiness. One may also wonder whether leisure time is as scarce as Linder suggests, considering the uses to which many people put it. Still, the Linder view can help us understand why many people, like his desperate Scandinavian, may find that extra income yields a smaller share of bliss than they had vaguely hoped it would.

The Linder view and the theory of the allocation of time can perhaps help us in another way. They tell us that as goods become cheap compared with time, the pattern of consumption should shift away from activities which are time-intensive and toward those which are goods-intensive. It would, of course, take quite an investigation to establish that this is so. Both Linder and Scitovsky, however, think it is and offer a variety of evidence to support their view. If one accepts it, there is a further implication. Goods-intensive activities are, by and large, directed to desires which, when met, lower people's levels of arousal. The routine satisfaction of such desires leaves us bored, dissatisfied, and in need of stimulation. But experience and activities which are sources of stimulation—the arts, literature, active sports, travel, artistic creation, companionship, and so forth—generally demand preparation and active involvement. They are time-intensive, but the rising price of time and the cheapness of goods seduce us to other more immediately comforting, but ultimately unrewarding habits.

3.4 Satisfaction in Work

We have so far looked at economic welfare and growth from the point of view of people as consumers. Following Scitovsky (1973), however, I can offer one more explanation of the Easterlin paradox, this time looking at welfare from the point of view of people in their roles as workers.

Standard economic theory tells us only two things about work:

(1) that the utility of marginal units of the work itself—not the earnings—must be negative, and

(2) that the total earnings from a job must be worth at least as much to the job holder as the burden which the total job imposes.

But economic theory tells us nothing about whether the day's work is, on the whole, a burden or a positive source of satisfaction, nor anything about how total satisfaction from work may differ among people or over time. In particular, it has little to say about the relation between the satisfaction afforded by the job itself and the pay it carries.[2]

That is economic theory. Yet we all know that jobs differ immensely in

---

[2] I say "little" rather than "nothing" because, between jobs which call for similar grades of skill and other capabilities, competition among workers and employers probably tends to establish pay scales which compensate workers for doing jobs that are relatively dangerous, tedious, noisy, dirty, or otherwise unpleasant. But the larger differences among incomes are associated with job differences calling for very different levels of skill, education, experience, responsibility, etc. Workers are, therefore, not able to compete freely for jobs which, besides carrying larger incomes, may also be more stimulating, safe, and generally pleasurable. There is, therefore, no theoretical presumption that income differences are inversely related to the burdens of work. As suggested in the text, the reverse is probably the case.

the degree to which they are themselves sources of exciting, challenging, stimulating activity, and in the opportunities they afford for companionship and interesting contact with other people. One may well believe, moreover, that there is a positive correlation between the degree of satisfaction or pleasure which people take in the performance of their jobs and the relative income, particularly the relative lifetime income they pay. The point to be stressed is that the connection is between goodness of job and *relative,* not absolute, earnings. If, as I believe, that is right, this is another reason why people who, at any time, are found in a high income bracket are more likely to report themselves happy than people in lower income brackets. When average incomes rise, however, there is no clear reason to expect that this will be accompanied by an improvement in the character of the work that people do. That depends on the nature of the technical progress which underlies the rise of incomes.

It is, of course, clearly the case that technical progress and capital accumulation have been associated with great changes in the nature of work. But it is not easy to generalize about the net effect of the changes in work on the satisfaction people take from it. In some respects, work has improved immensely. It has become lighter, cleaner, safer, and it is conducted in pleasanter surroundings. Jobs are more secure, and workers are better protected from the arbitrary actions of superiors. On the other hand, the kind of technological progress on which growth rests involves increasing specialization which at once extracts more intense effort and greater efficiency from people and at the same time seems to reduce the interest and variety of the work and often cuts off workers from meaningful contact with their fellows.

Query: Do these two kinds of changes in the nature of work correspond again to the distinction drawn by psychology, and by Scitovsky, between comfort and stimulus, with the further implication that the satisfaction from greater comfort is evanescent, being subject to erosion by habituation? I believe so. Yet the whole subject is open to question. My characterization of the two kinds of secular trends in the nature of work may itself be wrong or inadequate. It may be roughly satisfactory as a description of the drift of developments during a very long period, say the last century, but be grossly mistaken as applied to the last 25 years. I have to leave the matter open.

4. What of It?

When people first meet the Easterlin paradox, there is a strong tendency to brush aside its message. Surely, they say, in a rich country people are *really* "better off" than in a poor country, no matter what they say about their feelings. Surely, they are *really* better off when the average income in their own country has risen than they were when it was lower, even if they feel otherwise. Who would choose to give up a higher income for a lower, or even be indifferent between the two? To a very large extent, this initial, almost instinctive rejection of the Easterlin paradox betrays our inability to keep separate the benefits that individuals can get when they rise on the scale of relative incomes from those that can be gotten from national or average growth and to distinguish the transitory satisfactions of tasting a higher income from the smaller long-term benefits of consuming it every day. When we reject the message of the Easterlin paradox, we are very likely identifying an absolutely high income with a relatively high income, and we are thinking not of living on a higher standard but of adjusting to it. Moreover, we do not easily absorb the fact that when people all have high incomes, they cannot really live like the more limited number who had such incomes in the past. We forget that consumption is only part of life, that work is another large part, and that the representative person's satisfaction from work does not necessarily rise with average income. In truth, our inclination to reject the Easterlin paradox is itself part and parcel of the whole growth syndrome. It simply reveals in another form why almost everyone strives for more money even though, in the end, a representative person may be little better off for getting it.

The very nature of the Easterlin paradox, therefore, means that we cannot deny its message simply because it offends our intuition. There remains a nagging doubt, however, and it has a substantial basis. That is because the surveys posed a question (are you "very happy" or "fairly happy" or "not so happy"?) which does not fully meet our needs. For the comparisons we have been making, we need to know whether a person who reports himself "fairly happy" in Italy is just as happy (or less happy or more happy) than a person who reports himself "fairly happy" in Sweden. When respondents report themselves very happy and fairly happy in the same frequencies at high income levels as similar respondents did earlier at lower incomes, are they, on the average, really just as happy—or happier or less happy? A direct answer to these questions demands interpersonal and intertemporal comparisons which the surveys could not make. We cannot be sure, therefore, that the quality or intensity of felicity which impels a Swede to describe himself as happy is not higher than that which permits an Italian so to describe himself. It is possible, therefore, that the findings which I call the Easterlin paradox are consistent with the view that their higher income level makes Swedes happier than Italians even if the proportions of people who report themselves as happy is the same, and similarly for the relation between happiness and increasing average income within a country. That possibility, it seems to me, does have plausibility, and, I believe, helps account for people's faith in growth and for their inclination to reject the moral of the Easterlin paradox.

Yet, the possibility is no more than that, and even if, as I suspect, it does point to something real and solid—people in America are *really* better off than in Italy—it does not mean that the significance of the Easterlin paradox itself vanishes. It remains true and important that the proportion in which people report themselves as happy does not rise over time with rising average income as much as we should expect it to do from a comparison between income levels at a given time and place. Nor do as many more people in a rich country say they are happy as one might expect from the reported connection between income and happiness in a poorer country. One may well grant that the technique of extracting reliable testimony from people about their states of happiness is still in its infancy. Much more thought and experimentation will be needed before we can be confident that we are measuring the impact of growth on happiness reliably. Still, the happiness surveys made so far are almost the only evidence we now have about the relation between economic growth and subjectively appraised human satisfaction.[3] There is no *prima facie* reason to discard their results. They are, moreover, no mere spurious statistical coincidence. Several persuasive considerations can be advanced to explain the statistical relations which the surveys yield. We are bound, therefore, to consider seriously what the surveys suggest, which is that the contribution of per capita income growth to average happiness is distinctly smaller than we have so far believed.

[3] The possible sensitivity of the evidence to the form in which questions are formulated is suggested by a recent Gallup Poll, completed since the present article was written. This poll surveyed people in 70 nations containing 90% of the population of the "free world." The survey asked each respondent to point to the step on a 10-point scale which best represented his feelings of satisfaction or dissatisfaction with a particular aspect of his life. A newspaper report interpreting the results (1976) states that Americans express a higher level of satisfaction [than do people in other regions] with important aspects of daily living, including family life, health, leisure time, housing, work, their communities, their standard of living, their education for work and for life and, finally, life in their nation today.

The results, however, are anomalous and puzzling when viewed as expressing a relation between levels of income and levels of satisfaction, since a somewhat larger proportion of the *lower* income population in the United States reported themselves as "highly satisfied" with these several aspects of living than was the case in the population at large in Western Europe. Differences between Latin America and Western Europe, moreover, are small and inconsistent. Essentially the same proportions reported themselves "highly satisfied" with their standard of living. This is a result consistent with the earlier happiness surveys, but not with the view that higher levels of average income are accompanied by higher levels of satisfaction. By contrast, the reported differences between levels of satisfaction in North

Suppose then that we suspend our impatience with paradox. Suppose the Easterlin data do tell us something real about people's feelings and about the somewhat limited capacity of national income growth to enhance life's satisfactions. Suppose the reasons for this failure are of the sort I have suggested. What of it?

Well then, many things could change. If growth is less important for welfare than we have so far supposed, other goals would rise in the scale of social priorities. We could strive harder to reduce income inequalities

---

America, Western Europe, and Latin America on the one hand and the Far East and Africa on the other are very large and consistent.

The tables, as published, follow[a]:

In the results reported below, the percentage for a given satisfaction represents the total score for the top three steps of the scale, and describes the "highly satisfied":

"HIGHLY SATISFIED"

	North America	Western Europe	Latin America	Africa	Far East
Your family life	73%	64%	60%	18%	18%
Your present health	63	51	48	33	18
Your leisure time	58	48	51	30	13
Your housing	55	49	37	14	14
Your work	49	40	22	7	7
Your community	47	42	38	17	13
Your standard of living	46	35	36	5	8
Your education for work	40	28	26	6	6
Your education for life	36	25	32	4	4
Life in nation today	36	29	38	18	12

The following table shows the satisfaction levels in the United States and differences by economic levels:

	National	Upper income	Middle income	Lower income
Your family life	73%	83%	77%	67%
Your present health	63	73	67	55
Your leisure time	59	58	61	58
Your housing	55	69	55	50
Your work	49	52	48	50
Your community	47	48	48	46
Your standard of living	46	64	45	39
Your education for work	40	47	42	37
Your education for life	36	43	38	32
Life in nation today	34	36	30	37

[a] Copyright 1976, Field Enterprises, Inc.

and to promote greater justice, if not greater happiness, among individuals and groups even if that means slower growth. If there is a conflict between income growth for the generations now living and the safety of generations yet unborn, we could take fewer risks with the long future. In choices between private income growth and the protection, provision, and enhancement of public goods, we could learn to appreciate better the relative value of the latter. We would recognize work as a source of satisfaction in itself and not just as a source of income for consumption. If we could learn what makes some jobs pleasurable and others burdensome, we could try to bring efficiency in production into better balance with the costs and satisfactions of the job itself. This is an effort now getting under way. To realize its potential will demand a difficult redirection of technological and administrative effort, and it will strain both our ingenuity and our social arrangements to provide incentives to reorient the goals of engineers and managers. If we recognized the limits of goods as distinct from activity as sources of consumer satisfaction, we could alter the balance between "work" time and "leisure" time and do more to prepare ourselves to make leisure time less passive and somnolent, more stimulating and actively pleasurable than it now is. That would require child-rearing, education, and *off*-the-job training whose spirit is different from that which rules today.

These are not exactly novel themes and to sound them again has a somewhat evangelistic flavor. But the Easterlin paradox gives them a new poignancy. The paradox tells us that it is harder for a nation than for a man to enter the Kingdom of Heaven just by getting rich. It does not say that it is impossible, but it provides new evidence that the wealth of nations lies not in its size alone but also in how it is produced, divided, and used.

References

Abramovitz, M. (1959). The Welfare Interpretation of Secular Trends in National Income and Product, in *The Allocation of Economic Resources: Essays in Honor of Bernard Francis Haley* (M. Abramovitz *et al.*, eds.). Stanford, California: Stanford Univ. Press.

Cantril, H. (1965). *The Pattern of Human Concerns*. New Brunswick, New Jersey: Rutgers Univ. Press.

Easterlin, R. A. (1974). Does Economic Growth Improve the Human Lot? in *Nations and Households in Economic Growth* (P. A. David and M. W. Reder, eds.), pp. 89–125. New York: Academic Press.

Fuchs, V. R. (1967). Redefining Poverty and Redistributing Income, *The Public Interest* **8**, 88–95.

Harrod, R. F. (1958). The Possibility of Economic Satiety—Use of Economic Growth for Improving the Quality of Education and Leisure, in *Problems of United States Economic Development*, Vol. I, pp. 207–214. New York: Committee for Economic Development.

Linder, S. B. (1970). *The Harried Leisure Class*. New York: Columbia Univ. Press.

Nordhaus, W., and Tobin, J. (1972). Is Economic Growth Obsolete? in *National Bureau of Economic Research, 50th Anniversary Colloquium V*. New York and London: Columbia University Press for National Bureau of Economic Research.

Pigou, A. C. (1932). *The Economics of Welfare*. London: Macmillan.

Pigou, A. C. (1951). Some Aspects of Welfare Economics, *American Economic Review* **41** (June).

Schumpeter, J. (1942). *Capitalism, Socialism and Democracy*, New York and London: Harper and Bros., Second Ed., 1947.

Scitovsky, T. (1973). The Place of Economic Welfare in Human Welfare, *Quarterly Review of Economics and Business* **13**, No. 3 (Autumn), 7–19.

Scitovsky, T. (1976). *The Joyless Economy*. London and New York: Oxford Univ. Press.

Department of Economics
Stanford, University
Stanford, California

The Property Rights Doctrine
and Demand Revelation
under Incomplete Information*

Kenneth J. Arrow

1. Introduction

The conditions under which the price system might not achieve optimal resource allocation have gradually been refined since they were first given reasonably accurate expression by Young (1913) in a review of Pigou's *Wealth and Welfare* (the first edition of what became *The Economics of Welfare*). Landmarks on the way to better understanding were the work of Knight (1924) and of Scitovsky (1954).

The basic thesis is that the optimal resource allocation will not be

* This work was supported by National Science Foundation under Grant No. SOC75-21820 at the Institute for Mathematical Studies in the Social Sciences, Stanford University.

achieved by a competitive market system if there are technological externalities. These are goods (or bads) for which no market can be formed.
The usual reason given is that the good is not property in law or in practice, the latter covering the cases in which the act of enforcing property
rights is itself costly and may therefore not be worthwhile. An excellent
survey of market failure and its implications is to be found in Bator (1958).

A conclusion which is usually drawn from the presence of externalities
not mediated through competitive markets is that the state has to intervene in some form to improve resource allocation, whether in the form of
taxes and subsidies or other regulatory forms. Such were the recommendations of Pigou (1952) after he had absorbed Young's critique; an enthusiastic formulation is that of Baumol (1952).

A recent counterattack has been that of the so-called "property rights"
school, starting with the well-known and important paper of Coase (1960)
and including the work of Buchanan, McKean, and others, as surveyed by
Furobòtn and Pejovich (1972). They start with the position, common to
all, that market failures are associated with lack of definition of property
rights. However, they then argue that in principle clear definition of property rights is sufficient to ensure efficiency. This position goes well beyond
the standard neoclassical position that competitive markets suffice for
efficiency. As is well known, defined property rights are only one of the
necessary conditions for competitive markets; large numbers (actual or
potential) of buyers and sellers, concavity of the production possibility
sets, and informed buyers are others. Scitovsky (1951, Chapters XV and
XVI) has given the classical characterization of competitive markets as
means of achieving efficiency.

The property rights theorists do not usually set out their underlying
assumptions with the utmost clarity. But it appears that the basic postulate is the same one that underlies the theory of cooperative games, in the
original formulation of von Neumann and Morgenstern (1947, Chapters V,
VI, and X) and in virtually all later developments [see, e.g., Luce and
Raiffa (1957, Chapters 6, 8, and 9)]. That is, whatever else may be true
about the outcome of the bargaining process, it will certainly be Pareto
optimal. The argument is obvious. Suppose A and B are both possible
outcomes of the game, achievable by suitable choices of strategies by the
players. Suppose the players can bargain about the choices of strategies,
including possible side payments, and suppose that every player prefers A
to B. Then clearly they will not stop at B, since, if nothing else is achievable, they can all improve by going to A.

What is not always recognized is that this argument depends crucially
on the unstated assumption that every player knows every other player's
payoff (utility, profit, whatever) as a function of the strategies played. In
the case of bargaining over externalities, the strategies might be offers and

counteroffer strategies, that is, plans beforehand to make a counteroffer as a function of the initial offer. If player I misperceives the payoff function of player II, then he or she may make an offer judged to be Pareto superior to the initial position but not in fact superior in player II's payoff function. Thus, getting stuck at a Pareto dominated point is no longer impossible.

In the traditional smoke case, suppose the landowners in the neighborhood of a factory own the property rights to clean air. (The opposite assignment of property rights leads to a similar analysis and discussion is omitted.) The factory owner must buy out the rights from all land owners before he can emit smoke. Each landowner has a reservation price for permitting smoke. Efficiency implies that the smoke be emitted if and only if the pure profits of the factory owner exceed the sum of the reservation prices of the landowners. It would appear that a mutually advantageous bargain will achieve the efficient allocation.

But the factory owner does not know the reservation prices of the landowners. If the land is used for residential purposes, then the reservation price is determined by the indifference surfaces of the residents, clearly private information. If the land is used for production, then the reservation price depends on the effect of smoke on productivity, and it is an essential virtue of decentralized private enterprise that businesses do not know in detail each other's production functions. By the same token, the landowners do not know the value of smoke emission to the factory owner; and, what is at least as important, no landowner knows the reservation prices of the other landowners. (A landowner might infer the reservation price of another landowner who was visibly identical to him in circumstances, by assuming it was the same as his own; but to the extent that landowners vary in land use and location relative to the factory, their mutual knowledge of reservation prices becomes correspondingly hazy.)

Consider then how bargaining might proceed. The factory owner might make an offer to each landowner. Since he does not know the reservation prices of the landowners, the offer might well be rejected by some as below the reservation price. This, by itself, is only a difficulty in the adjustment process, for the factory owner has now acquired information about the reservation prices. But a more serious problem is that a landowner might reject the offer even if it is above his reservation price, to convey the idea that it is still higher, for he knows that the factory owner cannot be sure of the deception. In turn, knowing this possibility means that the factory owner cannot draw any inference from a refusal.

Suppose instead the landowners initiate the offers. Independently of each other, each landowner states a price at which he is willing to yield his rights to clean air. Even if, and perhaps especially if, each landowner has a fairly good idea of the factory owner's profits and of the reservation prices of others, he will be tempted to set a price much higher than his true reservation price. Each one will attempt to garner for himself the entire surplus in the economy, the excess of the producer's profits over the sum of the reservation prices (assuming it is positive and large relative to any one landowner's reservation price). Indeed, precisely this situation actually occurs in land assembly, where a large plot of contiguous land is needed, and the odd shapes of some department stores and office buildings testify mutely to failures to achieve efficient resource allocation.

The second case brings out more fully the essential identity between the achievement of efficiency through bargaining and the well known "free-rider" problem in efficient allocation of resources to public goods. In the second case, each landowner may be tempted to ask for much more than his reservation price, relying on the others not to ask too much; similarly, in the public goods case, each may be tempted to understate his benefits if his taxes are related to his statement.

This connection reminds us of the recent literature, which suggests the possibility of overcoming the free-rider problem by appropriate incentives (Clarke, 1971; Groves and Loeb, 1975; Green and Laffont, 1977). These incentives have been referred to as achieving, "demand revelation" [the term is due to Tideman and Tullock (1976), who give a most spirited interpretation and an argument for practical implementation].

The dominant theme in this work has been the search for strategy-proof incentive structures. The agents are supposed to send messages which reflect or purport to reflect their valuations. In addition to the initial resource allocation problem, a system of rewards and penalties as functions of the messages is created; the resulting game is supposed to be such that the message sent by an agent reflects only his valuations and is independent of his guesses as to the evaluations of others. If the preference orderings of the agents over the possible outcomes are unrestricted a priori, then indeed there is no possible mechanism which will guarantee strategy-proof behavior, as brilliantly shown by Gibbard (1973) and, independently, by Satterthwaite (1975). However, strategy-proof procedures may be possible if the orderings are restricted, for example, by the assumption that there are no income effects, so that any rewards or penalties are additive to the results of the bargaining procedure. This assumption is in fact the basis of most of the demand revelation literature and will be made here.

[There is a close relation between the existence of strategy-proof procedures and the existence of social welfare functions. In fact, as shown by Maskin (1976, Chapter III), the two problems are essentially equivalent, in that an a priori restriction on the agents' preferences which permits one problem to be solved also permits the other to be solved.]

The demand revelation procedures do indeed yield efficient decisions, with, however, a curious qualification. The decision made is indeed efficient, but the rewards and penalties do not in general add up to zero; to ensure against infeasibility, it is in general necessary to permit resources to go to waste, in the sense that the sum of the penalties exceeds the sum of the rewards. Green and Laffont (1977) have shown that this lack of balance is necessary.

I wish to suggest a different approach to demand revelation, which achieves efficiency and avoids the waste of resources in the incentive payments. As might be expected, it makes stronger assumptions, in this case, assumptions about the expectations that each agent has about each others' valuations.

In Section 2, I will exhibit one possible formalization of the bargaining process which would lead to efficient allocation when the agents know each others' utility functions. Section 3 illustrates how efficiency fails to be achieved when this knowledge is absent. In Section 4, the general approach to demand revelation under incomplete information will be discussed. In Section 5, I show how this approach can be used to develop a demand-revealing game for which truthful revelation is a local equilibrium point (in the sense of Nash) and for which all the side-payments balance. Section 6 is supplementary; it shows that the utilitarian criterion ensures that the collective decision rule has a responsiveness property assumed in Section 5.

2. A Formalization of Bargaining

We are accustomed to proofs of the optimality of allocation resulting from the market under a competitive price regime. The rules of the system in equilibrium are well defined, and the propositions are clearly stated. What is meant by an assertion, whether by Coase or by von Neumann and Morgenstern, that unrestricted bargaining with well-defined property rights will lead to efficient allocation? What are the rules of the game and how do we determine its outcome?

We have to describe bargaining as a series of permitted moves and then an equilibrium concept which determines when no agent will wish to change his or her strategy. This turns out to be a difficult task, and most proposed solutions have some unsatisfactory qualities.

In game-theoretic language, the problem is to devise a noncooperative game whose equilibrium point (in the sense of Nash) is an efficient allocation of resources. Thus, each agent will have the right to change unilaterally, but the game is so devised that at some efficient allocation no agent will in fact find it preferable to change.

I confine discussion to the case of two agents, Estragon (E) and Vladimir (V). To simplify further, assume that there is only one private good and one public good (or externality-producing activity). Suppose first that the public good is resource-using. Let x_E be the amount of the private good going to Estragon, x_V the amount of the private good going to Vladimir, and y the amount of the public good. Total initial resources are w, and there is no production. An allocation, then, is feasible if and only if

$$x_E + x_V + y = w. \tag{1}$$

Assume that the two individuals can have any feasible allocation they agree to. If they do not agree, suppose that there is no public good ($y = 0$) and that each keeps his initial stock of the resource for private use, $x_E = w_E$ and $x_V = w_V$, where w_i is the initial resource holding of agent i ($i = E$, V). We shall refer to the allocation (w_E, w_V, 0) as the disagreement payoff and denote it by A^d.

Let $U^i(x_i, y)$ be the utility of agent i if he receives x_i of the private good and the amount of the public good is y. An efficient resource allocation then satisfies the well-known Samuelson condition, that the sum of the marginal rates of substitution of the public good for the private for the two individuals equals 1:

$$\frac{\partial U^E}{\partial x_E} \bigg/ \frac{\partial U^E}{\partial y} + \frac{\partial U^V}{\partial x_V} \bigg/ \frac{\partial U^V}{\partial y} = 1. \tag{2}$$

Equations (1) and (2) constitute two equations in the three unknowns, x_E, x_V, y, and define the Pareto frontier. However, because of initial holdings, the contract curve is restricted in addition to the allocations which satisfy the conditions of *individual rationality*,

$$U^i(x^i, y) \geq U^i(w_i, 0) \qquad (i = E, V); \tag{3}$$

i.e., no agreement will make any individual worse off than he could be without agreement. Note that the disagreement payoff A^d satisfies these conditions by definition.

Consider now the following simple procedure: Estragon proposes an allocation, that is, x_E, x_V, and y, satisfying the feasibility condition (1). Vladimir can accept or reject it. Suppose that Estragon knows Vladimir's utility function. Vladimir will accept if and only if the proposed allocation is individually rational from his point of view. Then clearly Estragon's optimal strategy will be to choose that allocation which maximizes his utility subject to the constraints,

$$x_E + x_V + y = w, \qquad U^V(x_V, y) \geq U^V(w_V, 0). \tag{4}$$

In general, the optimal allocation to Estragon subject to (4) will be better for him than the disagreement point (w_E, 0), and therefore he will not choose an allocation which will be rejected by Vladimir, while among those which Vladimir will accept, Estragon will, of course, choose the best from his viewpoint.[1,2]

The outcome of this procedure is clearly Pareto efficient by definition, since it maximizes the utility of one agent for a given level of utility for the other. Hence, there is a game whose equilibrium is Pareto efficient. The outcome, it must be noted, is not the competitive equilibrium.

3. The Failure of Bargaining under Privacy

One of the virtues of decentralization is the respect for privacy. The utility functions of different individuals cannot easily be known to each other. Indeed, since they have meaning only in terms of observable behavior, there may be no way of transmitting utility functions from one agent to another. There is in general no way of forcing an individual to reveal his utility function; if he knows that this knowledge will be used in some allocation process, what he will transmit will or at least can be designed to affect that allocation favorably to him.

Let us analyze the outcome of the procedure of the last section with one additional complication: Estragon does not know for sure what Vladimir's utility function is. More specifically, suppose that it could be one of two utility functions, $U_a{}^V(x_V, y)$ or $U_b{}^V(s_V, y)$, and Estragon does not know

---

[1] Wilson (1978) has given a procedure for any number of economic agents which will achieve efficient allocation by means of a noncooperative game; the procedure above is the special case of Wilson's when there are but two agents.

[2] The procedure given in the text is not quite standard in game theory. The game has been described in so-called extensive form. It is usual to reduce games to normal form, in which each agent describes his potential behavior at any point for every possible history of the game up to that point. These descriptions or *strategies* are thought of as chosen simultaneously at the beginning of the game. Then the equilibrium point is a choice of strategy by each agent such that neither could gain by changing if the other player does not change. In the game described above, Vladimir's strategy, in this sense, would be a statement describing which allocations he would accept if offered by Estragon. But then if he should choose a strategy of accepting only one allocation, Estragon's optimal strategy in reply would be to make that offer if it is at least as good for him as the disagreement allocation; and given that offer, Vladimir should announce that he would accept it if it is at least as good for *him* as the disagreement allocation. Hence, any individually rational allocation could be achieved as an equilibrium in this sense.

In the text, and in the work of Wilson (1978), the last player is not allowed to formulate a strategy in advance but rather is required to accept or reject previous offers on the basis of a comparison with the disagreement allocation. This concept of equilibrium, in which the second player is optimizing given all previous history, has been termed a *perfect* equilibrium by Selten (1975); it is the game-theoretic counterpart of the principle of optimality in dynamic programming.

which. Let us go further, and represent his uncertainty by an assignment of probabilities; Vladimir's utility function is U_a^V with probability p_a, U_b^V with probability p_b, $p_a + p_b = 1$. These probabilities may be regarded as objective facts or as subjective probabilities of Estragon's.

Now consider Estragon's choice problem. If he chooses a feasible allocation (x_E, x_V, y) which Vladimir would accept for either utility function, then the probability of acceptance would be one. Clearly, among such allocations, Estragon would choose the best from his point of view. Hence, one possible candidate for his choice would be

$$A^* = (x_E^*, x_V^*, y^*) \qquad \text{maximizes} \quad U^E(x_E, y)$$

$$\text{subject to} \quad x_E + x_V + y = w, \tag{5}$$

$$U_a^V(x_V, y) \geq U_a^V(w_V, 0),$$

$$U_b^V(x_V, y) \geq U_b^V(w_V, 0).$$

Another possibility would be to consider a broader class of feasible allocations, those which Vladimir would choose if his utility function were U_a^V. Again, among these, Vladimir would choose that one which maximizes his utility. This allocation might happen to satisfy also the condition that $U_b^V(x_V, y) \geq U_b^V(w_E, 0)$, in which case it would be the allocation A^*. If we disregard this possibility, we have another candidate for Estragon's choice,

$$A^a = (x_E^a, x_V^a, y^a) \qquad \text{maximizes} \quad U^E(x_E, y)$$

$$\text{subject to} \quad x_E + x_V + y = w, \tag{6}$$

$$U_a^V(x_V, y) \geq U_a^V(w_V, 0).$$

Note that Estragon will prefer this policy to any other which is rational for Vladimir under U_a^V because, if rejected, the payoff to Estragon is independent of the offer. Since the probability of acceptance is p_a, the expected utility of Estragon is

$$p_a U^E(x_E^a, y^a) + p_b U^E(w_E, 0) \tag{7}$$

Symmetrically, of course, Estragon can choose an allocation which would be acceptable to Vladimir if his utility function were U_b^V. He would choose the best:

$$A^b = (x_E^b, x_V^b, y^b) \qquad \text{maximizes} \quad U^E(x_E, y)$$

$$\text{subject to} \quad x_E + x_V + y = w, \tag{8}$$

$$U_b^V(x_V, y) \geq U_b^V(w_V, 0),$$

and the expected return to him would be

$$p_a U^E(w_E, 0) + p_b U^E(x_E^b, y^b). \tag{9}$$

Finally, Estragon could, if it were desirable, choose an allocation which Vladimir would reject whether his utility function were U_a^V or U_b^V. But Estragon would know that the disagreement allocation would result, an allocation he could also obtain by offering it, since it would satisfy all the individual rationality conditions for Vladimir. In that case, he would do at least as well by choosing A^*, so that we can assume that Estragon will always choose an allocation which satisfies Vladimir's individual rationality condition for at least one possible utility function.

Estragon then chooses that one of the three allocations A^*, A^a, A^b which makes his expected utility as large as possible; the expected utility of A^* to him is $U^E(x_E^*, y^*)$, since there is no uncertainty in that case, while the expected utilities of A^a and A^b are given by (7) and (9), respectively. Given all values of the utilities, the choice depends on p_a, being A^a if p_a is sufficiently large, A^b if it is sufficiently small; there may also be an intermediate range in which A^* is chosen.[3]

If A^a is offered and in fact Vladimir's utility function is U_a^V, the allocation will be Pareto efficient. But there is a probability p_b that the disagreement allocation will be the equilibrium. Hence the system cannot guarantee efficiency; indeed, p_b might easily be nontrivial and the inefficiency of the disagreement point very considerable. Similarly, if A^b is offered, there is a probability p_a of winding up at the disagreement allocation. Finally, A^* is inefficient whichever utility function Vladimir has; hence, if it is offered, there will be inefficiency with probability 1.

Thus, it can be seen that a procedure which would achieve a Pareto efficient allocation if each agent knew the other's utility function will have a positive probability of falling short of efficiency if this knowledge is absent.

4. Bargaining as a Game of Incomplete Information

The game analyzed in the last section is one of incomplete information in the sense introduced in an important series of papers by Harsanyi (1967–1968). It can be reduced to a game in standard form by introducing, for each agent, a chance move which determines his utility function, the

---

[3] For those interested in the detailed results, it will be easy to verify the following statements. Define $V^a = U^E(x_E^a, y^a) - U^E(w_E, 0)$, $V^b = U^E(x_E^b, y^b) - U^E(w^E, 0)$, $V^* = U^E(w_E^*, y^*) - U^E(w_E, 0)$. Let V be half the harmonic mean of V^a and V^b. Then there are two cases: (1) if $V^* > \bar{V}$, then Estragon chooses allocation A^a if $p_a > V^*/V^a$, A^b if $p_a < 1 - (V^*/V^b)$, and A^* in the intermediate range; (2) if $V^* < \bar{V}$, then A^* is not chosen for any value of p_a, while A^a is chosen if $p_a > V^a/(V^a + V^b)$, and A^b otherwise.

outcome of the move being revealed to him but not to other agents. (In the particular game just discussed, uncertainty about Estragon's utility function is irrelevant, since Vladimir has to respond passively to Estragon's proposal; but in general, allocation games will be more symmetric.) The probabilities of different utility functions are part of the rules of the game and are known to both (or, more generally, all) agents. It might be asked why Vladimir, who comes to know his own utility function, has to know the *ex ante* probabilities; in the particular game in fact he does not have to know, but more generally, he should know what probabilities about his utility functions are in Estragon's mind.

The question to be posed is: Can we find a set of rules, a game, in which each agent is to announce his or her utility function, the allocation of resources is a function of the announcements, and the rewards are such as to induce each to announce truly? The answer to be demonstrated here is that such a game can be devised if (1) income effects are neglected, and (2) the probabilities of different possible utility functions for the agents are known and are independent of each other.[4]

It should be remarked that there has been a shift from revelation of indifference maps to revelation of utility functions. The reason is that once probabilities are introduced, the aim of each agent in the bargaining game is to maximize *expected* utility according to the conventional Bernoulli–Ramsey–von Neumann–Morgenstern hypothesis. The results will not be invariant under monotone transformations of the utility functions, since such transformations alter attitudes toward risk-bearing.

The absence of income effects means that the utility function is linear in income (and therefore, in particular, implies risk-neutrality toward income). This is a serious limitation, though one that is common to the entire demand-revelation literature.

More specifically, we model the making of a public decision, a variable x in some domain. (The decision might include the allocation of private goods, but it is the choice of public goods and externalities that is most in mind here.) Agent i has a utility function for the decision; the form of this function is known to all up to some parameters which are private. Let ρ_i be the parameters of the ith agent; his utility function then is $U^i(x, \rho_i)$. Individual i has a net increment of income t_i (which may be negative); then his utility is $U^i(x, \rho_i) + t_i$.

---

[4] After working out the ideas to be presented, I found that the representation of incentives for satisfactory bargaining as a game of incomplete information had already been used by d'Aspremont and Gerard-Varet (1975). The ideas are essentially the same; their utility functions, arising out of a pollution problem, are more specialized, and this fact permits some simplification.

Since there could be infinitely many parameters, the restriction of the utility functions U^i to a class of known form in unknown parameters is no real restriction.

Each individual makes an announcement of his parameter values, which may or may not be true. For example, in a pollution problem, the manufacturer may announce the unit cost of antipollution measures to him while the neighbor announces the damage due to unit pollution. If the issue is whether or not to build a bridge, each agent may be asked to announce the value to him of the bridge. Let r_i be the announcement by agent i.

There is specified a rule for making the decision as a function of the announcements, $x(r_1, \ldots, r_n)$, where n is the number of agents. At the moment we leave the rule unspecified; it might be derived on the hypothesis of maximizing the sum of the agents' utilities on the assumption that their announcements are true, a case we will consider in Section 6.

Each agent i has a probability distribution over the true parameter values of other agents. Let ρ^i be the parameters of all individuals other than individual i: $\rho^i = (\rho_1, \ldots, \rho_{i-1}, \rho_{i+1}, \ldots, \rho_n)$. Suppose the ith agent assumes that everyone else will tell the truth (he does not of course know what those parameters are but knows their distribution). If he announces r_i, then the social decision is $x(r_i, \rho^i)$. In the absence of any money transfers, his utility will be $U^i(x(r_i, \rho^i), \rho^i)$; but, since he does not know ρ^i, he would be induced to maximize

$$E_{\rho^i}[U^i(x(r_i, \rho^i), \rho_i)], \tag{10}$$

where, as the notation indicates, the expectation is taken over ρ^i. One would like to see that $r_i = \rho_i$ for all ρ_i; that is, we would like to have individual i be induced to reveal his private parameters truthfully if everyone else did so. If this held for all i, truth-telling would be an equilibrium point of the game.

There is no reason so far for truth-telling, as we well know from the literature on the free-rider problem in the theory of public goods. The demand-revelation literature suggests that we modify the payoff to individual i by assessing a change in income as a function of his announcement. Specifically, we will prescribe a function $T_i(r_i)$ for each individual, which is the amount he pays if he makes the announcement r_i. This income has to go somewhere; it would be inefficient to throw it out if positive and there is no source to supply it if negative. Hence, we add a specification that the income dispensed by one agent is paid out to all other agents. That is, we specify functions, $T_{ij}(r_j)$, the amount paid by individual j to individual i if j's announcement is r_j. These functions are defined only if $i \neq j$, of course. By definition,

$$\sum_{i \neq j} T_{ij}(r_j) = T_j(r_j). \tag{11}$$

From the viewpoint of individual i, then, his utility is decreased by his payments, $T_i(r_i)$ and increased by the payments made to him by others, $\sum_{j \neq i} T_{ij}(r_j)$. Therefore, once the functions T_i, T_{ij}, satisfying (11) are selected, and each agent chooses his announcement r_i, the net payoff to individual i is

$$U^i(x(r), \rho_i) - T_i(r_i) + \sum_{j \neq i} T_{ij}(r_j), \tag{12}$$

where $r = (r_1, \ldots, r_n)$. Each agent must choose an announcement r_i for each possible true value of the parameters ρ_i; that is, a *strategy* for i is a function $r_i(\rho_i)$. Once the strategies are selected by the agents, the expected utility to agent i is the expected value of (12) over the parameters of other agents, ρ^i. Let r^i be the announcements of agents other than i, and $r^i(\rho^i)$ the strategies of agents other than i. Then agent i's expected utility is

$$E_{\rho i}\{U^i[x(r_i(\rho_i), r^i(\rho^i)), \rho_i]\} - T_i(r_i(\rho_i)) + E_{\rho i}\left(\sum_{j \neq i} T_{ij}(r_j(\rho_j))\right). \tag{13}$$

An equilibrium point is a specification of a strategy $r_i(\rho_i)$ for each agent, such that if every agent $i \neq j$ chooses $r_j(\rho_j)$, then (13) is maximized for agent i by the choice of the strategy $r_i(\rho_i)$. This is the same as saying that, for each particular value of ρ_i, the corresponding value of the strategy $r_i(\rho_i)$ maximizes (13).

5. The Demand-Revelation Game

A truth-telling strategy is given by $r_i(\rho_i) \equiv \rho_i$ (i.e., identically in ρ_i). A truth-telling equilibrium is one where each agent is playing a truth-telling strategy. Our problem is to find functions T_i, T_{ij} so that truth-telling is an equilibrium.

Define $F^i(r_i, \rho_i)$ to be the expected payoff to agent i, when all other agents are telling the truth. This is defined by setting $r_j(\rho_j) \equiv \rho_j$ in (13); for a given ρ_i, we also replace $r_i(\rho_i)$ by r_i:

$$F^i(r_i, \rho_i) = E_{\rho i}[U^i(x(r_i, \rho^i), \rho_i)] - T_i(r_i) + E_{\rho i}\left(\sum_{j \neq i} T_{ij}(\rho_j)\right). \tag{14}$$

At an equilibrium, agent i chooses r_i to maximize $F^i(r_i, \rho_i)$. Assume now differentiability of all relevant functions, and also assume that the optimum choice is not at a boundary. Also, for simplicity, assume ρ_i, and therefore r_i, are one-dimensional variables; this restriction is solely expository and can be removed with only notational changes. Then r_i satisfies the condition $\partial F^i/\partial r_i = 0$. This condition in fact defines r_i for each value of ρ_i and therefore defines the strategy $r_i(\rho_i)$. Since the last term in (14) is independent of r_i, optimal behavior for agent i is defined by

$$E_{\rho^i}[U_x{}^i(x(r_i, \rho^i), \rho_i)x_{r_i}(r_i, \rho^i)] - T_i{}'(r_i) = 0. \tag{15}$$

To have a truth-telling equilibrium, the solution of (15) in r_i should be ρ_i for all ρ_i. That is, (15) should hold with r_i replaced by ρ_i for all ρ_i:

$$T_i{}'(\rho_i) = E_{\rho^i}[U_x{}^i(x(\rho_i, \rho^i), \rho_i)x_{r_i}(\rho_i, \rho^i)]$$

for all ρ_i, or, if we replace the variable ρ_i by the variable r_i,

$$T_i{}'(r_i) = E_{\rho^i}[U_x{}^i(x(r_i, \rho^i), r_i)x_{r_i}(r_i, \rho^i)] \tag{16}$$

for all r_i.

Equation (16) supplies a complete solution of the problem, if one exists. It defines the function $T_i(r_i)$, up to an irrelevant constant of integration. The right-hand side is well defined by the conditions of the problem. The transfer function T_{ij} does not affect the behavior of any individual and therefore can be chosen arbitrarily, subject to the condition that the transfer to all other individuals equals the payment required; see (11).

The right-hand side has a simple interpretation. If the true value of the parameter ρ_i is in fact equal to the announcement, then a perturbation dr_i in the announcement will change the social decision by $x_{r_i} \, dr_i$ and therefore change the individual's utility by $U_x{}^i x_{r_i} \, dr_i$. This product depends, however, on the true values of other individuals' parameters ρ^i; hence, from agent i's point of view, he must consider the expected marginal utility. The payment function T_i has to be fixed to just offset any resulting incentive to change from r_i to $r_i + dr_i$.

Thus, each agent will find that truth-telling satisfies the first-order conditions for a maximum. We must, however, check to see that the second-order conditions are also satisfied.

The derivative $\partial F^i/\partial r_i = F_{r_i}^i(r_i, \rho_i)$ is given by the left-hand side of (15). By our construction of T_i, we know that $F_{r_i}^i(r_i, \rho_i) = 0$ when $r_i = \rho_i$, that is,

$$F_{r_i}^i(r_i, r_i) \equiv 0$$

identically in r_i. Total differentiation with respect to r_i yields

$$F^i_{r_i r_i}(r_i, r_i) + F^i_{r_i \rho_i}(r_i, r_i) \equiv 0. \tag{17}$$

In order that truth-telling be optimum for individual i, given that all others are telling the truth, it is necessary that the first- and second-order conditions for a maximum in r_i be satisfied at $r_i = \rho_i$, that is, that $F^i_{r_i}(\rho_i, \rho_i) = 0$, which is guaranteed by construction, and that $F^i_{r_i r_i}(\rho_i, \rho_i) < 0$. Since these conditions must hold for all ρ_i, we can replace ρ_i by r_i, and require that they hold for all r_i. From (17), then, we require that $F^i_{r_i \rho_i}(r_i, r_i) > 0$ for all r_i.

In (14), note that the second and third terms are independent of ρ_i. If we differentiate (14) with respect to ρ_i and that derivative with respect to r_i and set $\rho_i = r_i$, we find that the second-order condition for individual i to have a truth-telling optimum is

$$E_{\rho i}[U^i_{x \rho_i}(x(r_i, \rho^i), r_i) x_{r_i}(r_i, \rho^i)] > 0.$$

This means that, on the average, for any given values of the utility function parameters of the others, if an individual is telling the truth, a shift in his parameter changes the amount of the public good, through the collective decision rule, and the marginal utility of the public good to him in the same direction. This is a minimum condition for the collective decision rule to represent positively the desires of the economic agents.

We can restate our results formally.

DEFINITION 1   A *collective decision rule* is a function which determines the amount of the public good for any specification of the utility function parameters of the economic agents.

DEFINITION 2   A collective decision rule is said to be *responsive* if, for any given individual, a shift in his parameter changes on the average his marginal utility for the public good and the amount of the public good in the same direction. More precisely, the expected value of the product of these changes, averaged over the utility function parameters of others, is positive.

THEOREM 1   Suppose

(1)   there are no income effects so that agent i has a utility function in the public good and other income of the form $U^i(x, \rho_i) +$ (other income),

(2)   the form of the utility function is known to all, but the value of ρ_i is known only to the agent i;

(3)   each agent has a probability distribution over the utility function parameters of others which is independent of his own parameter value;

(4)   the collective decision rule is responsive.

Consider the following social decision procedure: Each individual chooses a strategy which associates to each possible value of his parameter an announced value of the parameter. The public good quantity is determined by the collective decision rule as a function of the announced values of the parameters. Finally, there are specified functions $T_{ij}(r_j)$ $(i \neq j)$, which specify amount of income paid by agent j to agent i as a function of j's announcement r_j of his utility parameter. These functions satisfy the condition

$$\sum_{i \neq j} T_{ij}(r_j) = \int E_{\rho^j}[U_x{}^j(x(r_j, \rho^j), r_j) x_{r_j}(r_j, \rho^j)] \, dr_j. \tag{18}$$

Then the truth-telling strategies, $r_i(\rho_i) \equiv \rho_i$, form a local equilibrium point of the social decision procedure.

Remark 1 By a local equilibrium point is meant that, given that others tell the truth, agent i will find that, for each value of ρ_i, the action $r_i = \rho_i$ is a local maximum. Examination of the second-order conditions cannot by itself show that the action is globally optimal for the agent.

Remark 2 Condition (18) is simply a restatement of (16), with i replaced by j and condition (11) substituted in. The constant of integration in (18) can be chosen arbitrarily.

6. The Utilitarian Decision Rule

I have so far only required that the collective decision rule be responsive. A natural condition is that the collective decision rule be defined by the condition that the amount of the public good be such as to maximize the sum of individuals' utilities. This rule is especially plausible if we maintain the assumption that utility is linear in money, for then the sum of utilities is the money value of net benefits. This rule will in fact imply that the collective decision rule is responsive if the utility functions are concave in the public good.

We are requiring that $x(r_1, \ldots, r_n)$ be defined as the value of x which maximizes the sum of utilities on the assumption that announcements are true:

$$x(r) \quad \text{maximizes} \quad \sum_{i=1}^{n} U^i(x, r_i), \tag{19}$$

where $r = (r_1, \ldots, r_n)$. Then $x(r)$ satisfies the identity in r,

$$\sum_{i=1}^{n} U_{x}{}^{i}(x(r),r_i) \equiv 0.$$

Partial differentiation with respect to r_i yields

$$\left(\sum_{i=1}^{n} U^i_{xx}(x(r), r_i)\right) x_{r_i}(r) + U^i_{xr_i}(x(r), r_i) \equiv 0.$$

Multiply through by $x_{r_i}(r)$,

$$\left(\sum_{i=1}^{n} U^i_{xx}(x(r), r_i)|\right) [(x_{r_i}(r)]^2 + U^i_{xr_i}(x(r), r_i)x_{r_i}(r) \equiv 0.$$

But, because U^i is assumed concave in x for each i, the first term is in gerneral negative, so that the second term must be positive. But this certainly implies that x is a responsive collective choice rule.[5]

THEOREM 2   If the collective choice rule $x(r)$ is defined so as to maximize the sum of the agents' utilities, then it is responsive.

References

Arrow, K. J., and Scitovsky, T., eds. (1969). *Readings in Welfare Economics.* Homewood, Illinois: Richard D. Irwin.

Bator, F. (1958). The Anatomy of Market Failure, *Quarterly Journal of Economics* **72,** 351–379.

Baumol, W. J. (1952). *Welfare Economics and the Theory of the State.* Cambridge, Massachusetts: Harvard Univ. Press.

Clarke, E. (1971). Multipart Pricing of Public Goods, *Public Choice* **11,** 17–33.

Coase, R. H. (1960). The Problem of Social Cost, *Journal of Law and Economics* **3,** 1–44.

d'Aspremont, C., and Gerard-Varet, L. (1975). Incentives and Incomplete Information. CORE discussion paper (unpublished).

Furobotn, E., and Pejovich, S. (1972). Property Rights and Economic Theory: A Survey of Recent Literature, *Journal of Economic Literature* **10,** 1137–1162.

Gibbard, A. (1973). Manipulation of Voting Schemes: A General Result, *Econometrica* **41,** 587–602.

Green, J., and Laffont, J. (1977). Characterization of Satisfactory Mechanisms for the Revelation of Preferences for Public Goods, *Econometrica* **45,** 427–438.

Green, J., and Laffont, J. (1977). Révélation des préférences pour les biens publics, *Cahiers du Séminaire d'Econometrie* **19,** 83–103.

Groves, T., and Loeb, M. (1975). Incentives and Public Outputs, *Journal of Public Finance* **4,** 211–226.

Harsanyi, J. (1967–1968). Games with Incomplete Information Played by "Bayesian" Players, I–III, *Management Science* **14,** 159–182, 320–334, 486–502.

---

[5] Laffont and Maskin (1978), in some unpublished work, have shown that the utilitarian rule actually implies that truth-telling is a global equilibrium point in this game; that is, if everyone else is telling the truth, then truth-telling is a global maximum strategy. They have also shown the close connections between the revelation mechanism developed here and the Groves mechanism and its generalization.

Knight, F. H. (1924). Some Fallacies in the Interpretation of Social Cost, *Quarterly Journal of Economics* **38**, 582–606. [Reprinted in Arrow and Scitovsky (1969, pp. 213–227).]

Laffont, J., and Maskin, E. (1978). A Differential Approach to Expected Utility Maximizing Mechanisms, Notes, Groupe de Travail, Economic de l'Information, Exole Polytechnique, Paris (unpublished).

Luce, R. D., and Raiffa, H. (1957). *Games and Decisions*. New York: Wiley.

Maskin, E. (1976). Social Choice on Restricted Domains, Ph.D. dissertation in Applied Mathematics. Harvard Univ., Boston.

Pigou, A. C. (1952). *The Economics of Welfare*, 4th ed. London: Macmillan.

Satterthwaite, M. A. (1975). Strategy-Proofness and Arrow's Conditions: Existence and Correspondence Theorems for Voting Procedures and Social Welfare Functions, *Journal of Economic Theory* **10**, 187–217.

Scitovsky, T. (1951). *Welfare and Competition*. Chicago, Illinois: Richard D. Irwin.

Scitovsky, T. (1954). Two Concepts of External Economies, *Journal of Political Economy* **62**, 143–151. [Reprinted in Arrow and Scitovsky (1969, pp. 242–252).]

Selten, R. (1975). Reexamination of the Perfectness Concept for Equilibrium Points in Extensive Games, *International Journal of Game Theory* **4**, 25–55.

Tideman, N., and Tullock, G. (1976). A New and Superior process for Making Social Choices, *Journal of Political Economy* **84**, 1145–1160.

von Neumann, J., and Morgenstern, O. (1947). *Theory of Games and Economic Behavior*, 2nd ed. Princeton, New Jersey: Princeton Univ. Press.

Wilson, R. (1978). A Competitive Model of Exchange, *Econometrica* **46**, 577–585.

Young, A. (1913). Pigou's *Wealth and Welfare*, *Quarterly Journal of Economics* **27**, 672–686.

Project on Efficiency on Decision Making
  in Economic Systems
Harvard University
Cambridge, Massachusetts

On Two Experiments in the Pricing of Theater Tickets

*William J. Baumol**

1. Introduction

Sometimes economists have the fortune, good or ill, of being given the opportunity to see put into practice what they have preached. Professor Scitovsky and I have, over the years, had a bond in our interest in the arts, and we have both tried to do whatever is possible for practitioners of the dismal science to smooth their path. This paper, a rather heterodox

* I should like to thank the Ford Foundation for support of the studies described here, which were carried out through the agency of the Theatre Development Fund of New York City and Mathematica, Inc. Above all, though, I must thank my wife, who was codirector of the studies.

entry for a volume of economic essays,[1] is an interim report on two experiments now underway in New York City, both of them intended to expand the audiences for live theater and to bring new types of attendees to it. One of them is also intended to introduce a novel method for the apportionment of subventions going to theatrical groups. The reader will readily recognize the insinuation of some of the economist's preconceptions, particularly his penchant for use of the market mechanism even in areas into which it would not have extended of its own accord.

The two experiments reported here span the extremes of the theater in New York City. One deals with the oldest and most established form of production in the United States–the New York commercial theater, while the other applies to off-off-Broadway and "ethnic theater," encompassing the city's most variegated, financially unstable, and burgeoning theatrical enterprises. For the first of these groups, the problem at issue was straightforward—rising costs and ticket prices which have not kept up with them have been a source of growing financial pressure, making it constantly harder to live with the large number of unsold seats which has been Broadway's most carefully kept military secret. The objective was to find customers for those seats without at the same time producing an offsetting reduction in the commercial theater's current sources of revenue.

For the off-off-Broadway theater, the problem is even simpler—it is a matter of channeling funds into this incredibly impecunious sector of the theater, but doing so in a way that is administratively feasible for the funding agencies, that minimizes unintended artistic interference by these agencies (which is usually an unavoidable by-product of the choice of types of group they finance most generously), but nevertheless provides some suitable incentives to the theaters.

2.   The Off-Off-Broadway Theater

Before turning to the nature of the program of support which is our main concern, it may be well to provide the reader with a brief description of the off-off-Broadway theater itself.

It is probably no exaggeration to say that never in human history has there been anything like the volume of creative activity now underway in this sector of the New York theater. Our calculations indicate that about 1000 new productions, a high proportion of them new plays, were presented in one year in that sector of the theater alone. (London, by con-

---

[1] Heterodox particularly because there proved to be little opportunity for rigorous statistical analysis so that most of the conclusions are unavoidably impressionistic.

trast, produced well under 100 altogether.) Today, altogether about 175 theatrical groups are in operation, and we have estimated their average number of new productions to be over 9 per year.

But quantity is not the essence of the matter. The fact is that off-off-Broadway is now a prime source for new plays, new approaches in production and direction, new talent, and new ideas for the live theater and the mass media, not only for the United States, but for the world. Theater professionals in many countries of Western Europe, Japan, Israel, Iran, and behind the Iron Curtain know the work of off-off Broadway and look to it for new directions. Off-off-Broadway groups tour abroad, are invited to international festivals, are feted by theatrical groups in foreign capitals, and one has even established branches in other countries. In the United States, outside circles specializing in the theater, its work is unknown. The audience for this branch of the theater is tiny. The median seating capacity in an off-off-Broadway theater is 100, and altogether we have estimated an entire season's attendance to be about 230,000, that is, less than 4% of the 6 million tickets sold annually on Broadway.

This is not because all the work of off-off-Broadway is experimental and bizarre. While some would undoubtedly strike the neophyte attendee as somewhat outré, a good deal of the work is conventional—performances by groups aspiring to offer good productions of good plays. And while some plays are amateurish, others meet the most exacting professional standards and more. There are groups that insist on a year and more of concentrated work on a production before they are prepared to show their work to the public.

While the total size of the audience for off-off-Broadway is comparatively small, it is reaching those traditionally not served by the standard theater. Completely new audiences have been attracted by approximately 20 ethnic theaters, mostly Black and Spanish-speaking, that are an important component of off-off-Broadway. Almost 10% of the audience is composed of retired people who can no longer afford to attend commercial theater. The largest part of the audience is composed of professionals in the theater and the allied arts.

The finances of these groups are even more extraordinary. Our sample of 62 off-off-Broadway groups indicates a median total expenditure in 1972–1973 of $23,000, with the lower and upper deciles respectively equaling $4000 and $112,000. This includes a full year's compensation of all artistic and administrative personnel, production costs, rent, advertising, and any other outlays. A budget of $30,000 is apt to cover over ten full productions per year.

Forty-two percent of the theaters do not pay most of their actors, and almost 70% of the actors are unpaid. Only the most successful of the theaters offer salaries that average as high as $50 per week and the figure has only recently reached this level. A salary of $10 per week is sometimes taken to be a considerable achievement. Administrators are paid somewhat more frequently, three-quarters of the theaters providing some compensation for this service, but here also the figures are low. In a subset of the most prosperous theaters for which we were able to obtain more extensive financial data, the average administrator was paid $7300 per annum (median, $6000). This is for 1973–1974.

Admission fees are also extraordinarily low for live theater (even in comparison with countries in which the theater is subsidized heavily). In our sample of 62 theaters, the median admission fee was $2.50, with some offering free admission or suggesting a contribution of $2.00 by each attendee.

In sum, off-off-Broadway provides an enormous volume of artistic activity and new ideas at very little cost to anyone other than those who supply it. We have estimated the total annual budget of all the off-off-Broadway theaters together to run to some $3 to $3.5 million, less than just the *production* (i.e., preopening) cost of four Broadway musicals. This means a cost *per production* for off-off-Broadway averaging some $3000. Or put the other way, it means that off-off-Broadway can perhaps provide 250 new productions for the cost of one Broadway musical! Certainly the off-off-Broadway productions are a bargain for everyone but the performers and the others whose contributed effort makes possible the (precarious) existence of the "emerging theater."

3. The Voucher Program for the Support of Off-Off-Broadway

In the fall of 1972, the Theatre Development Fund, a nonprofit organization for the encouragement of work in the theater, inaugurated a new program of support for the off-off-Broadway theater, along lines that had been suggested independently by several persons, including the present author. The proposal was intended to select a number of different groups such as students or blue collar workers whose attendance it was desired to stimulate, and, in effect, to let them decide by their own attendance on the distribution among individual theatrical groups of support funds provided by private foundations and other granting agencies.

Specifically, as now instituted, the voucher program operates by inviting applications from members of a number of eligible groups—union members, students, teachers, clergymen, retired people, etc. Each such person can purchase from the Theatre Development Fund (TDF) books of vouchers as they become available (as the requisite funding is obtained by

TDF). Each such voucher costs the applicant $1.00 and it is usable in lieu of admission charge at any off-off-Broadway theater that has requested to be and has been declared eligible. Almost 150 theaters have received voucher money this year. The theater which has accepted vouchers as admission payments returns them to TDF, and receives in return for each not the $1.00 which was paid for them by the attendee, but $2.50. Thus, in effect, each voucher holder carries with him $1.50 in subsidy to the theater he decides to attend.

The voucher program was intended to achieve a number of different objectives:

(a) *Voucher attendees* are intended to receive from the program not only some subsidy for their attendance, but also some degree of influence over the policies of the theaters themselves. For example, it was hoped that the program would stimulate a number of performing groups to make a deliberate effort to make themselves attractive to students or to other special groups eligible for voucher participation.

(b) *Theaters* would, it was hoped, benefit not only by receiving some additional funds, but also by receiving these funds in a way that would not submit them to the particular tastes of foundation personnel whose preferences among performing groups as expressed in their allocation of funds inevitably serve to impose pressures upon the theaters to adapt themselves to that aesthetic orientation.

(c) Foundations were expected to benefit by being freed from decisions which they often prefer not to make—the determination of the precise amount of money to be granted to each applicant group. As it is organized, the granting organization is left with two instruments of control over the use of its funds (in addition to the choice of the total budget allocated for the purpose). It can decide what groups are to be eligible to purchase vouchers, and it can decide which theaters are eligible to participate. But once having exercised these two choices, the rest is in the hands of the attendees and the ability of the theaters themselves to influence those attendance patterns.

From the economists' point of view, the remarkable feature of the program is the injection of a quasi-market mechanism into the field of philanthropic support. The issue here is a delicate one. Presumably, the objectives of a subvention program would be undermined if the entire matter were left in the hands of the market. For then grants would simply flow to the productions that are most popular, that are least in need of funds, and which, from some widely accepted points of view, are those that merit such support least. Surely there would be few advocates of a subvention program, the bulk of whose funds were to flow to successful

Broadway musicals. Thus, a pure market mechanism for the allocation of support funds to the theater is unlikely to attract many enthusiasts. On the other hand, the complete absence of such a mechanism minimizes the motivation of theater groups to devote effort to the attraction of audiences, to seek to communicate with audiences effectively, and to provide programming which is attractive to any substantial group.

The voucher program was intended to sail between this Scylla and that Charybdis. By a foundation's selection of groups eligible to purchase vouchers and the right it retains to exclude particular theaters from participation, it can either prevent or limit the subvention of those who are judged not to merit it, either on financial or aesthetic grounds. In particular, by selecting for eligibility particular groups, such as members of minorities, whose attendance it was anxious to promote, the foundation could even help to stimulate the growth of a new type of theater, which not only has barely existed in the past, but which until recently virtually did not have the means to come into existence.

4. The Voucher Audience

After the voucher program had been in existence for nearly $1\frac{1}{2}$ years, we undertook a study which was partially intended to provide a preliminary report of its operation. This proved more difficult than had been anticipated, partly because of the very poor condition of financial records of many off-off-Broadway theaters, the extreme frequency with which groups are born and die (sometimes only to rise again), and the great variation in the magnitude and character of the activities of the individual theater from one year to another. Moreover, because the program began on so modest a scale (providing some 3% of the total estimated budget of the theaters), it was very difficult to separate out its effects from those of the far larger injections of funds from other sources of support.

One of the first steps we planned was a series of interviews with voucher users, theatergoers, and other attendees of the off-off-Broadway theater. Altogether some 350 such interviews were conducted by telephone from a randomly selected sample of voucher purchasers, in theater lobbies, and from a sample of theatergoers who declined to purchase vouchers.

Now it should be pointed out that attendees of live performances in theater, music, or dance are a remarkably homogeneous group. Their incomes are relatively comfortable. For example, over 57% of Broadway audiences earn over $15,000 per annum and nearly 25% earn more than

$25,000 (Playbill, 1973), and we have independent evidence that the figures for other art forms are very similar. Well over half of the adults in these audiences are professionals (Baumol and Bowen, 1966, p. 458). They are extraordinarily well educated: consistently more than half the women in these audiences have attended college and more than half the men have attended graduate school!

It has been found extremely difficult to modify these patterns. Free concerts bring only a tiny addition to the approximately 3% blue-collar workers who normally attend. Independent surveys in various European countries where extensive subsidies have long been provided show that the audience composition there differs negligibly from our own. It was hardly to be expected, then, that the voucher program would effect a revolution in audience composition, and looking only at averages it seems to have had little consequence at all.

The voucher users were found to have a median age of 40, which is not very different from that of the Broadway audience. The median educational level was completion of four years of college, falling short of completion of graduate school by only a few percentage points. Median income was about $18,000, probably even a bit higher than that of the patrons of the commercial theater.

Yet vouchers were able to attract at least two special audience groups, one of them rather surprising. The efforts of the Black and Hispanic theaters and their supporting community groups did apparently succeed in bringing in new audiences from among these ethnic groups, but this was accomplished only by bending the rules of the voucher program and in a number of cases by permitting direct distribution of vouchers to members of such organizations and neighborhood groups. The other special group of attendees which our survey showed to have been attracted by vouchers are older persons who have long enjoyed the theater but who feel their retirement income is insufficient to permit them to continue to attend higher-priced performances. Thus our survey showed 9% of voucher users to be aged 60 and over, while the comparable total Broadway figure is only 5%.

On the other hand, there are a number of impecunious attendees of off-off-Broadway theater who have not been reached by the voucher program. Our surveys of audiences in the lobbies showed that well over 30% of the audience earned less than $7000 per year, many of them writers, actors, poets, and others with professional interest in the theater. Most of these had not heard about the voucher program, and in fact many of them were not eligible for it since they were not students, union members, or members of any other groups that had been declared qualified.

5. Other Consequences of the Program

In studying the budgets of the individual theaters, one of the conclusions that emerged quickly from the figures was that the voucher program is particularly well adapted to the dispersion of funds among a large number of highly diverse groups. The major funding sources for off-off Broadway other than their own box offices (which yield one-third of their expenses) are the New York State Council on the Arts (providing 19% of total budget in 1972–1973), the National Endowment for the Arts (13%), and private foundations (13%). Groups such as these tend to have their favorites. Some 40% of the theaters in our sample received support from two of the three foundation sources mentioned and 10% received support from all three sources. Yet some of the theaters in the sample with outstanding reputations and excellent reviews (some of them winners of Obies, which are the off-off-Broadway annual rewards for outstanding artistic contributions) received support from none or at most one of these sources.

All private foundations together provided support to only 24 of the groups in our sample of 62. The National Endowment for the Arts offered funds to 18 of the groups, and only the New York State Council on the Arts reached more than a majority of the groups, a total of 42 of them. By the time its first full season of operation had drawn to a close, the voucher program had also brought income to over 80 off-off-Broadway groups, and in the next season the number of theaters it was helping had reached 127.[2]

The point is that in an area specializing in experimental effort of one sort or another, there must be some way to provide support quickly to new groups before they can establish an extensive record of artistic accomplishment or, for that matter, are able to present extensive financial records. The mechanism of the standard foundation procedure with its careful case-by-case investigation is simply not adapted to this sort of undertaking. On the other hand, the evidence suggests that the voucher program is able to channel funds quickly and easily throughout this segment of the theater.

Another fact that emerged, somewhat unexpectedly, was the relatively low administrative cost of the voucher program. Because it does not require examination of the budget of any theater group or extensive evaluation of its proposals, the bulk of the administrative work can be left to the computer which, in effect, acts as a seller of vouchers and as a record

---

[2] In total, the voucher program provided $50,000 to the theaters during its first (half) season of operation. During the next season, 1973–1974, it provided $100,000 in subvention money. The 1974–1975 total was $140,000.

keeper for eligible purchasers and eligible theaters. It has proved possible to operate the program for a total annual cost of $50,000 to $60,000, with the capacity to handle a much larger operation with only small increments in cost.

Moreover, for a small foundation, or a foundation which has no staff specializing in the arts, the program represents an even less expensive way to provide funds to a number of performing groups, for it can contribute to the agency that operates the voucher program (the Theatre Development Fund in the case of New York City).[3]

Yet the results show also that, after a point, there can be diminishing returns to the channeling of an excessively large proportion of support funds through a voucher program. Despite the opportunity for selectivity in the audience and theater groups declared eligible, there does remain some tendency for voucher funds to flow most heavily to more traditional and "popular" sorts of fare. For example, the theater which received by far the preponderance of voucher funds in the first full season of operation of the program is one that specializes in highly traditional performances of the classics and which can in no sense be considered experimental. TDF was indeed somewhat embarrassed at the disproportionate flow of funds to that one group and has since imposed a ceiling on the amount of voucher funding that can be received by any one theater.

The voucher program has also proved able to stimulate the theaters to devote effort toward attracting the voucher audience. While the $2.50 they receive from each voucher is no more than their typical admission charge and often less than that amount, they often have unsold seats and are therefore happy to get any such addition to their revenues. Indeed, some of their voucher income may represent a replacement of what were formerly complimentary tickets. Moreover, those theaters whose normal ticket price is $4 or $5 are likely to charge some of the difference as a supplementary attendance fee to voucher users. In any event, the theaters themselves have indeed made some effort to publicize the program. Of 27 theater groups in which interviews were conducted, 20 advertise in newspapers and mention TDF vouchers in their advertisements. Eighteen of the theaters send mailings advertising their presentations to the list of voucher holders which is made available to them by TDF. It is noteworthy that at the inception of the program, when the voucher budget was smaller and the theaters received only $2.00 per voucher, many of them indicated

---

[3] The off-off-Broadway program is no longer the only voucher program in operation. TDF has been offering separate vouchers for dance companies for over a year. Recently in Buffalo, New York, a voucher program was inaugurated for a more heterogeneous group of performing organizations, Chicago has its program, and proposals for such programs are under consideration in other localities.

that they had been far more reluctant to undertake additional mailings or to devote other types of extra effort for the purpose.

6. Concluding Comment on Vouchers

The main conclusion to be drawn from the evidence of the voucher program's brief period of operation is that it works. For nearly two years now it has operated remarkably well with little friction. It has brought support to a large and diverse group of organizations and seems to have contributed somewhat to the influence of audiences upon the performing groups. The evidence indicates most strongly that it has made life easier for the disbursing organization whose administrative costs have been kept low and which has been spared the distasteful job of arriving at aesthetic judgments it does not care to make and, worse still, of translating those judgments into specific pecuniary figures.

7. The Second Experiment: The Discount Ticket Booth—Background

As has already been indicated, two of Broadway's main economic problems are its large number of unsold tickets and its reluctance to admit their existence. In a month-by-month study extending over three theater seasons, we found that the revenues of Broadway productions on the average ranged from 60 to 70% of "capacity gross"; i.e., evaluated in monetary terms, 30–40% of capacity goes unsold on the average. Nor is it merely "flops" whose tickets go unsold. After much prodding, we were finally given access to data on day-by-day sales extending over a two-week period on nine productions, most of them reasonable "hits." Using the rather loose definition which takes anything less than 100 tickets unsold to constitute a "sellout," of the 132 performances in our sample, 109, or some 83%, were not sold out. Indeed, there was not a single sellout of any performance on a Monday, Tuesday, Wednesday, or Thursday evening (Baumol, 1972, pp. 25–28).

In addition to its unsold seats, Broadway has been plagued by the fact that its costs have been rising at a significantly more rapid rate than its ticket prices. For example, in current dollars, the average "top price" to a dramatic production rose from $3.59 in 1927–1928 to $8.77 in 1968–1969, i.e., it went up by a bit less than 2.5 times (the price of musicals rose even more slowly). On the other hand, from a sample of seven dramas in the earlier of these years and five in the latter,[4] average production costs for a "straight play" had risen more than sevenfold, from $16,300 in the earlier year to $115,000 in the latter.

8. The TKTS Discount Booth Arrangements

The natural solution in such circumstances is a reduction in ticket prices in order to attract a larger audience, preferably by means of a discriminatory mechanism that brings with it little loss in those revenues that would have accrued in the absence of the price innovation. As a matter of fact, several such discriminatory provisions were already in use considerably earlier. About four years ago a "student rush" program was instituted. Under its provisions, shortly before curtain time, tickets are put on sale at substantial discounts to students presenting ID cards and persons with Medicare identifications. A system of "two-fers" has been in operation for even longer. These special passes for failing productions are left at student unions, bars, and other miscellaneous repositories. The holder of such a pass is entitled to purchase, *in advance* and for certain specified times of performance, two tickets for the price of one.

Extending and somewhat modifying these ideas, in June 1973 the Theatre Development Fund opened a discount box office at 47th Street and Broadway, right in the heart of the theater district. It is located on a small square separating Broadway and Seventh Avenue, where those who pass by can hardly avoid noticing it and the long lines of people that frequently stand before it.

The discount box office accepts allocations of tickets from Broadway, off-Broadway,[5] and Lincoln Center productions including the Metropolitan Opera. The tickets are sold *only on the day of performance.* They are priced at one-half their nominal value plus a small service charge. The half-price is remitted to the theater while the service charge covers the cost of operation of the box office. Purchasers are offered no amenities,

---

[4] For the earlier figures, see Berheim, (1932, Chapter 34). For the ticket price data and the more recent cost figures, see Baumol (1972, pp. 30, 37).

[5] Note the single "off" in the name of this category. Soon after World War II, off Broadway evolved as an experimental theater movement. It gradually became pretty much an establishment activity with admissions close to those of Broadway and relatively little if any innovative activity, distinguished from Broadway only in the smaller size and dispersed location of its theaters. It was virtually destroyed by the latest contract with Actors Equity. Almost all the theaters that now have off-Broadway union arrangements are nonprofit and noncommercial.

not even protection from the elements, until they are within a few yards of the ticket windows. There they also find a listing of all the productions to which tickets are available. Thus, TKTS[6] does incidental service as a central box office[7] at which buyers can pick and choose among shows.

Participation by producers has been fairly substantial. Usually some two-thirds of the shows running are represented at TKTS. A few smash hits have just had no tickets to offer, and several producers who disapproved of the entire idea on the ground that it would habituate patrons to "cheap theater" sedulously boycotted the institution altogether.

Measured in terms of the volume that had been anticipated, TKTS was an instant success and has continued to perform superbly. Starting off with sales of about 7000 tickets per week, sales have since risen (with an occasional dip) to more than twice that amount. In its second season of operation, it can be anticipated that TKTS may well contribute over $4 million to participating theaters or nearly 10% of the total Broadway gross.

Sales do not seem to fall off in bad weather. Despite the absence of shelter for patrons, demand is brisk over the Christmas–New Year season and the ensuing months, and is also heavy in the summer months that are traditionally considered slack periods.

9. Effect on Audience Composition

To determine whether the discount box office was working, three issues seemed to be central:

(a)   Was TKTS attracting a different type of attendee?

(b)   How much of a net increase in attendance was TKTS producing?

(c)   Was it making a net contribution to theater revenues despite the reduced prices at which it was selling tickets?

In effect, there is a fourth question implicit in this last:

How successful has the discriminatory pricing policy pursued by TKTS been in keeping its new market separate from the more traditional Broadway market?

Audience composition was studied with the aid of some 1600 questionnaires filled out at the box office by a reasonably random sample of its

[6] TKTS is a pseudoacronym for the institution, whose full title is The Times Square Theatre Centre.

[7] It should be noted that a central box office has been advocated by persons in the theater industry for at least 50 years. However, the collection of individualists who compose the industry found it impossible to agree on any such measure. The TKTS box office was established only because it was organized by an independent agency.

customers. Overall, the audience exhibited most of the same characteristics we had come to expect: they were well educated, had comfortable incomes, and were primarily professionals.

However, there were differences. TKTS patrons were considerably younger, better educated, and slightly less affluent than the overall Broadway audience. TKTS users included a higher share of professionals than the overall Broadway audience (60 versus 56%) and a higher proportion of blue collar workers (5 versus 3%). The median age of TKTS patrons was 30, while that of the Broadway audience was 40. Some 70% of the former and 45% of the latter have completed college. The median income of TKTS users was $15,800, while that of the Broadway audience was $17,100. It may be slightly suggestive to think of these responses in price elasticity terms. In calculating such elasticities, one cannot take the pertinent price change to be a 50% price cut. For, TKTS patrons must purchase tickets of whatever price category happens to be available. On the basis of the interviews, we learned what category of seat (orchestra, balcony, etc.) the TKTS patron normally purchased when buying from another source. We were able to calculate that the average price of a ticket purchased elsewhere by this group was about $7.00, while at the TKTS box office the average price received for a ticket (excluding service charge) was $4.50 (full price $9.00). This gives us an average price reduction of $(7 - 4.5)/[0.5(7 + 4.5)] = 43\%$. We then obtain the pseudoelasticities of audience composition (Table I). Thus, composition of TKTS patrons was in a number of respects substantially different from that of the typical Broadway audience.

There was, however, one very great difference which we know to be significant, though we are not in a position to document its magnitude. TKTS has clearly made a substantial contribution to last minute "impulse" buying. While we do not have the data, it is quite clear that Broadway's advertising of its sellout smash hits has led to the sale of a very high proportion of its ticket volume to patrons who are willing to

TABLE I

Percent Changes in Selected Audience Characteristics over Percent Change in Price

Characteristics	TKTS patrons	Broadway audience	Percent difference	Pseudo-elasticity
Percent professionals	60	56	6.8	0.16
Percent blue collar	5	3	50.0	1.16
Median age	30	40	−28.6	−0.67
Percent college graduate	70	45	43.5	1.00
Median income	$15,800	$17,100	−7.9	−0.18

commit themselves well before the date of performance, typically weeks and even months in advance.

At TKTS one *cannot* buy before the day of performance. Moreover, the fact that TKTS serves as a central box office means that the buyer can be quite certain of getting tickets to something, and therefore the trip to the theater district in search of last-minute tickets becomes less risky. The result is clear. In our interviews, over 60% of the TKTS patrons indicated they had decided to purchase tickets no more than 2 days before their date of attendance.

10.   Effect on Volume and Revenues

Unfortunately, it is very difficult to carry out any sort of sophisticated statistical analysis on theatrical data because of their basic heterogeneity. We cannot conduct a straightforward comparison of sales of tickets to plays which utilize TKTS and those which do not, because there are obviously other reasons for differences in their popularity and changes in their popularity. Moreover, a time series analysis is not easy because interest in a production tends to dwindle with the passage of time, and the weather, seasonal patterns, and other influences inject a great deal of noise into the data. Thus, our analysis of the revenue and attendance effects of TKTS was deliberately as simple and unsophisticated as we could make it.

Two analyses, completely independent in method and data, were in fact carried out, and happily their results were completely consistent. The first was based on a study of revenue data for participating and nonparticipating theaters for a period of 10 weeks before and 10 weeks after the opening of the discount ticket booth. The second analysis was based entirely on information obtained from our interviews.

The first of these calculations was carried out by Professor Stephen Goldfeld, using data on weekly grosses taken from *Variety,* for all but two of the productions that were running at the time that TKTS opened (the two were rejected because their participation in the program was too erratic to permit them to be classified easily). The sample consisted of seven participating and four nonparticipating productions. Because there is more temptation for producers to use TKTS when the box office sales of a production are declining, we expected sales of participating productions to be declining faster than those of nonparticipants *both before and after* the opening of the box office, and the data in fact confirmed this. The problem was to separate out this decline from any effect of the sales by TKTS. Breaking the data into four 5-week periods and comparing the figures, it turned out that for participating productions, for every $1 spent in the first 5-week period before the opening of TKTS, 90¢ was grossed in the second 5-week period, and 83¢ in the 10 weeks immediately following the opening. (For nonparticipating productions, the results were much flatter, with the figures respectively $1, 97¢, and 95¢.)

Of the 83¢ to participating productions, roughly 9¢ came from TKTS and the remainder from other sources. If one is willing to make the assumption that in the absence of TKTS the percentage loss in sales from the first 5 weeks to the second would have continued thereafter, then in the absence of TKTS box office sales of participating theaters would have been 77¢ for every dollar of gross in the initial 5 weeks. If one adds to this the slight seasonal decline evident for the nonparticipating theaters, this estimate is reduced to 75¢. In other words, under this assumption, of the 9¢ attributable to TKTS, only 1–3¢ would have shown up at the box office anyway. Thus between 67 and 89% of TKTS revenues represented a net contribution to box office income.

With alternative tests of this variety yielding results at least equally strong, it was estimated, in sum, that of the $2 million paid to the theaters by TKTS during its first year of operation, between $1 and $1.6 million was a net addition to sales.

Our second and independent estimate was obtained from figures on past attendance of current TKTS users and the length of time they had been using the box office. From interview data it was calculated that an average TKTS user had attended Broadway performances an average of about 5.4 times during the preceding year, while for newcomers to the booth the previous average attendance was only 2.9 times. Assuming that the latter figure characterized the attendance of all persons when they first used the booth, to bring the overall average up to the calculated 5.4 for both new and old patrons together, this means that the typical TKTS user must go to the theater far more often than he or she did before beginning to use the booth. Indeed, it is easy to show that this difference must be 11.9/2.9, i.e., of the order of 4 to 1.[8]

Thus, recalling that we are dealing with an average price reduction of 43% (see Section 9), this gives us an apparent arc elasticity figure of about 2.8. Of course, this figure need not represent what would happen if all

---

[8] Let P_0 be the proportion of new box office users, P_1 the proportion who have been using it one month, etc., where the figures were $P_0 = 37.09, P_1 = 12.58, P_2 = 5.96, P_3 = 5.30, P_4 = 5.30, P_5 = 2.65, P_6 = 10.60, P_7 = 2.65, P_8 = 3.31, P_9 = 2.65, P_{10} = 5.96, P_{11} = 5.96$. Let x be the rate of attendance of TKTS patrons, with 2.9 the pre-TKTS-use rate of attendance and 5.4 the average attendance. Then we must have $P_0(12/12)(2.9) + P_1[(11/12)(2.9) + x/12] + \ldots + P_{11}[(1/12)(2.9) + 11x/12] = 5.4$, whose solution is $x = 11.9$. Thus, the ratio of the new attendance rate to the old is $x/2.9 \cong 4/1$.

Broadway ticket prices were reduced 43%. It may in good part reflect the public's reaction to a clearly labeled bargain,[9] and to the convenience in having a central ticket box office where the buyer can see the available choices on display.

In any event, we can now complete our second calculation of the revenue contribution of TKTS. Since TKTS users, on the average, bought $7 tickets previously, and now pay the theaters $4.50 per ticket on the average, this means that every 2.9 visits to the theater yielding $20.30 (= $7.00 × 2.9) per year was replaced by TKTS providing a purchase of $53.55 (= $4.50 × 11.9). In other words, every dollar of gross brought in by TKTS yielded to the theaters a net return of 62¢. Of the $2 million total grossed through TKTS, about $1.25 million was a net contribution—a figure completely consistent with our previous estimate of $1–$1.6 million.

Obviously, TKTS does then seem to be making a net contribution to theater audience and theater income. It is apparently an effective device for price discrimination, with the separation of the pertinent markets somewhat imperfect but by no means so great as to undermine its workings.

11. Concluding Comment

This discussion was intended to show that economic analysis can be helpful to the arts directly, and to illustrate some of the ways in which it can be useful. It can help in the design of new programs, basing itself on some of our welfare notions and on the policy predilections to which they lead. It can also help in the analysis of the consequences of some of these policies, at least getting beyond the most obvious statistical pitfalls in the evaluation of their results. It may be added, in conclusion, that all of this work was done at the request of various segments of the theater, that the results have elicited considerable interest, and that the response has been reasonably gratifying.

References

Baumol, W. (1972). *Basic Report, Study of the New York Theater*. New York City Cultural Council.

[9] There seems to be evidence that a label announcing "5¢ off" on a package of soap increases sales significantly more than a straightforward reduction equal in amount. There are many possible explanations other than "irrationality." The "5¢ off" label provides or appears to provide information while the shopper may simply never notice the straightforward reduction. Moreover, the label suggests that the reduction is temporary, making it attractive to stock up on the product before its price rises again.

Baumol, W. J., and Bowen, W. G. (1966). *Performing Arts: The Economic Dilemma.* New York: Twentieth Century Fund.

Berheim, A. L. (1932). *The Business of the Theater.* New York: Benjamin Blom.

Playbill (1973). *Playbill* Survey. New York: Metromedia, Inc.

Department of Economics
Princeton University
Princeton, New Jersey

and

New York University
New York, New York

From Growth to the Millenium:
Economics and the Transformation
of the Idea of Progress

*Paul A. David**

1. A Puzzle for Social Science

Most of the academic economists in my acquaintance express some impatience with polemics against "growth," and puzzlement over the

* A sketch of this paper was presented at the American Academy of Arts and Sciences Planning Conference on "The Transformation of the Idea of Progress," February 10–12, 1977, San Diego, California; the paper in substantially its present form was presented to the Conference on Resources in Economic History (convened by W. N. Parker) at Villa Serbelloni, Bellagio, Italy, April 12–18, 1977. Helpful comments were received from participants in both conferences. I also have benefited immeasurably from the opportunity to discuss this subject with Moses Abramovitz, and to read a draft of his contribution to this volume. While Abramovitz has done his utmost to keep me from error, he must be absolved of all complicity in the views represented here. Financial support under NSF Grant No. SOC 75-08444 is gratefully acknowledged.

59

fashion these lately have come to enjoy in intellectual circles. To give my colleagues their due, theirs is not the reaction of certifiable growth-maniacs. Rather, they take the view that the rising chorus of discontent and dismay occasioned by the prospect of continued material progress (as it used to be called) has succeeded in drawing attention to conceptual issues that have been thoroughly understood by several generations of economists, refurbishing these well-worn questions by interjecting an array of empirical assertions whose validity remains unestablished. In short, they are inclined to dismiss the "limits to growth" literature in its various forms as having been compounded largely of old truths and new falsehoods. Whatever one may say concerning the merits or injustices of this characterization—and it seems beside the point for me to try deciding the matter here—impatience usually is of little help to understanding. Hence the economist's persisting puzzlement over the growing currency of these ideas in the industrialized societies of the West.

As the phenomenon in question still lies mainly in the realm of social thought, and thus outside the narrow purview of an economist's professional competence, some diffidence on my part in essaying its causes may be forgiven—indeed, applauded. Certainly, I would be proceeding under less of an intellectual handicap had the corpus of classical and neoclassical economic analysis been more than only marginally touched by nineteenth century conceptualizations of societal progress. Yet, as much as Auguste Comte did for John Stuart Mill's own intellectual development, non-Marxian economics remains essentially an ahistorical social science. And within such a framework it is awkward to come to grips with the possibility that, as a consequence of the rapid pace of material progress itself, we are now witnessing an incipient realization of the paradoxical transformation of ideology envisaged by J. B. Bury.

Recall that it was Bury's (1932) observation that the Idea of Progress achieved its ascendancy by overcoming "the illusion of finality." But he eventually asked whether this ideology could be immune from its own negation of finality:

> Will not that process of change, for which Progress is the optimistic name, compel "Progress" too to fall from the commanding position in which it is now, with apparent security enthroned. . . . A day will come, in the revolution of centuries, when a new idea will usurp its place as the directing idea of humanity. Another star, unnoticed now or invisible, will climb up the intellectual heaven, and human emotions will react to its influence, human plans respond to its guidance. It will be the criterion by which Progress and all other ideas will be judged. And it too will have its successor [p. 352].

Is that day dawning—rather sooner than Bury seemed to have anticipated? If so, why at this juncture, and not at some other? What is the relation of this "new idea" to the Ideology of Progress as formerly conceived, and among what social groups may it come to exercise a strong appeal? These are questions properly addressed to an historical social science, which may account for some of the difficulties that conventional economists have in confronting them.

2. Material Progress, Economic Welfare, and Social Welfare

Conventional economic analysis, "bourgeois economics" if you like, has its share of conceptual deficiencies. But a failure to distinguish between "more" and "better" is not among them. It may be helpful therefore to begin with some insights drawn from welfare economics.

Material progress, or "economic growth" as it is called nowadays, takes its meaning from a conception of the interest of society. The conventional view embraced by economists derives from the utilitarian doctrine that the interest of society lies in satisfying the wants of the individuals who compose it. It is their satisfactions which comprise "welfare." The Physiocrats and Adam Smith took the position that human happiness was promoted by increased opulence and the liberty to enjoy as well as profit from it. But economists since Pigou generally have been careful to draw a distinction between *social welfare* and the narrower concept of *economic welfare*, which is taken as referring to "that part of social welfare that can be brought directly or indirectly into relation with the measuring rod of money [Pigou, 1952, ed., p. 11]." National product or income, in turn, is taken to be the objective, quantitative counterpart of economic welfare. By now few social scientists are unaware of the fact that the conventional national income accounts do not provide a fully comprehensive, utterly coherent measure of aggregate economic performance. That indexes of real national income growth also abstract entirely from crucial distributional questions, of course, is more widely recognized. Those economists who have concerned themselves primarily with the study of secular change, however, have traditionally been most sensitive to the uncertainties and ambiguities involved in interpreting real national income per capita as a basic index of long-term economic progress.

For purposes of evaluating short-run movements, the view taken is that changes in economic welfare can be presumed to affect social welfare in the same direction, and may be fairly confidently gauged by reference to measures of aggregate or per capita output. When the sources of short-term variations in measured economic growth are considered, variations that will arise primarily from changes in unemployment and the intensity of utilization of available stocks of resources, the foregoing empirical presumption hardly seems unreasonable. When one comes to think about economic growth processes of a more sustained character, less confidence can be placed in the presumption that the dominant effect of economic causes is on the quantity of output, and that the satisfactions potentially or actually derived from changes in output overshadow those effects which flow from concomitant alterations in social organization, in the structure and location of industry and population, in the nature of work and other aspects of the human condition. Expressions of doubt among economists on this score are scarcely of recent origin, even in the literature informed by modern welfare theory. In a deservedly influential essay written two decades ago, Abramovitz (1959) pointed out that

> when we compare generations and half-centuries, we cannot escape the fact that the causes which produce large differences in output also shape the nature and organization of work and modify the substance of our material opportunities, liberties, and security, and, therefore, the satisfaction we can obtain from these aspects or consequences of economic activity and organization [pp. 3–4].

This, however, is a viewpoint grounded in an historical, developmental conceptualization of the process of long-term economic growth, and it is necessary to acknowledge that many economists have found it quite attractive to work within a rather different, indeed, an antithetical paradigm of growth. During the late 1950s and the 1960s there flourished a fashion for mathematical growth theories that were preoccupied with generalizing upon, and working out the full implications of von Neumann's distinctly ahistorical vision of an unchanging economic structure undergoing "balanced," "quasi-stationary" expansion. The interest generated in this line of inquiry was not unrelated to the contemporary real-world phenomena of economic growth. But, even so, there were some economists whose intimate knowledge of "growth theory" led them to identify the latter as the theory of steady state expansion. They hastened to insist that, however useful the notion of a steady state growth path might be for analytical purposes, and however comforting it might be to seize upon that fiction as a warrant for setting aside doubts about the firmness of the links joining increasing output to greater social welfare, this branch of dynamic analysis had little to do with economic history or empirical issues of economic development (cf., e.g., Hahn, 1971, p. viii).

While doubt and controversy concerning the nexus between economic welfare and social welfare is generally engendered by perceptions of the structural changes that are, historically, the concomitants of economic growth, there is some reason to suppose that dissension on this score may become more pronounced as higher levels of real income are attained. The argument goes something like this. Personal hopes and fears having to do with immediate economic circumstances appear to constitute the single most salient area of human concerns, dominating even voiced concerns about health and family matters. Such generalizations receive a measure of support from the findings of Cantril (1965) and others. American cross-sectional data and some international comparisons surveyed by Easterlin (1974, pp. 94–95, 114) suggest that whereas familial and person health concerns do not diminish in prominence as individuals reach higher income levels, economic concerns do become somewhat reduced in importance. Correspondingly, the proportion of the population for whom some other areas of concern are most prominent becomes enlarged. But there is no comparable area of salience discernible within this latter category of concerns: for some, emotional maturity counts uppermost; for others, it is world peace, the enjoyment of leisure time, job satisfactions, personal or social acceptance, and so forth. Thus, to put it baldly, increased affluence may systematically erode the basis for social consensus on the desirability of material improvements, and increase the weight people assign to conditions of their existence which—taken in toto—are not systematically affected for better or worse by the processes of change associated with sustained economic growth.

A further, rather easy elaboration of this hypothesis may be considered of interest for its relevance to the peculiar historical circumstances of the post World War II era. We might suppose that the circumstances of youth exercise an especially potent influence in forming the subsequent pattern of human concerns. In the United States and the industrialized countries of Western Europe, the rearing of an unusually large cohort of (baby-boom) youngsters during a period of unprecedentedly rapid economic growth and remarkably sustained prosperity may have temporarily brought into existence a large segment within the now-adult population who do not concur with their parents' generation in assigning overriding importance to immediate economic circumstances. Moreover, for reasons already noticed, it may well be the case that the individuals forming this segment of the population have yet to find some common point of focus among their increasingly salient "nonmaterialist" concerns, except in the consensus that these diverse individual aspirations will not all be equally well served by further economic growth. Here, then, is a potential market—but possibly only a transiently exploitable opportunity—for antigrowth polemicists who can elaborate upon the distinction between improving economic welfare and increasing human happiness. Yet sufficient additional opportunities for those who would ply this trade are created by the unbalanced character of economic growth itself.

3. Unbalanced Growth and the Dubious Nature of Economic Progress

The fact that economic growth historically has entailed structural changes in the array of goods and services produced, and in the relative market valuations placed upon them, gives rise to two sorts of difficulties or "hitches" in economic analysis. One sort of "hitch" is that the economic welfare content of pronounced changes in per capita output measures becomes uncomfortably ambiguous. The other sort consists of the logical contradictions that can be created by indefinitely extrapolating a persisting pattern of unbalanced expansion. Such contradictions, when embedded in concrete models, give specific form to visions of the process of economic growth that Schumpeter (1954) described as "hitchbound" rather than "hitchless."

Members of the first of these two classes of difficulties are referred to as index-number problems. They are endemic in all aggregation procedures where aggregation is really necessary. In an economy undergoing balanced, or steady state growth, the production and consumption of all outputs (goods, *and* bads such as effluvient discharges) would be increasing at the same rate; any element in the set would serve equally well as an index of the growth of the aggregate, whatever principle of aggregation were adopted. Unbalanced growth occasions the need to construct meaningful aggregates. Following the logic of Pigou's proposal to render incommensurable quantities commensurable by applying "the measuring rod of money," economists have settled upon the use of some set of relative prices as the weights to be used in constructing measures of aggregate real income or product.

There is a sophisticated rationale for the use of prices as weights in this connection. It rests upon a fundamental theorem: that the relative prices generated in a perfectly competitive economy would reflect not only relative social marginal costs of production, but the relative marginal utilities derived by individuals in an equilibrium situation characterized by "Pareto optimality." The latter refers to a "welfare-efficient" allocational state in which the economic welfare of no individual could be improved except at the expense of reducing the economic welfare of some other member(s) of the society. No more satisfactory principle of weighting has been proposed. Still, substantial discomfort with it is created by acknowledgment of the growing disparities between the world in which we live and the hypothetical model of a perfectly competitive equilibrium-seeking system of producers and consumers whose individual economic welfare can be affected *only* through the medium of market transactions, and not by nonmarket externalities of production and consumption.

Be this as it may, we have yet to come to the index-number problem.

The latter arises when one asks which relative prices, among the alternative price configurations generated in the process of economic change, are to be taken as the standard in evaluating the movements of aggregate production or real income? In general, the answer to the question "How much economic growth has occurred?" will not be invariant with respect to the weighting scheme that has been selected. Moreover, in a comparison of two bundles of goods, unless the quantity of every commodity purchased has increased or at least remained unchanged, it is quite possible that the measured change in real income (real aggregate expenditures) will show an increase when one of the corresponding sets of prices is employed to perform the aggregation, and a decrease when the alternative set of prices is thus employed. The more pronounced the change in the structure of consumption (or output), and the more pronounced the correlation between relative movements of prices and quantities, the more likely it is that such diametrically conflicting evaluations will arise.

In other words, the shifts in commodity consumption and price structure that have been part and parcel of the rapid economic growth experienced in the industrialized nations during the past 25 years, have tended to heighten the range of ambiguity caused by the index-number problem. And in so doing, rapid economic growth has exacerbated doubts concerning its economic welfare content. At the individual level, people may perceive this in terms of being able to recall having consumed a basket of goods very different in composition and correspondingly different in relative valuation from the one presently within their command. Live theater is now attended only rarely, whereas television dramas are watched far more frequently than formerly was the case. But compared to the cost of an evening before the television set, the cost of an evening at the theater is now much greater than it used to be. Our representative individual did not have it within his power to chose to live with one of these relative price regimes rather than the other. But the macroprocess of growth has now posed for him the problem of evaluating its "meaning." He must either cling to an autonomous and invariant set of preferences, or, alternatively, choose between the socially formed vantage points of the present and past—as these are mirrored in relative market valuations of commodities—before he can determine whether he has become economically better off or worse off.

Index-number problems such as this create further ambiguities when one begins to debate whether particular goods and services properly are to be treated as positively valued final outputs, rather than omitted, or subtracted from conventional measures of aggregate production. Are the services of private automobiles used by commuting workers a final good, or an intermediate input (hence a cost) required by spatial location or production and consumption activities? Are the regulatory and protective services of governmental agencies similarly intermediate inputs, the costs of running a complex, highly interdependent urbanized society? Are national defense expenditures to be omitted from measures of economic welfare on the ground that these are "regrettable necessities" which unfortunately do not contribute to improving the human lot? There is ample room for ethical disagreement over these questions, and some nice philogophical issues would be involved in deciding them (cf. Nordhaus and Tobin, 1972).

But the point here is that the way they are resolved would not be of any consequence for the measurement of economic growth if everything were growing "in balance." The fact that these debated uses of productive capacity appear to have been expanding relatively rapidly during the present century, and may continue to do so in the future, has thus served to further deepen the penumbra of doubt and controversy that has come to surround our available indices of material progress. This increased uncertainty concerning the proper interpretation of the recent historical record is hardly diminished by the observation that nonmarket uses of time also have increased vis-à-vis the allocation of time to market production. For, on some standards of valuing nonmarket time, it appears that a fully comprehensive per capita measure of economic welfare (MEW, a là Nordhaus and Tobin) would be found to have more closely approximated the rate of growth in the conventional net national product measures during the present century than was the case in former times.[1] On this reading of the long historical record (which draws upon my unpublished work with Abramovitz), the overstatement of the rate of economic welfare improvement represented by net national product per capita has become progressively less pronounced, although there is no assurance of the continuation of this trend in the American economy.

The second class of "hitches" occasioned by an awareness of the unbalanced character of modern economic growth are quite different from those just considered. They encourage immediate doubt about the future by focusing attention upon some supposedly ineradicable obstacle to sustained material progress. The paradigm for these hitchbound visions is, of course, the dismal Ricardian picture of convergence to a stationary state

---

[1] When time devoted to all nonmarket uses (other than eating and sleeping) is valued at its constant 1800 shadow price (its opportunity cost in the production of conventional, market goods), a per capita measure of economic welfare for the United States—aggregating the real value of nonmarket time and real net sustainable private domestic product—is found to have grown at the average annual rate of 0.31% during the era 1800–1890. This amounts to only one-fourth of the concurrent growth rate of real GNP per capita. The comparable per capita MEW growth rate during 1890–1967 is 1.29% per annum, representing almost three-fourths of the per capita GNP rate.

in which population growth and net investment cease when (and because) average income is driven downward to a basic subsistence level by the pressure of population upon a fixed stock of land. The majority of economists are chary of embracing such pessimistic visions, perhaps because they share Schumpeter's view that the obvious deficiency of the early "dismal scientists" was their lack of imagination and inability to perceive what was happening to future production possibilities—as a consequence of many technological developments underway during the age in which they wrote.

The simpler versions of exhaustible-resource-bound models of growth that have surfaced once more are, therefore, largely the creations of scientists and engineers. In the work of Meadows *et al.* (1972), the proximate limiting factors are the stocks of depletable natural resource deposits, and, after those, unpolluted bodies of water and breathable air. A more universal pessimistic vision—whose logic even economists are prepared to acknowledge—is the thermodynamic reformulation offered by Georgescu-Roegen (1971), in which the role of the limiting stock is taken by the finite amount of low entropy matter available to a closed system.

With regard to all but the lattermost of these formulations, economists have been quick to ask just how the stock is operationally defined and whether it is truly exhaustible. Can environmental degradation be reversed at some cost? One also wants to know about the prospects for technological improvements that could effectively augment the size of discoverable stocks (cf. e.g., Beckerman, 1974). Further, the ease with which the services of reproducible stocks can be substituted for those of nonreproducible stocks turns out to be quite critical in determining whether or not particular exhaustible resources would prove to be an obstacle to sustained growth. Finally, with respect to this whole class of models, economists have questioned the temporal relevance of the cited limits. If there exist irremovable obstacles to sustained material progress—or sustained existence of a stationary state, in the case of the prospective heat-death promised us by the Second Law of Thermodynamics—then it is certainly not irrelevant to ask whether the limits are imminent as well as immanent. Is the end so close, and being approached at so rapid a rate in real time, that these concerns should dominate current thinking on matters of social policy?

A parallel logical structure may be recognized in Baumol's (1967) formulation of the macroeconomic implications of unbalanced productivity growth, which is envisaged as causing production costs to rise more rapidly in the service sector than in primary and secondary productive activities. And parallel questions of empirical relevance may be raised. The measurement of productivity change in the service industries is itself fraught with difficulties, so that the global premises of the model must remain in some doubt. But put that sort of carping criticism to one side. Will the impossibility of reducing the man-hours required for the playing of Beethoven string quartets really form a final impediment to the continuation of economic progress? The difficulty to which Baumol was directing notice, of course, was the tendency for the price of live performances of the arts to rise in relation to the price of other commodities, threatening their replacement by recordings, videotapes, or other, still less perfect, substitutes. But then the problem is not so much one of a production limit to growth, as it is the index-number ambiguities that surround the assignment of welfare meaning to the process of change. This surely is also the way one should read Linder (1970) on the effects of the rising opportunity cost of time, in creating the paradox of a "harried leisure class." And the same may be said with regard to Scitovsky's (1976) perception of a systematic tendency of modern technological progress to reduce the relative prices of goods that are better suited for use in satisfying peoples' needs for comfort than their needs for stimulation. This insidious sort of unbalanced productivity change in the limit draws the unwary affluent consumer into a condition which leaves him more bored than pleased—victim of the "joyless economy."

Hirsch, in *Social Limits to Growth* (1976), managed to construct an archetypal impasse that synthesizes many of the foregoing variations on the unbalanced growth theme. As people obtain more of the only kinds of goods the supply of which can be expanded without immediately foreseeable limits, according to Hirsch, they will more ardently seek "socially limited," or "positional" goods. Fundamentally, to caricature a rather more subtle argument, when peoples' immediate physiological wants are satisfied by material progress, they begin to hanker after territory and slaves. In bourgeois society, this drive has been sublimated to the point that it looks like the quest for a larger backyard in low-density suburbia, an unspoiled view of the beach, and domestic help. But the supply of these (so-called positional) goods that can be made available to all the members of a closed society will not expand. Indeed, Hirsch discerned a still greater perversity in the workings of the affluent economies: the congestion at the beach caused when everybody has the time and the means to get there, and the negative effect of rising income upon the supply of work, ultimately results in a diminution of the quality-adjusted stock of positional goods. This then becomes the absorbing barrier which eventually sops up society's physical and psychic resources until, presumably, the process reaches a nonprogressive equilibrium state where individuals' aspirations have been replaced by the dominant sensation of frustration and inevitable self-defeat.

It seems to me that these gloomy parables are not meant to be taken literally. Certainly no more than was Ricardo's. His dismal dynamics is best read as an artful elaboration of the vision projected by the first edition of Malthus' *Essay,* and designed to convert the young Reverend's retort to Godwinian utopianism into a persuasive polemic against the English Corn Laws. But Ricardo was a meliorist reformer in the Enlightenment tradition. Recent antigrowth polemicists have a different purpose in developing parables around the contradictions of indefinite unbalanced growth. By insisting that things cannot go on like this forever, they direct attention to the inevitability of a terminus and the necessity of a transition to some new state of affairs. Whether or not the specific models are parametrized so that the point of terminus can be fixed in real time, the vision of its existence is elevated to the status of a dominant idea that should guide human thought and action now and for the immediate future. If this, the Ideology of Limits, is the "new idea" which presently is laying claim to the place formerly occupied by the Ideology of Progress, I think it is worth remarking upon its striking resemblance to a much older conceptual system: millenarianism.

4. The Ideology of Limits and the Future of Middle-Class Millenarianism

"Millenarian" is a term used typologically to characterize religious movements that expect imminent, total, ultimate, this-worldly, collective salvation (Talmon, 1968, pp. 349–362).[2] The label has been affixed to a wide assortment of historical movements, but my identification of the emergent ideology of "limits of growth" as millenarian in its conceptual characteristics in frankly speculative. In these brief observations I have neither the desire nor the space to overstate the case.

The nub of it is simple enough: the millenarian tradition derives from Jewish apocalyptic literature and the Revelations of St. John, echoes of which reverberate clearly in the writings of the modern ecodoomsayers. The apocalypse is close at hand, and believers must live in tense expectation and preparation for the Day—and for the salvation on earth that is to follow. The view of salvation itself is revolutionary and catastrophic, for millenarianism is dominated by a sense of deepening crisis, the solution for which only can be redemption of an ultimate kind. And this impending salvation is conceived of as ultimate and temporally irrevocable. Time

---

[2] In the following, I conform to *Webster's Third New International Dictionary* in using the term "millenarianism," rather than the shortened form "millenarism" favored by Talmon.

appears as a linear process that leads to a final future, an *Endzeit*. By merging historical and nonhistorical, mythical, conceptions of time in this way, millenarianism represents a mode of posthistorical thinking, encouraging flight from historical consciousness toward the desired recapture of the past viewed as a golden age. This feature of millenarianism may account for the parallelisms to be found in economists' discussions of long-term growth, for such discussions themselves oscillate between the historical and ahistorical time conceptions embedded, respectively, in "development theory" and "growth theory."

The more profound the crisis, and the more complete the impasse, the more radical must be the break with society's past experience if the faithful are to transcend the disorder. Ample room is thus afforded within the millenarian conceptual system to those whose fundamental optimism regarding the perfectibility of man predisposes them to see beyond the apocalypse to the endless salvation. The new dispensation is to bring about not merely improvements, but final solutions. Meliorist economic prescriptions in the liberal tradition, therefore, are illusory. Worse still, they may even be subversive of preparation for the complete transformation in which answers will be found for all the vexing allocational problems which externalities create in decentralized, market economies. The ultimate ethical and political issues of achieving distributive justice too, will be resolved—if only because the need to settle these questions will become compelling as a means of allocating the ultimately limited stocks of resources that are available to mankind. Indeed, in this last regard, the ultimate solutions are not less but the more to be desired because they require a moral revolution. Here is Daly (1973), describing the "enormous and revolutionary" social and economic implications of the coming stationary state:

> The central concept must be the stock of wealth, not as presently, the flow of income and consumption. Furthermore, the stock must not grow. For several reasons the important issue of the steady state will be distribution, not production. The problem of relative shares can no longer be avoided by appeals to growth . . . the arguments justifying inequality in wealth as necessary for savings, investments and growth will lose their force . . . the focus will be on the distribution of the stock of wealth, not on the distribution of the flow of income. . . . It is hard to see how ethical appeals to equal shares can be countered. . . . The steady state would make fewer demands on our environmental resources, but much greater demands on our moral resources. . . . But in an age of rockets, hydrogen bombs, cybernetics, and genetic control, there is simply no substitute for

moral resources, and no alternative to relying upon them, whether they prove sufficient or not [p. 19].

Along with a typical vagueness regarding the steps by which the redemption is to be brought about, another suggestive characteristic of millenarian ideology is its definite collective orientation. Individualistic preparation for the Day is unavailing, and solutions that engage egotistical impulses (such as economic self-interest) rather than encouraging the moral perfection of mankind, are inimical to the enjoyment of salvation by the faithful *as a group*. Listen to Hirsch (1976) in this vein:

> The only way of avoiding the competition in frustration [caused by the quest for positional goods] is for the people concerned to coordinate their objectives in some explicit way, departing from the principle of isolated individual striving in this sphere. That is to say, only a collective approach to the problem can offer individuals the guidance necessary to achieve a solution they themselves would prefer. The principle is acknowledged in the standard liberal analysis, but confined to the exceptional case. . . . By collapsing individual and total opportunities for economic advance into a single process grounded on individual valuations, the standard view has obscured a significant change in the nature of the economic problem. . . . Getting what one wants is increasingly divorced from doing as one likes [p. 10].

Repeat this last sentence several times, and its rather authoritarian overtones become discomfortingly resonant, as the author himself eventually acknowledged:

> It follows that just as centralized or coordinated action is needed to relate specific individual actions to the social interest in the presence of externalities, so some measure of deliberate direction is needed to encourage reorientation of individual action in general. . . . This is far from saying that either individual motives or behavior can be controlled, at least without abandonment of primary liberal values. Subjugation of individual judgment on moral issues and behavioral choices to the thought of some Charman Mao would remove the heart of individualist autonomy. Thought control remains the most horrifying threat in the collectivist intrusion. Yet if individual orientation is outside our area of influence, we are left with an impasse. We know what needs to be done and cannot or dare not do it [pp. 179–180].

What does not follow, however, is that "we" will get to exercise a deliberate choice about the matter. This worrisome train of thought brings me, finally, to the still more tenuous speculation that the current fashionableness which antigrowth ideology is enjoying in some circles could become transformed into a significant social movement of a diffusely religious and possibly rather authoritarian complexion. Historical experience generally supports the proposition that millenarianism, as an active force in guiding social movements, emerges as the religion of deprived groups—the lower social strata and oppressed and persecuted minorities (cf. Mannheim, 1929–1931). But poverty and pariah status have not been the only elements in the picture (cf. Talmon, 1968, pp. 354–357). More recent studies of millenarian movements draw attention to the predisposing influence exerted by the formation of marked discrepancies between expectations and the means of satisfying them, whether because expectations have been unrealistically inflated or because social and economic transformations have placed "traditional" goals beyond reach. Millenarianism also may be born out of a search for a tolerably coherent system of values, a regained sense of dignity and self-respect under conditions in which rapid social and economic changes undermine the effectiveness of traditional norms as guides to action, causing cultural disintegration and individual disorientation. Comparative historical analysis has underscored the important role played by immigrant groups and itinerant workers in the development of militant millenarianism. Rather than concentrating upon the economic and social status of such groups, it has been thought more relevant to lay stress on the fact that the individuals in question were not firmly embedded in well-integrated kinship groupings, nor given effective political organization and protection within cohesive local communities.

To date, the ideology of limits of growth has manifested itself most clearly in polemical writings emanating from the professoriate and directed largely to the concerns and frustrations of the newly affluent. But that is no ultimate disqualification. Many studies of millenarian movements have noticed the prominent leadership roles played by "secondary elites," and their followers have not always been drawn from the lowest strata of the less privileged. So, however paradoxical it may seem, the development of a middle-class millenarian antigrowth movement, conditioned by the relative deprivation of frustrated expectations, the disorientation produced by the rapid erosion of "outmoded" value systems, and the isolation of the geographically and socially mobile, may remain a perturbing and not wholly implausible possibility for the future.

References

Abramovitz, M. (1959). The Welfare Interpretation of Secular Trends in National Income and Product, in *The Allocation of Economic Resources* (M. Abramovitz *et al.*). Stanford, California: Stanford Univ. Press.

Baumol, W. J. (1967). Macroeconomics of Unbalanced Growth: The Anatomy of Urban Crisis, *American Economic Review,* **57** (June), No. 3, 415–426.

Beckerman, W. (1974). *Two Cheers for the Affluent Society, A Spirited Defense of Economic Growth.* New York: St. Martin's Press.

Bury, J. B. (1932). *The Idea of Progress.* London: Macmillan.

Cantril, H. (1965). *Patterns of Human Concerns.* New Brunswick, New Jersey: Rutgers Univ.

Daly, H. E. (ed.) (1973). *Toward a Steady-State Economy.* San Francisco: Freeman. (The passages quoted are from the editor's Introduction.)

Easterlin, R. A. (1974). Does Economic Growth Improve the Human Lot? Some Empirical Evidence, in *Nations and Households in Economic Growth* (P. A. David and M. W. Reder, eds.). New York: Academic Press.

Georgescu-Roegen, N. (1971). The Entropy Law and the Economic Problem, *Distinguished Lecture Series,* No. 1, 1971, The Univ. of Alabama [reprinted in Daly (1973), pp. 37–49].

Hahn, F. (ed.) (1971). *Readings in the Theory of Growth.* London: Macmillan.

Hirsch, F. (1976). *Social Limits to Growth.* Cambridge, Massachusetts: Harvard Univ. Press.

Linder, S. B. (1970). *The Harried Leisure Class.* New York: Columbia Univ. Press.

Mannheim, K. (1929–1931). *Ideology and Utopia: An Introduction to the Sociology of Knowledge.* New York: Harcourt, 1954. [A translation of *Ideologie und Utopie* (1929), and of the article "Wissenssoziologie" (1931).]

Meadows, D. H., *et al.* (1972). *The Limits to Growth.* London: Earth Island Ltd.

Nordhaus, W. D., and Tobin, J. (1972). Is Growth Obsolete? in *Economic Growth.* New York: Nat. Bur. Econ. Res.

Pigou, A. C. (1952). *The Economics of Welfare,* 4th ed. London: Macmillan.

Schumpeter, J. A. (1954). *History of Economic Analysis.* London and New York: Oxford Univ. Press.

Scitovsky, T. (1976). *The Joyless Economy, An Inquiry into Human Satisfaction and Consumer Dissatisfaction.* London and New York: Oxford Univ. Press.

Talmon, Y. (1968). Millenarism, in *International Encyclopedia of the Social Sciences* (D. L. Sills, ed.), Vol. 10. New York: Macmillan and The Free Press.

Department of Economics
Stanford University
Stanford, California

Appraisal of Project Appraisal*

János Kornai

1. Introduction

After a few pioneering experiments, the application of cost–benefit analysis for the appraisal of projects of developing countries has spread widely in the past years. The basic thought of the analysis is this: instead of private profitability, the social benefits and costs of the project envisaged must be determined in such a way that current prices are replaced in the calculation by accounting prices (shadow prices) reflecting social effects.

It is not the task of the present study to summarize the full history of

* The author acknowledges with appreciation the support he received from the United Nations Food and Agriculture Organization (FAO). He expresses his gratitude to A. Simonovits, Institute of Economics, Budapest, who assisted him in the elaboration of the Appendix.

doctrines of this methodology; we will not investigate intellectual priorities either. It is doubtless, however, that—as regards application in the developing countries—the school is mainly attached to the names of Little and Mirrlees (1968, 1974). Their books had very considerable influence and helped to integrate earlier experience.

The methodology of project appraisal based on cost–benefit analysis has penetrated deeply into the activities of a number of international organizations. The first edition of the book by Little and Mirrlees (1968) was published as an Organization for Economic Cooperation and Development (OECD) manual—the international organization dealing with the relations between advanced capitalist countries and developing countries. Manuals of a similar spirit were published by the United Nations Industrial Organizations (UNIDO) (Dasgupta et al., 1972) and the World Bank (IBRD) (Squire and Van Der Tak, 1964). The United Nations Food and Agriculture Organization (FAO) has no printed manual of similar importance to that of UNIDO. In one of its mimeographed brochures, however, FAO (1971) also invited the application of cost–benefit analysis.

Cost–benefit analysis with shadow prices has become a *school of thinking* in the project appraisals of developing countries. I will call it the *CB school*. It is doubtlessly influential. Maybe it is not even the actual selection of investments that is influenced by it but rather the thinking of economists engaged in planning in developing countries.

The subject of this study is the critical appraisal of the CB school.

The question has already prompted quite a volume of literature. Not only manuals with positive recommendations have been published but also a considerable number of critical comments and polemical essays. Three separate layers of discussion can be discerned.

In most cases, such problems are treated as *tertiary;* e.g., how could the shadow wage rate or the shadow exchange rate be better determined within the shadow price systems used in cost–benefit analyses? In such cases, the disputants are practically in full agreement over the fundamental principles of the methodology. They have no doubt that it is right to examine isolated investment plans by means of cost–benefit analysis and that shadow prices must be applied. A considerable part of the literature treating the question may be placed in this category. As a matter of fact, the differences which exist between the various manuals mentioned previously also belong to this category. Although there are slight differences between the methodologies recommended by UNIDO, IBRD, OECD, and FAO, they appear only in the tertiary strata. In their basic principles, all the enumerated manuals agree.[1]

---

[1] This is justly emphasized in the study of Lal (1973): "The author concludes that in principles most of the suggested methods are equivalent, given the same basic assumptions about the economic environment."

There is also a *secondary* stratum of the discussion, in which the critics question whether it is right to examine the benefits and costs of an isolated project torn out of the whole of the economic system, and do it in such a way that the linkages with other parts of the economy are represented exclusively by shadow prices. In the dispute, sectoral or economy-wide planning is contrasted to analysis done on the project level. This part of the dispute is in most cases closely correlated with the polemic which opposes mathematical planning methods with the less-sophisticated procedure of project analysis. Many doubt whether such complicated planning problems can be solved by such simplistic calculation as is recommended by cost–benefit analysis.[2]

This dispute undoubtedly touches on theoretical problems of a more essential character than the previously mentioned tertiary stratum. If, however, we want to get to the roots of the questions, the *primary* subject will be discussion of the *theoretical foundations* of cost–benefit analysis.

Believers and critics agree that the theoretical background of the CB school is the modern welfare economics that has emerged following Pigou. Those who consider the propositions of welfare economics self-evident truth have not and cannot have theoretical doubts about the CB school, and, necessarily, they may raise technical questions of detail only with regard to practical applications. The present writer is one of those who is full of doubts regarding modern welfare economics, and *exactly for* this reason also doubts the CB school.

The examination of the *primary* problems is the main subject studied here. The theoretical bases of the CB school will be treated first. To a lesser extent, the group of questions classified as *secondary* will also be discussed; i.e., project analysis versus sectoral or economy-wide planning, and nonmathematical efficiency calculation versus mathematical planning. *Tertiary* problems will not be discussed.

It is pertinent at this point to state the practical final conclusion of my train of thought. The CB school claims that decision-makers should consider cost–benefit analysis carried out with shadow prices as the fundamental criterion of selection. This then may be supplemented by (or linked with) other analyses, e.g., sectoral or economy-wide planning, but the appraisal or projects by means of cost–benefit analysis is at least as important, or even more significant, than sectoral and economy-wide planning.[3]

I suggest that *this demand should be rejected as exaggerated and unjustified.*

At the same time, I do not propose that CB methods should be excluded

---

[2] A characteristic example of the secondary layer of criticism is the article by Rudra (1972).

[3] The CB school will assign a greater role to sectoral planning in a sector producing normally untraded goods.

from the array of analytical tools. Let us use it, but let us mark a more modest place for it; let us regard it as one of many tools.

Arguments to support this practical suggestion will be presented. The discussion is divided into three parts: the theoretical bases of the CB school; the measurement of economic performances; and the relation between planning, market, and cost–benefit analysis.

2. Theoretical Roots

2.1 The Course of the Analysis

The CB school, as mentioned in Section 1, is a branch of modern welfare economics, i.e., a special practical application of it to planning in developing countries. On the other hand, modern welfare economics itself is in a close intellectual relationship with Walrasian general equilibrium theory and with neoclassical economic thought in general. Welfare economics has grown out of the Walrasian tradition, while separating from it to a certain extent owing to critical considerations.

In comparison to traditional neoclassical economic thought, the CB school may be qualified as *enlightened orthodoxy*. It is *orthodoxy* because, to use the word in fashion, it lives in the neoclassical paradigm, it thinks in the conceptual framework of the latter, and feels most of its basic assumptions to be above dispute. At the same time, it is *enlightened*, because it sees quite clearly that reality is different from the Walrasian world. Therefore, it builds up a shadow world identical with the Walrasian ideal and expects the decision-makers to act as if this world were real.

The theoretical examination of the CB school will be carried out in three steps.

Step 1   We shall outline a theoretical model which will be called the "welfare equilibrium model." The main assumptions of the model will be stated. This model conforms to the CB methodology in the following sense: *if* we accept the assumptions of the model, *then* the CB model will become justifiable deductively.

Step 2   It has to be clarified which assumptions of the "welfare equilibrium model" are *necessary* to support the CB methodology. What are the premises on which we must agree in order to accept the methodology?

Step 3   The "necessary premises" clarified in Steps 1 and 2 will be analyzed critically. If the reader can be convinced that these premises should be refused, then—in accordance with Steps 1 and 2—the exaggerated claims of the methodology must be rejected.

The aim, therefore, is to pick out from the previously cited manuals the ultimate theoretical implications of CB methodology. Unfortunately, the CB school itself gives little help. Its leading representatives are prominent scholars of theoretical economics, who obviously could write the theoretical foundations of their methodology in a rigorous form. Unfortunately, however, this has not been done. It is true that the CB school openly declares its relation to modern welfare economics and general equilibrium theory, but neither overlappings nor deviations are accurately described; the axiomatic formulation and the mathematical deduction of the theoretical basic propositions are missing.[4] The present author cannot, of course, undertake to do all of this for the CB school and is not sure that he would be able to do it; but it is sure that the "CB model" he built would not be authentic. But, finally, this is not the task of the *critics* of the CB school, but of its *followers*. Therefore, I chose a more modest—and certainly less convincing—procedure. Instead of presenting a detailed mathematical discussion, I shall argue only verbally in Section 2.2, according to the nature of this study. Instead of complete deductions, I can refer only in general terms to the popular statements of the new welfare economics evolved following Arrow and Debreu. In addition, the mathematical appendix is an illustration of (but not a complete mathematical deduction of) the ideas discussed in Section 2.2.

2.2   Step 1: The "Welfare Equilibrium Model"

Let us imagine a perfectly centralized economy in which production, investments, and consumption are planned down to the smallest detail with the aid of huge computers. The initial scarce resources are given for the system. The convex production functions are also given. Finally, a *social welfare function* is given, which is concave. If the practical problems of data collection and computation are now disregarded, there exists—on the plane of mental experiment—an ensemble of production, investment, and consumption activities, with which the social welfare function will

---

[4] For example, the book by Little and Mirrlees (1974), although containing several technical appendixes, does not give a summarizing theoretical appendix which treats the foundations of the methodology in axiomatic form.

Mishan (1967) surveys welfare economics; Prest and Turvey (1967) give an account of cost–benefit analysis. Both works are frequently referred to: they may be considered the most representative surveys of the two interrelated subjects. Yet a rigorous treatment of the theoretical foundations of cost–benefit analysis is not to be found in either.

It is possible, of course, that there exists a work which has accomplished this task, but, unfortunately, it has not come to my attention.

attain its maximum.[5] The concavity of the welfare function and the convexity of the set of production, investment, and consumption programs guarantees that there exists one and only one optimum production–investment–consumption plan. Let us name it the *centralized optimum program*.

To this centralized optimum activity program belongs one and only one centralized *optimum shadow price system*.[6]

Now let us imagine another system, one with completely decentralized production–investment decisions. In this system, independent *organizations* (e.g., enterprises or state authorities) isolated from each other decide on production and investment. All the initial scarce resources of society are allocated among the organizations. The production functions of the organizations are convex. Each organization will determine its production and investment plan in such a way that its *social profit function* should attain its maximum. The social profit function of the organization is concave. The *social price system* used in the computation of the social profit function comes exogenously to the organization. Let us call the optimum production–investment plan of the organization the *decentralized optimum program*.

The following statement can be demonstrated:

The ensemble of the optimum programs of decentralized organizations is identical with the centralized optimum program, if the centralized optimum shadow price system is applied for the social price system used in the decentralized decision. There is one unique price system with which this identity exists.

Let us accept this as the *basic proposition of welfare equilibrium*. I would like to stress once more that the theorem is not rigorously "deduced." A complete and exact description of the model has not been given, but rather an outline of the train of thought.[7]

In the world of the model just outlined and, in case of prevalence of the basic welfare equilibrium proposition, the application of the CB method-

[5] "It has been assumed so far that the reader has an intuitive idea of the meaning of social cost and benefit. For a more precise idea it is necessary to understand the general nature of what has been termed 'the economic problem' that is the maximization subject to certain constraints of some combination of social objectives: the way in which these objectives are combined is expressed by what is known as 'the objective function'" [Little and Mirrlees, 1974, p. 38].

[6] A constructive algorithm was worked out by M Scarf and T. Hansen for the computation of the optimum shadow price system (Scarf, 1973).

[7] The static model described in the Appendix is a special case of the vaguely described but more general model already discussed. It may, however, help the reader in finding the linkages between the underlying assumptions of the CB methodology and the assumptions of modern mathematical general equilibrium theory.

ology accomplishes optimum decentralization. *If* the centralized optimum shadow price system is used for the cost–benefit analysis for isolated projects, *then* the ensemble of the decentralized decisions will lead to the maximum value of the social welfare function.

We said "if–then." Therefore, let us now pinpoint the most important axioms that serve as foundations for the "welfare equilibrium model."

AXIOM 1   There exists a social welfare function.

AXIOM 2   The objective of decentralized decision-makers is to maximize the social profit function.

AXIOM 3   Production functions are convex. The social welfare function is concave. The social profit functions of the organizations are concave.

Axioms 1–3 are not sufficient to deduce the basic welfare equilibrium proposition; some additional (but from the economist's point of view less questionable) assumptions are also needed. It is, however, clear from the literature (and from the Appendix as well) that these axioms are necessary to the derivation of the basic proposition. This will lead us to Step 2.

2.3   Step 2: The Necessity of the Axioms

Is it true that Axioms 1–3 are *necessary* to demonstrate, in the deductive way, the justification of the CB methodology?

What would happen if we rejected Axiom 1 and did not presume the existence of a social welfare function "dictated from above" or "accepted by consensus"? Most works on modern mathematical equilibrium theory do not apply this assumption, but postulate only the existence of individual preference orderings. In that case, as is well known, only a weaker theorem is reached: the Pareto optimum states of economy can be determined. Yet, at a given date—degenerate cases disregarded—the number of Pareto optimum states is infinite. In such a case, we would not have one unique global optimum program to deal with, but a set of Pareto optimum programs and, together with it, a set of the Pareto optimum shadow price systems. The CB methodology, however, is not content with such indeterminacy. Instead, it suggests that there exists one *unique* optimum shadow price system, on the basis of which every decision-maker is able

---

To the reader who would like to deal in more detail with the mathematical formulation of the problem, without, however, getting lost in the sea of literature treating mathematical equilibrium theory, I would recommend the article by Bator (1957). Although the model treated there is not the same as the one presented here, it is quite close. For example, the first part of the article also applies strong convexity assumptions. It assumes that there exists a welfare function which society tries to maximize. The article also treats the utilization of the price system for decentralized decisions.

to select unambigously the socially optimal projects. For uniqueness, therefore, it is indispensable that one and only one social welfare function should exist, from which, if maximized—with given scarcities—the optimum shadow price system will be unambiguously determinable.

It is true that manuals conceived in the spirit of the CB school stress the practical difficulties of determining the optimum shadow price system. A sharp distinction must be made, however, between the inexactitute of the practical computation of a uniquely determined variable and the theoretical indeterminacy of that variable. With regard to the optimum shadow price system, the CB school as a whole recognizes the former but not the latter.[8]

Axiom 2 is also indispensable for the support of the CB methodology. This is trivially obvious. We *must* presume that decision-makers are able to maximize not their private profit at actual prices but, instead, the shadow profit. If we did not presume this, the recommendation of the methodology would be meaningless and empty.

Finally, Axiom 3 is also by all means necessary to guarantee the uniqueness of the solution. If production functions are not convex, and if the social welfare function and the social profit functions of organizations are not concave, the existence of only one optimum shadow price system cannot be guaranteed. It cannot be guaranteed, either, that, counting with optimal shadow prices, only one ensemble of decentralized optimum decisions exists.[9] Yet, as mentioned in connection with Axiom 1, one of the most important features of the CB methodology is that it suggests acceptance of a *unique* optimum shadow price system, and not the experimentation with multiple, equally good price systems.

2.4 Step 3: Criticism of the Axioms[10]

Axioms 1–3 have been named *axioms* to stress that such assumptions do not even require verification in the eyes of the followers of the school. It is

[8] There are, however, certain differences between the members of the school. Some authors admit that there are insurmountable difficulties and hence are satisfied with partial comparability of alternatives. Accordingly, they go further in restricting the role of cost–benefit analysis to comparisons within a sector or within the authority of a single agency (see, e.g., Dasgupta *et al.*, 1972). Nevertheless, I think that the problems of a unique shadow price system still remain in this restricted domain.

[9] In past decades, a number of successful efforts have been made to weaken rigorous convexity assumptions. These, however, have led to theorems—otherwise of interest—that do not obtain uniqueness of solution, but consider the set of equilibrium states, or the set of Pareto optima, or the set of other states of specific characteristics.

[10] There is a partial overlapping between the set of axioms underlying Walrasian general equilibrium theory and CB methodology. For a more detailed criticism of the former see Kornai (1971).

in the nature of these axioms to be the self-evident starting points of a deductive train of thought, as e.g., the Euclidean axioms are self-evident starting points of the whole mental construction of Euclidean geometry. In fact, however, none of the axioms expresses a self-evident truth.

Let us begin by examining Axiom 1. There is a huge volume of literature on the problem of the welfare function.[11] I do not think I can add anything new on the subject. All the same, it is important to stress a few thoughts from the many kinds of criticism of the welfare function, in connection with cost–benefit analysis and the decisions affecting the projects of developing countries.

Welfare functions are usually interpreted in different manners. In the broadest interpretation, the welfare function expresses "social interest." Yet "social interest" does not exist as such a general term. Every real society, as also, naturally, that of developing countries, consists of interest groups.[12] These are divided according to numerous criteria:

(1) There are everywhere social classes separated from each other as a consequence of their conditions of propriety, income and wealth, social status, and political power. There can be sharp conflicts between the layers separated according to classes, ownership, income, wealth, status, and power.

(2) Separate interest groups are formed by different generations. On questions of sharing burdens between present and future, the proportions of the material incentives to producers, of family allowance and of pensions, in decisions on income distribution, consumption, and investments, the interests of the young, the middle-aged, and the aged may deviate.

(3) Interest groups are also formed according to geographical regions.

(4) In a state with several nationalities, conflicts of interest may occur between nationalities. In certain cases, religious groups are also separated.

(5) People identify, to a certain extent, their interests with those of the institution at which they work. On this account, conflicts may arise between "agrarian" and "industrial" interests, or between smaller branches within these spheres.

We cannot list here all criteria of division and separation. An individual may belong, in accordance with the various criteria, to several interest

---

[11] See Mishan (1967, 1972) and Arrow and Scitovsky (1969), i.e., the collection composed of the important articles of welfare economics. It contains, among others, the contributions—already considered classic—of A. Bergson, O. Lange, K. J. Arrow, N. Kaldor, T. Scitovsky, P. A. Samuelson, H. Hotelling, J. Hicks, and others.

[12] My criticism on this point overlaps the thought evolved by Stewart (1975).

groups not excluding each other, such as worker, young, living in the capital, and industrial.

"Social interest" is an undefinable category. What can happen in reality is that only a compromise can be reached in the conflict between different classes and interest groups. By "compromise" I do not mean a fifty–fifty agreement by any means. The compromise reflects current relative strengths. It may express the dominance and superiority of one group, or it may be more balanced, depending on the actual social and political situation. In any case, compromise is a function of power relationships.

The formulation in which the "welfare function" is the expression of "social interest" is misleading because it creates illusions. It gives the impression that there exists some kind of social interest interpretable as such, and that the politically neutral economist can reflect it in the optimum shadow price system.

Let us take the other, narrower interpretation of the welfare function. Accordingly, the welfare function does not reflect "social interest," but what the political party or parties in power, i.e., the government, declares as such. Let us consider any country in the Third World. A party or parties in power does not represent the "whole society" but only a part of it: a class or some classes, or strata. At some places this is admitted, at others concealed. If the government in question wants to create a successful permanent inner stability, it usually makes serious efforts to achieve a wide social compromise, possibly making concessions to some classes and groups. Whatever way is chosen, there exists, obviously, some power and some official government policy. As opposed to the preceding wider interpretation, no political illusion will be created if one says: the efficiency calculation is carried out by the economist in such a way as to make a particular partial decision to serve the global official government policy.

In this regard, two questions may be raised.

(1)   Does the economist act correctly if he serves official government policy? Obviously, no answer of general validity can be given, since this depends on the actual government policy of the country in question. Let us assume, therefore, that the economist has settled the question in his own political conscience.

(2)   Can the official government policy be reflected by a welfare function? Opinions differ.[13] I think that reflection is not feasible. The consistency postulates that must be satisfied by a preference ordering so that it can be unambiguously represented by a utility (or, at the collective decision level, welfare) function are well known. However, the sequence of

---

[13] An affirmative answer is given to the question, e.g., by Frisch (1957).

state political decisions does not satisfy these consistency postulates. No priorities invariant over time can be discovered in a place in which political tendencies and governments change often. But even in countries in which the government is apparently lasting for a long period, priorities may vary.

If we observe the activities of a government actually in power in a developing country, we shall see that it tries to achieve simultaneously objectives that are contradictory to each other. It would be impossible to assign any stable weights to these objectives. The truth is that ad hoc solutions are resorted to as influenced by the current home and foreign political situation. Decisions are made by succumbing to the currently most intensive exterior and interior pressures and by resisting weaker pressures. Sometimes the problem is caused by the inconsequence of the government. At other times, the problem is the rigid insistence of the government and its inertia in asserting the same priorities, although these ought to have been long since modified.

For the reasons just outlined, I cannot imagine that the official economic policy of developing countries could be truly reflected by some kind of state welfare function. In the final analysis, therefore, Axiom 1—the assumption of the existence of a social welfare function—does not appear acceptable in either the wider or the narrower interpretation.

My main objection to Axiom 2 is that it appears naive. The decision-maker—whether an individual or a corporation—has his own interests. This does not hold only for the owner of a private enterprise, whose decision is obviously influenced by profit interest. According to experience, the leaders of state enterprises or even of state authorities are inclined to identify their own interests with those—real or assumed—of their "own" enterprise or authority. Many of them do so without any financial interest, quite unselfishly. They represent partial viewpoints not less combatively and narrow-mindedly than those whose service of partial interests explains itself by a direct personal financial profit.

Now, if the decision that would be made in the interest of the decision-maker's own institution deviates from the one suggested by the cost–benefit analysis based on "impartial" shadow prices, the decision-maker will use every means to assert the former. Anybody who has taken one close look into the "witches' kitchen" of economic calculations knows that it is not true that they are carried out with absolute impartiality. "First calculation, then selection"—that would be the desirable principle. A reverse order is, however, quite frequent. Selection is made and then calculation is carried out in such a way that it will demonstrate the alternative selected to be more advantageous than those that are to be rejected. An adroit economist can always do that, without even expressly falsifying numbers. It is enough to select them cleverly and classify them adequately. In the analysis of costs or of direct or indirect effects, much depends on how the data background is selected. What is more advantageous: if a short, or a long time series is taken as basis, or, if instead of a time series a cross-section pattern is applied? Also, whether domestic or foreign figures are used? After all, cost–benefit analysis allows quite a large degree of flexibility, even if prescriptions of very detailed manuals are observed.

The basic idea of the CB methodology is to analyze isolated projects, torn out of the whole of national economy. To the project, however, necessarily belong living people, who have direct personal interests and who will inevitably influence the calculation itself. I think that is the reason why the method of project appraisal by means of cost–benefit analysis affected the thoughts of economists more than the actual choice of real decision-makers.

There remains the criticism of Axiom 3. This should be easy, since the arguments against strict convexity assumptions are well known to all. It is enough to think of the important role played by increasing returns to scale in every investment, and especially in developing countries. That is to say, in such a country the establishment of one single factory may be equivalent to the introduction of a whole new industrial branch, leading to economies of scale. Yet it is not worth going much into the criticism of Axiom 3. Why think about whether the social welfare function is concave, if we doubt the very existence of the function? Why discuss the shape of social profit functions, if it is questionable whether it can be attained that actual decision-makers of organizations will try to maximize, in reality, exactly this function?

Does not the rejection of Axioms 1–3 lead to the refusal of *all* kinds of economic calculation? It does not, but the raising of the question leads us to the next subject: the more general examination of the measurement of economic performance.

3. Measurement of Economic Performance

3.1 Scalar versus Vector Measurement

The economist educated in the neoclassical school is apt to see in planning a problem similar to the determination of the production of a profit-maximizing enterprise. The difference is that, instead of one single enterprise, there is the whole national economy to consider, and instead of private profit, there is the social profit to be maximized—otherwise the tasks are of a similar nature.

The capitalist entrepreneur (at least according to the neoclassical textbook) observes one single *scalar* measure in considerations for decision-making: profit. He adds up all his revenues, and deducts from them the total of his expenditures. The planner should do the same thing. He should assign artificial weights to the various social benefits and costs so that they become additive. In my opinion this is an unnatural way of comparing economy-wide decision alternatives. I shall quote a Hungarian example. One of the dilemmas of economic policy is: What should be the proportions of living standards in towns and in villages? For a long time there was a large gap; agricultural living standards were far behind those of industry. There are quite a number of instruments in the Hungarian socialist economy that influence the proportions: industrial wage policy, state price policy, taxation, allocation of state investments, etc. In forming the policy, a series of aspects must be considered:

(1) Labor supply in industry and in agriculture. A specified growth path is planned in each sector. The considerable backwardness of agricultural living standards would strengthen migration to industry, and thus an increased agricultural labor shortage would occur.

(2) Housing. Low living standards in villages may result in migration to urban areas to such an extent that the increasing demand for housing cannot be satisfied fast enough by city housing, and then congestion may become unbearable in city transport, trade, and other services.

(3) Transport problems. Should every industrial worker live in town? Or shall we accept the fact that part of them commute from village to town? This may be a burden to people living in a village and working in town; it also increases the tasks of the transport sector, yet it does ease the congestion in the large city.

(4) Political views. The two different living standards affect the relationship between people of the town and those of the village, i.e., between industrial workers and the peasantry. The different living standards may increase or decrease tensions between the people.

The preceding list does not contain all aspects of the question. It is, however, sufficient to indicate that a complex network of problems is involved here. Whatever the government's decision, consequences will follow in several dimensions, which must be considered one by one. The final result of the considerations was that the government made efforts to reduce the difference between the living standards of workers in towns and those in villages. At present, for the first time in the history of the Hungarian economy, the gap is more or less closed, at least as regards current incomes.

The planner educated in the neoclassical tradition would consider as a natural order of succession that decision-makers assign—*before* policy formation, *a priori*—1 : 1 weights to the level of town and village consumption in the social welfare function. In real planning, however, these weights are not given a priori. The 1 : 1 rate is not the *input* of the policy formation process, but its *output*, which is determined as the final result of a many-sided analysis.

Little and Mirrlees (1974) point out that difficulties may arise in determinating the welfare function if the economist expects the political decision-maker also to give his preferences numerical weights. Maybe the politician is wary of doing so because this would be much too revealing.[14] It is possible that a fear of openly confessing political priorities also has a role in the reticence of decision-makers. My own experience, however, makes me doubt if this is the main reason. The main reason is that this is an *unnatural* form. The adding up of qualitatively different effects, i.e., their unification in a unique scalar measure, is the fixed idea of neoclassical economic thinking. This obsession may be traced back to several factors and several kinds of thinking habits. One thought that is hidden behind this practice is *the principle of the general substitutability of effects.* According to this principle, the individual—or, if the whole national economy is involved, the society—may be fully compensated for some disadvantage by another advantage. It is true that there is compensation and substitution, but only between certain limits. Ultimately, *complementarity requirements* assert themselves. People want better food *and* better clothing *and* better housing conditions *and* better other services, etc. The city dweller is not compensated for the housing shortage or for overcrowded buses by the fact that industry produces relatively more consumer goods as a result of a wider industrial employment.

It is not justifiable to add up different effects with a plus or minus sign and thereby unify them. A physician would never think of expressing the general state of health of a patient by one single scalar indicator. He knows that good lungs are not a substitute for bad kidneys. The physician thinks about health as a "vector" and not as a "scalar." Why cannot the economist also shift at last to that way of thinking?

Another factor encourages the economist toward scalar measurement to which reference is often made: the *simplification* of decision preparation; *"economizing"* the mental capacity of decision-makers. It is difficult to draw a comparison between two vectors, especially if there is no simple

---

[14] This is mentioned, e.g., in regard to the regional planning problem. Little and Mirrlees (1974) point out how difficult it would be in a multiregion state to openly declare: consumption generated in region *"P"* is worth one and one half as much as that in region *"R"*. ". . . even in a unified state it is not easy to imagine a government agreeing to such a vare-faced quantification of the regional problem [p. 58]."

relation of domination between them, while it is absolutely simple to compare two real numbers.

This is true, of course. Yet, in every difficult decision problem, people have become used to comparing a vector with a vector and not a scalar with a scalar. If one has several offers for a job, one will consider the wages offered, whether the work promises to be interesting, the distance of the working place from one's home, and the transport connection; if the information is available, one will also consider what the boss as well as the colleagues will be like—and then the decision is made. But one never assigns weights to the importance of all these criteria and, computing a weighted average of the expected effects, then makes a decision about the job to be selected. Why are political decision-makers to be spared the difficulties of vector comparison, which no one is spared in the countless decisions of life?

Finally, there is a third factor to explain the idea of scalar comparison: the grave impression made on everyone by the functioning of the *market* and especially on the market expert: the economist. The market is a peculiar mechanism, which renders qualitatively different products and services comparable and that in a scalar, i.e., monetary, form. If the market can do this with such a number of things, why could not the economist do the same with *everything* without restriction in his cost–benefit analysis?

3.2 Pecuniary versus Nonpecuniary Measurement

Cost–benefit analysis is a heroic experiment in translating every favorable and unfavorable effect into the language of pecuniary terms. That means that cost–benefit analyses follows the market not only in that it has a common scalar measure, but it borrows expressly the measurement system of the market and measures everything in money.

If the market as a social phenomenon is approached in a historical view, it can be stated that there are no eternally valid borderlines between market-regulated allocation processes and nonmarket allocation. Ever since the market appeared in history, there have always been spheres that have remained entirely outside market influence, or at least have been little affected by it. This is so in most societies with the choosing of one's spouse, partner, and friends, and with commitment to a party, a religion, etc. It is not necessary to assert that these are no less important choice problems than those taking place in the market. And, if the market enters such areas (wife, lover, friend, or statesman to be bought for money), the moral sense of most of us would judge this as degeneration.

It is difficult to forecast anything general for the coming few decades. Two opposing tendencies are prevailing simultaneously: the market sphere intrudes earlier nonmarket spheres and, vice versa, market processes are becoming nonmarket processes. Considering only advanced capitalist countries, it is found that military service as a civic duty is now replaced by a mercenary army in the United States (otherwise quite an old historical invention). At the same time, education and health service become partly or totally free in a number of capitalist countries, which entails their nonmarket allocation. In socialist countries, there is an extremely large sphere of services allocated by state or social authorities outside of the market. At the same time, the reforms of past years in socialist countries enlarged the reach of the market. The current borderlines are questionable. It must be noted, however, that there have always been and there will always be allocation processes outside of the market. This is the normal order of society. It is an unnatural effort to transform every allocation—even if only on the patient cost–benefit sheet—into a "quasi-market" allocation based on pecuniary calculation.

Besides, the question is not only about the borderlines of market and nonmarket allocation processes, but also about the fact that positive market transactions also have nonmarket effects. The employment of labor is a market action in the first approach: the enterprise buys labor for money. Some of the consequences of unemployment may be very naturally expressed in monetary terms: so much production is lost, and the unemployed lose so much in wages. It may be the latter is partly or fully compensated for by unemployment benefits. Yet unemployment also means human humiliation and defenselessness, not only to the actually unemployed but also to those employed but menaced by unemployment. What is the dollar equivalent of this "deficit" of humiliation and defenselessness?

There is much talk about water and air pollution. What is the "worth" in yen of the health of a Japanese living on the coast, endangered by eating the fish poisoned through industrial pollution?

These are unnatural, perverse questions, to which only unnatural and perverse answers can be given. There are, of course, effects not measured conventionally in pecuniary terms that can also be—with adequate calculation—expressed quite easily in such terms; e.g., what is the value in money of higher education, measured either on the side of input in higher education, or on the side of higher income available through higher education? At the same time, there are effects against the pecuniary expression of which common sense, or moral sense, or both, protest. This is another weighty argument for the following principle:

Let us not strive to integrate every social benefit or cost into one unique pecuniary indicator. Instead, let us carefully separate effects and describe them by a vector of suitable indicators.

Some components of the vector are added up by benefits and costs measured at actual prices. Other components are counted by benefits and costs calculated at shadow prices—in cases where it can be done "naturally." Finally, additional vector components are measured in other, nonpecuniary units.

Market and nonmarket allocation, monetary and nonmonetary measuring lead to the last subject for discussion: the relationship between the market and planning, and, consequently, of the role of cost–benefit analysis.

4. The Market and the Plan: The Place of Cost–Benefit Analysis

4.1 Complementary Regulations

The market is an indispensable element of every modern society based on labor division. Experience has shown that it will not disappear even after the revolutionary transformation of capitalist conditions rooted in the private ownership of production means. The market also functions in a socialist economy.

It is true that (as has already been mentioned) the scope of the market changes in history. Its regularities are deeply influenced by the actual social, economic, and political environment: the functioning of the other components of the economic control system. Yet whatever the conditions in which it functions, its importance lies in that it is a *real* market and not just a shadow market existing only on the paper of economic calculations. The market is a real market if the buyer spends money and the seller receives money. The buyer's interest is to spend less money for the article, while the seller's interest is to receive more for it. The real market functions in the framework of this contradiction.

I have no illusions about the market. I know very well that it is not "perfect." A real market price does not express exactly "how much a certain product is worth to society." The rent paid for resources does not reflect exactly their "relative scarcity." There may be not only small and temporary but also large and permanent deviations between the real market price and the so-called social valuation. If we think that the price wrongly orients those who make their choices relying on the price signal, we may try to change the actual price. This may be done in various forms: by government price fixation, taxation and subsidies, support or hindering of cartel formation, etc. It is not within the scope of the present study to take a stand on these questions, but the following principle must be stated: those who do not like the actual price should try to achieve a *change* in the *actual* price. The problem cannot be avoided by replacing the actual price we do not like with a shadow price we prefer. Shadow prices may play a useful role, but only as analytical tools in the hands of the planner. We cannot expect, however, as already discussed, that microunits (firms, local authorities, etc.) will base their *actual* decisions on financially non-binding *accounting* prices.

In my opinion, the market should not be left to itself. The government may intervene in it, and does in fact in every modern society.[15] Besides, the market may be supplemented by planning and other government control activities of a nonmarket character. But within the sphere of market action, it should be a *real market* with real prices.

Planning is, in the vision of the CB school, a faint repetition of the market: a kind of ghost market with ghost prices and wages which are more advantageous than the real ones.

The CB school's "planning" is a language whose grammar and basic vocabulary are identical with those of the market, and which differs from the market only in its accent. Yet the real historical role of planning is not just that. Planning is a "separate language" with its own vocabulary and grammar. It is not a faint repetition of the market, but a supplement with its own purpose. A *living* market must be supplemented by *living* planning.[16]

The main aspect of planning is the *primal* aspect, if I may express it in the language of mathematical programming. The targets of production, investment, consumption, and domestic and foreign trade must be known beforehand. One must try to coordinate all these closely related processes. In parallel with the physical processes, their accompanying monetary processes, i.e., the flows of incomes and expenditures, must also be coordinated. All this, of course, must be completed by the *dual* aspect: the planning of future prices and wages. But these are not hypothetical prices either. The planning of prices means that there is consideration beforehand of what changes could be and ought to be achieved in future *actual* prices, wages, exchange rates, and interest rates.

---

[15] The study of shadow prices and their comparison with actual prices may help to correct the latter and to determine government price policy.

[16] In his classical article on externalities, Scitovsky (1954) underlined the complementary character of market and planning: "The proper co-ordination of investment decisions, therefore, would require a signaling device to transmit information about present plans and future conditions as they are determined by present plans; and the pricing system fails to provide this. Hence the belief that there is need either for centralized investment planning or for some additional communication system to *supplement* the pricing system as a signaling device.

"It must be added that the argument of this section applies with a special force to underdeveloped countries."

Planning is therefore a wide prognosis and organized exchange of information on the one hand, and a preliminary coordination of interests and activities on the other hand. All this, if well done, will improve the economic efficiency and reduce the frictions of adaptation. However, the whole thing is but an *ex ante* coordination which will later be exposed to the test of practice. In the market sphere it is the actual market, and in the nonmarket sphere it is the other allocation processes (e.g. allocation by authorities, administrative selection, etc.) that will realize actual coordination and adaptation. They will do it either by faithfully following the plan or by correcting it. It may also happen that forces active in society will resist the plan and therefore the goals included in the plan will not be adhered to.

In real planning, as later in the real market and in other real nonmarket allocation processes, the representatives of different interests meet. It is true that this usually takes place in a very "professional" form: with economic and technical argumentation. If, however, one takes a closer look at the arguments, it is found that big enterprises, ministerial planners, ministers, the leaders of geographical regions, trade unions, etc., all try to assert in planning the "interests" of the segment "represented" by them. This may seem alarming to those who believe that planning is a strictly impartial process which deduces its figures from facts independent of human interests. In reality, however, planning is a social process in which human beings take part. Finally, the plan is obtained out of this clash of interests.

4.2 The Two Interpretations of Planning

The various views on planning and project appraisal are summarized in Fig. 1. Figure 1a shows the neoclassical (welfare economics) ideal of planning. According to this, planning is nothing else but the solution of the "economic problem" (i.e., allocation of scarce resources to attain maximum utility) on an economy-wide level. It presumes the existence of a social welfare function. The objective is to reach the maximum social welfare.

While this fundamental starting point is shared by all those holding the neoclassical view, there are differences between them regarding methods. This is shown by the branching in Fig. 1. According to some, the "economic problem" can be solved only by an optimization mathematical model, or, at least, the solution can be approached only in this way (Fig. 1a, lower left rectangle). Others hold the view that the problem must be solved exclusively by isolated project appraisal, i.e., by cost–benefit analysis (Fig. 1a, lower right rectangle). There are also intermediate opin-

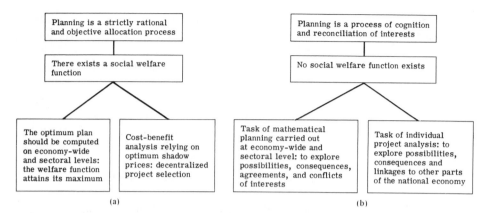

Figure 1 Two interpretations of planning.

ions, recognizing the usefulness of both procedures, but laying more stress on one or the other.[17]

The basic conception of welfare economics accepted, the various views harmonize quite well with each other. Arguments are restricted to opinions about the best means or combination of means for "planning technology," which is, finally, not a very fundamental question.

In Fig. 1b, I show the concept of planning that I accept, together with many other economists. As can be seen, it is not the "planning technology" that makes this concept different from the other concept, since both mathematical planning and project analysis also appear in this scheme, i.e., in the procedures. The point of difference is in the interpretation of the social function of planning. It does not begin with the sterile ideal of "rationality." The question here is not about the just, fine, and good planning, with every participant a "Homo oeconomicus." Instead, it approaches planning in the realistic way and poses the empirical question: What is planning in practice? First, it is a *cognitive* process; its participants try to explore possibilities and to state in advance what the consequences of effectuating this or that possibility would be. The task is, therefore, to enrich this exploration process as much as possible. Second, planning is a process of *reconciliation of interests*. It tries in advance to coordinate activities that would otherwise adjust to each other through conflicts. Planning may help in overriding the interests of particular

[17] Little and Mirrlees (1974, pp. 84–92) are in this category. They emphasize that planning is to be interpreted mainly on the macrolevel and in perspective (and also in the sectoral context for the case of nontraded goods), while it cannot say much about sectors producing traded goods and even less about details within such sectors.

groups to enforce more general goals of the political decision-makers and planners. Planning can fulfill these functions well if it clearly reveals the tensions and contrasting interests to be expected.

The fulfillment of both functions may be promoted by mathematical planning on economy-wide and sectoral levels (and within it by optimization models, nonoptimizing simulation examinations, and input–output analysis) as well as by project appraisal. The latter is—without sectoral and economy-wide analysis—by no means sufficient for planning. On the other hand, it may be a useful supplement to plan calculations of a wider scope.

The final question to be posed in this study is: What then is the place of cost–benefit analysis in planning? I think it has an important role to play—although much less important than the one assigned to it by the most ardent followers of the CB school.

4.3 The Place of Cost–Benefit Analysis

Before directly answering the question just mentioned, let us see objectively what has been the actual role of cost–benefit analysis up to now. I think that, as has been pointed out already, it has not fundamentally influenced actual decisions. If it has exerted an advantageous effect, it has not been expressed so much in the choice of certain projects as in the education of planners and decision-makers. It has accustomed preparers of decisions concerned with projects, and planners in general, as well as specialists of international organizations, to examine each project within comprehensive social interrelationships; to consider not only direct profitability counted at current prices, but to try to examine thoroughly the whole series of expectable direct and indirect effects. What will be the consequence of the project from the aspects of employment, foreign trade, and, in general, the economic growth of the developing country? Cost–benefit analysis virtually develops in those who practice it "conditioned reflexes" to such complexity of analysis. I see its main future role in this educational and disciplinary effect. A carefully carried out cost–benefit analysis enforces the regular collection of data in connection with all positive and negative effects, and thus supplies rich material for decision preparation.

Beyond this educational effect asserting itself, in the long run cost–benefit analysis has also a direct use. If it is carried out in several variants under alternative economic assumptions and maybe alternative numerical hypotheses, it may facilitate the many-sided comparison of the advantages and disadvantages of projects to be considered. No one unique salutary cost–benefit indicator is necessary. Instead, a set of indicators which describe in detail the economic and social consequences of the choice should be fixed in advance. The indicator vector should not be too big. I shall mention only for illustration that 15–30 indicators are already apt to demonstrate effects widely and in detail. In a project appraisal, the numerical value of these indicators must be determined. Their determination and comparison should be the main task of cost–benefit analysis (more exactly, of the cost–benefit analysis *interpreted in a wider sense* in accordance with the study).[18] Within these limits, cost–benefit analysis may successfully promote the tasks of planning: cognition and reconciliation of interests.

Appendix

Introduction

We discuss a *static* equilibrium problem, which therefore can be regarded only as a special, simple case of the more general "welfare equilibrium problem" outlined in Section 2.2. It serves as a mere *illustration* of some ideas explored in Section 2.2. Being a static model, it does not deal with investment, interest rate, time horizon, intertemporal perferences, and some other dynamic phenomena related to project appraisal.

No claim of originality is made regarding this Appendix. On the contrary, the aim here is just to show the linkages between the problem discussed in Section 2.2 and modern Walrasian theory. In notation and in the specification of the problem, we follow mainly the classic paper by Arrow and Hurwicz (1960), and in the formulation of assumptions, theorems, and proofs we refer to the fundamental work by Arrow and Hahn (1971). (We slightly modified the notation of the former to adjust it to the setup of the latter.) Instead of presenting proofs, we give concrete references to the Arrow–Hahn theorems. The reader can easily check for logical validity by recalling the Arrow–Hahn proofs.

Notation

x_j is the level of activity j, $x_j \geq 0$, $1 \leq j \leq m$.

$g_{ij}(x_j)$ is the input (resp. output) of commodity j at activity level x_j. In the case of input (output), g_{ij} is negative (positive), $1 \leq i \leq s$.

y_i is the consumption of consumer good i, $1 \leq i \leq n$, $n \leq s$.

ξ_i is the initial stock of commodity i.

---

[18] A good example of such studies is that of Alexandratos *et al.* (1975).

Balance Inequalities

$$y_i \leq \sum_{j=1}^{m} g_{ij}(x_j) + \xi_i, \qquad 1 \leq i \leq n \qquad \text{(consumer goods)},$$

$$0 \leq \sum_{j=1}^{m} g_{ij}(x_j) + \xi_i, \qquad n + 1 \leq i \leq s \qquad \text{(intermediate commodities)}.$$

Welfare Function

$$W(\mathbf{y}) = W(y_1, \ldots, y_n).$$

DEFINITION   An optimal production–consumption pair $(\bar{\mathbf{x}}, \bar{\mathbf{y}})$ is a pair of feasible production and consumption vectors (i.e., $\mathbf{x}$ and $\mathbf{y}$ satisfying the balance inequalities). The welfare function attains its maximum at the optimum consumption level: max $W(\mathbf{y}) = W(\bar{\mathbf{y}})$.

Assumptions

In the following enumeration, the first number refers to the chapter and the second number to the assumption of Arrow and Hahn (1971).

A.3.1   There exist x_j^0 such that $g_{ij}(x_j^0) \geq 0$, $1 \leq i \leq s$, $1 \leq j \leq m$.

A.3.2–3.3 $g_{ij}(x_j)$ is strictly concave.

A.3.4   If $\mathbf{x}$ is feasible and $g_{ij}(x_j) \geq 0$ for every i and j, then $g_{ij}(x_j) = 0$ for every i and j.

A.3.5   There exists a feasible $\mathbf{x}$ for which all balance inequalities hold strictly.

A.4.1 $y_i \geq 0$, $1 \leq i \leq n$.

A.4.2   There exists a feasible vector $\hat{\mathbf{y}}$ such that $\hat{y}_i < \xi_i$ if $\xi_i > 0$, and $\hat{y}_i = 0$ if $\xi_i = 0$.

A.4.4 $W(y)$ is a strictly quasi-concave function. There is no $\mathbf{y}^0$ such that $W(\mathbf{y}^0) \geq W(\mathbf{y})$ for all $\mathbf{y} \geq 0$. (The assumption is equivalent to the Arrow–Hahn assumption 4.4, at least regarding our theorem.)

A.5[19]   For each feasible $(\mathbf{x}, \mathbf{y}, \xi)$ triple, there exists a feasible $(\mathbf{x}', \mathbf{y}', \xi')$ triple such that $W(\mathbf{y}') > W(\mathbf{y})$ and $\xi_i' > \xi_i$ if $\xi_i > 0$, and $\xi_i' = 0$ if $\xi_i = 0$.

[19] Our Assumption A.5 is implied in Definition 5.4 of Arrow and Hahn (1971).

Deduction of the Proposition

Let us assume that there exists at least one optimal $(\bar{x}, \bar{y})$ pair. Then, according to Theorem 9 of Arrow and Hurwicz (1960), there exists an optimal relative price vector of dimension s: $\bar{p} \geq 0$ ($\Sigma_{i=1}^{s} \bar{p}_i = 1$), the dual solution of the problem such that $\bar{x}_j$ will be the optimal solution of the profit-maximizing problem of activity j:

$$\sum_{i=1}^{n} \bar{p}_i g_{ij}(x_j) \to \max.$$

Since A.4.4 and A.5 are true for every optimal production–consumption pair, strict equality holds in all balance inequalities; therefore, $\bar{p} > 0$.

According to Definition 5.1 of Arrow and Hahn (1971), $(\bar{x}, \bar{y}, \bar{p})$ is a competitive equilibrium, and according to Theorem 5.5 such a competitive equilibrium does *exist*. Since there is only one aggregate consumer, according to Theorem 9.4 the competitive equilibrium is *unique*.

In summary, the following proposition can be regarded as proven:

PROPOSITION   (a)   There   exists   a   unique   optimal   production–consumption pair.

(b)   There exists a unique optimal relative price vector as the dual of the optimal production–consumption pair.

(c)   Each component of the optimal production vector can be determined by the solution of a profit-maximizing problem, in which profit is computed by using the optimal relative price vector.

Interpretation of the Proposition

Now let us return to the farmework of Section 2.2. The preceding proposition has the following interpretation:

The decision-makers decide separately on each activity j. The decentralized decision-makers maximize social profit, accounted on optimal shadow prices $\bar{p}$. The optimum activity level $\bar{x}_j$ is determined. The ensemble of decentralized decisions will yield the optimum production–consumption pair, and the social welfare function attains its maximum. In other words, we arrive at the welfare equilibrium proposition of the paper—at least for a simple aggregate-consumer static world.

The reader may verify that the set of assumptions presented in this Appendix implies—in addition to some technical assumptions without special economic significance—Axioms 1–3 discussed in Section 2.2.

References

Alexandratos, N., *et al.* (1975). *An Economic Model for the Planning of Forest Sector Development Strategy in Peninsular Malaysia.* Rome: FAO.

Arrow, K. J., and Hahn, F. H. (1971). *General Competitive Analysis.* San Francisco–Edinburgh: Holden-Day–Oliver & Boyd.

Arrow, K. J., and Hurwicz, L. (1960). Decentralization and Computation in Resource Allocation, in *Essays in Economics and Econometrics,* Chapel Hill, North Carolina: Univ. of North Carolina Press.

Arrow, K. J., and Scitovsky, T. (eds.) (1969). *Readings in Welfare Economics.* London: Allen & Unwin.

Bator, F. M. (1957). The Simple Analytics of Welfare Maximization, *American Economic Review* **47**, 22–59.

Dasgupta, P., Marglin, S., and Sen, A. (1972). *Guidelines for Project Evaluation.* New York: UNIDO.

FAO (1971). *General Guidelines to the Analysis of Agricultural Production Projects* (mimeographed), Rome.

Frisch, R. (1957). *Numerical Determination of a Quadratic Preferences Function for Use in Macroeconomic Programming.* Oslo: Inst. of Economics, Univ. of Oslo.

Kornai, J. (1971). *Anti-Equilibrium.* Amsterdam: North-Holland Publ.

Lal, D. (1973). *Alternative Project Selection Procedures for Developing Countries* (mimeographed). Washington, D.C.: International Bank for Reconstruction and Development.

Little, I. M. D., and Mirrlees, J. A. (1968). *Manual of Industrial Project Analysis in Developing Countries,* Vol. II. Social Cost–Benefit Analysis, Paris: OECD.

Little, I. M. D., and Mirrlees, J. A. (1974). *Project Appraisal and Planning for Developing Countries.* London: Heinemann.

Mishan, E. J. (1967). A Survey of Welfare Economics, 1939–59, in *Surveys of Economic Theory,* Vol. I, pp. 154–222. London–New York: Macmillan–St. Martin's Press.

Mishan, E. J. (1972). *Cost–Benefit Analysis.* London: Allen & Unwin.

Prest, A. R., and Turvey, R. (1967). Cost–Benefit Analysis: A Survey, in *Surveys of Economic Theory,* Vol. II., pp. 155–207. London–New York: Macmillan–St. Martin's Press.

Rudra, A. (1972). Use of Shadow Prices in Project Evaluation, *Indian Economic Review* **7**, 1–15.

Scarf, H. (1973). *The Computation of Economic Equilibria.* New Haven, Connecticut: Yale Univ. Press.

Scitovsky, T. (1954). Two Concepts of External Economics, *Journal of Political Economy* **17**, 143–151.

Squire, L., and Van Der Tak, H. (1964). *Economic Analysis of Projects.* Washington, D.C.: International Bank for Reconstruction and Development.

Stewart, F. (1975). A Note on Social Cost–Benefit Analysis and Class Conflict in LDCs, *World Development* **3**, 31–39.

Institute of Economics
Hungarian Academy of Sciences
Budapest, Hungary

The Size Distribution of Income: How Has It Changed?*

Mordecai Kurz

1. Introduction

Although income distribution is probably the most engaging issue of economic policy, modern economic theory has failed to develop a body of knowledge which will adequately explain the forces determining this distribution. This does not mean that theories have not been developed to deal with the issue, but it is clear that little, if any, convincing body of knowledge has been established as a consensus in the discipline.

* This work was supported by the National Science Foundation under Grant No. SOC75-21820 at the Institute for Mathematical Studies in the Social Sciences (IMSSS), Stanford University. The author greatly benefited from suggestions by Professor Paul David, Professor Paul Taubman, and the members of the seminar on income distribution at the IMSSS. An earlier version of this paper appeared in the Hebrew language in the *Israel Quarterly Tax Review*, No. 37–38.

The reason for this state of affairs appears to be deeply rooted in the nature of the Walrasian model of a market economy. In the competitive model, the distribution of physical endowment is a given datum and the distribution of income is simply an outcome of the competitive mechanism depending on prices and marginal productivities. Thus, in the Walrasian system, the question of *why* individual *j*'s income is such and such is equivalent to the question of why the prices of his endowments are such and such. Focusing on the functional distribution of income, the relative shares of capital and labor in a competitive equilibrium are simply determined by the conditions of technology and the abundance of supply.

An important aspect of the Walrasian system is that it cannot explain the formation of taxation and public expenditures. The idea of considering the public sector as a competitive Lindahl equilibrium is rather difficult to accept since it flies in the face of a reality in which most people pay taxes (or receive transfer payments) at a level that bears no relationship to the level of public goods which they enjoy, in addition to which the free-rider question makes the association between taxation and the production of public goods, at best, highly suspect.

The few theories which did not start from the competitive assumptions succeeded in providing some important insights into the distributive mechanism. The original work by Pareto (1897) and subsequent work on the Markov process theories of income distribution (Champernowne, 1943, 1973; Simon, 1955; Mandelbrot, 1960, 1961) attempted to explain why the tails of the distribution can be approximated by the Pareto distribution. The support for a log-normal distribution came from such diverse writers as McAlister (1879), Kalecki (1945), and Roy (1950, 1951). These are very interesting contributions in their ability to improve our understanding of the statistical properties of the distribution with particular emphasis on its skewness and the nature of its tails. These studies fail, however, on two counts: first, income is distributed neither according to the Pareto nor to the log-normal distributions; and second, they fail to explain the forces determining the distribution of income in the first place.

The Marxian "exploitation" notions, which found expression in the writing of the various Marxist economists, contain many interesting ideas, but this body of knowledge will not be evaluated here. As the reader will note later, an attempt will be made to provide a quantification of the notion of "power" and of its use in achieving income redistribution. To this extent the classical line of thought will be followed and the Marxian writings regarded as a very fertile source of ideas. Yet, one body of writing which is indirectly related to the Marxian theory received an extensive following among Western intellectuals, and that is the theory of the "Welfare State." This vast body of writing by academic as well as political thinkers has regarded the major changes in the distribution of income in Western societies during the past half century to have been due to the development of the welfare state. Moreover, the empirical evidence appears to be overwhelming: between 1900 and 1975 the size of the public sector in the Western economies grew from a negligible fraction to the range of 30 to 50% of national income. In his writings on the welfare state, Myrdal (1960) has thus concluded that our society is moving toward a stage which is *beyond* the welfare state. Yet, since it is generally agreed that the most essential element of the welfare state and government intervention is the redistribution of income toward greater equality, the empirical question still remains open: What were the true accomplishments of the welfare state with regard to this objective? Moreover, what are the logical bases for the theory of the "welfare state" as a stage in the economic development of modern societies and to what extent is such a theory supported by the historical evidence?

2. The Logical and Historical Foundation of the Theory of the Welfare State

All the writers on the subject of the welfare state cannot be reviewed here; it will thus be convenient to pick one good representative of this body of writing, of which the book *Beyond the Welfare State* by Myrdal (1960) is an example. Myrdal states in his introductory chapter that he intends to stay away from ideological and perhaps semantic arguments regarding the "free" or "planned" economy. This should clarify his contrasting the old order of liberal economics with the welfare state in which state intervention in economic life is extensive, not as an ideological matter but rather as a practical reflection of the day-to-day functioning of the economy.

So, if the welfare state is a true social reality, what is it, what are its origins, and why did it develop during the twentieth century?

Myrdal tells us that as a matter of historical perspective, state intervention preceded state planning and the process itself was almost unnoticed. More specifically, Myrdal (1960, pp. 21–22) argues that state intervention was originally intended only to meet emergencies. However, the acts of intervention induced state planning which emerged as an entirely different matter. The twentieth century, however, brought with it a series of international crises in the forms of World War I, the Great Depression, the collapse of the gold standard, World War II, and other forces that, according to Myrdal, caused the failure of the market economy and led to state intervention. Based on the "crisis theory" of social change, Myrdal (1960) thus concludes that the process cannot be reversed:

> No country today—and certainly not the United States—is willing any longer to accept a level of economic activity and employment determined by the automatic repercussions, through the banking system, of changes in its international payment situation. To put it another way: no country is prepared to abstain from interfering in the "free" economy. No country is now in a position to allow monetary matters to remain outside economic policy—or even outside politics. . . .
>
> This is indeed a reason why so many social changes are as irreversible as the reaction when sodium is thrown into water. And this particular chain of events, which has led us away from the relatively high degree of automatism which in the nineteenth century ruled monetary matters, definitely has such a character [pp. 28–29].

But now we need to understand why the welfare state came to be. What are the basic internal forces which made its appearance, according to Myrdal, inevitable?

First, Myrdal reviews the fact that the liberal idea of perfect competition was never a reality, and during the twentieth century, market structures have been so altered that a new form was needed. More accurately, Myrdal (1960) says in one of the most revealing passages of the book:

> This perfect market was understood, of course, never to have existed. A more important thing, however, of which we are also all aware, is that for a long time reality has been moving steadily further and further away from this liberal idealization. Technological and organizational developments have in many fields been increasing the size of the units in relation to the markets. At the same time, in all other fields the individual units have found the means by which to combine.
>
> They have thereby come into a position where they can influence the markets and manipulate the prices. The markets and the prices have more and more lost their character of being given and objective conditions, outside the influence of the individuals units, which merely have to adjust to them. The markets have become consciously "regulated" by the participants.
>
> And when the atomism has gone, then the assumed static institutional frame is no longer protected, but can be influenced, as can the price formation taking place within that frame. Instead of obediently

adjusting themselves to a given framework of society and accepting the burdens and rewards as they come out from the working of the forces within this framework, the individuals begin to cooperate in order to influence this process and, going even further, to adjust the framework itself according to their own interests.

When this happens on a large enough scale, a fundamental institutional change has occurred in the position of the human beings in relation to each other and to the community. I do not need to recall to what extent practically all markets are manipulated at the present time. Many markets are dominated by one or a few sellers or buyers. But, apart from these cases, almost every individual person in any one of the Western countries who has something to sell or who earns an income or seeks a profit, is associating himself with his compeers with the intention of influencing the conditions under which he is acting.

This development compels the state to large-scale measures of intervention. They become necessary simply to prevent the actual disorganization of society, which would result from the organization of the individual markets, if this development were not controlled and coordinated. And they are needed in order to prevent those who have acquired a stronger bargaining power from exploiting the others [pp. 31–33].

However, for Myrdal (1960) the transformation from the liberal era to the welfare state is also a change in philosophy, psychology, and attitudes. He argues that when "rational hedonism" is actually practiced, it does not lead to a free market economy but rather to its breakdown [p. 34]. We finally arrive at the heart of the program of the welfare state which is obviously income redistribution, and Myrdal (1960) thus tells us:

The urge for economic equalization is everywhere present, and it is commonly proclaimed as a principle. Its sphere of operation is not limited to taxation and to redistributional expenditure schemes like those for various forms of social insurance. It enters into, and determines, the scope of all other state intervention. . . .

The rational basis for this general interest of people in the lower income brackets in intervention is that, when private relations become public relations in the Western countries, now so firmly dedicated to equality, there is a better chance that the poor man's concerns will be looked after. Income distribution has the form of a pyramid with a broad basis and a narrowing top. In a democracy with effective universal suffrage, this is one of the explanations why we are steadily proceeding in the direction of government control and direction. Even the conservative and liberal parties will have to become the vehicles for this development, or else disappear from the political scene [pp. 38–40].

Myrdal visualizes the "free" market economy as containing essential conflicts which will be resolved in the completely coordinated and managed welfare state in which income distribution is equalized. Although Myrdal recognizes the loss of individual "rights" in favor of state power, he holds the view that people indicate a preference for this outcome since the welfare state is to be a better society. Moreover, after greater equality is achieved, the high degree of conflict of the free economy will give way to "harmony" of interests in the welfare state:

> The examples I have given of a trend towards a convergence of attitudes and ideologies—in regard to the now largely undisputed, and consequently almost automatic, progress of further redistributional reforms, to which could be added educational and health reforms, etc., and the virtual disappearance of the nationalization issue—point to the increasing political harmony that has come to exist much more generally between all the citizen groups in the advanced Welfare State. The internal political debate in those countries is becoming increasingly technical in character, ever more concerned with detailed arrangements, and less involved with broad issues, since those are slowly disappearing [p. 77].

To sharpen the exposition, the essential points of the "Welfare State" theory of economic development in general and as given by Myrdal (1960) in particular are summarized:

(1) State intervention and economic planning have come about because special interests in the pluralistic society used the power of the state to advance their own interests. This has been a very slow process, but was accelerated by the economic and political crises of the twentieth century.

(2) Technological and institutional developments have caused increased market concentration and price manipulation to a point where growing monopoly and oligopoly power resulted in a gradual breakdown of the competitive markets and called for extensive state intervention to mediate and regulate the competing forces.

(3) In a long discussion which has not been quoted, Myrdal argues that innovative, rational, and creative people will always find ways to avoid competition, thus subverting the market mechanism and destroying the market economy, which gives rise to the regulated welfare state. Myrdal

thus concludes that for a free market economy to function, people must be traditionalistic, inhibited, nonquestioning, and conventional.

(4) Equalization or economic egalitarianism in the welfare state is a "basic" urge which is uniformly and universally agreed upon as a principle. In this way it becomes an important force in increasing state intervention on behalf of the weak.

(5) In the advanced welfare state, political harmony is expected to prevail since all the strife among the various population groups would end, making most political debates largely technical.

The most striking features of Myrdal's writing are the lack of empirical support for the claims made and some basic flaws in logic. A few points of this nature are now considered. The argument that state intervention developed as a needed mediator among growing giants who gradually took over the markets has no empirical support since it is far from clear that market concentration is higher in 1976 than in 1900. Moreover, sheer industrial size is far from implying "power," as the ailing railroads of the twentieth century will indicate. Thus, as a general proposition, it is not generally agreed that the relative power of the various industrial actors in the different markets has increased during the last half century.

The claim that state intervention is intended to lead to industrial harmony and increased efficiency appears to be supported neither by fact nor by logic. If anything, state intervention in a great many cases such as that in Britain of recent years may have increased economic strife, since the state itself is composed of a great many political interests and when these interests are injected into any specific situation of conflict, they may enlarge the conflict and delay its resolution. This means that in conflict situations state intervention may create interconnections among conflicts when such connections were not there to start with, and by establishing these relations the state makes the resolution of conflicts more difficult.

It is important to remember that Myrdal wrote his book in 1960 when the issue of nationalization was very hotly debated. Thus, Myrdal often identified "intervention" with "nationalization," thinking that when nationalization reaches an advanced stage, it will be associated with industrial tranquility and efficiency compared to the inefficient market economy. Unfortunately, neither industrial harmony nor efficiency has been attained. In fact, the evidence seems to suggest that the degree of industrial inefficiency rises with the degree of centralization. It is not proposed here that this must be the case on any conceptual grounds; rather, it is a simple empirical observation that seems to contradict Myrdal's prediction. Similarly, Myrdal's views regarding the international markets seem to be contradicted by the simple fact that the international monetary mechanism and trade of the 1970s are functioning better than ever. With regard to human attitudes, Myrdal's argument about people's attitudes and psychological make-up is interesting, but then why did the welfare state arrive only in the twentieth rather than the nineteenth century?

A striking piece of empirical evidence which must be examined is the phenomenal rise in the size of federal, state, and local governments. Start by noting that the welfare state theorists did not make a distinction between public intervention in regular markets with the intent of *removing* individual rights in general, and property rights in particular, and those public interferences which are carried out in order to *ensure* individual and property rights. Public interference to ensure proper flow of market information (securities, drugs, insurance, etc.), public actions to regulate externalities (pollution), and public regulation of industries with declining cost are all interferences which aim to preserve individual rights and establish the proper legal boundaries between conflicting property rights. It then follows that the "interference" of the public sector in the economy does not necessarily mean "nationalization" or that the government "plans" or "coordinates" economic activities. Furthermore, a growing number of socialist economies are moving toward greater decentralization with a growing dependence upon the market mechanism, which is exactly contrary to Myrdal's view of the functioning of markets.

In the historical context of the capitalist economies, one suspects that it was in the nineteenth and early twentieth centuries that we have seen the greatest interferences with the proper functioning of markets in which the interferences were accomplished by a small class of powerful individuals using their own economic resources in addition to the power of the state to distort the functioning of markets in their own favor and thus to infringe upon the rights of others. It took a century of political developments to provide the individual with protection of the law that would ensure his market rights on all levels: as a small consumer the protection against fraud, as a small investor the protection against legal embezzlement, as a member of the community the protection against environmental decay caused by externalities produced by profit-maximizing firms, and as a voter the guarantee of freedom to exercise his political rights. With these accomplished, markets can function today more effectively than in earlier times. With this perspective in mind, one may find Myrdal's record of the historical evidence rather unacceptable.

On the quantitative level, we may note that a very extensive part of the growth of the size of the public sector does not represent "interference," "nationalization," or a tendency to "plan" or "coordinate" in the Myrdal sense, but rather is a part which acts either at the purely redistributive level or establishes the production of public goods or redistribution through the existing decentralized economy. These items include all national defense, all educational programs, social security and welfare, medical plans of various categories, veteran's benefits, and the interest on the national debt. Clearly, the totality of these items is a very large fraction of the national budget. Combining these facts with my earlier argument, it is clear that a large public budget does not mean public "interference" in the Myrdal sense, and a "large" government does not necessarily do what Myrdal predicts that it would do.

We can thus turn to the final and the essential acid test of the welfare state: income redistribution. Myrdal's belief that egalitarianism and equality have been elevated to universal principles agreed to by all has no supporting evidence. However, all will agree that the nature and extent of actual income redistribution is the ultimate test of the viability and meaning of the proposed theory of the "Welfare State." If, in fact, egalitarianism is a universal principle and our societies are already moving *beyond* the welfare state, then income redistribution during the past two generations must have been dramatic; i.e., if we consider the period 1936–1976 which was the 40 years in which the most dramatic "welfare state" legislation was put into effect, we should expect dramatic changes in income distribution during this time. The reader may consult any elementary textbook on public finance to find out *that such dramatic changes did not take place!* [See, e.g., Atkinson (1975, Chapter 4).] Historical evidence will be presented for the United States not necessarily because the experience there is the same as anywhere else but rather because the United States has gone through some of the stages of social legislation and growth of government which Myrdal discusses. Thus, we regard the United States as an example only. Further, by examining the evidence, some new propositions will be developed, on which the positive part of this paper (Section 3) shall be built. With this in mind, consider the historical evidence in the United States. The data in Table 1 include direct transfers of income, but exclude taxes paid and all the direct and indirect benefits of public expenditures received by the various groups. For the sake of our discussion, the changes over time in the distribution of income *after taxes and after direct and indirect transfers* are needed. Unfortunately, such information is not available. The following conclusions, however, can be drawn from the data at hand:

(1) The share of the *lowest* quintile before taxes and other public expenditures from which it is a major beneficiary has increased from about 4 to about 5%. Since this quintile pays no taxes and receives a relatively higher fraction of other public expenditures, it is clear that the share of this quintile increased from 1936 to 1976.

(2) The share of the top quintile decreased from about 50 to 45%

TABLE 1

Distribution of Family Personal Income before Taxes by Income Quintile, All Consumer Units, Selected Years[a,b]

Quintile	Old series						New series			
	1935–1936	1941	1944	1947	1950	1956	1961	1964	1970	1971
Lowest	4.1	4.1	4.9	5.0	4.8	4.8	4.6	4.2	4.6	4.8
Second	9.2	9.5	10.9	11.0	10.9	11.3	10.9	10.6	10.7	10.8
Third	14.1	15.3	16.2	16.0	16.1	16.3	16.3	16.4	16.4	16.4
Fourth	20.9	22.3	22.2	22.2	22.1	22.3	22.7	23.2	23.3	23.3
Highest	51.7	48.8	45.8	46.0	46.1	45.3	45.5	45.5	44.9	44.6
Total	100.0	100.0	100.0	100.0	100.0	100.0	100.0	100.0	100.0	100.0
Top 5%	26.5	24.0	20.7	20.9	21.4	20.2	19.6	20.0	19.2	19.1
Percentiles 81–95	25.2	24.8	25.1	25.1	24.7	25.1	25.9	25.5	25.6	25.6

[a] *Survey of Current Business,* Table 10 (October 1974).
[b] Percent of income.

before taxes. Both taxes and other expenditures will reduce further its share. Thus, we can definitely conclude that its share declined. However, note from the last two lines in Table 1 that one may conclude that this decline did not occur in the entire top quintile but rather *in the top 5%* whose share declined from about 26 to 19%, leaving the percentiles 81–95 *unchanged.*

We are unable to determine from Table 1 what happened during the period at hand to the three quintiles (second–third–fourth) which contain 60% of the consuming units; i.e., what happened to the middle of the distribution? There is, however, some information which, fragmentary as it may be, may provide some help. Consider first the evidence available (Musgrave and Musgrave, 1973, Table 16.5). From Table 2, we see that the comparison of the shares of the second quartile before and after taxes and transfers indicates that this share is the *same.* On the other hand, the share of the third quartile is lower after taxes and transfers, contrary to the data *before* taxes (Table 1), which indicates a slight rise in the share of the third and fourth quintiles between 1936 and 1971. This means that taxes by themselves tend to neutralize the increased share recorded for the third and fourth quintiles in Table 1. Now consider the evidence presented in a recent study by Reynolds and Smolensky (1975), in which they calculate the distribution of income after all taxes and transfers. Unfortu-

TABLE 2

Distribution of Family Income by Quartiles—1968[a]

	% Income without taxes and transfers	% Income after taxes and transfers
Lowest 25%	1.9	6.6
Second 25%	15.1	15.4
Third 25%	28.0	26.0
Highest 25%	55.0	52.0
All	100.0	100.0

[a] Data from Musgrave and Musgrave (1973).

nately, they carry out their analysis only for the years 1950, 1961, and 1970. The results are presented in Table 3. The Reynolds–Smolensky figures are not comparable to the data presented earlier, but they do confirm the view that after taxes and transfers *the center of the distribution has changed very little.*

This leads to the third conclusion:

(3)   Considering the distribution of income after taxes and transfers, the share of the second quintile has either remained unchanged or may have increased by a very small amount. There is, however, absolutely no evidence that after taxes and transfers the relative shares of the third and fourth quintiles have changed over the last two generations.

I could not find comparable data for the bottom 5%. It is widely believed that the changes within the lowest quintile were not uniform and by far the greatest change occurred in the relative share of the bottom 5%.

The empirical findings can thus be summarized as follows:

(1)   During the period 1939–1971, the distribution of income after transfers and taxes in the United States has changed only slightly.

(2)   During this period, the entire change in the distribution of income

TABLE 3

Estimated Shares of NNT after Taxes, Transfers,
and Government Expenditures

	1950	1961	1970
Lowest 20%	7.2%	8.7%	7.9%
Middle 60%	54.8	56.3	55.5
Highest 20%	38.0	35.0	36.6

Mordecai Kurz

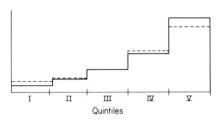

Figure 1   Histogram of the distribution of income after taxes and transfers: 1936,—;
1971, - - -.

after taxes and transfers occurred in the two extreme tails, lowering the
relative share of the top 5%, raising the share of the bottom 5–10%, and
leaving essentially unchanged the share of the 85–90% of the consuming
units.

These empirical realities are summarized in Figs. 1 and 2. Figure 1 is a
histogram of the post-tax and post-transfer distribution of income by quintiles. Figure 2 shows the distribution of income after conceptual normali-
zation for the mean; thus I visualize the changes as shown.

The empirical facts presented here are very important for the analytical
development presented in Section 3. It is therefore clear that the intellectual challenge at hand is not only to explain why the distribution of income
changed so little during the period at hand, but also *why the distribution
changed in the way that it did!*

Returning, however, to complete the review of the theory of the welfare
state, it appears that, in spite of the analysis and predictions of its sup-
porters, the "welfare state" in the sense of Myrdal is a fiction that never
existed: the propositions regarding its emergence have no logical or empirical foundation, and its intellectual construction has only limited use.

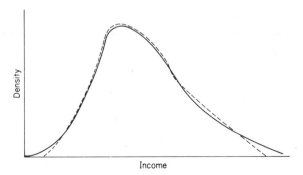

Figure 2   Diagrammatic representation of the change in the distribution of income
after taxes and transfers: 1936,—; 1971, - - -.

Moreover, it is views like Myrdal's and those of other liberal or social–democratic theorists that have retarded the development of a proper theory of income distribution. Myrdal and other theorists writing on welfare economics employ such ideas as "historical forces" or notions of "social cohesion" that make the "state" into an entity with resources, objectives, desires, preferences, aims, and means to achieve them. Thus, Myrdal's characterization of the state acting to achieve anything is the same as the characterization of a consumer or a firm in neoclassical economics. The democratic state has never been such an entity, and no useful theory of income distribution can emerge from this view, since the state represents nothing but the compromises achieved by the conflicting interests within it.

If making the state into an entity which distributes income according to its own preferences will not lead to an acceptable theory of income distribution, what will? A new approach to the theory of income distribution is now proposed, which aims to derive the distribution of income from the underlying economic and political forces which constitute the framework of economic activity.

3. The Aumann–Kurz Theory of Income Distribution

Aumann and Kurz (1977a, b) developed a new theory of income distribution and proposed a specific but simplified model for its application. The theory will be reviewed here briefly and the simple model reported by Aumann and Kurz (1977a) described.

Aumann and Kurz begin their analysis by assuming the existence of a democratic process and a basic constitution which defines individual rights, including property rights. Each individual is thus endowed with certain resources which can be used for consumption and production, but, in addition, the individual has his vote and the right to his own property. In a free market economy in which prices are endogenously determined, the distribution of income will be an automatic outcome of the endowment of each person and the prevailing prices. To achieve redistribution, individuals must act via the political mechanism. They can form pressure groups, political parties, and other associations, all of which we call "coalitions," and such coalitions aim to reach the minimum size that is sufficient to allow the group to enact whatever redistributive laws it wishes to make in accordance with the voting rules laid down in the constitution. The power to pass redistributive laws, however, is not irreversible; any politically dominant coalition may find itself displaced by a differently composed majority coalition with correspondingly different legislative proposals. Thus, in the process of social bargaining, the formation of alternative coalitions should always be viewed as a threat of potential alternative actions which may be taken by other groups. As noted, Aumann and Kurz assume that every majority coalition may pass any redistributive proposals it may wish to enact, and that these represent the set of alternative threats that it has against its opponents. What must now be brought to bear are the potential threats of the minority. What Aumann and Kurz assume is that the minority may refuse to cooperate with the majority and call for a general strike of its members against the majority. Thus, the idea of "property rights" is translated into the right of a potentially oppressed minority to refuse to work or make its capital or other resources available to the system as a whole.

As political–economic tactics, strikes are familiar from labor-management relations, while tactics of civil disobedience are common as political moves. What is done in the Aumann–Kurz theory is to accept the view that such strategies are at the bottom of most economic threats and, combined with the democratic process, they constitute the essential reason for a social compromise. When formalized into a game of conflict, the solution is an income distribution which emerges as an endogenous outcome of the game.

Obviously, one may think of other threats and counterthreats which are commonly employed in our economies, and these may influence the final distribution as well. This is true, and Aumann and Kurz simply set the stage for further developments of the theory. When one considers the simple model in which some of these ideas are embodied (Aumann and Kurz, 1977a), it will become clear that this is only the start of a new scientific development, and much further work may be expected. Let us then turn to this simple model and examine how to apply it to our problem.

The development of the model starts with the definition of a set T of individuals with utility functions $u_t(y)$, $t \in T$, where y denotes income, thus making "income" the only variable to be considered.[1] As noted earlier, every member t of this economy starts with his own potential endowment $e(t)$ which should generally be viewed as the unobservable resources of individual t. A measure μ defines the "size" of every coalition S. Also, if a coalition S is formed, then its aggregate resources will be $e(S) = \int_S e(\tau)\mu(d\tau)$, and it may be able to use these resources for direct redistribution, production and redistribution, etc. It is not necessarily advisable to think of $e(t)$ as pretax income, since pretax

---

[1] Aumann and Kurz (1977b) extended the model to deal with a multicommodity economy. The income distribution results are not altered.

income is already *an outcome* of the redistribution struggle due to the fact that redistribution is achieved via many means, taxation being only one. Thus, if a law is passed that prevents you from using your land for one purpose or another, your "pretax income" is already affected by this redistributive law.

In forming a coalition S, individuals can achieve two things:

(1) They can combine their resources $e(S)$ to make better use of them jointly and then redistribute the outcome. In the simple version, Aumann and Kurz ignore production, although it can easily be incorporated.

(2) If S has a number of members which exceeds 50% of the total, then S can use its power to pass any legislation that will benefit S and reduce the share of the minority (i.e., the coalition $T \backslash S$).

Formalizing this model and adopting the Shapley–Nash–Harsanyi solution concept, Aumann and Kurz show that the final income distribution $y(t)$ must satisfy

$$y(t) + u_t(y(t))/u_t'(y(t)) = e(t) + c, \tag{1}$$

where

$$c = \int_T \frac{u_\tau(y(\tau))}{u_\tau'(y(\tau))} \mu(d\tau). \tag{2}$$

Let the elasticity of u_t be denoted by ϵ_t. Thus,

$$\epsilon_t = u_t'(y(t))y(t)/u_t(y(t)).$$

Then (1) and (2) can be expressed as

$$y(t) = \frac{\epsilon_t}{1 + \epsilon_t} e(t) + \frac{\epsilon_t}{1 + \epsilon_t} \int_T \frac{y(\tau)}{\epsilon_\tau} \mu(d\tau). \tag{3}$$

It is then clear that the final, postredistribution income $y(t)$ is determined by two factors:

(1) the initial wealth $e(t)$ of the individual, which contributes $[\epsilon_t/(1 + \epsilon_t)]e(t)$, and
(2) the individual's voting power which contributes $[\epsilon_t/(1 + \epsilon_t)]c$.

What this theory suggests is that important changes in income distribution will occur only because of changes in the way the democratic process functions and because of changes in the legal structure defining property rights. The term "property rights" must be understood in the deep constitutional sense which defines the set of actions which are available to the individual. It appears to me that no drastic changes in the basic, individual property rights have occurred in the United States since 1936. Extensive legal developments around this question did take place, but these concentrated on the interpretation of the basic constitutional principle when externalities occur and opposing property rights conflict. These developments tried to identify in a clearer manner the boundaries of individual property rights. Even cases of conflict between private property rights and the "public interest" due to externalities (such as pollution) should be interpreted as raising an issue of finding the exact boundaries among the differing and perhaps contradictory property rights of all members of society.

The situation is dramatically different on the political side of the equation. We now argue that important political changes took place, and these are due to economic forces which are analyzed here. We believe that during this half century we have observed a dramatic rise of individuals exercising their political rights and groups forming political organizations to make their demands known. Since, earlier in this century, various oppressed groups began to seek the removal of economic and legal barriers which prevented them from voting, these movements finally gained sufficient momentum to secure an almost complete abolition of effective restrictions on voting and other forms of political participation. This political drive was clearly part of a much broader process in which a growing number of political interests found ways to express themselves. This increased political participation required massive organization, leading even to cases of protest and civil disobedience as was the case during the antiwar protest. In our earlier terms, we would interpret all this to mean that individuals and groups are exercising their voting rights more effectively today than during the earlier part of this century. All these facts obviously represent a very complex set of phenomena, but what we seek now is that element which can be incorporated in the theory proposed here. In order to do that, one may start by asking why these events did not occur earlier. Why recently and not 100 years ago?

We do not believe that a satisfactory answer to the preceding question should suggest that people's attitudes have changed and, by preferring a more egalitarian society, they have adopted "equalization" as a basic principle, resulting in their being prepared to fight for a society with greater equality.

A better answer will concentrate on the process by which coalitions are formed and what it takes for a group of people to act together. Clearly, they need to communicate and organize, and, in the process of doing so, massive resources may need to be expended in order to achieve effective joint action. Thus, for coalitions to exercise their power, they need to form, but they will not form if the cost of forming will consume their limited resources. In this context, the two dramatic changes of the twentieth century are simply the rise of income and the dramatic decline in the cost of *information, communication, and organization.* In terms of the preceding discussion, think of the voter registration movement in the South without the automobile, the cheap telephone, the inexpensive newspaper and radio advertising, in addition to the rising resources of the organizers. What would have been the effect of Martin Luther King without television, radio, and recording technology? In our opinion, the antiwar movement would have never expanded from the grounds of the universities had it not been for the technology of television. These are only very dramatic examples of how the relative cost of transmitting information, communicating, and organizing have sharply declined over the last half century.

Note that the Aumann–Kurz model did not take into account the cost of coalition formation. What we shall now show is that if this cost is introduced into the model, then the model will be capable of making a prediction of how changes in the cost of coalition formation will alter the distribution of income. We will then argue that this prediction explains the data for the last 40 years as presented earlier here.

4. The Effect of Changes in the Cost of Organization and Communication

To examine the hypothesis proposed, the Aumann–Kurz theory will be modified to include the cost of coalition formation. Thus, consider a coalition S. In the early formulation, if S is formed and if $e(S)$ is the total amount of resources available to S, then it can select a new distribution $x(t), t \in S$, of these resources in such a way that

(a) $u_t(x(t))$ is the utility of each member t, and

(b) $\int_S x(\tau)\mu(d\tau) \leq e(S)$.

However, if this coalition must incur organizational and informational cost $g(S)$, then one needs to replace (b) with the condition

(b′) $\int_S x(\tau)\mu(d\tau) \leq e(S) - g(S)$.

Note first that $e(S) - g(S)$ may be positive or negative. If $e(S) - g(S) < 0$, then there is no reason for coalition S to form at all since it will need to spend on organizing itself more than the resources it has. Moreover, even if $e(S) - g(S) > 0$, this coalition may be "weak" in the sense that the totality of its net resources is rather small. Also, if the utility functions $u_t(y)$ demonstrate steep slopes around the origin and a sharply declining marginal utility of income, then the existence of organizational costs will tend to weaken the bargaining power of members of S.[2]

This discussion clarifies the fact that the existence of organizational costs reduces the effectiveness of the poor coalitions with a small amount of resources $e(S)$. It is also clear that increasing the amount of initial resources $e(S)$ or reducing the amount of organizational costs $g(S)$ has the same effect!

Assume that communication and organizational costs are simply proportional to the *size* of the coalition S and do not depend upon the characteristics of members of S. This may be a simplified assumption since the presumption ought to be that, for example, it is easier to communicate with and organize educated people and that it is easier to intimidate uneducated people. Disregarding this, assume that there exists a parameter $k > 0$ such that $k < e(t)$ for all t and $g(S) = k\mu(S)$, where $\mu(S)$, as before, measures the "size" of coalition S. With this assumption it can be shown that if $y(t)$ is the solution to the *modified Aumann–Kurz* model, then $y(t)$ must satisfy

$$y(t) + u_t(y(t))/u_t'(y(t)) = [e(t) - k] + c. \tag{4}$$

Since k can be interpreted as the marginal organizational cost (i.e., the organizational cost per person), from the strategic point of view, the effect of such costs is equivalent to lowering the real income level of each participant by a fixed quantity k. We now wish to examine how changes in k alter the distribution of income $y(t)$. In order to keep the computations simple, assume that the utility functions of the population take the form

$$u_t(y) = y^{\alpha+\beta t}, \qquad 0 \le \alpha + \beta t \le 1, \quad 0 \le t \le 1, \tag{5}$$

where $T = [0,1]$, and for this family of utility functions calculate

$$y(t) + y(t)/(\alpha + \beta t) = c + [e(t) - k] \tag{6}$$

or

$$y(t) = [(\alpha + \beta t)/(1 + \alpha + \beta t)]\{c + [e(t) - k]\}. \tag{6'}$$

In examining the effect of changes in k on the distribution of income, we need to know something about the distribution of the utility functions u_t in the population. This follows from the fact that in this theory the final distribution of income depends, among other things, upon the distribution of people's attitudes toward risk (reflected in the expression u_t/u_t'). If, for example, all the rich people [people with high $e(t)$] *also* happen to have

[2] See the notion of "the fear of ruin" developed by Aumann and Kurz (1977a).

certain types of utility functions, then the distribution of income will be different from the case in which the distribution of utility functions u_t and endowments $e(t)$ are independent in some sense. The specific sense to be employed here can be stated as follows:

ASSUMPTION OF INDEPENDENCE OF TASTES AND WEALTH   Let $\epsilon_t = y(t)u_t'(y(t))/u_t(y(t))$. Then, over the population as a whole,

$$\int_T \frac{\epsilon_\tau}{1 + \epsilon_\tau} e(\tau)\mu(d\tau) = \left[\int_T \frac{\epsilon_\tau}{1 + \epsilon_\tau} \mu(d\tau) \right] \bar{e}, \tag{7}$$

where $\bar{e} = \int_T e(\tau)\mu(d\tau)$.

Next examine the effect of changes in k on the distribution of income.

Let S^* be any group of people. Define

$$\eta(S^*) = \frac{\int_{S^*} y(\tau)\mu(d\tau)}{\int_T [e(\tau) - k]\mu(d\tau)},$$

that is, the relative share of group S^* in total income.

The aim is to establish the expression $d\eta(S^*)/dk$, but first consider the following proposition:

PROPOSITION $dy(t)/dk < 0$ for all t.

Proof   Since

$$y(t) + y(t)/(\alpha + \beta t) = c + [e(t) - k],$$

we have

$$\frac{dy(t)}{dk} = \frac{\alpha + \beta t}{1 + \alpha + \beta t} \left(\frac{dc}{dk} - 1 \right) ;$$

but since

$$\int_T y(\tau)\mu(d\tau) = \int_T e(\tau)\mu(d\tau) - k,$$

it follows that

$$\int_T \frac{dy(\tau)}{dk} \mu(d\tau) = -1.$$

This proves that

$$\frac{dc}{dk} - 1 = - \left[\int_T \frac{\alpha + \beta\tau}{1 + \alpha + \beta\tau} \mu(d\tau) \right]^{-1},$$

and thus

$$\frac{dy(t)}{dk} = - \frac{\alpha + \beta t}{1 + \alpha + \beta t} \Big/ \int_T \frac{\alpha + \beta \tau}{1 + \alpha + \beta \tau} \mu(d\tau) < 0.$$

This proposition shows that when organizational costs are reduced, *everybody gains* in the absolute sense, since fewer resources are spent on organization of the political mechanism. The deeper question to be explored is who are the *relative* gainers and losers?

To analyze this, we avoid a rather complex set of calculations and state without proof that if $S*$ is any coalition, then a change in k alters the relative share of this group [i.e., $\eta(S*)$] in the following way:

$$\frac{d\eta(S*)}{dk} = \frac{1}{(\bar{e} - k)^2} \left[\int_{S*} \frac{\alpha + \beta\tau}{1 + \alpha + \beta\tau} [e(\tau) - \bar{e}]\mu(d\tau) \right.$$

$$\left. + \left\{ \int_T \frac{\alpha + \beta\tau}{1 + \alpha + \beta\tau} [e(\tau) - \bar{e}]\mu(d\tau) \right\} \frac{\int_{S*} \frac{\alpha + \beta\tau}{1 + \alpha + \beta\tau} \mu(d\tau)}{\int_T \frac{\alpha + \beta\tau}{1 + \alpha + \beta\tau} \mu(d\tau)} \right].$$

First, note that

$$(\alpha + \beta\tau)/(1 + \alpha + \beta\tau) = \epsilon_t/(1 + \epsilon_t),$$

and by assumption (7),

$$\int_T \frac{\epsilon_\tau}{1 + \epsilon_\tau} [e(\tau) - \bar{e}]\mu(d\tau) = \left[\int_T \frac{\epsilon_\tau}{1 + \epsilon_\tau} \mu(d\tau) \right] (\bar{e} - \bar{e}) = 0;$$

therefore,

$$\frac{d\eta(S*)}{dk} = \frac{1}{(\bar{e} - k)^2} \int_{S*} \frac{\alpha + \beta\tau}{1 + \alpha + \beta\tau} [e(\tau) - \bar{e}]\mu(d\tau). \tag{8}$$

Formula (8) states the simple result that in the absence of correlation between wealth and tastes, the effect of changes in k on the relative distribution of income depends upon the distance of $e(t)$ from the mean $\bar{e}$. To interpret this, consider the following cases.

Case 1 The group $S*$ consists entirely of the lowest 10 percentiles of initial income. Thus, $e(t) < \bar{e}$ for all t, and therefore we have $d\eta(S*)/dk < 0$, indicating that the share of $S*$ will rise whenever k falls. Moreover, the larger are the differences $e(t) - \bar{e}, t \in S*$, the larger is the expression $\int_{S*}[e(\tau) - \bar{e}]\mu(d\tau)$, and this results in a larger effect of changes in k. This means that the greatest effect is to be found in the tail.

Case 2   The group S^* consists entirely of the top 10 percentiles of initial income. Thus $e(t) > \bar{e}$ for all t, and we have $d\eta(S^*)/dk > 0$, indicating that the share of S^* will fall whenever k falls. Again, the larger are the differences $e(t) - \bar{e}$, $t \in S^*$, the larger is the effect of changes of k on $\eta(S^*)$. This again shows that the greatest effects are to be found in the tail.

Case 3   The group S^* consists of a group of people with $e(t)$ evenly distributed around $\bar{e}$. For these people, $d\eta(S^*)/dk \simeq 0$, and no change in their relative share is to be expected. This means that no substantive change occurs in the center of the distribution.

In general, the theory predicts that a reduction in k will lead to increased equality, but what is interesting is to see how the increased equality is to be achieved; the prediction is that it will be the extreme tails at which the change will occur, leaving the center of the distribution essentially intact.

I propose that these results provide a simple and unified explanation of the empirical facts regarding the nature of the change in income distribution during the past two generations. I have been unable to obtain any reliable data for the pre-1929 period. However, the proposed theory says that in order to understand any changes in income distribution, one should seek to understand the changes in the balance of political power within the society as well as the underlying legal structure which defines property and individual rights.

To some, the view proposed here may be regarded a bit pessimistic, but this is not so. It is an attempt to integrate both political and economic factors into a unified theory of income distribution. On the methodological level, the proposed view suggests that no useful theory of income distribution will ever emanate from the artificial construction of the "social welfare function," and the discussion of an "optimal income tax" is, at best, useless.

5.   Some Qualifications

I have attempted to show that a great deal of the literature on modern economic development of the advanced Western economies provides an inadequate explanation of the observed changes in the distribution of income. In proposing an endogenous theory of income distribution, I am suggesting a new approach to this theory. In doing so, I have tried to indicate that the predictions of the model are consistent with the historical data. However, we must keep in mind that many other forces operated on the distribution of income during the period of study. These include the changes in the age distribution of the population, in the amount and distribution of human capital, and in the process of household formation. All such factors have been ignored in the simplified proposed model.

On purely theoretical grounds, it is clear that the nature of social bargaining may be more complex than I proposed, and the existence of such phenomena as discrimination and strong customs which prevent some people from joining some coalitions (some workers may refuse to join their employers) suggest that the solution concept which was adopted is not satisfactory. Moreover, there are many dynamic considerations that have been ignored, in addition to problems of increasing returns to scale in production and the presence of important public goods.

Yet, income distribution is endogenously determined and the factors proposed in the model play some role in the determination of the distribution of income. It is surprising how much the simple model proposed helps clarify many issues involved, and we may only hope that future work will proceed to close the open gaps.

References

Atkinson, A. B. (1975). *The Economics of Inequality*. London and New York: Oxford Univ. (Clarendon) Press.

Aumann, R. J., and Kurz, M. (1977a). Power and Taxes, *Econometrica* **45**, No. 5, 1137–1161.

Aumann, R. J., and Kurz, M. (1977b). Power and Taxes in a Multi-Commodity Economy, *The Israel Journal of Mathematics* **27**, No. 3–4, 185–234.

Champernowne, D. G. (1943). A Model of Income Distribution, *Economic Journal* **68**, 318–351.

Champernowne, D. G. (1973). *The Distribution of Income*. London and New York: Cambridge Univ. Press.

Kalecki, M. (1945). On the Gibrat Distribution, *Econometrica* **13**, 161–170.

Mandelbrot, B. (1960). The Pareto Levy Law and the Distribution of Income, *International Economic Review* **1**, 79–106.

Mandelbrot, B. (1961). Stable Paretian Random Functions and the Multiplicative Variation of Income, *Econometrica* **29**, 517–543.

McAlister, D. (1879). The Law of the Geometric Mean, *Proceedings of Royal Society* **29**, 367–376.

Musgrave, R. A., and Musgrave, P. B. (1973). *Public Finance in Theory and Practice*. New York: McGraw-Hill.

Myrdal, G. (1960). *Beyond the Welfare State*. New Haven, Connecticut: Yale Univ. Press.

Pareto, V. (1897). *Course d'Économie Politique*, Vol. II. Lausanne.

Reynolds, M., and Smolensky, E. (1975). Post-Fisc Distribution of Income: 1950, 1961 and 1970 (mimeographed), Madison, Wisconsin (May).

Roy, A. D. (1950), The Distribution of Earnings and of Individual Output, *Economic Journal* **60**, 489–505.

Roy, A. D. (1951). Some Thoughts on the Distribution of Earnings, *Oxford Economic Papers* **3**, 135–146.

Simon, H. A. (1955). On a Class of Skew Distribution Functions, *Biometrika* **42**, 425–440. (Reprinted in H. A. Simon, *Models of Man*. New York: Wiley, 1957.)

Department of Economics
Stanford University
Stanford, California

Welfare Criteria, Distribution, and Cost–Benefit Analysis

I. M. D. Little*

Tibor Scitovsky's name is unbreakably linked by "welfare criteria" with those of Kaldor, Hicks, and myself. For this I am partly to blame. He may not therefore agree that this is a very appropriate subject for an essay in his festschrift. But welfare criteria are surely part of welfare economics, and there can be no doubt that this latter is one of the subjects which have been graced by his writing.

Scitovsky (1941) quickly introduced the concept of distribution into the subject of how one determined whether there was a change in welfare; the national product, real income, or what-have-you. If the Kaldor–Hicks hypothetical compensation criterion declared Q_2 to be bigger than Q_1, it might also proclaim Q_1 to be bigger than Q_2—and most people seem to

---

* I am indebted to Mr. Kevin Roberts of Nuffield College for comments.

agree that good criteria should not have such unlimited discretion. The essential reason why this apparent contradiction arose was that there might be a significantly different distribution of wealth or utility before and after the change, and that the potential gain or loss from a change or its reversal was dependent on the distribution from which one started.

It seemed to me to be an obvious step to combine a judgment about the merits of a change in the distribution of utility with an estimate of the sign of the potential net monetary benefits—both for the change from Q_1 to Q_2 and for the reverse change from Q_2 to Q_1. This would not only avoid contradiction, but would also—which is more important—provide an acceptable criterion for a beneficial change. However, this seemingly obvious step has been the subject of a debate which has lasted for a quarter of a century (even longer than the Cambridge–Cambridge argument, despite the far greater simplicity of the issue).

The step has been condemned or criticized by most writers on the theoretical welfare economics, and by some of them very often in many articles. It has received explicit support only from Sen (1963) and Ng.[1] As the debate smoulders mainly in the *Economic Journal* and *Oxford Economic Papers,* the antis appear to have it. Since the *Economic Journal* debate of December 1963, I have not written on the subject. Once a decade is enough. But explicit criticism continues (e.g., Mishan, 1965; Nath, 1969), and so some further comment seems justified, especially as it can be argued that the Little criterion is, in fact, the basis of much—even most—applied welfare economics.

I advanced as a sufficient condition for an improvement (assuming that everyone could not benefit from the change) that both the redistribution should be good (strictly, not bad) and either the gainers could compensate the losers, or the losers be unable profitably to bribe the gainers to oppose the change.

Unfortunately, I cannot avoid including yet again one of the diagrams from *A Critique of Welfare Economics* (Fig. 1). The diagram is in ordinal utility space, and the curves are loci of points traced out by making lump sum transfers from Q_1 and Q_2, respectively. The curves are called utility possibility curves (UPCs), but might also be called compensation curves or redistribution curves. Assuming Pareto preferences, a move from Q_1 to Q_2 is indicated if H is preferred to Q_1, and from Q_2 to Q_1 if J is preferred to Q_2.

I defined the statement "Q_2 is a better distribution (of utility) than Q_1" as equivalent to "there is a point H, attainable by lump sum transfers from Q_1, which lies to the southwest of Q_2 and is preferred to Q_1." (Preferred by whom? By whomever makes the judgment!) I attached no meaning to

---

[1] Y.-K. Ng, Little's Welfare Criterion: A Proposed Rehabilitation (mimeographed).

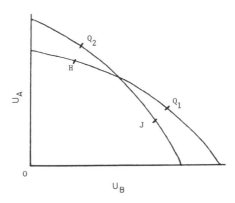

Figure 1 [From Little (1957).]

any comparison of rays through the origin; e.g., no sense was attached to such a statement as "any point on OHQ_2 is *distributionally* better than any point on OJQ_1."

The main objections to this analysis have been twofold; first, that it *leads to* contradictions, and second, that it is futile. The first of these can be summarily dismissed. If Smith's preferences are Paretian, and JpQ_2, and HpQ_1, then $Q_2pHpQ_1pJpQ_2$, whence transitivity (and my criterion) *disclose* Q_2pQ_1 and Q_1pQ_2. There is something wrong with Smith, not me![2,3]

This brings me to the objection that the analysis is futile, because, if one can rank points on the same utility possibility curve, one can also rank

[2] Contradictions arising out of a conflict between more equality somehow defined and a Paretian improvement have nothing to do with my analysis, although Mishan and Nath associate them with my name: all these demonstrations show is that certain distributional preferences cannot be consistently held together with Pareto preferences. Nath also manufactures contradictions by assuming that the preference holder has consistent but non-Paretian preferences, while I assumed Paretian preferences. It does not seem to be playing the logical game to remove someone's assumption, and then cry "How's that!"

[3] Kennedy (1963) suggested that an examiner who compares candidates in a roundabout way using two different principles—by analogy to a Pareto and a distributional judgment—should be dismissed as unreliable. I do not see the appositeness of this analogy. I do not think that northeasterly moves in utility space are all that fundamentally different from northwesterly moves. He also seemed to suggest that having to use a third point might muddle him up—i.e., genuinely *lead to* contradictions. Yet one of the most common forms of ethical discourse is as follows. Someone says he prefers A to B. His discussant says—but I am sure you prefer B to B' (for that is an example of a principle which I cannot believe you do not accept). Now are you really sure you prefer A to B'? The discussant suspects his friend of being muddled, and hopes B' will disclose this, and make him rethink and perhaps revise his position. The intermediate point is introduced to remove contradictions, not lead to them.

points such as Q_1 and Q_2 directly (Kennedy, 1952–1953). This is harder to deal with, and my previous defence has been called lame.

Perhaps some clue as to whether or not it is futile is to see whether it is used. The application of welfare economics in a piecemeal manner—that is, the application of welfare economics—has come to be called social cost benefit (SCB) analysis. (That SCB analysis has been mainly applied to investments is neither here nor there; there is in principle no difference between a SCB analysis of an investment project, a tax change, a change in the output of some commodity, etc.) What do SCB analysts do? What do they advocate?

That which seems to be common to all SCB analyses is the use of the Kaldor–Hicks criterion. The Scitovsky double criterion may be employed, but this is rare. (It is implicitly assumed that the curves do not cut.) Analysts answer the question whether the utility possibility curve after the change passes southwest or northeast of Q_1—this often being described as a test or economic efficiency. This is tantamount to saying that points such as H and J are relevant.

Disagreement now begins. One school of thought says that economists should not weight the gains and losses, which should be simply added to establish the position of J relative to Q_1. At this stage, on this view, there is no attempt to locate Q_2 in utility space, or even in monetary space. It is enough to establish that its UPC goes above or below Q_1.

If distribution is to be taken into account, at least by the decision maker, if not the economist, it can be done more or less precisely. My impression is that actual SCB analyses seldom describe the gainers and losers at all precisely (such a description would have to categorize thousands or millions of people into groups which are of interest to the decision maker—such groups might or might not be mainly income or wealth groupings), and seldom ascribe a monetary value to their gains or losses. If the compensation test is passed, the decision-maker may decide, with very limited information, that any redistribution would not be bad. If so, he sanctions the change, implicitly deciding that economic welfare would be increased.

It seems to me that this sort of application of welfare economics can be tolerably well described as an application of the Little criterion. If the decision-maker was comparing Q_2 and Q_1 directly, he would surely want a better description of Q_2 than he is usually given; moreover, if his distributional judgment was a direct comparison of the merits of Q_2 and Q_1, he should not have required the economist to assure him about "efficiency." The economist in turn should not expect a distributional judgment from the decision maker, but a direct welfare judgment, based on as precise a description of Q_2 as possible. In fact, the "efficiency" and "distributional" elements are usually regarded as separable. I rationalized the separation by taking redistribution to *mean* a movement along a UPC. If we assume that the preference holder is Paretian and consistent, this is, I believe, the only way of separating (and then combining into a dual criterion) efficiency and distributional judgments. And such dual criteria are undoubtedly used.

However, Mishan (1973) has recently shown that two points such as Q_1 and Q_2, lying on *different* and intersecting "point" UPCs (i.e., the maximum utility loci of sets of goods), have nevertheless a common point UPC because it is always possible to find some set of goods such that both Q_1 and Q_2 would lie on the UPC of that third set. Given his own definitions, this means that a "distributional comparison" can be made between Q_1 and Q_2—a comparison not involving a point such as H or J.

This would seem to imply that if one has to ask for a distributional comparison anyway, then nothing more is required. Dual criteria again become redundant, together with compensation tests and SCB analysis as generally practiced.

It seems to me that this ingenious analysis, so far from resolving any paradox, is a red herring which further confuses the issue. It is unreasonable to interpret a distributional comparison of two points as a welfare comparison of them regarded as lying on the UPC of some arbitrary and hypothetical set of goods, chosen on purely theoretical grounds. The importance of a point such as H is that it would actually be reached from Q_1 by lump-sum transfers—it is a point that would be attained by redistribution. Q_2 cannot be reached from Q_1 by redistribution, except in fairyland. Welfare criteria are attempts to reconcile real world judgments with theoretical analysis; this purpose is not helped by imaginary and unidentified sets of goods.

Mishan seems to have an obsession with sets of goods.[4] I have repeatedly emphasized that the appropriate way to define a UPC for the purpose of a contemplated economic change is with reference to a set of factors of production in an environment which is given (apart from the contemplated change) and not with reference to a set of goods—because H must be a point that would *actually* be reached by redistribution. However, it is probable that Mishan's new theorem could be proved for a set of factors of production. But this would not make things any better, for the set of factors of production which would bring Q_1 and Q_2 onto a common UPC would still be imaginary and unidentified.

---

[4] Mishan also seems to possess two hats—a welfare criterion hat and a SCB hat. Wearing the latter he writes about compensation, and bases "pure" SCB analysis entirely on the Kaldor–Hicks criterion without making the strange claim that the gainers must be able to overcompensate the losers with the actual set of goods that would be produced at Q_2. It is also difficult to reconcile his "resolution of a paradox" with compensation tests at all.

A more pertinent case can perhaps be made for saying that dual criteria are, or should be, irrelevant. With much more research than is usual, and the proper presentation of information on the distribution of gains and losses, the decision-maker could locate Q_2 in monetary space, and hence in his own mind in utility space. He can then make a direct comparison. The question which then arises is whether he would add up the individual gains and losses. If he adds them up, he regards H or J as relevant. I suspect he would usually add them up, or complain if the analyst had not done this for him.

The decision maker surveying the vector of gains and losses might also think it would help him to multiply by a vector of weights. Supposing he does, the question still arises whether he would not also want to know the unweighted total. Again I would suspect (and hope) that he usually would.

In either of the preceding cases, he may make a direct comparison of Q_1 and Q_2. If so, there is no call to ask what is meant by a distributional judgment, and the Little criterion is not required. But, if I am right, points such as H and J remain relevant. Why should they be relevant? Suppose Q_2 is judged to be better than Q_1, but the UPCs are as shown in Fig. 2. A Paretian would not want to move to Q_2 if H is attainable. If one could make lump-sum redistributions, H *would* be attainable. One cannot—but altering the tax system in a feasible way might still get one northeast of Q_2. A sketch such as Fig. 2 may show up the fact that Q_2 is better than Q_1—say, locating an industrial estate in a poor remote region rather than in a richer accessible region—mainly for distributional reasons, in which case it might be a good idea to look at alternatives. Points such as H and J are now relevant, not so much because they give meaning to the use of a dual criterion, but because they point up the need to consider alternatives which may be better than the change proposed.

I am not against producing a distribution of the gains and losses. Nor am I against applying weights. These direct comparisons [as, e.g., advo-

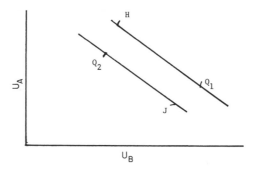

Figure 2   [From Little (1957).]

cated by Kennedy (1952–1953) and Meade (1959)] are also advocated by Little and Mirrlees (1974). But it should always be remembered that an increase in welfare as determined by such a direct comparison is not a sufficient reason for doing something. A negative unweighted expected present value may suggest that there could be better alternatives—in other words, compensation tests are not redundant, even when direct welfare comparisons are made.

But the dual criterion of a compensation test plus a distributional judgment—the Little criterion—will continue to be employed. It uses less information, and in practice that is important. On a more theoretical level what I showed was that one can find an interpretation of the distributional judgment, which is logically watertight. Welfare criteria, including those which use weighting systems, are concerned with creating and analyzing dialogues between facts and values. One therefore must concern oneself with meanings to be attached to various kinds of value judgment, including distributional judgments. The meaning I attached to a distributional judgment concerning a change from Q_1 to Q_2 may seem a little bizarre to some, but it did not in my opinion do great violence to what any noneconomist might mean. Therefore I think I was justified in claiming that a satisfactory basis for applying welfare economics had been provided—in those ordinal days of long ago.

References

Kennedy, C. M. (1952–1953). The Economic Welfare Function and Dr. Little's Criterion, *Review of Economic Studies*.

Kennedy, C. M. (1963). Two Comments, *Economic Journal* (December).

Little, I. M. D., (1957). *A Critique of Welfare Economics*, p. 104. London and New York: Oxford Univ. Press (Clarendon).

Little, I. M. D., and Mirrlees, J. A. (1974). *Project Appraisal and Planning for Developing Countries*. London: Heinemann.

Meade, J. E. (1959). Review of *A Critique of Welfare Economics, Economic Journal* (March).

Mishan, E. J. (1965). The Recent Debate on Welfare Criteria, *Oxford Economic Papers* (July).

Mishan, E. J. (1973). Welfare Criteria: Resolution of a Paradox, *Economic Journal* (September).

Nath, S. K. (1969). *A Reappraisal of Welfare Economics*. London: Routledge and Kegan Paul.

Scitovsky, T. (1941). A Note of Welfare Propositions in Economics, *Review of Economic Studies* (November).

Sen, A. (1963). Distribution, Transitivity and Little's Welfare Criteria, *Economic Journal* (December).

Nuffield College
Oxford, United Kingdom

The Place of Ethics
in the Theory of Production

M. W. Reder

1. Introduction

In a model of production in which information is costless and agree-ments are costlessly enforced, there is no place for ethics or other disposi-tional attributes of the persons who own the instruments. The attitude of a person from whom one buys an object or a service becomes a matter of concern only if he may disclose more or less information about the attri-butes of what he sells or about his behavior in various contingent future states of the world.

I shall argue that certain patterns of conduct are "more ethical" than others, that it is more efficient that the ethical standards (morality) among a group of transactors be higher rather than lower,[1] that the marginal private product of ethical conduct, while positive, is less than the marginal social product, and that important institutions of training and socialization are designed to overcome this gap.

I do not presume to offer a complete theory of ethics. Ethics is considered only as it refers to conduct toward other individuals (including fictitious individuals such as corporations) with whom a person enters into voluntary agreements. The ethical standard discussed is a slightly generalized version of the injunction, "keep your word"; in a phrase, it is "morality as trustworthiness." It does not encompass obligations to God, country, "the poor," etc.

2. The Meaning and Measure of Ethical Conduct

Ethics does not refer to acts divorced from intent, or to intentions unrelated to actions. This is why I shall speak of ethical *conduct* rather than ethical *behavior*. Rather than start with a general and rather abstract definition, I shall proceed by means of example.

Consider the very simple case of an unsecured loan. Obviously, it is moral to repay it. But the difference in utility between repaying and defaulting will vary with the borrower's wealth level when the loan falls due, and with the punishment for defaulting. Punishment the same, diminishing marginal utility of wealth ensures that the greater the borrower's wealth level on the repayment day, the less utility he will gain by defaulting.[2]

In this simple case, the *morality* of a borrower is some increasing function of the amount of wealth he would forego rather than default. [Explicitly, I include in wealth capitalized potential earnings through (market) work.] Roughly, the morality of the borrower is measured by the wealth loss he would bear rather than default.

In measuring the (potential) wealth gain from a given act of default, it is necessary to subtract the cost of resisting the (unsuccessful) attempts to collect the debt that will be made. Henceforth in discussing the wealth

[1] I use "morality" and "ethics" interchangeably. This is mainly to avoid the awkwardness of speaking of a degree or extent of conformity with an ethical standard.

[2] Implicitly, this statement defines the borrower's utility function $U = U(W, X_1, \cdots, X_n)$ so that it includes arguments other than wealth W; e.g., specifically, it includes reputation and the psychic tranquillity of a clear conscience. If one so wishes, he may define wealth to include all sources of utility, but then he will have to distinguish between "alienable" wealth—i.e., sources of utility that could conceivably be used in exchange—and other types of wealth. W refers to alienable wealth and explicitly *includes* the market value of available time.

gain from a default or other act of malfeasance, I shall be referring to the net gain after deducting the cost of resisting attempts at enforcement of the agreement.

Part of the deterrent to defaulting is the loss of reputation as a (good) credit risk which will result in having to pay more in order to borrow a given sum for a given period. In one sense, this loss of reputation is a loss of wealth; i.e., one can collect damages for a (false) report that causes such loss. However, neither in a census of wealth nor in an ordinary financial statement would one include "good reputation." Consequently, I shall lump reputation together with other sources of "inalienable wealth," and treat them collectively as "that which is sacrificed" by defaulting. In other words, I do not distinguish among the pain of a bad conscience, the loss of social acceptance, and the deterioration of one's credit rating as deterrents to violation of agreements and (therefore) as a prop for morality.

Let us write a morality function in which M measures morality, W (alienable) wealth, and S the maximum wealth sacrifice an individual will make rather than default on a loan contract of specific size and terms; e.g., a \$100 unsecured promissory note for 1 year at $i\%$ interest:

$$M = M(W, S), \qquad M'_W < 0, \qquad \text{and} \qquad M'_S > 0. \qquad (1)$$

$M'_S > 0$ means that an individual will be considered to be more ethical (moral), the greater the (maximum) amount of wealth he will sacrifice rather than default on a loan contract, initial stock of wealth constant. $M'_W < 0$ means that a given S indicates lower morality, the greater one's wealth; i.e., an S of \$1000 indicates a lower morality for a millionaire than for a man whose wealth is \$2000.

To compare the morality of (different) individuals owning different W's, or of the same individual in different situations where his W's differ, it would be necessary to posit a specific form for (1). One possibility would be

$$M = M(S/W), \qquad M' > 0; \qquad S \leqslant W, \qquad (1a)$$

i.e., to make morality vary with the proportion of wealth that will be sacrificed rather than default. However, this is merely a suggestion; detailed investigation of the properties of (1) is beyond the scope of this paper.

For the purpose at hand, it will suffice to posit that one or more forms of (1) can be found, each applicable to sufficiently large groups of individuals to be descriptively useful. Granted this assumption, we can (for example) describe the moral level of an individual by such statements as: "he would be willing to sacrifice $X\%$ of his wealth, at a wealth level of W_0, rather than default on a debt."

2.1 Conceptual Difficulties

In principle, one would like to measure the M of a particular individual (or group) without reference to the type of agreement used to measure it, or to the identity of the party (or parties) with whom the agreement is made. In practice, this will rarely be possible, given that individuals with specific amounts of wealth will vary in their concern to honor agreements depending upon both the identity of the creditors and the terms and subject matter of the agreement. For example, one may say that A is very trustworthy about money, but likely to betray confidences.[3]

Thus an individual may have not one but many M's, and anyone interested in analyzing or predicting his behavior will need to consider which is applicable. This will create no analytical problems provided the number of M's is not unmanageably large. Except where the contrary is specifically indicated, an M will be (hypothetically) measured on an agreement with an unspecified party; i.e., it is assumed that M may vary with the nature of the agreement but not with the individuals involved. Where this does not apply, an individual's M's will vary in yet another dimension.

The argument presented is predicated upon the assumption that the many facets of morality have a very strong "first principal component" and that the other significant principal components are few in number. For example, the expected value of a bet that an individual will honor an agreement will depend primarily upon his individual morality and, secondarily, upon a limited number of characteristics of the agreement and of the other party (or parties); e.g., whether they are members of the same group.

It is not hard to generate conundrums in which an individual is involved in mutually incompatible commitments. In such cases, measuring morality by fidelity to agreements encounters obvious difficulties. Among these,

---

[3] I do not assume that all dimensions of morality can be measured by amounts of wealth that would be sacrificed rather than violate an agreement. This would be true only if all sources of utility could be exchanged on markets. To illustrate the point, consider the "pain-acceptance" standard of morality. The moral virtue of a member of an espionage group might be measured by how many turns of a thumbscrew he would accept before giving information about his fellows. Clearly, M and thumbscrew rankings, across individuals, may vary widely.

This fact is not disturbing: an M score is only one, though an important, attribute of an individual; i.e., knowledge of an individual's M score would be of use in dealing with him and in analyzing his behavior.

an outstanding example is the problem of "honor among thieves." The more faithful the members of a group of thieves are to their mutual commitments, the more efficient their combined efforts, and the worse for honest men. Obviously, similar problems arise in connection with hired killers, cartel members, and other participants in antisocial agreements.

I would resolve such difficulties as follows: it is not argued that morality is always conducive to *social welfare,* but only that it fosters *production.* If a group of parties is engaged in activities that reduce the social product, then greater morality among them may be counterproductive from the viewpoint of society as a whole. But it will increase the *private productivity of the group in question.*

In other words, the usefulness of this concept of morality is conditional upon the cooperative activity of individuals having negligible (adverse) impact upon others. Where this condition fails, the notion may lose interest. I make no claim that for all purposes and under all circumstances Eq. (1) is a satisfactory basis for constructing a useful measure of morality. Its value can be determined only in use, case by case.

2.2 Long-Term Service Agreements

Now let us consider another type of agreement: the long-term, partially unwritten service agreement. The loan agreements discussed in the previous section are, quite literally, contracts and enforceable in the courts. In contrast, what we now consider as "agreements" are at best only partially enforceable in a court. One important member of this category is the employment agreement (or contract) which is so vague in its implications for the employee's behavior that its implementation is a major part of the employer's job.

Consider the important case where both employer and employee invest resources in creating firm-specific human capital whose yield is a stream of productive services to the employer and a stream of earnings and promotions to the employee. The employee's performance will depend upon a sequence of events that determines his environment and the development of his capacities, as well as upon his own efforts. His compensation will depend, not only upon his own performance (current and past), but upon the various events that determine the employer's present and prospective demand for his services, his (the employer's) concern with honoring the implicit commitment made at the time of initial hiring, and his ability to implement his concern.

In short, each party has a concern with the "morality" of the other in that the return upon his own investment in the joint venture is greatly affected by it. It is not really expected that either party will accept unlimited loss because of the implicit agreement, and it is recognized that, beyond certain limits, failure to perform up to expectation by one party is ground for termination by the other without violating the initial understanding. Obviously, the vagueness of such mutual understandings invites disagreement as to their interpretation. Nevertheless, some courses of conduct would clearly violate the intent of the agreement.

Because of this, both workers and employers acquire reputations as more or less well-intentioned or reliable—ethical—quite apart from their abilities. A summary measure of the characteristics referred to as "good" is M, here interpreted as the upper limit to the employee compensation or employer profits that would be sacrificed rather than violate the spirit of an agreement. While I believe that concern with protecting one's reputation for ethical behavior has an effect upon the labor market behavior both of employers and employees, I do not propose to stress this effect.

Rather, I wish to emphasize that because this concern is known to be limited, each party engages in otherwise counterproductive behavior to protect himself from the (somewhat) unethical behavior expected of the other. Thus an employer uses resources to supervise and monitor the performance of workers to limit "shirking."[4] Less resources would be so used if the (expected) morality of workers were higher. Similarly, a worker will try to prevent his employer from learning how much he can produce per time period to prevent the employer from demanding more output as a condition of honoring their implicit agreement.[5] If workers believed employers were more "fair"—ethical—about rewarding greater effort, there would be fewer attempts to disguise work capacity.

Another example of a long-term service agreement is the service warranty associated with the purchase of a durable good. The mutual distrust of the parties to such transactions is notorious. As a result, sellers try to devise warranties that will prove attractive to buyers, yet protect them from being saddled with the cost of offsetting the effect of "improper" or "excessive" use. If the ethics of buyers were (thought to be) better, more attractive warranties could be offered at given prices, generating more sales. Conversely, buyers refrain from purchases they would make if they fully trusted the warrantors.

2.3 Moral Standards and the "Quality" of Social Interaction

In a wide variety of everyday contacts, behavior is adjusted to protect oneself from being cheated. Whether or not one counts one's change; demands a receipt to record a payment; demands or is required to make a

---

[4] The concept of shirking is discussed by Alchian and Demsetz (1972).

[5] This is, of course, an old story. The classic description is that of Mathewson (1931).

deposit to reserve availability of a commodity unit; is allowed to try an object before purchase; requires commitments to be made in writing, recorded, and the like; is required to identify oneself in order to be admitted; all reflect distrust of those with whom one is dealing.

The extent of these precautions, and the time and trouble they entail, varies inversely with what the moral standard of the "typical" individual is believed to be. Notoriously, it is believed that these standards have declined in the United States during the past 10 years, and precautions to limit the resulting losses have increased accordingly.

The incentives to imperfectly moral conduct, and the precautions that are prompted by awareness of them, are very similar to the incentives to commit crimes and to the self-protective activities thereby inspired (Becker, 1968). Indeed, part of what is termed unethical behavior is also criminal. However, much of what is unethical is not criminal—or even tortious—and awareness of such behavior influences a great part of normal productive activity.

Consider the nature of this influence, and some of its cost. In addition to the private efforts at self-protection from commercial deception already mentioned, there is a substantial amount of government activity aimed at protecting those presumed likely to be deceived. Thus, numerous government agencies have been created to expose or prevent misleading advertising or promotional claims in the selling of securities, bank loans, products of all kinds (especially those putatively bearing upon health or safety), educational programs, etc.

The common purpose of defaulting on a contract, shirking on the job, breaching a warranty, making false or misleading statements about a product or service, is to profit by failure to fulfill an expectation of performance that one has created. In all these cases, morality consists in refusing to profit and/or bearing loss rather than permitting the nonfulfillment of an expectation that one has created. The maximum size of the loss one would bear (profit forego), measures morality.[6]

Clearly this measure is not all-purpose; moralists may wish to distinguish among different promises depending upon the circumstances under which they are made; how solemn were the assurances given, how great is the loss of the disappointed party and how well he can afford it, etc. To such important matters, this criterion is irrelevant: it bears only upon how morality affects economic activity—production.

---

[6] A conceptual limitation of our measure of morality should be noted here: default is a binary concept; one does or does not default. While it would not be difficult to generalize our measure to allow for partial default, such generalization would not advance the present discussion.

3.   The Productive Effect of Moral Conduct

The economic loss from "imperfectly moral" conduct arises from the misinformation to which it gives rise. As here defined, immorality always involves deception; fully divulged intentions are never "immoral."

Assume, for simplicity, that prices are known costlessly and with complete accuracy. Then informational errors result in inappropriate combinations of inputs being used because decision makers have been misled as to their expected performances. Some informational errors are not random; they result from the purposive misinformation given by resource owners to increase the prices they can obtain from the sale or rent of their property. The effect of such misinformation is

(1)   to transfer wealth from buyer to seller, and
(2)   to lead buyers to obtain a smaller output from given resources than would be technically possible.

But, normally, buyers are not naive. They are aware that sellers are not completely honest, and accordingly take precautions to limit the extent to which performance will fall short of promise. The precautions include monitoring, gearing payment to performance, requiring precise and complicated contracts that are cheaper to enforce—though not to devise—than simple verbal agreements, and so on. (Where the buyer is a renter of a durable instrument, the owner-seller also will take precautions to ensure reasonable usage.)

In effect, ethical imperfection adds to information cost. It is a source of error with a known (direction of) bias which can be reduced, but only at a cost. The cost incurred to reduce this bias (i.e., to improve performance under agreements) is a deadweight loss that could be avoided if suppliers were "perfectly ethical."[7] Failing this impossible standard, the marginal return to self-protection from the disappointing performance of a supplier (acting under an agreement) may be assumed to vary inversely with his level of morality; i.e., the more moral a supplier, the less the expected loss from his failing to live up to expectations, and the lower the expected return to an additional dollar devoted to self-protection therefrom; *ceteris paribus,* the smaller will be the number of dollars that will be used in this manner (to provide self-protection).[8]

If a supplier were believed to be of superior morality, it would be to the

---

[7] That is, if suppliers acted as though fulfilling the expectations inspired by an agreement was the only activity that gave them positive utility, until said expectations were (completely) fulfilled.

[8] Throughout this paper, I abstract from risk aversion, which would complicate the argument without in any way advancing it.

advantage of a buyer to pay some premium to contract with him rather than with a less moral (but otherwise identical) competitor, recouping the extra cost by using fewer resources to police the contract. But, of course, suppliers are aware of this and invest in building reputations for morality to the extent that it is *privately* profitable to do so. Presumably, such investments are made by exhibiting fidelity to the spirit of contracts; e.g., by foregoing the gains attainable through default and the like.

Assume, plausibly, that the extent of such reputation building is an increasing function of the private return it yields. The factors that augment such private returns are

(a) speed of the spread of information about the morality of suppliers,
(b) clarity about the behavioral implications of morality,
(c) retentiveness of the memory of the typical buyer for information relevant to immoral behavior, and
(d) punitiveness of the community for immoral conduct.[9]

Increases in any of these will tend to increase the private return to investment in a moral reputation.

In equilibrium, then, each transactor will establish some level of moral repute that will be determined by his capacities,[10] his utility function, and the various parameters that determine the private return to a moral reputation. If everyone's capacities and utility function were the same, the (compensating) price differentials that offset differences in moral reputations would disappear along with the differences in morality. But in reality such differences persist, reflecting the cost and returns to superior observance of the spirit of agreements.

The productivity of superior morality lies in the value of the resources that would otherwise be used to disguise "immoral conduct," by those engaged in it, and of the resources used to detect and defend against such conduct by potential victims. Further gains in the productivity of a given body of resources arise from the greater range of contracting parties, and complexity of contract forms, whose utilization is privately profitable at higher levels of morality.

Empirical measurement of differences in morality across individuals,

---

[9] This is in addition to any legal punishment that may be involved. The expected value of the legal punishment is assumed to be deducted from the gain from an immoral act.

[10] For example, some producers of relatively little skill may do best by promising more than they can usually deliver, charging more than a "repeat customer" would pay and operating a "one sale to a customer, no repeats" low moral style of business. Others of great skill may charge much higher prices, have lower volume, but deliver fully on promises and obtain their customers largely through repeat sales and referrals; this type of producer would probably be highly moral.

groups of individuals, or whole societies is well beyond anything intended here. However, a few of the phenomena that have been attributed to the operation of changing or differing moral standards may be mentioned both to fix ideas and also to suggest approaches to empirical research.

(1) Trading and/or lending among parties far removed in space, or among whom communication and/or performance monitoring is otherwise difficult, can be carried out more efficiently where the parties trust each other, i.e., where they act as though high standards of morality obtained. For example, it is often alleged that, prior to the twentieth century, the activity and success of Jews in trading and banking was facilitated by their adherence to higher moral standards (in honoring loan contracts) than those generally prevailing among Gentiles.[11]

The (alleged) prevalence of higher moral standards among members of some ethnic groups than among others should be associated with various measures of group cohesiveness (e.g., prevalence of endogamy). Cohesiveness would be associated with relatively fast transmission of information within the group; with consensus on propriety of conduct and power to punish offenders (by casting them out). These are the same factors that make for large (private) returns to a reputation for moral conduct. One would conjecture that, *ceteris paribus,* group cohesiveness would be associated with a comparative advantage in productive activity associated with forms of agreement requiring trust.

(2) Tendencies for members of an ethnic group to employ or transact with others of the same group may be explained by the greater ability of fellow ethnics to curb shirking. To the extent that this is valid, it accounts for some of the "economic segregation" described by Becker and attributed by him to a taste for discrimination (Becker, 1974). Such tendencies will vary with the cohesiveness of the group. Group cohesiveness facilitates the spreading of information (publicity) about misconduct, and increases the disutility (loss) to an offender from group sanctions. The tendency toward ethnic segregation would presumably be stronger in jobs where the premium upon morality, and the opportunity for malfeasance, was greater.

(3) The legal form of economic organization is obviously influenced by

---

[11] I am speaking here of moral standards that vary with the identity of the individual to whom one is committed. Clearly such variations exist as they bear upon agreements among members of the group (family, tribe, nation, etc.) and agreements between group members and outsiders. This causes no conceptual problems, so long as the moral standard applies to the obligation itself given only a (very) few generic characteristics of the other party (parties). If a moral standard were permitted to vary with one's personal feelings toward the individual to whom one happened to be obligated, moral obligations would become indistinguishable from expressions of personal regard.

the morality of the people who seek to raise capital, and by the costs of compelling them to honor their agreements. Technical economies of scale may be frustrated by low moral standards that make debts to nonmembers of family or tribe uncollectible. As Marshall (1920) put it:

> the great body of the shareholders of a joint-stock company are, save in a few exceptional instances, almost powerless. . . . It is a strong proof of the marvellous growth in recent times of a spirit of honesty and uprightness in commercial matters, that the leading officers of great public companies yield as little as they do to the vast temptations to fraud which lie in their way. If they showed an eagerness to avail themselves of opportunities for wrong-doing at all approaching that of which we read in the commercial history of earlier civilization, their wrong uses of the trusts imposed in them would have been on so great a scale as to prevent the development of this democratic form of business. There is every reason to hope that the progress of trade morality will continue, . . . and thus collective and democratic forms of business management may be able to extend themselves safely in many directions in which they have hitherto failed . . . [pp. 303–304].

4. Private and Social Returns to Morality

Obviously, a reputation for moral behavior has commercial value. Equally obvious is the fact that most people do not trust most other people, unmonitored, to honor obligations completely. Because of this they use substantial amounts of resources to specify the details of agreements, and to police them. Use of these resources (lawyers, judges, supervisors, time clocks, record systems, notaries, etc.) could be greatly reduced, if transacting parties would agree to honor the spirit of their agreement and simply shake hands. The resource saving to the two parties combined, from substituting this mode of "enforcing" agreements to those currently used, is clear. Why, then, does not this more efficient mode of transacting drive out the more costly methods through the normal competitive process?

The answer is that these "agreements to honor agreements" would (themselves) have to be policed, and we have no more confidence in the sanctity of second-order agreements than of first order, so that the expenditures on enforcement would not be saved, but merely diverted to the second-order agreements. (Analogous statements apply to third- and higher-order agreements.) Thus, voluntary contracts will not enable us to obtain the gain in net output (i.e., save resources used to disguise and to detect violations of agreements, to self-protect against the consequences of such violations, and so on) that would be attainable if agreements were always honored.[12]

The underlying rationale for this "waste" of resources is that it is privately profitable to engage in some degree of "cheating" on agreements, and to use resources to disguise the fact; it is profitable to assume that those with whom one transacts do likewise. In other words, moral hazard exists, and is rationally guarded against, in any agreement and not only in insurance contracts. But the extent of this hazard depends upon the disutility of cheating and the disutility, to the typical member of the community, of dealing with cheaters. For brevity, let us refer to this disutility as the *moral tone* of the community; moral tone rises with the disutility.

From the preceding argument, it follows that a community would be able to obtain a greater output from given resources with a given technology if its moral tone were higher. But voluntary contracting will not enable it to alter its moral tone; all that voluntary contracting can accomplish is to induce more moral conduct, at the price of imposing greater sanctions upon immoral conduct, moral tone given.

The advantage to a community of a high moral tone can be readily seen if we consider the effect of an unquestioning belief that a supernatural force would unfailingly punish the breach of an appropriately sworn oath. Agreements, ratified by appropriate oaths not to break them, would be enforced without cost. A community in which this belief prevailed would, *ceteris paribus,* have a larger net output than one where it did not. The government of such a community could profit from this difference by charging a higher immigration fee than would otherwise be possible.[13]

5. The Production of Moral Individuals

If a community were collectively rational it would try to raise its moral tone. To effect this, it would be necessary to *produce* transactors who were more moral. (Use of punishments and rewards is no substitute; they affect behavior, *given* preference functions. The problem is to alter the

---

[12] I am abstracting from "honest" differences of interpretation of agreements, the opportunity for which increases with their complexity. Certainly mendacity and ambiguity of obligation interact to lower the moral tone of a community more than would be properly attributable to the sum of their separate effects.

[13] I omit consideration of the effect that the immigrants might have on the moral tone of the community.

preference functions themselves.) To understate the matter, the technique of producing better and worse "character" in individuals is not well understood. However, there is a strong consensus which I think would be widely shared in all societies, that character is somehow produced in childhood and youth; i.e., in the "formative years." Accordingly, one would expect that the Central Authority (not necessarily the state), would be much concerned in this production process; and it is and has been.

In principle, the family *could* assume full responsibility for rearing its young, including their socialization. In practice, the church, state, or both have actively participated in this process. I will not speculate upon why they have, in fact, so often participated but merely note that there has always been a very good reason for such participation. The reason is the difference between the marginal private and social product of morality.

In most societies, there is a conflict between what is in the interest of an individual or his immediate family, and his various obligations to God, Caesar, creditors, or their cultural analogs. The official moral doctrine stresses the importance of fulfilling obligations and the punishment that awaits the defaulter. It is within the family and the peer group that one learns the "facts of life" which involve the fine art of how, and how far, to shirk social obligations in the interest of self and immediate kin.[14]

The part of education that consists in impressing his moral duties upon the individual is not small. And if left to the family alone, or its hired agents (teachers), the social interest in teaching the nature and importance of social obligations would tend to be neglected. Hence the involvement of church, state, or their amalgam in the process of character formation. To venture a bold conjecture, the concern with character formation is a major reason for the dominant role played by the central authority of society (church, state, or other) in the production of education. In particular, it explains why profit-seeking firms have not been permitted to become major producers of that part of education that is admixed with character formation.[15]

In the previous two paragraphs, I have identified fulfillment of duty or obligation with morality (as already defined). This is deliberate: morality is the special case of fulfilling obligations where obligations are voluntarily

[14] This may sound as though I thought that both schools and families had effective methods for directing character development; I entertain no such notion. All that I assume is that both have some limited ability to impart behavioral instruction that, on average, influences children to behave in the general manner desired by the instructor.

[15] In societies with several religions, the state has often permitted each religious group to operate its own educational system. But it has been the church that has acted as the agent of the group that has run the program, not individual families, and what the church taught had to be at least tolerable to the state.

(e.g., contractually) assumed for a consideration. By contrast, in most societies throughout history, obligations have been determined by one's status, which reflected a combination of age, birth order, and lineage. In Marxian terms, our "morality" is "bourgeois morality:" "pay your bills" rather than "noblesse oblige."

The concern of the central authority in promoting morality often may have been to maintain a desired distribution of the social product, as well as (or even more than) to increase its size. In feudal Europe, the obligations it wished to sanctify included taxes, tithes, dues, etc. But this in no way detracts from the proposition that in a society in which production requires voluntary agreements, it is in the interest of the central authority to produce a population whose tastes are such as to make contract compliance a pleasure.

I would not wish to conclude before explicitly disavowing the idea that producing a higher moral tone is costless. One need not be terribly familiar with twentieth century literature, or psychiatry, to recognize that rigid conformity to a punitive code of ethics may create very unhappy people. A high moral tone with ostracism of bankrupts, prompt firing of shirkers, "shame upon him who loses his job," etc., will reduce the cost of enforcing agreements and, *ceteris paribus,* increase net social product as measured in the social income accounts. But its cost may be an appreciable increase in general "up-tightness."

References

Alchian, A., and Demsetz, H. (1972). Production, Information Costs and Economic Organization, *American Economic Review* (December), 777–795.

Becker, G. S. (1968). Crime and Punishment: An Economic Approach, *Journal of Political Economy* **76**, (March/April) No. 2, 169–217.

Becker, G. S. (1974). *The Economics of Discrimination,* 2nd ed., pp. 23–27. Chicago, Illinois: Univ. of Chicago Press.

Marshall, A. (1920). *Principles of Economics,* 8th ed. New York: Macmillan.

Mathewson, S. B. (1931). *Restriction of Output among Unorganized Workers.* New York: Viking.

Graduate School of Business
University of Chicago
Chicago, Illinois

Rationing and Price as Methods of Restricting Demand for Specific Products

*Walter S. Salant**

1. Introduction

The Arab embargo on oil exports to the United States in late 1973 and early 1974 and the subsequent professed policy of the United States to cut consumption of oil products revived an old question: the relative desirability of restricting demand by rationing or by charging higher prices to consumers and other users. That question was debated vigorously during World War II, and probably whenever "shortages" (i.e., excess demand)

* I am grateful to my colleagues Arthur Okun and George Perry for helpful suggestions on a previous draft and greatly indebted to Stephen W. Salant, whose criticisms of that draft led me to eliminate or reduce the emphasis on some points and to reorganize the paper.

became acute. The demand-restricting role of price has been recognized by economists since early in the history of classical economics and has been a continuing element in the successive refinement of explanations of how the system of market prices works, both in the theory of general equilibrium and in discussion of the welfare aspects of competitive markets, but it appears not to be widely recognized by the general public. Economists usually assume that where excess demand or supply develops at a going price in a competitive market, a new price will reestablish market equilibrium by its influence on both the amounts demanded and the amounts supplied. Although this idea is rudimentary to economists, the lay public apparently recognizes and accepts only the role of price in inducing supply, not its role in limiting demand. A rise in price accruing to the seller generally meets with little objection if it is believed to be necessary or even merely effective in inducing an increase in output, but if it is not believed to be effective in that way, it is widely regarded as at best useless and at worst an antisocial act the only effect of which is to "rob" the public. A deliberate policy of raising prices to consumers for the purpose of reducing purchases, even if the proceeds of the increase do not accrue to the seller, meets positive resistance and often elicits a demand for rationing.

The objection usually made to raising the price to consumers is that price increases are inequitable; they concentrate the cut in consumption unduly on the poor, who may no longer be able to afford the product in question, and spare the rich, who are better able to continue their purchases, even though they may be satisfying mere whims while the poor may have to forgo satisfying more urgent needs. If consumption must be cut, the argument goes, the cut can be more equitably distributed by rationing based on some definition of "need," which does not impose an undue burden on the poor.

The prevalence of this objection to price increases is anomalous in a society that, in general, acquiesces in the use of prices to allocate most of the goods and services that the economy produces. It is true that because price squeezes some poor consumers out of the market, it has been rejected as a means of allocating some products in nearly all countries with market economies. Its rejection is implied by the adoption of the food stamp plan, rent subsidies, and similar devices to make goods and services available at less than market prices in the United States and other countries. Similarly, education and medical care are provided free in many countries.[1] Nevertheless, the use of price to distribute food among

---

[1] It may not be amiss, however, to point out that the original purpose of the food stamp plan was to dispose of surplus farm products in the interest of removing a depressing influence on their prices, not to relieve the plight of those too poor to buy them. See, e.g., the summary history of the plan in *Congress and the Nation* (1965).

the vast majority of the population and to distribute clothing and most other necessities among the entire population is widely accepted. Why should inequality of income and wealth be regarded as any more relevant to the method of allocating products for which excess demand has suddenly developed, either because of a reduction in supply at the prevailing price or an increase in demand, than for the vast bulk of existing products, which would also be in excess demand at prices lower than those prevailing?

Scitovsky (1942) offered an answer to this question at the beginning of his World War II article on rationing. He observed that

> failure of the [pricing] system, in time of peace, to fulfill this function equitably, or to provide the poor with the necessities of life, usually leads to a demand for mitigating inequalities of income. Today, in time of war, it is widely felt that the same problems would be solved more easily by rationing—that is, by distributing scarce necessities independently of the market mechanism. What is the reason for this changed view? [p. 114].

His answer to his own question was as follows:

> Public opinion tends to accept the distribution of effective demand as equitable if it leads to an egalitarian, or nearly egalitarian, distribution of *all* necessities. Inequalities of income and wealth, however great they may be, will not be considered oppressive as long as *all* necessities are cheap and plentiful enough to be available in sufficient quantities even to the lowest income groups. Conversely, even slight inequalities of income will be regarded as unjust if *one* or more necessities are short—that is, so scarce and expensive as to become the privilege of the well-to-do [p. 114, my italics].

It should be noted, as Scitovsky warned his readers, that he did not define a commodity as "short" when the demand exceeds the supply at the existing price, which is the usual economic definition. Instead, he applied the adjective "short" only to "necessities" and said that "a necessity is short if it is so scarce as to become the privilege of the rich when distributed by the ordinary market mechanism." This definition enabled him to argue that

> a shortage can be eliminated not only by increasing supplies but also by mitigating inequalities in the distribution of effective demand. The extent to which inequalities must be mitigated in order to eliminate shortages, therefore, is *independent of the number* of necessities that are short and depends only on the supply and demand conditions

of the necessity that is the most short. The elimination of one single but severe shortage may require the complete equalization of effective demand. No shortages (in our sense) could arise if the distribution of income and wealth were completely equal [p. 114, Scitovsky's italics].

This argument led to his explanation of why rationing was demanded in wartime but not in peacetime:

Remembering that the elimination of only one single shortage may require the complete equalization of income and wealth, we immediately see that if the shortages are few and severe, it is simpler to distribute the short necessities independently of the market mechanism [p. 115].

Thus Scitovsky concluded that the explanation of the anomaly turns on rationing's being simpler than mitigation of inequalities of income and wealth as a means of making necessities available to the poor.

His statement about when the distribution of effective demand is accepted as equitable and when it is regarded as oppressive (in the second quotation above from his article) appears plausible, as far as it goes, and the whole argument is ingenious. But it is not entirely persuasive, perhaps because it is not complete. It does not take into account that what is regarded as a necessity and what is not depends largely on the consumption to which the general public has become accustomed, and this in turn depends largely on the combination of relative prices and the distribution of income and wealth to which they have become accustomed, however unequal the latter is. It appears that the *suddenness* of an increase in the relative price of a widely consumed commodity must be included in the explanation of pressure for rationing in a society that generally accepts allocation by prices.

When it becomes necessary to reduce the consumption of a commodity that has come to be regarded as a necessity, rationing, with the price of the rationed commodity kept below market-clearing levels, has the merit of allocating substantial reductions of consumption in a way that is regarded as more equitable than allocation by price increases. It does, however, involve administrative costs. Moreover, it also involves a loss of the "economic efficiency" that economists normally associate with prices lower than those that would clear a market in which there is perfect competition among consumers in this sense: it results in a situation in which it would be possible, at the existing distribution of income among consumers, to make some of them better off without making others worse off.[2] The purpose of this paper is to weigh these alternative ways of allocating a scarce commodity and to propose a theoretically efficient and administratively manageable method of distributing them which would, I think, generally be regarded as equitable, thereby in effect mediating and perhaps resolving the current controversy about allocation of gasoline and other petroleum products.

In order to confine the comparison of price and rationing to their relative merits as methods of restraining demand, the effect of price in inducing supply is here ignored; in effect, I assume (for the purpose of analysis) that the price-elasticity of supply is zero. The price increase that will be compared with rationing takes the form of an excise tax (or an increase in an existing one), the total revenue from which is redistributed to the public in amounts unrelated to their current consumption of the taxed commodity. (A distribution of the revenue related to consumption of course would offset the effect of the tax.) The prices discussed will be those paid by users, not those received by producers, which are less by the wedge that the excise tax places between these two prices. It should be noted that insofar as raising the price received by producers actually would increase production, the comparison of rationing only with a price rise caused by increased excise taxation biases the comparison against the price alternative; it not only excludes the possible effects of higher prices to producers in eliciting greater supply but, in the general case, opens the possibility of actually reducing supply, since an increase in excise taxes may reduce the return received by producers.

2. Rationing with Nontransferable Coupons

It was mentioned briefly that in the case of commodities for which there is perfect competition among consumers, it is economically efficient to charge them the market-clearing price. Since this implies that when the supply of a commodity is reduced, thereby raising the price that would just clear the market, economic efficiency calls for raising the actual price to consumers, this proposition about economic efficiency needs to be clearly understood. If the price clears the market (i.e., induces consumers, when they are free to buy as much as they want, to buy in the aggregate exactly the amount available), each consumer will buy an amount that equates his marginal valuation to the price. As a result, the

---

[2] This definition of economic efficiency paraphrases Scitovsky's definition except that the reference to the given distribution of income has been added (Scitovsky, 1971, p. 58).

total amount will be distributed among them in such a way that no consumer can exchange the commodity in question for others with another consumer in a way that leaves them both better off, which is what is meant by "economically efficient." Such a distribution does not occur when a commodity is sold subject to a ceiling price less than the market-clearing price and is rationed under a system that prevents consumers from selling their unused rations. As Scitovsky (1971) says, such a system "deprives the consumer of freedom to determine his rate of purchases" and, as a result,

> keeps some consumers from buying as much as they want of rationed goods and hence from equating their marginal valuations of the rationed goods to the prices of these goods. Therefore, different people's marginal valuations of a rationed commodity are likely to be different [p. 62].

As a result, a consumer whose marginal valuation of the last unit exceeds the ceiling price would be glad to pay something to enlarge his ration, while another consumer who valued part of the rationed amount at less than the ceiling price and therefore did not use his entire ration would be glad to sell the unused portion of his ration. A system that prohibits the transfer of ration coupons prevents transactions that would make both parties better off. It is in this sense that such a system is economically inefficient, at least if there is no black market.

The combination of sales at a price below the market-clearing level and suppression of the resulting excess demand by rationing with nontransferable coupons creates a conflict between the interest of the individual in consuming and the interest of society in economizing on use of the product. This argument, applied to oil, was stated effectively by Friedman (1973):

> The higher prices would give each of the 210 million residents of the United States a direct incentive to economize on oil, to find substitutes for oil, ... The only alternative is exhortation backed by compulsion: artificially low prices accompanied by governmental rationing. This method induces each of us to oppose the general interest rather than to further it. Our separate incentive is to wangle as much as we can from the rationing authorities [p. 130].

To state this case more precisely, for consumers who would have consumed less than the ration before the shortage, the incentive to economize on the product is only the ceiling price (which may be no greater than the price before the shortage). This incentive is less than it would be if the price rose. Moreover, while consumers who would have consumed more than the ration are (legally) forced to economize down to the ration, their incentive to economize further is also limited to the ceiling price. Thus the incentive to economize is less than it would be if an excise tax were levied.

Rationing requires the creation and continued operation of an administrative organization that is probably more costly in its use of real resources than the collection and enforcement of a new excise tax, and is certainly more costly than an increase in the rate of an existing excise tax, such as the existing federal tax on gasoline (unless the increase raises the tax so high as to induce substantial illegal selling without payment of the tax). The price method, by invoking the self-interest of would-be buyers, avoids the need for administrative organization, the use of manpower, and other real economic costs that rationing requires.[3] This saving of real costs constitutes a third argument in support of the price alternative.

The economic inefficiency of rationing with prohibition of transfer of coupons would be reduced by black market activities in the form of either sale of ration coupons or of the rationed product itself by consumers who do not want the entire ration for their own use. But the sale of ration coupons would be illegal under the system of nontransferable rations assumed, and the sale of the commodity itself to people who have used their full ration and therefore have no ration coupons would be illegal under any rationing system, even if the commodity were sold at the ceiling price. It would be doubly illegal if it were sold at above the ceiling price, as it would be.[4] That such a system provides a strong inducement for engaging in illegal activities is a further deficiency. In contrast, the use of price to constrain demand avoids the standing incentive to corruption that always exists when the law seeks to prevent people from doing what they want to do and can do by successful bribery, by theft of ration coupons, or by other illegal means.

---

[3] To prevent sales of the product without surrender of the coupons, a rationing system generally requires a flow-back of coupons not only from consumers to retailers but upstream through the entire redistributive system in exchange for the flow of the product downstream. This system forces a seller to obtain coupons for all sales of the rationed product since without them he would be unable to replenish his stock because his supplier, in turn, must obtain coupons in selling to him. This flow-back requires a ration banking system and, when the coupons have flowed back to an early stage, their return to the rationing authority along with an accounting at the earliest stage to show that the ration coupons transferred in one direction represent an amount of the product equal to the product transferred in the opposite direction. This system involves administrative costs of which the ordinary consumer is generally not aware. For a full account of the systems used in World War II, see Kershaw (1947).

[4] It may also be noted that, in the case of gasoline, sale of the commodity by consumers would be dangerous.

What rationing with nontransferable coupons can do that price increases to consumers cannot do is to ensure that a product remains accessible to the poor. That, as we have seen, is the ground for the widespread demands for rationing that so frequently arise when the supply of a massconsumed product is suddenly reduced.

All of the differences between the rationing and price methods of constraining purchases discussed so far relate to continuing considerations, i.e., characteristics of the two methods that would continue to operate as long as the excess demand continued. In addition to these considerations are some that arise during the initial period of a shortage and are associated with the suddenness of its impact or with its duration.

One such consideration is the urgency of the need to curtail consumption. Demand is generally less responsive to price increases in short periods of time than in longer ones because consumers need time to make the adjustments associated with economizing on the scarce product, whether these adjustments take the form of changing their habits or of finding other ways of satisfying the wants served by the product that has become short. The latter kind of adjustment, especially, may be expensive and time consuming. As a result, a price increase may take some time to have its full effect in reducing market demand, and may have very little immediate effect. At first sight it may appear that rationing would have no such disadvantage; the curtailment of consumption occurs immediately when the rationing goes into effect. Rationing may therefore appear to be preferable if the need to cut consumption is immediate. In the case of rationing with nontransferable coupons, however, this conclusion is not so clear as it first appears to be. Any practicable distribution of nontransferable rations will give some people larger rations than they can afford or wish to use. If the total rations distributed are no greater than the amounts to be consumed, the failure of some people to use their entire rations will result in cutting consumption excessively. A system of rationing that cuts consumption of a commodity in short supply by more than the shortage justifies is sure to cause an outcry and may threaten the acceptability of the system. The rationing authority, foreseeing that some rations will be unused, will know that it should allow for this fact by issuing rations in a total amount exceeding what it intends the consumption to be by the proportion of unused coupons to intended consumption. Although it could probably forecast that proportion fairly accurately after experience had accumulated, at the outset of a shortage it could only guess what that proportion would be. If it underestimated the portion that will be unused, it would have cut consumption by more than it intended. If it overestimated that portion, it would have cut consumption by less, with the result that at first inventories would be reduced by more than was intended and then, if it were not feasible to correct the error in time, some holders of ration coupons would find that they could not obtain all the goods that their ration coupons entitled them to buy. Errors in either direction at the outset of a rationing program would be likely to endanger its public acceptance.

Thus, both a price increase and rationing with nontransferable coupons have the disadvantage in the early stages of their use that the degree to which they restrict consumption may be slight and in any case is uncertain.

Another argument against the use of the price method is that it may stimulate or add impetus to a rise in the general price level, an effect that may be avoided by rationing and price ceilings. This argument can have validity only in a situation of general inflation such as the world has been going through in the past decade and, even then, only in the case of products important enough to have significant effects on the general price level, either directly or indirectly, such as oil products. It is rational to consider the effect on the consumer price index and to take that effect into account if it would be great enough to have a serious effect on the general price level that could not be offset. It appears, however, that even in the limited situations to which it applies, the validity of the argument is uncertain for several reasons.

While a rise in the price at which a given quantity of a specific product is supplied raises its price relative to the prices of other products, it does not necessarily raise the general level of prices above what it would otherwise have been. It is true that in an economy which strongly resists decreases in prices, an increase in a major price is unlikely to be offset by decreases in other prices, even under policies that attempt to restrain expansion of aggregate money demand, as it would be offset in a world of more flexible prices. Resistance to price decreases, however, implies only that increases in some prices tend to raise the general price level in situations where actual decreases in other prices would be required to offset them, i.e., when the general level of prices would have been approximately stable but for the specific price increases whose effects we are considering. When the general price level is rising, all that is required to offset the effect of an increase of one price is a smaller increase in other prices than would otherwise have occurred. Thus, the downward rigidity of money prices does not of itself imply that the increase of a specific price will accelerate the rise in the general price level. While it may increase some prices, it also may restrain increases in other prices. The latter possibility does not seem to be ruled out by past experience, so the effect of specific price increases on the general price level in an inflationary environment is an open question.

Even if an increase in an important specific price does not induce offsetting effects on other prices and therefore does raise the general level, however, it is doubtful that a one-time increase, such as results from imposition of an excise tax, raises the *continuing* rate of inflation. If not offset by a fall or slower rise of other prices, it does raise the general price level, thereby raising the rate of its increase for as long as its indirect repercussions on other product prices filter through the economy, but whether it produces a continuing increase in the rate of inflation over a longer period depends on the vulnerability of the price level to one-time inflationary shocks. In general, one-time price increases give a continuing impetus to inflation only when they set off increases more rapid than would otherwise have occurred in money wages per unit of output or in the money returns to other factors of production. A recent analysis of the evidence on this issue through 1974 indicates that such an effect, if it exists at all, is small. [5]

Moreover, if it is regarded as important to prevent even a one-time (though stretched out) boost in the consumer price index, there are generally other ways to minimize or avoid it, such as reducing other federal excise taxes or, as was suggested by Arthur Okun at President Ford's summit conference in September 1974 and elsewhere, using the revenues to subsidize cuts in state and local sales taxes.

The preceding discussion has led to the conclusions that, compared with raising prices to consumers by excise taxation, rationing with nontransferable coupons and with a ceiling price set below the market-clearing level has the advantage of ensuring that a "necessity" does not become unavailable to the poor and that various initial costs of adjusting to the shortage are not concentrated on them, but that it also has several continuing disadvantages: it is economically inefficient; it not only fails to

[5] This statement is based on the finding by Perry that changes in consumer price indexes have had only minor effects on money wages in the United States and Canada, and still less effect in eight other industrial countries. Perry did find a positive response of wages to changes in the private nonfarm deflator, but such changes reflect changes in value added per unit of output, which is a price received by producers. He found that increases in these prices did affect wages through their effect on the ability and willingness of employers to pay higher wages. This influence would not operate when price increases are caused by increases in excise taxes. (See Perry, 1975.) Perry's finding regarding effects of changes in the consumer price index was based on data through 1972 but held through 1974. Between November 1974 and November 1976 the portion of all workers covered by major collective bargaining contracts whose contracts included cost-of-living-adjustment clauses increased from 51 to 60.6%. The existence of such escalator clauses does not necessarily magnify the effect of a price increase in raising wages, however, because their inclusion may reduce the agreed increase in basic wage rates below what it otherwise would have been. In fact, wages set by contracts containing such clauses have risen less in recent years than those set by contracts that do not contain them (see LeRoy, 1977).

invoke the self-interest of consumers in furthering society's objective of economizing on use of the scarce product but sets their self-interest against that objective; by doing that, it creates inducements to illegal activities; it involves more costly administration than does an increase in excise taxation and in addition, because of the inducement it offers to illegal activity, involves greater costs of enforcement. Rationing has the additional characteristic of not affecting the price level, while the effect on the price level of an increase in an excise tax on an important product is uncertain but any effect it does have appears, on what evidence is available, unlikely to be a continuing one.

3. Rationing with Transferable Coupons

It is possible, however, to retain the major advantage of such a rationing system and to eliminate its disadvantages, despite setting a ceiling on the price of the short commodity at less than the market-clearing level, by allowing the rations to be transferred. When consumers may buy and sell ration coupons, a free market for them will develop. In such a system, consumers of the rationed commodity who, in the absence of rationing, would consume more than their rations at the ceiling price of the commodity may still do so by purchasing unused coupons from other consumers who are willing to sell them, thereby supplementing their initial allotment. Because such consumers must pay for the coupons as well as for the commodity with respect to amounts exceeding their initial ration, the effective price of quantities exceeding the initial ration is higher than the ceiling price. At the same time, this system gives every consumer a right of first refusal of the rationed amount at the ceiling price, which the price method of constraining demand does not do. This system thus appears to be a halfway house between a price increase without rationing and rationing with nontransferable coupons combined with a ceiling on the price of the scarce commodity.

The right of first refusal to buy some of the rationed product at the ceiling price, combined with the ability to buy additional amounts at that price plus the market-determined price of additional coupons, appears to establish two prices for the rationed product, one for quantities represented by the initial allocation of coupons and the other for amounts in excess of that. But this appearance is deceptive. While it is true that the out-of-pocket costs per unit are different, all units have the same opportunity cost (difference in cost between buying and not buying the product). Consumers who buy an amount of the product within their initial allocation not only pay the ceiling price but forgo the proceeds of selling the coupon, which they could realize to the extent that they refrain from using all of the initial allotment. Therefore, consumption of any amount, even within the quantity represented by their initial allotment, makes their economic position lower than it would be if they consumed less. The difference, per unit of the rationed product, is the sum of the ceiling price of the product and the per unit equivalent of the price of the coupon, just as it is for those who buy coupons and consume more than the initial allotments represent. Thus, there really is only one price in the true sense of the amount per unit that buyers give up.

Because there is only one price in this sense, the money incentive to economize on the product is the same for all quantities of the product— those equal to and less than the initially allotted ration as well as those in excess of it—and for all consumers—those who would buy the amount equal to or less than their initially allotted ration as well as those who would buy more.

The transferability of the ration increases the incentive to economize even for consumers who, under a system of nontransferable rations, would not have bought less than their ration. The reason is that, with nontransferable rations, for every unit reduction of their purchases they only save the purchase price of the commodity, but when the rations are transferable they not only save that amount but earn the per unit equivalent of the sale price of their unused coupons. They therefore have an incentive voluntarily to reduce their consumption further below their initially allotted ration than they would reduce it if their unused rations were useless. Thus, in comparison with a rationing system in which coupons are not transferable, a system which permits them to be sold provides a greater, or at least a more widely distributed, incentive for consumers to economize.[6]

This does not imply, of course, that the aggregate consumption of the commodity will be less. The freedom to transfer the coupons affects only distribution of the given amount of the commodity among consumers: it enables consumers of higher income or more intense demand for the commodity to consume more than their initially allotted ration but at a premium price, which they must pay to those who consume less than their

[6] It is difficult to justify calling the aggregate incentive "greater." Although consumers who, under either system, would not use all of their ration have a greater incentive to economize when the rations have a market value than when they have none, those who would like to use more than their ration are subject, under a system prohibiting transfers, to an absolute (legal) compulsion not to do so. In effect, their "incentive" to economize is infinite. Aggregating the change of incentives as we go from nontransferable to transferable coupons thus requires evaluating the sum of the increase from zero in the incentives of the first group of consumers and the decrease from infinity for the second group, which is impossible.

initially allotted ration and sell the unused portion. In effect, the issuance of ration coupons is an egalitarian distribution of supplementary money income that is of limited use when the coupons are not transferable, but is of general use, like any other disposable income, when coupons are transferable. Their transferability permits a redistribution of this supplementary income from (a) those who, either because they are well off or because they have an intense want for the product, have a strong market demand for it and thus buy ration coupons to (b) the poor and to those with moderate or weak demand for the product, who are sellers.

Such a system probably would also be less costly to administer than one in which ration coupons are not transferable. Although it would be necessary under both systems to enforce a prohibition against sale of the product without receipt of coupons, the transferability of coupons would eliminate the need to enforce the prohibition against their sale and purchase, which is a saving of real resources.

If sales and purchases of ration coupons were permitted, a market for them would develop, with dealers who would buy coupons from would-be sellers and sell them to would-be buyers. This activity would also involve some use of real resources. This social cost must be set off against the saving of resources permitted by not having to enforce the prohibition against transfer of coupons in a system of nontransferable rations. But this dealing function or brokerage function would probably be performed by the sellers of the rationed product, and at a cost in use of real resources that would probably be much less than the resources saved by not having to enforce a prohibition of transfers. Therefore, the transferability of coupons would probably save real resources on balance.

4. Excise Taxation with Revenue Distributed like Rations

The fact that there is really only one price to consumers under a system of rationing with transferable coupons leads to the conclusion that there must be some excise tax that would result in a price to consumers exactly equal to the cost per unit that they incur in buying the commodity under a system of ceiling prices and rationing with transferable coupons. That cost (the sum of the ceiling price and the per unit equivalent of the free market price of the coupons) is equal to what the market-clearing price of the product would be if the same total quantity were supplied without rationing, so the equivalent excise tax would be one equal to the market price of the per-unit value of the coupons.

There may still seem to be a difference between the two systems because, under this rationing system, both rich and poor consumers can buy amounts represented by the initial allotment of coupons without being worse off than if they had bought the same amount before the shortage. The reason they are able to do so is that, as was noted earlier, a distribution of transferable coupons is in effect a disbursement of additional income. Insofar as this increment of income is distributed more equally than ordinary income, the inequality in the distribution of total income (ordinary income plus income in the form of coupons) is reduced. But obviously there is also some distribution of the revenue from an excise tax that can produce the same result. Evidently, it would be a level of excise tax equal to the price at which coupons settle combined with a distribution of the resulting tax revenue to consumers proportionate to the initial allocation of ration coupons. Thus, the appearance that the two systems necessarily affect consumers in different ways is also deceptive; the two procedures can be made to allocate the scarce product in the same way.

The issuance of transferable rations to consumers of the scarce commodity and the alternative of distributing the revenue from an excise tax in the same way would both increase the demand of these consumers for goods in general (i.e., both would have an income effect), but this increase would be distributed over the whole range of commodities and would offset only partially, and probably only slightly, the decrease in demand for that commodity caused under both systems by the increase in its relative price to the consumer (i.e., the substitution effect).[7]

The only inherent difference between the two systems, apart from costs of administration, is that rationing with transferable coupons fixes the total quantity that may be bought and allows the price increase (in the form of the price of coupons) corresponding to that quantity to be determined in the market, while the excise-tax method allows the quantity to be settled in the market. Since it is the quantity demanded that the government wishes to control, rationing appears to have an advantage from the point of view of assuring accomplishment of the objective. This advantage would be especially important where the need to restrain consumption arises suddenly and is urgent, e.g., because inventories are low. With coupons that are transferable, all rations issued would be used, so the authorities would know that they could issue them in amounts exactly equal to what they intend to have consumed without the risk of discrediting the program that we found to exist under rationing with nontransferable coupons.

If, as appears likely, the continued operation of the rationing system (as

---

[7] There would be some inflationary effect compared to the situation before the shortage. That this must be the case becomes clear when it is recognized that the reduction in supply that created the shortage is a reduction in real income, while the increase of taxation combined with return of the revenue to consumers leaves their money income unchanged.

distinguished from its initial costs) would involve higher real costs of administration than would continued operation of excise taxation and distribution of the revenue, the ideal procedure—at least when demand for the product is to be constrained for more than a relatively short period—appears to be to begin with rationing through transferable coupons, to observe where the price of coupons settles in the market, and then to replace the rationing system and price ceiling by an excise tax equal to the per-unit equivalent of the market-determined price of the coupons, distributing the revenue to recipients of the rations so that each one gets a dollar amount equal to the number of physical units of the product represented by the initially allocated ration multiplied by the free market price of the ration coupons (expressed per unit of the product). This tax and revenue-distribution procedure would result in the same total consumption and the same distribution of the product as would occur under rationing with transferable coupons, but it would save the excess of the real cost of administering the rationing system over the real cost of administering the excise tax and the distribution of its revenue.

If the market value of ration coupons were not included in the price of the product in computing the consumer price index, the replacement of such a rationing system by an excise tax would raise the price index and, if the product is sufficiently important or the excise tax sufficiently high, the effect on the index might be perceptible. If this were the case and if, in addition, the economic situation were characterized by inflationary momentum and the increase was likely to aggravate it enough to offset the saving of costs and other advantages of the excise tax, the rationing system could be retained until that danger was judged to have disappeared.

Another disadvantage of an excise tax, compared to rationing with transferable coupons, arises from its not directly fixing the quantity consumed. If the demand for the product at a given price is unstable, it is more difficult to control the quantity demanded by a tax than by rationing. It could be done only indirectly, by changing the tax rate. The minor aspect of this difficulty in the United States is that under present law it would require legislation to change the tax rate, so that changes would lag behind the need for them. This would not be a serious problem if there were substantial inventories of the product; even if there were not, the law could be changed to give the President discretionary power to alter the excise tax on the specific product within limits set by the Congress. The more serious difficulty in the case of a product with unstable demand is that nobody would know how much the tax should be changed to maintain consumption at the quantity desired. Where there is serious danger that demand for the product is likely to be so unstable that it cannot be cushioned by variations in inventories, therefore, rationing with transferable coupons may be the better alternative.

References

Congress and the Nation (1965). Vol. I, 1945–1964, pp. 740–741. Washington, D.C.: Congressional Quarterly Service.

Friedman, M. (1973). *Newsweek* (November 19).

Kershaw, J. A. (1947). *A History of Ration Banking* (Historical Reports on War Administration, General Publ. No. 2). Washington, D.C.: Office of Temporary Controls, Office of Price Administration.

LeRoy, D. (1977). Scheduled Wage Increases and Escalator Provisions in 1977, *Monthly Labor Review* (January).

Perry, G. L. (1975). Determinants of Wage Inflation around the World, *Brookings Papers on Economic Activity 2:1975*, 408–409 and 413–435.

de Scitovszky, T. [*sic*] (1942). The Political Economy of Consumers' Rationing, *Review of Economic Statistics* **24** (August), 114.

Scitovsky, T. (1971). *Welfare and Competition*, Rev. ed. Homewood, Illinois: Richard D. Irwin.

The Brookings Institution
Washington, D.C.

What Price the National Income?

M. FG. Scott

1. Introduction

In the Note to Chapter IV of *Welfare and Competition,* Scitovsky (1971) explained with his customary lucidity the economic significance of changes in real national consumption, as measured in the usual way by deflating current values by either Paasche or Laspeyres index numbers of prices of consumption goods. He took the view that the same method could also reasonably be applied to measure real government expenditure (or public consumption), but not to measure private capital formation. His unwillingness to extend the method to the latter stemmed from his view that the widespread existence of imperfect competition would make the prices of intermediate goods (including capital goods) understate their true marginal value in terms of consumption goods. Whereas consumers

163

(and governments) could reasonably be regarded as price takers, so that relative prices of consumption goods would give a reasonable measure of marginal rates of substitution in consumption, the same could not be said of producers. The existence of monopolistic profit margins would then lead to the systematic understatement just mentioned and to be further discussed.

We shall discuss what price index should be used to deflate national investment expenditure and so, by implication, national income as a whole. Our chief concern is not the existence of imperfect competition, but the correct index to use even if there were universal perfect competition. It is conventionally assumed that the correct procedure is analogous to that used for consumption. The national income statistician is thus enjoined to measure the quantities of the various capital goods purchased and to revalue them at base year prices. Confronted by the seemingly intractable problem of allowing for quality changes in capital goods, the statisticians have done their best to produce the index numbers required of them, while confessing that their estimates are very uncertain. Some (as we shall see presently) have asserted that it is a mistake to attempt to allow for quality changes at all except insofar as they are matched by changes in cost. We believe that the correct solution to this problem is much simpler than has generally been realized.

In our view, investment expenditure should either be regarded as so much consumption foregone or, alternatively, as the net present value of so much future consumption gained. In a perfectly competitive equilibrium situation, the two would be equal. Both meanings imply that investment expenditure should be deflated by a price index of consumption.[1] Our argument is explained with the aid of an arithmetical example in Section 2, and at the end of it we make some allowance for Scitovsky's point as well as for some other factors which lead to discrepancies between actual investment expenditure and its cost in consumption foregone or value in consumption gained.

A great advantage of viewing investment in this way is that it enables one to deal with two problems of measuring the real national income which have not hitherto been satisfactorily resolved. In Section 3, we consider the first of these: how to allow in an open economy for gains or

---

[1] The idea of deflating savings or investment by a price index of consumption has been mentioned or proposed by several writers, but does not yet seem to have been accepted by what may be called the "national income establishment" (Denison, 1957, footnote 13, p. 227; Kuznets, 1957, p. 276; Hicks, 1965, p. 303; Little, 1950, p. 228; Usher, 1976, pp. 324–329). One reason for this may be that, in all the works cited, apart from the very recent one by Usher, the idea is mentioned almost by way of aside. Denison, for example, relegates it to a footnote with the remark that it has "not as yet been seriously recommended for national income measurement." To avoid misunderstanding, the proposal here *is* seriously recommended for national income measurement!

losses from changes in its terms of trade. Several different methods have been suggested, but, we argue, all involve arbitrary conventions with no satisfactory justification in economic logic. Once we recognize that the problem is essentially that of determining the correct way to deflate net investment abroad, the solution, we suggest, is clear: it should be deflated by an index of the price of consumption.

If this is accepted, the same solution can be used to solve the second problem, that of deflating net property income and transfers from abroad. This is discussed briefly in Section 4.

In Section 5, we generalize our procedure to the measurement of all real outputs. If it is correct to measure the real output of capital goods by deflating their current value by an index of the price of consumption, may it not be equally correct to measure the real outputs of other intermediate goods, exports, and consumption goods in this way? We point out the close affinity of this suggestion to that of constant purchasing power (CPP) accounting, which is probably the best practicable way of correcting company accounts for the distorting effects of inflation. If the accountants' proposals for CPP accounting were to be adopted, as well as our own, it should be easier to reconcile micro- and macroaccounts of the economy. This, as we point out by way of conclusion, is but one of the ways in which conventional procedures in national accounting need to be changed.

2. Changes in Real Investment and National Income in a Closed Economy

In order to simplify the argument and to bring out the main points as clearly as possible, we at first assume a closed economy in which there is perfect competition and no government or taxes. We relax these assumptions later. We want to measure the increase in real national income between two periods, 1 and 2, in which prices differ. National income Y equals national expenditure on consumption C and investment I.[2] The conventional procedure is to revalue the expenditures of one period at the prices of the other period, so that the index of real national income is either the Laspeyres quantity index

$$Y_{2.1}/Y_1 = (C_2/p_c + I_2/p_i)/(C_1 + I_1) \qquad (1)$$

or the Paasche quantity index

$$Y_2/Y_{1.2} = (C_2 + I_2)/(p_c C_1 + p_i I_1), \qquad (2)$$

[2] We do not attempt here to justify this equation, although it can be justified if one defines income as the maximum rate of real consumption that can be expected to be maintained indefinitely. For further discussion, see Scott, (1976a).

where p_c and p_i are index numbers of prices of consumption goods and investment goods, respectively, in period 2, with period 1 set equal to unity.[3]

We propose a different (and simpler) procedure, namely, to use only one price index for the whole of national expenditure, that being the price index of consumption goods. Our proposed measures are then[4]

$$Y_{2.1}/Y_1 = [(C_2 + I_2)/p_c]/(C_1 + I_1), \tag{3}$$

$$Y_2/Y_{1.2} = (C_2 + I_2)/(p_c C_1 + p_c I_1). \tag{4}$$

The reason for using a price index of consumption goods to deflate both consumption and investment expenditures can be stated very simply, and is, indeed, the crux of the argument. Investment may be regarded either as so much consumption sacrificed or as the net present value of so much consumption gained. If we assume that the net present value of all investment is zero, and that all expectations are fulfilled, so that the consumption sacrificed exactly equals the net present value of the consumption gained, then it does not matter in which of these two ways we regard investment. In either case, it represents a certain amount of consumption whose value, in relation to actual consumption in the same period, is given by the current value of the investment. Hence the *quantity* of investment in any period is really a quantity of consumption either sacrificed or gained.[5]

We can state the argument in a slightly different way. Investment goods are really *intermediate* and not *final* goods. The only final goods are consumption goods. In measuring national income, we are not interested in the output of or expenditure on intermediate goods as such. We are interested only in expenditure on investment goods or in savings insofar as they represent future expenditures on consumption goods or present sacrifices of such goods. Hence, it does not matter how many or what kind of capital goods our sacrifice of consumption enables us to buy. That is only

---

[3] This formulation involves a further simplification (not essential to our argument), since it assumes a unique price index p_c for consumption goods, and also one, p_i, for investment goods. This would be true if, for example, all consumption goods prices rose in the same proportion, and likewise all investment goods prices rose in the same proportion which, however, might differ from that of consumption goods.

[4] Given our further simplifying assumption that there is a unique index of consumption goods prices p_c, it is clear that the two measures coincide. However, this is not important for our argument, and it would not hold in the general case in which Paasche and Laspeyres price index numbers of consumption goods differed from each other.

[5] This begs the question of how to measure the quantity of consumption. We shall simply assume that this can be done in the conventional way by Laspeyres or Paasche quantity index numbers, as did Scitovsky in *Welfare and Competition*. Since then he has written *The Joyless Economy* which, to say the least, makes one uneasy with such a simple solution.

an intermediate stage in the process. We can look either at the sacrifice itself or at what it finally achieves in the way of extra consumption.

A simple arithmetical example may clarify the argument, and also relate it to the old controversy over whether one should or should not allow for quality changes in capital goods in valuing investment (or capital) at constant prices (see, e.g., Denison, 1957; Ruggles and Ruggles, 1961). In Table 1, we portray a closed economy in two periods which we wish to compare. Output and prices of consumption goods are the same in each, but the quantity of investment goods produced has doubled and their prices halved, leaving the income of the economy unchanged in money terms. What has happened to its real income?

We must first state precisely what is meant by the doubling in quantity of investment goods, and explain why their price has fallen. The investment goods produced in period 2 are, we may suppose, physically identical with those produced in period 1. The reason why their price has fallen is that, on the one hand, the cost of producing them has fallen (for reasons about which we need not inquire) and, on the other hand, their value as investments has also fallen because wages have risen. We do not really need to inquire why wages have risen, but may suppose, for example, that the labor force is smaller and the capital stock greater in period 2 than in period 1. We shall also assume, for simplicity, that interest rates are unchanged. The main point is that, despite the unchanged physical nature of investment goods, we observe a fall in their price which is consistent with an equal fall in both their cost and their value.

Existing methods of calculating the output of investment goods, expenditure on them, and the national income would all show the result in one or another of the last two lines of Table 1, and hence conclude that real output and income had increased from period 1 to period 2. This is so whether one values output or expenditure at the prices of period 1 or period 2, although the *extent* of the increase differs.

Existing methods regard a physically identical machine in period 2 as

TABLE 1

Arithmetical Example for a Closed Economy

Period	Consumption C			Investment I			Income Y
	Quantity	Price	Value	Quantity	Price	Value	Value
1	80	1	80	20	1	20	100
2	80	1	80	40	0.5	20	100
2 at prices of 1			80			40	120
1 at prices of 2			80			10	90

representing the same amount of real output or expenditure in period 2 as in period 1. This is certainly the case if one adopts the procedure whereby goods produced in period 2 are valued at what they would have *cost to produce* in period 1, if one wants to make the calculation at period 1 prices; or, alternatively, if goods in period 1 are valued at what they would cost to produce in period 2, for a calculation at period 2 prices. According to Denison (1957), this procedure

> is in fact the only one for which estimates exist because of the characteristics of the price indexes used for deflation. . . . In the case of producers' durable goods, only those changes in specification involving differences in production costs between the old and new type capital goods are generally taken into account; in such cases the adjustment is based upon the cost differential [p. 224].

Denison (1957) does not recommend this method solely on grounds of its practicability (although he regards that as conclusive—see below). He also believes that "It is worthy of consideration on its own merits and not merely as a statistically imposed substitute for some other measure [p. 222]." He admits that the resulting estimates do not enable one to equate zero net investment with "keeping capital intact." For that to be possible, he thinks, one must allow for quality differences *other* than those directly measured by cost differences. However, despite this, he believes the estimates are interesting because they provide a useful measure of capital as an *input*. The analyst must be prepared to allow for changes in output per unit of capital input, but at least he has available a good measure of the input. Yet is this really so?

If we return to our arithmetical example, we may ask in what sense has the rate of capital input in period 2 doubled compared with period 1? Denison would presumably reply that it has doubled because twice as many identical capital goods are being added to the capital stock in period 2 as in period 1. However, is that what is meant by "capital input"? Surely the fundamental meaning of this is the same as saving, and saving is measured by the quantity of consumption foregone. Given our assumption of perfect competition, it seems reasonable to say that the quantity of consumption sacrificed, and hence the quantity of capital input, is the same in period 2 as in period 1.[6] We submit that this is a more interesting

---

[6] Of course, if a large change were made in investment, relative prices of consumption and capital goods would change. Hence we cannot be sure that the increase in consumption which would have resulted had investment been reduced to zero in period 2 would have been exactly the same as in period 1. However, the difference could go either way, and there is no reason to think that it would be large. It need bear no relation whatsoever to the relative quantities of investment goods in the two periods.

definition of capital input than Denison's, and that it accords much better with the needs of economic theory and analysis. The Denisonian concept, which is probably widespread, is that capital is, in some sense, a physical factor input like labor and land. This writer believes that this idea has been responsible for a great deal of confusion and misdirected effort. However, we shall not pursue the topic further here[7] but will pass on to consider the other method of measuring the quantity of investment—that which allows for quality changes.

According to this method, the value of a machine in period 2 at period 1 prices is to be found essentially by measuring its marginal product in period 2 at period 1 prices. Since, in our arithmetical example, the marginal product of each machine has halved (as shown by the halving of net present value which is equal to price, by assumption) the value of investment in period 2 at period 1's prices is unchanged, despite the doubling in the quantity of machines. It then appears that the real national income has not changed from period 1 to period 2. We believe that this is the correct conclusion. The real national income surely *is* the same in both periods since real consumption is the same *and* the net present value of future consumption gained through saving is also the same in real terms. This also agrees (given our assumptions of equality between cost of machines and net present value) with the conclusion reached by valuing investment in terms of real consumption foregone.

Why does Denison reject this method of valuing investment at constant prices? He admits that it is theoretically attractive, but believes it to be utterly impracticable. This seems to be because he conceives the task of the national income statistician who applies the method to be that of actually measuring the marginal product of each piece of investment. This would certainly be a hopeless undertaking. If, however, one is prepared to make the same bold assumptions here as one implicitly does in any value measure of output or income—namely, that producers' and consumers' valuations are reasonable approximations to marginal rates of transformation and substitution—then the task is much less daunting. All one has to do, then, is to deflate investment by the best index number of consumption goods prices available, in the manner already described.

To summarize, given our assumptions, the following conclusions can be drawn from our arithmetical example:

(a)   If one regards national income (or output) as the sum of consumption and saving, the latter being consumption foregone, changes in the real national income are best measured by deflating changes in its money value by an index of consumption goods prices.

[7] For further discussion, see Scott (1976a).

(b)   The same is true if one regards national income (or output) as the sum of consumption and the net present value of investment in terms of the extra future consumption it yields.

(c)   The measurement of real national income does not require an attempt to measure changes in the quantity of capital goods purchased, whether or not adjusted for quality changes. Existing procedures which attempt to do the latter may yield incorrect results, as the arithmetical example shows.[8]

We conclude this section with a brief discussion of the effect of relaxing some of our assumptions.

The existence of a government, with taxes and subsidies, leads to the following modifications (at least!). First, "consumption" must now be defined so as to include collective consumption. The relevant price index is then one which covers both private and public consumption. Second, indirect taxes drive a wedge between marginal costs and prices. Since taxes on consumer expenditure tend to exceed those on investment expenditure (which is, indeed, sometimes subsidized), investment expenditure at market prices may understate the value of consumption at market prices foregone. It may also understate the net present value of investment in terms of the extra future consumption at market prices it yields for two reasons. First, the private yield of investment may be less than the social yield at factor cost, because of direct taxes on profits and dividends. Second, the social yield at factor cost may be less than that at market prices because of indirect taxes on output. Subsidies to investment, however, would tend to offset this. If one took the definition of national income in (a), one might attempt to allow for different rates of indirect tax or subsidy so as to get a better estimate of consumption foregone. One might equally attempt adjustments using the definition in (b), but the estimates would be more difficult to make and also (since they would relate to an uncertain future) more uncertain. In any case, it would almost certainly no longer be true that the two different definitions would be equivalent, as in our example.

The existence of widespread imperfect competition may, just like indirect taxes, drive a wedge between marginal cost and price. This case was considered by Scitovsky (1971) who concluded that, as a result, the prices of capital goods (and of intermediate goods generally) would "systematically understate consumers' marginal valuation of the marginal contribu-

---

[8] Furthermore, procedures which do attempt to allow for quality changes, but take a narrow view of them, might easily make no adjustment in our example on the seemingly reasonable grounds that the machines in period 2 were physically identical with those in period 1. This would, of course, lead to the same error as the method which did not adjust for quality changes.

tion of these goods to final output [p. 402, footnote 13]." Consequently, the market value of investment would understate the net present value of the extra future consumption which it would yield, which is relevant to definition (b) of national income. What about definition (a)? It is not clear, in that case, that the market value of investment would give a biased estimate of the value of consumption foregone. There is no obvious reason why the average monopolistic profit margin on investment goods should differ from that on consumption goods. Hence, while imperfect competition may make estimate (b) more inaccurate, it may not greatly affect estimate (a).

There is, furthermore, another way in which imperfect markets, imperfect mobility, the cost of information, and supply inelasticities generally may affect (b). In the writer's view, it is unrealistic to assume that the *average* investment has zero net present value. Most self-respecting businesses would only undertake investments which were expected to yield positive net present values. Because of the supply inelasticities, etc., mentioned previously, any investment is likely to be subject to diminishing returns, which means that, although marginal increments in it may have zero net present value, the investment as a whole will not.[9] If this is accepted, it constitutes yet another reason why the net present value of investment in terms of the extra future consumption yielded by it is likely to exceed the market value of the investment, but it does not substantially affect the latter as a measure of consumption foregone.

In general, it seems likely that the market value of investment is likely to understate both the market value of consumption foregone (because of indirect taxes) and the net present value of future consumption gained (for a variety of other reasons as well). For these reasons, national income on either definition (a) or (b) is likely to exceed the conventionally measured figure. Nevertheless, the proportionate *change* in real national income may still be given, at least to a first approximation, by the procedure we have suggested, so long as both the proportionate understatement of consumption foregone or gained and the share of investment are about the same in both periods.

3. The Open Economy: Allowing for Changes in the Terms of Trade

The procedure suggested for measuring changes in real income and investment can be applied to an open economy whose terms of trade have changed. A number of countries produce estimates of real national in-

[9] This is quite consistent with the widespread existence of economies of scale. For further discussion see Scott (1967).

come which are adjusted for changes in the terms of trade, and several writers have discussed how this adjustment should be made, putting forward procedures which differ in various respects [see Bjerke (1968), Cambridge Economic Policy Group (1975), Courbis (1969), Hibbert (1975), Burge (1961), Geary (1961), Nicholson (1960), Stuvel (1959); the article by Hibbert is a useful survey of the others]. Our own procedure differs yet again, and has a logic which, it is claimed, the others lack. We first explain our own procedure, and then compare it with some of the others. Again, to simplify matters we assume no government, perfect competition, and zero net present values for all investments.

Let us now consider the arithmetical example in Table 2, in which we have still further simplified matters by assuming no domestic investment and unique price index numbers for consumption, exports, and imports.[10] The most important point to grasp is that the surplus on the current balance, exports minus imports, equals net investment abroad.[11] It is therefore treated in precisely the same way as net domestic investment. Since the price index of consumption in our example is the same in both periods, and since the current value of net investment abroad is also the same, its value at constant prices is likewise unchanged. Given our assumptions, this unchanged current value represents an unchanged real sacrifice of consumption and, equally, an unchanged real net present value of future consumption gained. It therefore represents an unchanged real quantity in the only sense which has economic significance for the country concerned. It is quite true, of course, that a smaller quantity of exports is being sacrificed combined with no change in the quantity of imports, but this all relates to intermediate transactions and, in measuring income, we are only concerned with the final result. We cannot, and should not, neglect the fact that exports in period 2 are worth more in terms of consumption, as also are imports. After these changes have been allowed for, the net result is that real net investment abroad is unchanged. Since consumption is also unchanged, real national income is unchanged.

Using the same symbols as in Section 2, our measure of real income in period 2 at the prices of period 1 is

$$Y_{2.1} = (C_2 + I_2 + X_2 - M_2)/p_c. \tag{5}$$

Before comparing this formula with those suggested by other writers, we must first express the argument in a form which will be more recognizable by those who are familiar with this subject. The usual approach is to start with a measure of real national *output,* so-called, which differs from real

---

[10] See footnote 3. We have also omitted the line showing period 1 at the prices of period 2. None of these further simplifications affects the essence of our argument.

[11] Exports and imports cover both goods and services. For the moment we neglect net property income and transfers from abroad. These are considered in Section 4.

TABLE 2

Arithmetical Example for Terms of Trade Case

Period	Consumption C			Exports X			Imports M			Current balance B, $X - M$	Income Y, $C + B$
	Q	P	V	Q	P	V	Q	P	V	V	V
1	80	1	80	40	1	40	20	1	20	20	100
2	80	1	80	20	3	60	20	2	40	20	100
2 at prices of 1			80			20			20	0	80

national *income* for an open economy whose terms of trade have changed. Real national output, which we may call Y', is conventionally measured as

$$Y'_{2.1} = C_2/p_c + I_2/p_i + X_2/p_x - M_2/p_m, \qquad (6)$$

each element being deflated by its own price index. In order to proceed from this measure of output to one of income, an estimate is made of the "gain" g, resulting from changes in the terms of trade between periods 1 and 2. The measure of income equals that of output plus the gain (which would, of course, be negative if the terms of trade worsened). Consequently,

$$Y_{2.1} = Y'_{2.1} + g. \qquad (7)$$

The difference between our measure of income, in (5), and other measures, in (7), is then

$$Y_{2.1}(\text{Scott}) - Y_{2.1}(\text{other}) = I_2 \left(\frac{1}{p_c} - \frac{1}{p_i} \right)$$

$$+ \left(\frac{X_2 - M_2}{p_c} - g - \frac{X_2}{p_x} + \frac{M_2}{p_m} \right). \qquad (8)$$

In what follows, we ignore the first term containing I_2 on the right-hand side of (8), since the argument concerning that is given in Section 2 and is not our concern in this section. We now consider the different suggestions which have been made about how to measure g and their implications for the second term in parentheses on the right-hand side of (8), which we henceforth refer to as DIFF. DIFF would be zero in all cases if there was zero net investment abroad, since then all methods are the same. [12] This at once shows that *the problem we are really discussing is how to deflate net*

---

[12] The fact that all methods give the same result if net investment abroad is zero can be seen by considering the values of DIFF in Eqs. (11), (13), (15), and (17). These are all zero if $X_2 - M_2 = 0$.

investment abroad. We summarize the results of the different methods in our arithmetical example in Table 3.

It is helpful, for comparative purposes, to give our own implicit measure of gain, although we regard the term as inappropriate since the definition of real output in (6) is not one we choose to adopt. With this qualification, we have

$$g(\text{Scott}) = (X_2 - M_2)/p_c - (X_2/p_x - M_2/p_m). \qquad (9)$$

The measure of g which has recently received the approbation of the official UK national income statisticians (Hibbert, 1975) is that advocated by Nicholson (1960):

$$g(\text{Nicholson}) = X_2(1/p_m - 1/p_x). \qquad (10)$$

The logic of this, it seems, is that the gain is the quantity of *imports* that could be purchased by the actual exports sent out in period 2 (i.e., X_2/p_m) *less* the actual volume of exports sent out (i.e., X_2/p_x). The writer does not find this a particularly significant figure to calculate. How does it compare with our own?

$$\text{DIFF}(\text{Scott} - \text{Nicholson}) = (X_2 - M_2)/p_c - (X_2 - M_2)/p_m. \qquad (11)$$

Equation (11) shows that, in effect, the Nicholson method is equivalent to deflating net investment abroad by the price index for imports, instead of, as we suggest, by the price index for consumption. Some may think that

TABLE 3

Arithmetical Example of Different Measures of Gain from Terms of Trade Change[a]

Method	g	DIFF(Scott − other)
Scott	20[b]	0
Nicholson[c]	10	10
Burge and Geary	6.7	13.3
Courbis	8	12
Stuvel[d]	16	4

[a] For definitions of g and DIFF, see text. The basic figures are in Table 2.

[b] This is simply national income in period 2 at the prices of period 1, which is 100, less national output in period 2 at the prices of period 1, as conventionally measured, which is 80.

[c] Also the method of the official United Kingdom national income statisticians.

[d] Also the method of the Cambridge Economic Policy Group.

this is preferable on the grounds that investment abroad earns foreign currency which is then used to buy extra imports. However, is this really a sensible way to look at it? For a start, if $X_2 - M_2$ were negative, we would be considering net investment by foreigners in the country, and, by the same argument, this should enable them to earn more of the exports of the country. The correct deflator would then appear to be the price index of exports, not imports. But this is still inadequate, since extra foreign currency earned need not be used to buy more from abroad. It can equally be used to sell less abroad, which suggests that both import and export prices are relevant. Even this, however, misses the real point. In the last resort, investment today is not made in order to get either exportables or importables tomorrow, but to get future consumption. Hence, as already argued, the best deflator to use is the consumer price index.

The Burge and Geary[13] method requires different measures of the gain depending on whether there is positive or negative investment abroad; thus,

$$g(\text{Burge–Geary}) = \begin{cases} X_2[(1/p_m) - (1/p_x)] & \text{if } M_2 > X_2, \\ M_2[(1/p_m) - (1/p_x)] & \text{if } X_2 > M_2. \end{cases} \quad (12)$$

g(Burge–Geary) is thus the same as g(Nicholson) if there is net borrowing from abroad. If there is positive net investment abroad, however, the Burge and Geary method is equivalent to deflating the current balance by export rather than import prices; i.e., if $X_2 > M_2$,

$$\text{DIFF(Scott} - \text{Burge–Geary}) = [(X_2 - M_2)/p_c] - [(X_2 - M_2)/p_x]. \quad (13)$$

This has no more logic to it than the Nicholson suggestion.[14]

The Courbis (1969) method is an attempt to meet some of the objections to the Nicholson method raised above by using a weighted average of import and export prices instead of just one or the other to deflate net investment abroad. Thus, if we write

[13] Burge (1961) and Geary (1961). It is interesting to note that Fabricant (1961), commenting on Burge and Geary, advocated that net investment abroad should be deflated by price index numbers of the capital goods purchased with the investments and not by any combination of export or import prices. This is a step in the direction we also advocate but, unless the additional step of using the price index of consumption is taken, the journey may never be started, since it looks too difficult.

[14] Geary himself (1961, Chapter 1, p. 7), drew attention to an objection to the Burge and Geary method advanced by Gaathon. This was that, using this method, the total gain of two countries trading with third countries need not equal the sum of their separate gains with those countries. This objection does not apply to the method Geary subsequently advocated which was a simplified version of that advocated by Courbis (1969). This subsequent Geary method involved deflating net investment abroad by the arithmetic average of export and import price index numbers, i.e., putting $a = \frac{1}{2}$ in the Courbis formula for p_t in the next paragraph in the text (Geary, 1961, Chapter 1, p. 8; Geary and Pratschke, 1968, p. 33).

$x = X_2/p_x, \qquad m = M_2/p_m, \qquad a = x/(x + m), \qquad p_t = ap_x + (1 - a)p_m,$

then

$$g(\text{Courbis}) = (X_2 - M_2)/p_t - (X_2/p_x - M_2/p_m), \qquad (14)$$

$$\text{DIFF(Scott–Courbis)} = (X_2 - M_2)/p_c - (X_2 - M_2)/p_t. \qquad (15)$$

There seems to be a bit more logic to using p_t rather than just p_x or p_m to deflate net investment abroad. However, p_t is still unsatisfactory for the reasons already given.

Finally, we come to the Stuvel (1959) method, which is close to, but not quite the same as, that of the Cambridge Economic Policy Group (1975, p. 91). [15] This amounts to deflating net investment abroad by p_y, the deflator for national output as conventionally measured, i.e., as in (6). Thus,

$$p_y = Y_2/Y'_{2.4}$$

and

$$g(\text{Stuvel}) = (X_2 - M_2)/p_y - (X_2/p_x - M_2/p_m), \qquad (16)$$

so

$$\text{DIFF(Scott} - \text{Stuvel)} = (X_2 - M_2)/p_c - (X_2 - M_2)/p_y. \qquad (17)$$

This method comes nearest to the one suggested here since, if C is a large element of Y, as it generally is, p_c and p_y are unlikely to diverge by much. Nevertheless, on grounds of economic logic, p_c is surely preferable. Indeed, Stuvel (1959) himself does not regard his own measure as being compellingly logical. Thus, he poses the problem as one of finding a suitable deflator for an item in the accounts which is not a commodity (good or service) flow:

> The problem one is faced with here is to select an appropriate price index for this purpose, since the non-commodity flows do not have specific price indexes of their own. As with so many problems in national accounting, this is one which can be solved only by introducing a convention, for in the last resort the choice is an arbitrary one [p. 283].

We claim that, unlike Stuvel's (or the other) procedures, the use of the consumer price index is *not* arbitrary. On the contrary, it makes perfectly

[15] Instead of using the deflator for national output as advocated by Stuvel (see text), the Group uses the deflator for domestic expenditure (at market prices), that is, the sum of private and public consumption and domestic investment. This only differs from the approach suggested here by its inclusion of domestic investment, and of all the methods considered is the closest to the one we propose.

good economic sense to regard net investment, whether at home or abroad, as a flow of consumption either sacrificed or gained, which should therefore be expressed in real terms by deflating by a consumer price index.

To conclude this section, we deal with an objection which has been made to Stuvel's method and which might be applied to ours. As Courbis (1969, p. 45) pointed out, Stuvel's method does not yield a symmetrical measure of gain from changes in the terms of trade. One country's gain is not necessarily equal to the rest of the world's loss. This, so far as it applies to our own procedure, can be seen from Eq. (9). If, for example, neither the price of imports p_m nor of exports p_x nor of consumption in the rest of the world changed, then the rest of the world would experience neither gain nor loss. If, however, the price of consumption p_c in the country concerned were to fall, the country would, according to (9), experience a gain. So the gain of the country would be positive and that of the rest of the world zero. By contrast, both Courbis's own measure of gain and that proposed by Burge and Geary are symmetrical. This can readily be seen by looking at Eqs. (12) and (14).[16]

Let us call the country A and the rest of the world B. Then using our proposed method, any change in either p_x or p_m *does* lead to equal and opposite gains or losses for A and B. This can be seen at once from Eq. (9), since the X of A is the M of B. The only apparent discrepancy arises through changes in p_c, which may differ in A and B, thereby producing an asymmetrical effect. But is that anything to worry about? There is no reason at all why A should not increase its real investment abroad while B does not increase its real borrowing from A. The investment abroad by A increases in real terms, so far as A is concerned, if it requires a bigger real sacrifice of consumption or if it yields more real future consumption. If the prices of traded goods rise relative to those of consumption goods in A, as in the example in the preceding paragraph in which p_x and p_m are unchanged but p_c falls, then an unchanged quantity of traded goods exchanges for a larger quantity of consumption goods in A. Hence, in A, investment abroad in real terms—in terms of the quantity of consumption sacrificed or gained—has increased. This is quite compatible with no change in the relative prices of traded goods and consumption goods in B, and so no change in the real borrowing of B from the point of view of B. We conclude, therefore, that the objection that our measure yields asymmetrical results is without force.

[16] In (12), we must use one of the pair of equations for one country, and the other for the rest of the world. Then, in both (12) and (14), remembering that the imports (exports) of one country are the exports (imports) of the rest of the world, we can see that the gain of one country will be equal and opposite to the gain of the rest of the world.

4. Net Property Income and Transfers from Abroad

It should be clear that, if our suggestion is followed, there is no particular problem raised by net property income and transfers from abroad. These are simply one of the elements in the current balance of payments, and it is the resulting balance, equal to net investment abroad, which we deflate by the consumer price index.

Others have not reached this simple conclusion, and have, instead, felt compelled to adopt what can only be regarded as one of Stuvel's "arbitrary conventions" to deal with this item. Thus, Nicholson (1960) has suggested that the sums involved should be deflated by import prices. The official United Kingdom national income statisticians have adopted this suggestion, whose logic is open to precisely the same objections as those raised in Section 3. It seems unnecessary to repeat the arguments here. We merely point out that this is one further example which shows how adopting our fundamental approach—that saving and investment represent consumption sacrificed or gained—enables one to deal tidily with items which, hitherto, have had to be (in effect) brushed under the carpet.

5. A Generalization to All Outputs and Concluding Remarks

In both the closed economy case of Section 2 and the net property income from abroad case of Section 4, we are, in effect, measuring an industry's contribution to real national income by the value of its output deflated by the price of consumption.

The closed economy case is perhaps the clearer example.[17] Here, conventional procedures would agree that changes in real national output and income must be equal. If we imagine a simple economy with only two industries producing, respectively, consumption and investment goods, and if stock changes are zero, then changes in the output of the consumption goods industry must equal changes in real consumption. It follows that changes in the output of the investment goods industry must equal changes in real investment. Hence, if our procedure is accepted for measuring the latter, changes in the output of the investment goods industry must be measured by deflating its value by the price of consumption.

This prompts one to ask whether a similar procedure should not be followed in measuring the output of any industry, whether producing consumption goods, intermediate goods, exports, or investment goods? Can we not apply a very similar argument to them all? Suppose, to take a simple example, that there is a disastrous strawberry crop one year result-

---

[17] Some would not regard net property income from abroad as the output of an "industry." However, if it is so regarded (and it is certainly one contributor to national income), then our procedures imply deflating its "output" by the price of consumption.

ing in a sharp increase in raspberry prices. The marginal utility of raspberries has therefore risen and each punnet of raspberries represents more utils, and more consumption, than in the base year when both crops, we may suppose, were normal. Does this not mean that raspberry output has risen on this account? Let us suppose that the value of nonraspberry output is the same as in the base year, that the quantity of raspberries is also the same, and that the average price of total consumption has not changed. Since raspberry prices have risen, the share of the raspberry industry in total output at current prices must have increased. According to conventional procedures, we would have to describe the situation as being one in which total output in real terms has increased,[18] in which the raspberry industry has increased its share of total output at current prices, but in which, nevertheless, raspberry output in real terms has not increased. It would seem to be just as reasonable to describe the situation as one in which raspberry output in real terms has increased.[19]

If we adopted this procedure, we could still analyze the change in output of any industry into a relative price component and a quantity component. This is, in fact, precisely what Stuvel (1959, pp. 283–285) suggested, the only difference being that he preferred the implicit price index of net domestic product to the price index of consumption which is our suggestion. Apart from that (and we would claim that the price index of consumption has a basis in economic logic which, as Stuvel himself admits, the other index lacks), his proposed analysis of "price-structure" effects seems eminently reasonable.

The proposals made here provide a solution to the problem discussed by Stone (1956) of finding suitable price index numbers to deflate noncommodity flows in the national accounts. As he pointed out:

> many of the transactions recorded in a system of social accounts do not represent commodity flows and cannot be thought of as the sum of prices times quantities. . . . Thus, for example, personal income and personal saving fall into the class of aggregates of noncommodity

[18] Because the value of total output has increased (being the sum of an increase for raspberries and no change on average elsewhere) while prices on average have remained constant.

[19] However, it should be pointed out that there could be price changes that one would *not* want to regard as indicating changes in output in any sense. For example, the rise in raspberry prices might be due, not to a shift in the demand curve for them (as above), but to a monopolistic restriction of their output, resulting in a move *along* the demand curve for them. In that case there would be a fall (instead of an increase) in consumers' surplus on raspberries, and an increase in monopolistic rent received by raspberry growers. Ideally, one would like to be able to distinguish one kind of price change from the other, but it is hard to see how this could be done in practice. For that reason, among others, one would still want to analyze changes in the value of output into price and quantity components, as is suggested in the text which follows.

transactions and so do national totals of income and product. The search for deflators of these totals is essentially the search for appropriate collections of commodities on which these sums of money might be spent and in relation to the changing cost of which they can, in an interesting way, be expressed in real terms [pp. 89–90].

After pointing out that a solution to this problem cannot be found solely through the requirement that accounts at constant prices must balance, he concluded that some other criterion must be used to determine the bill of commodities whose price should be used, and that "the most appropriate bill of commodities is given by the final purchases of the economy in a given period. These purchases comprise the current and capital purchases of all sectors . . . [p. 95]." His conclusion is thus the same as that of Stuvel, and both are close to our own except that we claim that the "most appropriate bill of commodities" is total consumption expenditure (private and public) and that this, indeed, *is* total final expenditure properly defined, since capital goods are really intermediate.

There is a further advantage in our procedure. Those who are familiar with the proposals originally made by accountants to deal with the problems raised by inflation for company accounts will realize that there is a close affinity between the ideas put forward here and those proposals, which were called constant purchasing power (CPP) accounting (Institute of Chartered Accounts in England and Wales, 1974). The fundamental idea underlying the latter is that the various flows in company accounts, and also the values in balance sheets, should all be adjusted in various ways *but by the use of only one price index, namely, that for consumption.* In the writer's view, this is not merely convenient but also, from an economist's point of view, theoretically sound and sensible. If their proposals had been adopted, it would have become much easier to aggregate national accounts from microaccounts, and the aggregates would have taken the form suggested here.[20]

In many developing countries price index numbers of consumer goods are calculated, but other price index numbers are either lacking altogether or very inadequate. National income data are also very poor. The best way to attack this situation may be to concentrate effort on two fronts: first, estimates of the relevant current value series; and second, better estimates of consumer prices (including prices of public consumption). Estimates of volume and price for investment, exports, imports, and the outputs of specific industries on conventional lines are still desirable, but they should, perhaps, be given a lower priority.

---

[20] The British Government did not, however, accept the accountants' proposals and approved, instead, those made in the Sandilands Report (Her Majesty's Government, 1975). For a critique of the latter and further defence of the use of a single consumer price index to adjust accounts for inflation, see Scott (1976b).

In order to prevent misunderstanding, we should in conclusion point out that we have been discussing only the best way to deflate current values to obtain estimates of real national income. We have not discussed how the current values themselves need to be modified if the fundamental proposition that investment is consumption sacrificed or gained is accepted. Some important modifications are required, and are discussed by the writer elsewhere (Scott, 1976a). It may appear at first sight that our suggestions imply that real national income and output are the same in an open economy, since we abandon the conventional procedure of deflating separate components of national expenditure separately as in Eq. (6), and substitute the simpler procedure of deflating all of them by the price index of consumption as in Eq. (5). But there are other differences between national output and income which we discuss elsewhere (Scott, 1976a), although for most large countries we would expect them to be small.[21]

Apart from that, there are many other changes which need to be made in the conventional measures of national output and income, and which have been discussed by others. One proposed change, which the writer had the pleasure of developing in conjunction with Scitovsky and Little (Little *et al.*, 1970), concerns the measurement of both the contribution of different industries to national output, and of national output as a whole, in countries where tariff and quota protection is high and uneven. The rationale of the procedure we suggested has since been questioned (Bhagwati and Hansen, 1972), but an adequate defense would take us too far away from the subject of the present paper. We mention it and the other changes here to make the point that the whole of national income measurement is now undergoing a process of reappraisal.

References

Bhagwati, J. N., and Hansen, B. (1972). In *Development and Planning: Essays in Honour of Paul Rosenstein-Rodan* (J. N. Bhagwati and R. S. Eckaus, eds.). London: Allen & Unwin.

Bjerke, K. (1968). Some Reflections on the Terms of Trade, *Review of Income and Wealth* (June).

Burge, R. W. (1961). In *Studies in Social and Financial Accounting* (International Associa-

---

[21] In Scott (1976a), we suggest that the best practical measure of income is output less depreciation and net unilateral transfers. Our proposed definition of depreciation (which differs from the conventional one) is such that, for a nation, it would depend mainly on *expected* changes in the terms of trade. Consequently, the effects of changes in the terms of trade on income would depend on whether or not they were expected. If they were expected, they should be allowed for in earlier periods in the figures for national depreciation (or appreciation). If they were not expected, they should be allowed for only when they occurred. Herein, we have throughout treated changes in the terms of trade as being *unexpected,* and as if they were once for all. This accords with current practice, and may be the best practical solution, since for most countries it would be difficult to make reliable predictions of changes in the terms of trade.

tion for Research in Income and Wealth) (Income and Wealth Series, 9) (P. Deane, ed.), Chapter 2. London: Bowes and Bowes.

Cambridge Economic Policy Group (1975). *Economic Policy Review* (February), Univ. of Cambridge, Dept. of Applied Economics.

Courbis, R. (1969). Comptabilité nationale à prix constants et à productivité constante, *Review of Income and Wealth* (March).

Denison, E. F. (1957). Theoretical Aspects of Quality Change, Capital Consumption and Net Capital Formation, in *Problems of Capital Formation* (Studies in Income and Wealth, 19). Princeton, New Jersey: Nat. Bur. of Econ. Res.

Fabricant, S. (1961). In *Studies in Social and Financial Accounting* (International Association for Research in Income and Wealth) (Income and Wealth Series, 9) (P. Deane, ed.), p. 51. London: Bowes and Bowes.

Geary, R. C. (1961). In *Studies in Social and Financial Accounting* (International Association for Research in Income and Wealth) (Income and Wealth Series, 9) (P. Deane, ed.), Chapters 1 and 3. London: Bowes and Bowes.

Geary, R. C., and Pratschke, J. L. (1968). *Some Aspects of Price Inflation in Ireland,* Paper No. 40 (January). Dublin: The Economic and Social Research Institute.

Her Majesty's Government (1975). *Inflation Accounting,* Report of the Inflation Accounting Committee, Cmnd. 6225 (September). London: HMSO.

Hicks, J. R. (1965). *Capital and Growth.* London and New York: Oxford Univ. Press.

Hibbert, J. (1975). Measuring Changes in the Nation's Real Income, *Economic Trends.* London: HMSO (January).

Institute of Chartered Accountants in England and Wales (1974). *Accounting for Changes in the Purchasing Power of Money,* provisional statement of standard accounting practice No. 7 (May).

Kuznets, S. (1957). In *Problems of Capital Formation* (Studies in Income and Wealth, 19). Princeton, New Jersey: Nat. Bur. Econ. Res.

Little, I. M. D. (1950). *A Critique of Welfare Economics.* London and New York: Oxford Univ. Press.

Little, I. M. D., Scitovsky, T., and Scott, M. FG. (1970). *Industry and Trade in Some Developing Countries,* pp. 70–76, 410–421. London and New York: Oxford Univ. Press.

Nicholson, J. L. (1960). The Effects of International Trade on the Measurement of Real National Income, *Economic Journal* (September).

Ruggles, R., and Ruggles, N. (1961). Concepts of Real Capital Stocks and Services, in *Output, Input, and Productivity Measurement* (Studies in Income and Wealth, 25). Princeton, New Jersey: Nat. Bur. of Econ. Res.

Scitovsky, T. (1971). *Welfare and Competition,* Rev. ed. London: Allen & Unwin.

Scitovsky, T. (1976). *The Joyless Economy.* London and New York: Oxford Univ. Press.

Scott, M. FG. (1967). Supply and Demand Refurbished, *Oxford Economic Papers* (July).

Scott, M. FG. (1976a). Investment and Growth, *Oxford Economic Papers* (November).

Scott, M. FG. (1976b). *Some economic principles of accounting: a constructive critique of The Sandilands Report.* London: Institute of Fiscal Studies.

Stone, J. R. N. (1956). *Quantity and Price Indexes in National Accounts.* Paris: Organization for European Economic Co-operation.

Stuvel, G. (1959). Asset Revaluation and Terms of Trade Effects in the Framework of the National Accounts, *Economic Journal* (June).

Usher, D. (1976). The measurement of real income. *Review of Income and Wealth* (December).

Nuffield College
Oxford, United Kingdom

Interpersonal Comparisons of Welfare

*Amartya Sen**

1. Introduction

In his insightful survey of welfare economics Scitovsky's (1951) main theme was the limitations imposed by the two assumptions that had become "axioms generally accepted by most people who were concerned with such matters," viz., "the ordinal nature of utility and the impossibility of interpersonal utility comparisons [p. 175]." He noted that even the most "obvious" recommendations of policy (e.g., measures based on preferring "prosperity" to "depression") involved interpersonal comparisons:

The overwhelming majority of people may be better off in times of prosperity; but there are some, however few, who live on fixed in-

* I have benefited much from discussions with Ken Binmore, Peter Hammond, Richard Layard, and Eric Maskin, and from the comments of an anonymous "quasi-referee."

comes or accumulated savings, and who in depression, can "pick up bargains," as one economist has put it, that are not available to them in times of prosperity. The economist, therefore, who favours prosperity and advocates a policy of full employment makes an implicit value judgement. He implies that the gain of those millions who benefit by prosperity is in some sense greater or more important than the loss of real income suffered by those few whose money incomes are fixed [pp. 177–178].

Things have changed a great deal since those bleak days when Scitovsky had rather little company in questioning the rejection of interpersonal comparisons. There have been many recent attempts to make systematic use of interpersonal comparisons of welfare. This paper is concerned primarily with interpersonal comparisons, and with cardinality only in that context. The chief intention is to clarify alternative *interpretations* of interpersonal comparisons as well as alternative formal structures of the *type* of comparability.

Statements on interpersonal comparisons can be broadly classified into *descriptive* and *prescriptive* types. Robbins' well-known attack on interpersonal comparisons as treated by utilitarians was essentially based on denying that there was any descriptive meaning of such comparisons, and not, as often supposed, based on asserting that such comparisons should not be made.[1] Robbins (1935) could see no way of settling differences of views on interpersonal comparisons "in a purely scientific manner [p. 139]." "Introspection does not enable *A* to measure what is going on in *B*'s mind, nor *B* to measure what is going on in *A*'s [p. 140]." Thus Robbins saw "no way of comparing the satisfactions of different people [p. 140]," and took interpersonal comparisons to be "essentially normative [p. 139]."

I would like to argue that *both* descriptive and normative interpretations of interpersonal comparisons are possible, but it is important that they be clearly distinguished from each other.[2] I would also argue that *several* descriptive interpretations are possible and these different interpretations must also be distinguished from each other. And there are several distinct normative interpretations as well. The problem is not one of poverty, but of an embarrassment of riches.

---

[1] Scitovsky (1951) too possibly misinterprets Robbins on this: "Considering that practically every economic change favours some and hurts others, Professor Robbins was in effect barring himself and his colleagues from any policy recommendation whatever [p. 176]." I believe I have been guilty of the same misinterpretation (Sen 1973a, pp. 81–83), as has been pointed out by Baumol (1975) in his review of Sen (1973a).

[2] See Sen (1970, Chapters 7 and 9), Jeffrey (1971), Waldner (1972, 1974), and Hammond (1977).

In Section 2 alternative descriptive interpretations are considered, while Section 3 is devoted to normative interpretations. Sections 4 and 5 are concerned with alternative formal structures dealing with different types of interpersonal comparisons (e.g., of "levels," of "gains and losses").

2. Descriptive Interpretations

At least three distinct descriptive interpretations can be distinguished, based respectively on (i) behaviorism, (ii) introspective welfare comparison, and (iii) introspective *as if* choice.[3]

The behaviorist approach has been explored by Little and more recently by Waldner and others, using comparative behavior as the basis for making comparative statements on mental states. Obviously, the behavior observed in this case is not choice based in the sense of "revealed preference," since we do not in fact have the option of becoming someone else. But there are other kinds of observation, e.g. "we generally associate certain facial expression with frustration," and the focus is on developing "theories connecting desires to observables other than choices [Waldner, 1972, p. 96]."[4] Little (1957) explains the rationale of the behaviorist approach for interpersonal comparisons in persuasive terms:

> We can say of a man that he is habitually miserable, or that he has a disposition to be miserable. Obviously we cannot be meaning that he has a disposition to be more miserable than he usually is. We mean that he has a disposition to be more miserable than men usually are. . . . if we say of a man that he is always miserable, basing our judgement on how he looks and behaves, and how we know we would feel if we looked and behaved like that, and on a wide knowledge of his character gathered by observing his behaviour and words in a variety of situations, and on the opinions of all his friends who similarly knew him well, then we would think it just nonsense to say that he might really be deceiving everyone all the time and be the happiest of men [pp. 54–55].

It has been noted that Little's approach was influenced by "the concept of mind" as developed by Ryle (1949).[5] This might have been the case, but

---

[3] On methodological issues involved in the distinction between "introspective" and "behaviorist" interpretations of personal welfare statements, see Majumdar (1962).

[4] Some choices must, however, be relevant for interpersonal comparisons under the behaviorist approach, e.g., the purchase of mourning dresses, not to mention tear-wiping tissues. For a more ambitious attempt at making interpersonal comparisons based on consumption behavior, see Muellbauer (1975).

[5] See, e.g., Banerji (1964). See also Little's (1957) Preface, p. vii.

Little's view is a good deal less extreme than Ryle's, especially in the treatment of introspection in interpreting behavior.[6] For Ryle (1949), mental states are not essentially different from behavior as such: "overt intelligent performances are not clues to the workings of minds: they are those workings." "Boswell described Johnson's mind when he described how he wrote, talked, etc., fidgetted and fumed [p. 57]."[7] Contrast this with Little's view that "we *use* different men's behaviour, in a wide sense of the word, to compare their mental states [Little, 1957, p. 54, italics added]."

There are several variants of the behaviorist approach, and Little's concentration on behavior as giving evidence on mind is, in this sense, a weak version. It contrasts, however, quite sharply with making interpersonal comparisons based essentially on introspection. The usability of the behaviorist approach even in this weak sense depends on the existence of *agreed* criteria firmly linking comparative behavior to comparative mental states, and this is no slight issue [on this see Waldner (1972)].

The approach of *introspective welfare comparison* interprets interpersonal comparisons as personal statements, each reflecting a particular person's thoughts in answering a question of the kind: "Do I feel I would be better off as person i in social state x rather than as person j in social state y?" They are descriptive statements, but they describe a particular person's thoughts on the subject, e.g., "I would hate to be in your position." The thought experiment involves placing oneself in the position of another, including considering that person's mental characteristics. Needless to say, in placing oneself in the position of another, note may be taken of that person's behavior and the light it throws on his mind, but the immediate reference in a statement of interpersonal comparison in this approach is to the author's own thoughts (no matter how they are derived). As a prelude to a moral exercise, the description of the results of such a thought experiment is frequently invited,[8] and the use of introspec-

---

[6] Compare Little (1957, pp. 54–57) with Ryle (1949, I.(1)).

[7] The concept of the mind as a separate entity from behavior, Ryle (1949) argued, was a "category mistake." Of the same kind as made "by a foreigner visiting Oxford or Cambridge for the first time," who "is shown a number of colleges, libraries, playing fields, museums, scientific departments and administrative offices," and who then proceeds to ask: "But where is the University? [pp. 17–18]." Or as made by "a foreigner watching his first game of cricket," learning "what are the functions of the bowlers, the batsmen, the fielders, the umpires and the scorers," who goes on to observe that "there is no one left on the field to contribute the famous element of team-spirit [p. 18]." (I must confess to being more persuaded that a foreigner has a tough time in Oxbridge, than that mind cannot be distinguished from behavior.)

[8] "Take physic, pomp,
    Expose thyself to feel what wretches feel,
    That thou mayst shake the superflux to them,
    And show the heavens more just [*King Lear*, III, iv. 33–36]."

tive comparison is certainly one of the oldest approaches to interpersonal contrasts.[9]

The approach of introspective choice is similar to this, except that the exercise of placing oneself in the position of another is not followed by the question, "In which position do I feel I would be better off?" but by the query, "Which position would I *choose?*" The two questions are not identical, even though identifying welfare with choice is an established tradition in economics, especially in the context of "revealed preference."[10] There are two different issues involved in this identification, viz., legitimacy and convenience. While considering person i in x to be better off then person j in y is an argument for choosing to be i in x rather than j in y in this *as if* choice, other considerations may well enter the arena of choice, e.g., pride or ethics. For example, "Of course, I believe I would be better off as a rich Brahmin rather than the poor untouchable I am, but I would not dream of wishing to be one of *them.*" Thus, interpersonal comparisons of welfare based on *as if choices* do raise some problems of legitimacy of interpretation.

Even if rankings revealed by choice and welfare rankings are identified, there is the important issue of *which* to take as the "primitive" concept. A preference for the so-called "operational" quality of choice seems to be a conspicuous characteristic of the economist's taste, and this is extended to introspective choice as well (Arrow, 1963):

> The ordinalist would ask what possible meaning the comparison could have to anyone; a comparison should represent at least a conceivable choice among alternative actions. Interpersonal comparisons of the extended sympathy type can be put in the operational form; the judgement takes the form: It is better (in my judgement) to be myself in state x than to be you in state y [p. 115].

The existence of a "conceivable choice," which does certainly help to contemplate the contrast, does not, however, oblige us to identify the alternative chosen as being necessarily better. Furthermore, the use of operationalism in this particular context raises some intricate questions of relevance. While there may be an obvious advantage in dealing with choice-based statements when the choices are of other perople and are also observable, it is not obvious that a similar advantage exists in the case of one's own introspection over *as if* choices. It does not seem to make much less sense to say "I feel I would be better off as i than as

---

[9] For examples of ethical treatises based on such introspective comparisons, see Kant (1785) and Sidgwick (1874), and more recently Hare (1952), Harsanyi (1955), Rawls (1958, 1971), Suppes (1966), and Pattanaik (1971), among many others.

[10] For critical appraisal of different aspects of the foundations of the revealed preference approach, see Hicks (1958, 1974), Sen (1973b), Scitovsky (1976), Wong (1978).

person j, so I would choose to be i and not j," than to say "I would choose to be i and not j, and so I must be better off as i than as j." The advantage of operational meaningfulness in taking choice as the primitive in this case is not really convincing.

Each of the three descriptive approaches considered here have some advantages and some problems. The contrast among them is of relevance to the formal structures for interpersonal comparisons to be proposed in Section 4, as will be discussed there. Meanwhile, before discussing the normative interpretations, it is worth examining how these various descriptive approaches cope with Robbins's query about how to "settle our differences in a purely scientific manner" when we differ on interpersonal comparisons of welfare of person i and person j.[11] In the behaviorist approach the answer is clear enough. The test has to take the form of contrasting observed behavior, e.g., whether we agree that person i is laughing away while j is weeping pitiably. In the weaker interpretation of behaviorism (e.g., as given by Little), there could be further arguments as to whether these behavior characteristics do give us legitimate clues as to their respective mental states, though in this we have been given rather little guidance as to how to conduct the argument beyond going through the more obvious questions, e.g., are they play acting?

In the stronger version of behaviorism, the comparison of mental states is not essentially different from the comparison of behaviors. Given a set of criteria relating behavior to mental states, the disputes can indeed take a scientific form of whether or not a certain behavior was observed. It is worth remarking here that the fact that different people may be thought to have different ways of "expression" may weaken the appeal of moral rules based on welfare comparisons on behavioral lines, e.g., giving a unit of income to the person whose face *lights up* most (under Benthamism), or to the person who *looks* in general unhappiest (under "maximin"). But this weak appeal of moral rules based on behaviorist interpersonal comparisons does not render statements on interpersonal comparisons of wel-

[11] It is interesting to note, in the context of the history of economic thought, that Robbins' denial of the fruitfulness of "scientific" arguments on interpersonal comparisons, while derived from his particular interpretation of such comparative statements, was related to his concentration on market behavior as the predominant source of information on preference and welfare, anticipating the approach of "revealed preference" to be developed later by Paul Samuelson. Robbins (1935) concluded "It [interpersonal comparison] is a comparison which is never needed in the theory of equilibrium and which is never implied by the assumptions of that theory. It is a comparison which necessarily falls outside the scope of any positive science [p. 139]." Robbins contrasted interpersonal comparisons with an individual's *personal* comparison of welfare levels in two situations as revealed by market behavior [p. 138]. Incidentally, as it happens, the information given by market behavior may be inadequate even for such purely *personal* comparisons of a given individual's welfare over two specified social states [on this, see Hicks (1974), especially pp. 14–15].

fare in this approach any less scientific. The statements in question are simply those of comparative behavior.

The picture is quite different with the two introspective approaches. If person 1 thinks that i is happier than j and person 2 holds the opposite, there is nothing to "resolve," since each is a personal statement of the respective author on the results of placing himself in the positions of i and j.[12] For descriptive statements on our feelings and thoughts on the subject, there is no need to "settle our differences," even though we could well discuss whether we have taken all the relevant aspects into account. If you say that given the choice you would have preferred to live in Pompeii of A.D. 79 rather than in London of 1979, and I boringly express a preference for London of 1979, we can discuss whether we have considered the relevant facts (e.g., whether you have heard of Vesuvius), but there is no need to "settle our differences." But note that the statements themselves are not moral ones, nor normative in the usual sense; they *describe* our preferences.

The moral relevance of interpersonal comparisons based on introspective comparison or introspective choice arises from moral rules that may be formulated *using* these comparisons, e.g., Bentham's rule of maximizing the welfare sum, or Rawls's rule of making the worst-off individual as well off as possible. But the comparisons themselves are descriptive.

The contrast can be brought out with a specific example, e.g., the "Weak Equity Axiom" (WEA) (Sen, 1973a):

> Let person i have a lower level of welfare than person j for each level of individual income. Then in distributing a given total of income among n individuals including i and j, the optimal solution must give i a higher level of income than j [p. 18].

On the interpretation of "introspective choice," "WEA amounts to saying that if I feel that for any given level of income I would prefer to be in the position of person j [with his tastes and his non-income characteristics] than in that of person i, then [in distributing a given total of income] I would recommend that i should get a higher income level than j [p. 19]." In this if–then statement, the antecedent which involves interpersonal comparison is purely descriptive, and the moral element comes in only in the requirement that the antecedent must lead to the recommendation specified. A similar picture holds for using WEA with interpreting inter-

---

[12] There is an analogy here with Ramsey's (1931) complaint about the nature of many arguments: "I think we realize too little how often our arguments are of the form:—A: 'I went to Grantchester this afternoon.' B: 'No, I didn't!' [p. 289]." It will be a pity to conclude from the conversation that the subject of going to Grantchester is, in Robbins's phrase, "essentially normative."

personal comparisons in terms of behaviorism, or of introspective welfare comparison.

3. Normative Interpretations

We turn now to normative interpretations. Robbins (1935) had argued for interpreting interpersonal comparisons in this way. "To state that A's preference [for n over m] stands above B's [for m over n] in order of importance . . . is essentially normative [p. 139]."

It should be noted, however, that any normative interpretation is entirely relative to the maximand chosen. For example, if the maximand is taken to be the utilitarian one of welfare *sum,* then the consequent interpersonal comparisons are of welfare *differences.* With the utilitarian normative form, the statement just quoted amounts to identifying A's welfare difference between n and m as greater than B's welfare difference between m and n.

On the other hand, if we take the Rawlsian maximand, viz., the welfare of the worst-off individual, then the interpersonal comparison is of welfare *levels.*[13] The statement quoted then amounts to stating that B in social state n is better off then A in social state m. Interpretation of A's preference for n over m and B's for m over n as their respective personal welfare rankings permits us to identify the following interpersonal partial ordering, represented in the form of a Hasse diagram (with a downward line indicating superiority)[14]:

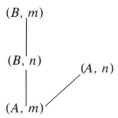

Similarly, with other normative maximands, interpersonal comparisons will take different forms, and there is no unique normative interpretation of interpersonal comparisons.[15]

---

[13] This is, strictly speaking, an apocryphal version of Rawls (1971), whose "Difference principle" judges advantage not in terms of *welfare levels,* but in terms of access to "primary social goods" (pp. 90–95). In this paper, however, we shall stick to the interpretation of the Rawlsian criteria popular among economists.

[14] The position of A in social state n is not ranked vis-à-vis those of B in m and n.

[15] The definiteness of Robbins's (1935, 1938) own normative interpretation arises from his taking the utilitarian form for granted; an example, I fear, of what he himself identifies so perceptively, in a different context, as "the accidental deposit of the historical association of English Economics with Utilitarianism [1935, p. 141]."

It must also be noted that on a normative interpretation of interpersonal comparisons, "basing" 2-person social welfare judgments on these comparisons will be purely tautologous, since these comparisons merely reflect those 2-person social welfare judgments. However, to base n-person social welfare judgments on these interpersonal values is nontautologous, since this would imply a particular class of restrictions relating 2-person judgments to n-person judgments.

For example, consider the Rawlsian maximin rule, which implies that if person i, who prefers n to m, is worse off in social state m than everyone in social state n, then socially n is better then m. On the corresponding normative interpretation of interpersonal comparisons, this amounts to saying that if person i's preference for n over m should prevail in the 2-person social welfare judgment for each pair (i, j) of persons including i and everyone else j one by one, then it must do so for the community as a whole. This is, of course, far from tautologous, and indeed it is easily checked that this relation does not hold for utilitarianism.[16] The utilitarian rule implies, on the normative interpretation of interpersonal comparisons, a different class of restrictions relating n-person judgments to 2-person judgments, and the contrast between the different classes of restrictions implied by different normative rules throw much light on the respective ethical approaches (d'Aspremont and Gevers, 1977; Deschamps and Gevers, 1976, 1978; Hammond, 1977; Maskin, 1976, 1978; Roberts, 1978).

4. Comparability Types: Formal Structures

The dichotomy between interpersonal comparability of *levels* of welfare—relevant for Rawlsian maximin rules (and more generally for criteria of equity)—and that of *units* of welfare—relevant for utilitarianism—was discussed elsewhere (Sen, 1970, 1973a).[17] The formal structures developed there is now presented with some extensions.

Let $W_i(\cdot)$ be any welfare function, defined over the set X of social states, attributable to person i. Denote the set of all positive monotonic transformations of $W_i(\cdot)$ as $M(W_i)$, and the set of all positive "linear"

[16] Cf. the axioms of binary build-up B and single-focus equity for n-member communities SFE(n), which hold for the Rawlsian maximin and lexicographic maximin rules but not for the utilitarian rule (Sen, 1976).

[17] See also Fine (1975), Blackorby (1975), Hammond (1976, 1977), Kelly (1976), d'Aspremont and Gevers (1977), Maskin (1976, 1978), Deschamps and Gevers (1978), Gevers (1979), and Roberts (1976, 1978). Hammond's (1977) analysis of "dual comparability" differs from the framework presented here in one essential respect, to be discussed in the next section.

(strictly, affine) transformations of $W_i(\cdot)$ as $A(W_i)$. Let L_i be the set of all welfare functions attributable to person i. If welfare is "ordinal," then $L_i = M(W_i)$; if "cardinal," then $L_i = A(W_i)$; if "ordinal-type" (Sen, 1970, p. 116), then $A(W_i) \subseteq L_i \subseteq M(W_i)$.

We define welfare being "transcardinal" as $L_i \subset A(W_i)$. This is more restrictive than cardinality in not permitting all positive "linear" transformations. A special case of this—we call it "homocardinal"—is L_i being the set of all *homogeneous*, positive "linear" transformations of W_i, denoted $H(W_i) \subset A(W_i)$. With homocardinality, the "origin" of a person's welfare function is not arbitrary and is invariant with respect to the permitted transformations, viz., multiplication of $W_i(\cdot)$ by any positive real number. (The interpretation may be to identify a distinguished point below which misery dominates—a concept of possible relevance for population policy; other interpretations are also possible.) This is sometimes called a "ratio scale."

The Cartesian product $L = \Pi_{i=1}^{n} L_i$ specifies all the possible n-tuples of individual welfare functions—one for each person—admissible *with respect to the measurability assumptions*. Interpersonal comparability assumptions may restrict the admissible set of n-tuples further, e.g., not being allowed to admit an n-tuple that "blows up" the welfare function of one person arbitrarily keeping those of others unchanged. The set of admissible n-tuples of individual welfare functions with respect to measurability *and* comparability assumptions together is given by specifying some $\bar{L} \subseteq L$.

Some distinguished cases of comparability types are clear enough.[18]

Noncomparability $\bar{L} = L$ Comparability imposes no additional restriction in this case, and each person's welfare function can be varied freely—within the restrictions imposed by the measurability assumptions—without reference to the welfare function of the others. $\bar{L}$ under noncomparability is denoted $\bar{L}(0)$.

Full comparability For any $\overline{W}$ in $\bar{L}$, $\bar{L}$ includes exactly all W in L such that for all i: $W_i(\cdot) = g(\overline{W}_i(\cdot))$, for some increasing function g (invariant with i), permitted by the measurability assumption. $\bar{L}$ under full comparability is denoted $\bar{L}(F)$.

Unit comparability For any $\overline{W}$ in $\bar{L}$, $\bar{L}$ includes exactly all W in L such that for all i: $W_i = a_i + b\overline{W}_i$, for some a_i and some $b > 0$ invariant with i. $\bar{L}$ under unit comparability is denoted $\bar{L}(1)$.

Level comparability For any $\overline{W}$ in $\bar{L}$, $\bar{L}$ includes exactly all W in L such

---

[18] All the distinguished cases covered here except the last two have been discussed in Sen (1970, 1973a). "Partial unit comparability" was called "partial comparability."

that for any i, j, and any $x, y \in X$: $\overline{W}_i(x) \geq \overline{W}_j(y)$ if and only if $W_i(x) \geq W_j(y)$. L under level comparability is denoted $\overline{L}(L)$.

Partial unit comparability $\overline{L}$ such that $\overline{L}(1) \subseteq \overline{L} \subseteq \overline{L}(0)$.

Partial level comparability $\overline{L}$ such that $\overline{L}(L) \subseteq \overline{L} \subseteq \overline{L}(0)$.

Partial full comparability $\overline{L}$ such that $\overline{L}(F) \subseteq \overline{L} \subseteq \overline{L}(0)$.

It may be remarked that full comparability makes interpersonal comparability just as "full" as the measurability of individual welfares will allow. With "ordinal" individual welfare functions, the comparability will not, thus, extend beyond level comparability, but with individual "cardinality," the units will be comparable also.[19] In fact, with "homocardinal" individual welfare functions, even interpersonal welfare *ratios* will be invariant under full comparability. Intermediate cases of measurability (e.g., "ordinal-type" or "transcardinal" individual welfare functions) will be similarly reflected in the interpersonal framework by full comparability.

The use of comparability assumptions is in terms of *invariance* with respect to the choice of a particular W from $\overline{L}$. The restriction is imposed on a "social welfare functional" (SWFL) (see Sen, 1970, p. 129).

SWFL   A social welfare functional is a functional relation F that specifies exactly one social ordering R for any W (an n-tuple of individual welfare functions): $R = F(W)$.[20]

Comparability restriction   For any $\overline{L}$, the social ordering R yielded by the SWFL for each $W \in \overline{L}$ must be the same.[21]

This type of framework can be used to examine analytically the links between comparability-cum-measurability assumptions and ethical structures for social welfare judgments (Sen, 1970, 1973a, 1976, 1977a; Fine, 1975; Blackorby, 1975; Hammond, 1976; d'Aspremont and Gevers, 1977;

[19] The case of full comparability discussed in Sen (1970, Chapter 7) corresponds to this, viz., to one with individual "cardinal" welfare functions. See also d'Aspremont and Gevers (1977), Maskin (1978), and Roberts (1978).

[20] In some cases the need for real-valued representability implicit in a W_i can be dropped, dealing directly with an extended ordering $\tilde{R}$ defined over the Cartesion product of X (the set of social states) and H (the set of individuals) (Sen, 1970, Chapters 9 and 9*). Such a function $R = f(\tilde{R})$—Hammond calls it a generalized social welfare function GSWF—is very close to a SWFL under the comparability restriction of level comparability, or of full comparability with *ordinal* individual welfare (see also Strasnick, 1976; Kelly, 1976; Hammond, 1976; Gevers, 1979; Roberts, 1976a).

[21] The measurability and comparability assumptions *restrict* the class of admissible ethical rules in terms of the "informational framework" (Sen, 1974a,b).

Deschamps and Gevers, 1976, 1978; Maskin, 1976, 1978; Gevers, 1979; Roberts, 1976, 1978).

How are the alternative *interpretations* of interpersonal comparability related to the choice of comparability types? As was discussed in Section 3, on the purely normative interpretation of interpersonal comparisons, the comparability type to emerge will depend on the normative maximand chosen. In particular, utilitarianism will yield partial unit comparability, and Rawlsian maximin, or the lexicographic maximin, will lead to partial level comparability.

As far as the descriptive interpretations are concerned, the picture is more complicated. The approach of "behaviorism" can be used to compare levels as well as differences, but the usual criteria linking behavior to welfare are not very exact [on this, see Waldner (1972)]. Partial full comparability seems to be the appropriate category, but precisely *how* partial the comparability will be must vary from case to case.

"Introspective choice" would seem to promise comparability of *levels* only. However, by considering lotteries, or generally by invoking (assumed) additive separability properties of these choices, a "cardinalization" can be achieved, which in this case will lead to full comparability. But the relevance of such cardinalization for social welfare judgments remains problematic since it incorporates the person's attitude to gambling or similar arbitrary characteristics reflected in the separable choices (Arrow, 1963, p. 10; Hammond, 1977). However, in the specific case of Harsanyi's model of "ethical judgments" with *as if* equiprobability of being anyone in the community (as part of the ethical requirement of "impersonality"), the attitudes to gambling may be thought to be relevant (Harsanyi, 1955, 1975). But full interpersonal comparability achieved this way is interpretable only in the context of choices over lotteries, and the temptation to interpret these utility differences as reflecting relative "urgency" of needs (Harsanyi, 1975, p. 319) may have to be resisted.[22]

"Introspective welfare comparison" can be applied to both levels and units. The comparison of levels is probably more easily made, but units can also be compared through ranking differences (Krantz *et al.*, 1971; Fishburn, 1970), or through higher-order rankings (i.e., rankings of alternatives, rankings of rankings, rankings of rankings of rankings, etc.).[23] Inability to go beyond a few stages in comparing higher-order differences, or higher-order rankings, will typically lead to partial full comparability, possibly with levels fully comparable and units only partially so.

---

[22] See Sen (1976), and also Harsanyi (1977) and Sen (1977c).

[23] See Sen (1977b). Cardinalization through higher-order rankings was jointly investigated with Ken Binmore, and is currently being further explored by R. Nader-Isfahani at LSE. For some related results, see Basu (1976).

5. Dual Comparability

For utilitarianism, concerned as it is with maximizing the sum of individual welfares, comparison of *units* is crucial and that of *levels* irrelevant. On the other hand, criteria of "equity" [e.g., the Difference Principle (Rawls, 1971), the Weak Equity Axiom (Sen, 1973a)], tend to use comparison of levels of welfare, and sometimes ignore comparison of units. This contrast between maximizing the sum of welfare and having a more equal distribution of welfare, which has some characteristics of an "efficiency–equity" contrast, relates closely to the dichotomy between comparability of units and that of levels, and the conflict can surface when *both* units and levels are comparable (Sen, 1973a).[24]

Hammond (1977) has recently explored the possibility of avoiding this conflict by using one set (n-tuple) of individual welfare functions $\{W_i\}$ for comparing levels of welfare and another set $\{V_i\}$ for comparing welfare units. As a criterion of equity, Hammond uses an axiom E which is a strengthened and generalized version of the Weak Equity Axiom. There are various versions of the Equity Axiom. The following is the most quoted (see Hammond, 1976).

E (Equity Axiom) If person i is worse off than person j both in x and in y, and if i is better off himself in x than in y, while j is better off in y than in x, and if furthermore all others are just as well off in x as in y, then x is socially at least as good as y.[25]

Hammond considers the problem of ranking alternative distributions of a given total income where each person i is better off whenever he has more income y_i. He calls a ranking procedure "equity-regarding" if it satisfies E. If the Equity Axiom is applied to $\{W_i\}$ and the utilitarian rule of ranking is used through $\{V_i\}$, then utilitarianism will be equity-regarding if

---

[24] Under every assumption of comparability with ordinal or cardinal individual welfares, the utilitarian rule generates a quasi-ordering R_u and the Rawlsian lexicographic maximin rule another quasi-ordering R_m, and both subsume the Pareto quasi-ordering R_p. Under noncomparability, $R_u = R_m = R_p$. Under unit comparability, R_u is a complete ordering but $R_m = R_p$. Under level comparability, R_m is a complete ordering, while R_u is not, but it coincides with the quasi-ordering R_s proposed by Suppes based on dominance which is also subsumed by R_m. See also Sen (1970, Chapter 9*) and Blackorby and Donaldson (1977) for related results.

[25] This can also be seen to arise from a preference for reducing inequality of welfare distribution in the relatively uncontroversial sense of "ordinal intensity," viz., if $a > b > c > d$, then (a,d) has more inequality than (b,c); on this class of criteria, see Sen (1976).

and only if a higher welfare W_i goes with a lower marginal utility V_i' for all y_i and all i.[26]

Problems of interpretation raised by Hammond's analytical results are not easy to handle. In what sense are $\{W_i\}$ and $\{V_i\}$ alternative representations of the same reality? Hammond imposes no restrictions on their relationship except that for each i, V_i must be a positive monotonic transformation of W_i, because "each represents consumer i's preferences." But this leaves the correspondence of the interpersonal comparisons of levels and units in $\{W_i\}$ and $\{V_i\}$ quite unrestricted. I shall call this case that of dual noncomparability (DN).

In the framework of interpersonal comparability presented in Section 4, based on Sen (1970), the comparability set $\bar{L}$ does typically include more than one n-tuple $\{W_i\}$, but all these admissible n-tuples are then used for comparing *both* levels and units (asserting only those rankings that hold for *every* n-tuple in $\bar{L}$). In Fig. 1, the set L of n-tuples permitted by the measurability assumptions is represented by the (circular) area, with the shaded region U representing its unit comparable subset $\bar{L}(1)$ and the shaded region L representing the level comparable subset $\bar{L}(L)$. The intersection Δ of U and L permits comparability of both units and levels. Consider any $\{W_i\}$ from Δ. Hammond's DN combines with it a $\{V_i\}$ that may come from anywhere in L. How is such a $\{V_i\}$ chosen? What characteristics make both $\{W_i\}$ and $\{V_i\}$ admissible but no other n-tuple? And why use one for comparing levels only and the other for comparing units only?

I would argue that dual noncomparability in this form can be interpreted both within the descriptive framework and within the normative framework, and each interpretation raises some problems. The descriptive approach first. Evidently, both $\{W_i\}$ and $\{V_i\}$ cannot reflect interpersonal comparisons under the *same* descriptive interpretation. Clearly then, under the descriptive approach, $\{W_i\}$ must be obtained from one descriptive interpretation and $\{V_i\}$ from another. To use them in the particular way proposed by Hammond, the descriptive interpretation underlying $\{W_i\}$ must be thought to be the relevant one for the equity criterion and that underlying $\{V_i\}$ the right one for utilitarianism. Such a contrast is certainly possible and need not imply schizophrenia, since the attractions of utilitarianism and equity criteria are not independent of the chosen descriptive interpretations of personal welfare comparisons, and these can differ.

[26] See Hammond (1977, Theorem 3.2). Hammond also considers the case of "intermediate" dual comparability with V_i obtained from W_i through multiplication by a positive number γ_i, and obtains the necessary and sufficient conditions for utilitarianism to be equity-regarding in this more restricted case [Theorem 3.3].

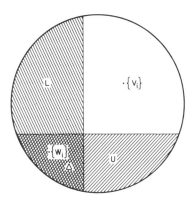

Figure 1

As an example, consider basing utilitarianism on behaviorist interpersonal comparisons and the equity criterion on introspective choice. Let the problem be one of giving a small gift to one of two persons. The question is, To whom? The rules now are the following.

Behaviorist utilitarianism Give it to the person whose behavior would indicate a greater gain (e.g., whose face would light up more).

Introspective choice equity Give it to the person in whose position you would rather not choose to be with or without the gift.

The different descriptive interpretations of interpersonal comparisons are now woven into the respective ethical imperatives.

Note that this approach to the interpretation of dual noncomparability goes beyond the freedom introduced in Hammond's analytical requirements: there is now no need even to presume that V_i is an increasing transformation of W_i, since comparison of levels of welfare of a given person i under one interpretation (e.g., behaviorism) may differ from that under another (e.g., introspective choice).

While this type of interpretation makes DN quite legitimate within the descriptive approach to interpersonal comparisons, it is not at all clear that this will help in avoiding a conflict between utilitarianism and equity. For avoiding such a conflict, what is needed is not the independence of $\{V_i\}$ from $\{W_i\}$, but a *very special kind of dependence* (though not a coincidence of the two). If, according to $\{W_i\}$, person i is better off in x than in y, j is better off in y than in x, and j is better off than i both x as well as in y, then the sum of individual welfares according to $\{V_i\}$ *must* be greater in x than in y. There is, of course, no reason whatsoever why such a thing must happen under two different descriptive interpretations. Thus while DN

may be legitimately interpretable under the descriptive approach, it need
not help much in resolving the conflict between utilitarianism and equity.
Consider now the normative approach. As discussed earlier, the normative values depend on the maximand chosen. A given set of ethical judgments can be used for normative comparison of individual welfare *units*
with respect to utilitarianism and also for normative comparison of individual welfare *levels* with respect of some level-oriented rule (e.g.,
lexicographic maximin, the Weak Equity Axiom, or Axiom E). If $\{V_i\}$ is
chosen consistently with the former and $\{W_i\}$ consistently with the latter,
then the two n-tuples can be used respectively for unit-comparing operations and level-comparing operations, reflecting alternative readings of the
same set of judgments. This would certainly reduce the possibility of a
conflict between utilitarian rankings based on $\{W_i\}$ and equity-regarding
rankings based on $\{V_i\}$. Indeed, the judgment of giving the *small* gift to
person i rather than j in the 2-person world would be interpreted under
utilitarianism as $V_i' > V_j'$, and under Rawlsianism (or the Equity Axiom)
as $W_i < W_j$. This would certainly help in making utilitarianism (based on
$\{V_i\}$) consistent with the pursuit of equity (based on $\{W_i\}$).

It should be mentioned, however, that this happy outcome is largely
tautologous. The *same* judgment is being interpreted here in Benthamite
and Rawlsian terms, respectively, and the coincidence reflects not a con-
gruence of Bentham and Rawls but of the same judgment expressed in two
different languages.[27] However, the approach in general is not entirely
tautologous. First, a set of normative judgments may not fully specify two
n-tuples $\{W_i\}$ and $\{V_i\}$, but only impose some constraints on the choices
of $\{W_i\}$ and $\{V_i\}$ respectively (see Section 3), and in using specific
n-tuples $\{W_i\}$ and $\{V_i\}$ satisfying these constraints to derive other judgments, problems of consistency can certainly still arise.[28] Second, even if
$\{W_i\}$ and $\{V_i\}$ were fully specified on the basis of judgments dealing with
2-person choice situations, the use of these n-tuples in n-person choice
situations raises problems of correspondence and consistency.

In making utilitarianism consistent with the usual criteria of equity, dual
noncomparability under the normative approach is, therefore, a help but
not a guarantee. The help is, however, more nominal than real. In contrast, DN under the descriptive approach is a real possibility and involves

[27] The possibility of taking one descriptive interpretation and one normative interpretation
also opens up the possibility of tautologous reconciliation, e.g., judgments based on level
comparisons derived from a descriptive interpretation being *translated* into unit comparison
under a normative interpretation.

[28] Note also that level comparisons can be derived with respect to several alternative
maximands, e.g., lexicographic maximin and lexicographic maximax, and equity regard may
or may not be reflected in these valuations. Similarly, unit comparison can arise from
nonutilitarian maximands as well.

no circularity, but it does not seem to be of a greal deal of help in resolving the conflict in question. Hammond's proposal of dual noncomparability would, therefore, appear to be of greater intrinsic worth—it draws attention to a real possibility—than of applied value in avoiding "efficiency-equity" conflicts of welfare distribution, for which it was, in fact, devised.

6. Concluding Remarks

The central problem in the theory of interpersonal comparisons of welfare seems to be an embarrassment of riches—there are many reasonable ways of making such comparisons and they need not coincide. Starting from the dichotomy of normative and descriptive approaches to interpersonal comparisons, several distinct interpretations have been presented, examined, and contrasted (Sections 2 and 3).

In addition to this problem of interpretation and procedure, there is also the question of the *type* of comparability to be used, e.g., whether of units only, of levels only, of both, of none, or partially of one or the other or both. Section 4 has been concerned with contrasting different types of comparability within a formal structure.

Finally, the possibility of basing level comparisons on one set of welfare functions and unit comparisons on another set ("dual noncomparability") proposed by Hammond (1977) has been examined in Section 5, both in terms of intrinsic merit as well as likely usefulness in serving the purpose for which the possibility was proposed. The former seems more satisfying than the latter.

References

Arrow, K. J. (1963). *Social Choice and Individual Values,* 3rd ed. New York: Wiley.
Banerji, D. (1964). Choice and Order: Or First Things First, *Economica* **31.**
Basu, K. (1976). Revealed Preference of Governments: Concepts, Analysis and Evaluation, Ph.D. dissertation, London School of Economics. London and New York: Cambridge Univ. Press (to be published).
Baumol, W. J. (1975). Review, *Economica* **42.**
Butts, R. E., and Hintikka, J., eds. (1977). *Foundational Problems in the Special Sciences,* Dordrecht and Boston: Reidel.
Blackorby, C. (1975). Degrees of Cardinality and Aggregate Partial Ordering, *Econometrica* **43.**
Blackorby, C., and Donaldson, D. (1977). Utility vs. Equity: Some Plausible Quasi-orderings, *Journal of Public Economics* **7.**
d'Aspremont, C., and Gevers, L. (1977). Equity and the Informational Basis of Collective Choice, *Review of Economic Studies* **46.**
Deschamps, R., and Gevers, L. (1976). Separability, Risk-Bearing and Social Welfare Judgments (mimeographed), Namur.

Deschamps, R., and Gevers, L. (1978). Leximin and Utilitarian Rules: A Joint Characterization, *Journal of Economic Theory* **17**.

Fine, B. (1975). A Note on "Interpersonal Comparisons and Partial Comparability," *Econometrica* **43**.

Fishburn, P. C. (1970). *Utility Theory for Decision Making*. New York: Wiley.

Gevers, L. (1979). On Interpersonal Comparability and Social Welfare Orderings, *Econometrica* **47**.

Hammond, P. J. (1976). Equity, Arrow's Conditions and Rawls' Difference Principle, *Econometrica* **44**.

Hammond, P. J. (1977). Dual Interpersonal Comparisons of Utility and the Welfare Economics of Income Distribution, *Journal of Public Economics* **6**.

Hare, R. M. (1952). *The Language of Morals*. London and New York: Oxford Univ. (Clarendon) Press.

Harsanyi, J. C. (1955). Cardinal Welfare, Individualistic Ethics, and Interpersonal Comparisons of Utility, *Journal of Political Economy* **63**.

Harsanyi, J. C. (1975). Nonlinear Social Welfare Functions, *Theory and Decision* **6**.

Harsanyi, J. C. (1977). Nonlinear Social Welfare Functions: A Rejoinder to Prof. Sen, in Butts and Hintikka (1977).

Hicks, J. R. (1958). The Measurement of Income, *Oxford Economic Papers* **10**.

Hicks, J. R. (1974). Preference and Welfare, in *Economic Theory and Planning: Essays in Honour of A. K. Dasgupta* (A. Mitra, ed.). London and New Delhi: Oxford Univ. Press.

Jeffrey, R. C. (1971). On Interpersonal Utility Theory, *Journal of Philosophy* **68**.

Kant, I. (1785). *Fundamental Principles of Metaphysics of Ethics* (transl. by T. K. Abbott). London: Longmans, 1907.

Kelly, J. (1976). The Impossibility of a Just Liberal, *Economica* **43**.

Krantz, D. H., Luce, R. D., Suppes, P., and Tversky, A. (1971). *Foundations of Measurement*, Vol. I. New York: Academic Press.

Little, I. M. D. (1957). *A Critique of Welfare Economics*, 2nd ed. London and New York: Oxford Univ. (Clarendon) Press.

Majumdar, T. (1962). *The Measurement of Utility*, 2nd ed. London: Macmillan.

Maskin, E. (1976). Decision-making under Ignorance with Implications for Social Choice (mimeographed), Jesus College, Cambridge.

Maskin, E. (1978). A Theorem on Utilitarianism, *Review of Economic Studies* **45**.

Muellbauer, J. (1975). Can We Base Comparisons of Welfare between Households on Behaviour? (mimeographed), Birkbeck College, London Univ.

Pattanaik, P. K. (1971). *Voting and Collective Choice*. New York and London: Cambridge Univ. Press.

Ramsey, F. P. (1931). *Foundations of Mathematics and Other Logical Essays*. London–New York: Kegan Paul–Harcourt.

Rawls, J. (1958). Justice as Fairness, *Philosophical Review* **67**.

Rawls, J. (1971). *A Theory of Justice*. Cambridge, Massachusetts–London and New York: Harvard Univ. Press–Oxford Univ. (Clarendon) Press.

Roberts, K. W. S. (1976). Possibility Theorems with Interpersonally Comparable Welfare Levels, *Review of Economic Studies*.

Roberts, K. W. S. (1978), "Interpersonal Comparability and Social Choice Theory," *Review of Economic Studies* (in press).

Robbins, L. (1935). *An Essay on the Nature and Significance of Economic Science*, 2nd ed. London: Macmillan.

Robbins, L. (1938). Interpersonal Comparisons of Utility, *Economic Journal* **48**.

Ryle, G. (1949). *The Concept of Mind*. Harmondsworth: Penguin, 1963.

Scitovsky, T. (1951). The State of Welfare Economics, *American Economic Review* **41**.

Scitovsky, T. (1976). *The Joyless Economy*. London and New York: Oxford Univ. Press.

Sen, A. K. (1970). *Collective Choice and Social Welfare*. San Francisco–Edinburgh: Holden-Day–Oliver & Boyd; distribution taken over by North-Holland.

Sen, A. K. (1973a). *On Economic Inequality*. London–New York: Oxford Univ. (Clarendon) Press–Norton.

Sen, A. K. (1973b). Behaviour and the Concept of Preferences, *Economica* **40**.

Sen, A. K. (1974a). Informational Bases of Welfare Approaches, *Journal of Public Economics* **3**.

Sen, A. K. (1974b). Rawls versus Bentham: An Axiomatic Examination of the Pure Distribution Problem, *Theory and Decision* **4** (reprinted in N. Daniels (ed.), *Reading Rawls*, Oxford: Blackwell, 1975).

Sen, A. K. (1976). Welfare Inequalities and Rawlsian Axiomatics, *Theory and Decision* **7** (reprinted in R. E. Butts and J. Hintikka, 1977).

Sen, A. K. (1977a). On Weights and Measures: Informational Constraints in Social Welfare Analysis, *Econometrica* **45**.

Sen, A. K. (1977b). Rational Fools: A Critique of the Behavioral Foundations of Economic Theory, *Philosophy and Public Affairs* **6**; also in H. Harris ed., *Scientific Models and Man*, London and New York: Oxford Univ. Press, 1979.

Sen, A. K. (1977c). Nonlinear Social Welfare Functions: A Reply to Prof. Harsanyi, in Butts and Hintikka (1977).

Sidgwick, H. (1874). *The Method of Ethics*. London: Macmillan, 1907.

Stransnick, S. (1976). Social Choice Theory and the Derivation of Rawls' Difference Principle, *Journal of Philosophy* **73**.

Suppes, P. (1966). Some Formal Models of Grading Principles, *Synthese* **6** (reprinted in P. Suppes, *Studies in the Methodology and Foundations of Science*. Dordrecht: Reidel, 1969).

Waldner, I. (1972). The Empirical Meaningfulness of Interpersonal Utility Comparisons, *Journal of Philosophy* **69**.

Waldner, I. (1974). Bare Preferences and Interpersonal Utility Comparisons, *Theory and Decision* **5**.

Wong, S. (1978). *The Foundations of Paul Samuelson's Revealed Preference Theory: A Study by the Method of Rational Reconstruction*. London: Routledge.

Oxford University
Oxford, United Kingdom

On Search and Equilibrium
Price Distributions*

J. E. Stiglitz

1. Introduction

In an intriguing section of his book *The Joyless Economy,* Scitovsky
(1976) makes two observations: there is a large dispersion of prices in the
American economy, and this dispersion is greater than in Europe. He
attributes the difference in the magnitude of the price dispersion to differ-

* I have benefited greatly from discussions with Tibor Scitovsky, particularly on the
subject of this essay. I am also deeply indebted to Steve Salop, with whom I have collabo-
rated extensively in working on the problem of equilibrium price distributions. An earlier
draft of this paper was presented at a conference at Bell Laboratories, February 1977.
Financial support from the National Science Foundation and IBM are gratefully
acknowledged.

ences in search intensity and suggests that the seeming preference of American consumers for European imports can be attributed in part to the closer correspondence, for those commodities, between price and quality, i.e., to the lower dispersion in the "quality adjusted" price.

> The American buyer of European imports benefits from the high standards which the careful European shoppers' finicky demand imposes on their producers; he does not have to be a careful shopper himself. In other words, he can be what is known as a free rider, enjoying the benefits of other people's careful shopping without paying his share of the cost, in terms of time and effort, that careful and aggressive shopping involves . . . [pp. 178–179].

Conventional economic theory has focused on the analysis of markets with zero transaction costs presumably in the belief that if these costs are not too great the equilibrium in the economy will look much like it would if there were zero transaction costs. As Scitovsky has suggested, this does not appear to be the case. The object here is to construct a simple model in which the effects of costly search on the market equilibrium can be assessed. There are many important questions on which we hope our analysis will shed some light: for instance, the fact that some individuals can act as a free rider on the search activity of others suggests that there may be an undersupply of search activity. Is that the case? Is it obvious that the widening of trade between Europe and America will, in the long run, give American consumers the benefit of the more careful European shopping? Is it not possible that, if exports to the United States became significant, in the long run the consequence will be that the European firms will respond to the lack of careful shopping on the part of American consumers by increasing price dispersion; that is, may not there be a negative externality imposed on the good shoppers as firms attempt to take advantage of bad shoppers, and may not this outweigh the positive externality imposed on the bad shoppers by the good shoppers?

Costly search (information) has several implications:

(a) It means that markets will be imperfectly arbitraged; a disturbance, say, in the demand in one submarket (location) may lead to the price there being different than the price in other submarkets.

(b) It means that individual stores will, in general, have some monopoly power. A store could, for instance, increase its price slightly above the price charged in other stores, and individuals who happen to come there may still purchase, because the cost of searching further exceeds the benefit of the slight reduction in price which they would thereby achieve.

These are obvious and well-known implications of costly search. But what is not so obvious are the implications of these observations for the market equilibrium, particularly when the markets are characterized by a large number of producers and there is free entry. Among the consequences are the following:

(1) There will, in general, not exist an equilibrium, if stores can charge nonlinear prices (Salop and Stiglitz, 1977c). In the attempt to exploit the monopoly power which costly search gives them, all stores pursue policies which, in the end, make it unattractive for any individual to enter the market.

(2) When each store charges a single price, all individuals have search costs and search is sequential (i.e., the individual purchases information about one store at a time); the equilibrium price is the monopoly price (Diamond, 1971).

(3) When search is not sequential, or when there are some individuals who obtain some information costlessly, equilibrium may be characterized by a price distribution.

There are three aspects to the construction of an equilibrium theory of price distribution (see Stiglitz, 1973). First, there must be some way of maintaining ignorance in spite of a flow of information. This may be done by assuming a flow of new entrants onto the market who have limited communication with the outside. [This is the approach taken by Stiglitz (1973) and Butters (1977).] Or there may be a continual source of exogenous disturbances to which the market must adjust (much of Mortenson's work (1973) and the Grossman–Stiglitz (1975, 1976) papers are of this character). Alternatively, firms may pursue random pricing policies, so that all the individual can learn is the probability distribution used by each store, not the price on a moment to moment basis. In this case the disturbances are, as it were, endogenous to the economy. This is the approach of Salop (1977), Shilony (1976), Salop and Stiglitz (1977a, b), and Stiglitz (1976b).

Second, if the free entry–zero profit condition is to be satisfied, firms with higher prices must have higher average costs. Here again there are two approaches. On the one hand, they could have higher costs of "acquiring customers" (or in the case of labor markets, higher costs of maintaining a given stock of labor). This is the approach taken by Stiglitz (1973) and Butters (1977).

Alternatively, they can have lower sales, with a conventional U-shaped average cost curve (Salop and Stiglitz, 1977a).

Finally, there needs to be an explanation of why some individuals pay different prices (receive different wages) than do others. There are two broad categories of explanations: individuals have different demand functions; Salop (1977) showed how a monopolist could act in a discriminating way by offering a price distribution, and Salop and Stiglitz (1977d) extended this to show how a monopolistically competitive equilibrium might be so characterized. On the other hand, individuals could, *ex ante*, be identical, but become different simply because of the randomness of the market. This is the case with the model of Butters (1977), where information about stores' location is distributed randomly, and in the model of Salop and Stiglitz (1977b), where individuals are different simply because of the luck they have in the store they have sampled.

The set of models with equilibrium price distributions is thus a rich one, and this paper represents a continuation of the exploration of the characteristics of such equilibria. In the model formulated here, we assume:

(a)   Individuals are identical except in their search costs; thus, the motivation for the price distribution is not discriminatory pricing.

(b)   There is no exogenous source of noise or disturbances; thus, in a socialist economy, there would be a single price.[1] The market itself creates the only source of imperfect information.

(c)   Stores have U-shaped cost curves, and the high-price stores sell lower quantities.

In the model, individuals live for two periods and have the option of making one search per period. Search is costly, and if they sample a low-price store the first period, they have the option of buying for storage for the second period. Thus, stores which charge low prices have larger sales than do stores which charge high prices. The interesting characteristic of this model is that *the only equilibrium may be one with a price distribution*. If all stores charged a high price (so it would not pay any individual to store), then it would pay some store to lower its price. But if all stores lowered their price (to any level below the monopoly price), since again there would be no storage, it would pay any firm to raise its price to the monopoly price.

2.   The Model

Individuals live for two periods and consume one unit each period provided the price does not exceed unity. If it does, they consume noth-

---

[1] In this sense, the model differs from that of Butters: In his model, given the technology of information distribution, some individuals would remain uninformed about the location of any store, and hence would be unable to purchase; there is some noise "intrinsic" to the model. Here there is no intrinsic noise.

ing. (These are standard assumptions in the search literature.) We assume that the cost of search is an increasing function of the number of searches in the period; for simplicity, we take the polar case in which the first search costs λc and the second search is prohibitively expensive. (This should be contrasted with the assumption made in most of the literature of constant costs per unit search, implying, for instance, no diminishing marginal utility of income or leisure.) Individuals do, however, have the option the first period of their life of purchasing for storage. We assume that a certain fraction of what is purchased spoils between the two periods. Thus, if the individual purchases the commodity at a price p, the total storage costs including interest are denoted by δp. (This assumes that storage costs are proportional to the expenditure on the good; if the major cost of storage were renting space, this would presumably be independent of the price paid. The model may easily be adapted to handle this.)

Individuals are all identical except for search costs. There is a distribution of λ, $F(\lambda)$; if F is differentiable, we write

$$F'(\lambda) \equiv f(\lambda).$$

We consider here only situations where there are at most two prices in the market equilibrium[2]: high-price stores, which sell only for current consumption, and low-price stores; if a young individual (an individual in the first period of his life) arrives at a low-price store he buys for storage as well as immediate consumption. It is also immediate that the high-price store charges a price of unity (at any price above that, its sales will be zero).

Let π be the percentage of firms charging the high price, and $1 - \pi$ be the fraction charging the low price, p^L. Then the reservation price $\hat{p}$ is just

$$\hat{p}(1 + \delta) = p^L(1 - \pi) + \pi + \lambda c. \tag{1}$$

At any price above $\hat{p}$, the individual would prefer to go to the market next period; at any price below $\hat{p}$, the individual buys and stores.

Thus, if all low-price stores charge the price p^L, the fraction of young individuals who purchase for storage is given by

$$1 - F[(p^L(\delta + \pi) - \pi)/c] = 1 - F(\hat{\lambda}), \tag{2}$$

where $\hat{\lambda}$ is the search costs of the individual who is indifferent between searching and storing. Hence, the total revenues are proportional to (dropping the superscript L)

---

[2] In the example below, it can be proved that there can be at most two prices. [The argument is the same as in Salop and Stiglitz (1977a).] However, more generally it appears that equilibrium with more than two prices is possible.

$$p[1 + \pi + (1 - \pi)F] + p(1 - F). \tag{3}$$

The first term represents sales for immediate consumption. If individuals randomly arrive at stores, a fraction π arrives at the high-price store; then $\pi + (1 - \pi)F$ of the individuals entering the market reenter it the second period (and purchase then only for their immediate consumption).

We assume, for simplicity, that the commodity being sold has zero cost of production. Hence, revenues and profits are identical.

There are now two conditions for an equilibrium. At a given π and p^L, each low-price firm must be maximizing its profits where it takes the number of individuals arriving at its store as exogenous, and the price of all other stores as given, but realizes that the number of young individuals who arrive that buy for storage will be affected by the price it charges; thus it maximizes

$$p[1 + \pi + (1 - \pi)F^*] + p\left\{1 - F\left[\frac{p(1 + \delta) - p^L(1 - \pi) - \pi}{c}\right]\right\}. \tag{3'}$$

Differentiating (3') with respect to p, we obtain (if F is differentiable)

$$2 + \pi(1 - F) = fp(1 + \delta)/c. \tag{4a}$$

The second-order condition requires

$$pf'(1 + \delta)/c + 2f > 0. \tag{4b}$$

In a simple example to be presented, F is not differentiable. It turns out then that the only possible equilibrium value of p^L is the reservation price for storage of the group which is at the margin of storing. (If stores charge more than that, they lose a discrete number of sales; if they charge less than that, they gain no customers, and hence revenues must be lowered; the reservation price is thus the profit maximizing price.) Hence, from Eq. (1),

$$p = (\pi + \hat{\lambda}c)/(\pi + \delta). \tag{4c}$$

Second, the high-price and low-price stores must have identical profits:

$$1 + \pi + (1 - \pi)F = p[1 + \pi + (1 - \pi)F + (1 - F)]$$

or

$$1 = p\{1 + (1 - F)/[1 + F + \pi(1 - F)]\} \equiv R(p, \pi). \tag{5}$$

Let $\tilde{p}(\pi)$ be the solution to (4). Then any solution π^*, $0 < \pi^* < 1$, to the equation

$$\rho(\pi) \equiv R(\bar{p}(\pi), \pi) = 1 \tag{6}$$

is an equilibrium with a price distribution [provided $\bar{p}(\pi) < 1$].

To see that such an equilibrium might exist, consider the case in which there are two groups with a fraction F with $c = 0$ and a fraction $1 - F$ with $c = \bar{c} < \delta$. Then

$$R = p(1 + [1 - F/1 + F + \pi(1 - F)]). \tag{7}$$

Setting $R = 1$, Eqs. (7) and (4c) define the equilibrium. Substituting (4c) into (7), we obtain

$$R(p(\pi),\pi) \equiv \rho(\pi; \delta, \bar{c}, F) = \frac{\bar{c} + \pi}{\delta + \pi} \left(\frac{2 + \pi(1 - F)}{1 + F + \pi(1 - F)} \right), \tag{8}$$

$$\rho(0) = 2\bar{c}/\delta(1 + F), \tag{8a}$$

$$\rho(1) = [(1 + \bar{c})/(1 + \delta)](3 - F)/2. \tag{8b}$$

The equilibrium value of π is found by setting $R = 1$, i.e.,

$$\pi^* = \frac{\delta(1 + F) - 2\bar{c}}{(1 + \bar{c} - \delta)(1 - F)}, \tag{9a}$$

$$p^* = \frac{\bar{c} + \pi^*}{\delta + \pi^*} = \frac{1 - \bar{c} + F(1 + \bar{c})}{2 - \delta + F\delta}; \tag{9b}$$

$$\begin{array}{lll} \pi^* > 0 & \text{if and only if} & \rho(0) < 1, \\ \pi^* < 1 & \text{if and only if} & \rho(1) > 1. \end{array}$$

The loci $\rho(0) = 1$ and $\rho(1) = 1$ (as functions of $\bar{c}$ and δ, for fixed F) are plotted in Fig. 1.

It is immediate that *there is a whole range of parameter values* (δ, c, F) *such that the only equilibrium entails a price distribution.*

In Fig. 2 we plot Eqs. (7) and (4c), denoting by p^0 the solution to (7) and by $\bar{p}$ the solution to (4c): since

$$\frac{dp^0}{d\pi} = (1 - p)^2 > 0, \qquad \frac{d\bar{p}}{d\pi} = \frac{\delta - \bar{c}}{(\pi + \delta)^2} = \frac{(1 - p)^2}{\delta - \bar{c}} > 0,$$

both loci are upward sloping but there is at most one intersection. Moreover, we can show that if there is an interior solution (i.e., $0 < \pi^* < 1$, $p^* < 1$), the p^0 locus crosses the $\bar{p}$ locus from above. This ensures that, under natural dynamic assumptions, the interior equilibrium is stable. We assume that the switch in "policy" from, say, a low-price store to a high-price store is slower than the adjustment in price, given that the store is a low-price store, to its optimal price (the former entails a discrete change in price, the latter may be continuous). Thus, at a given π, the

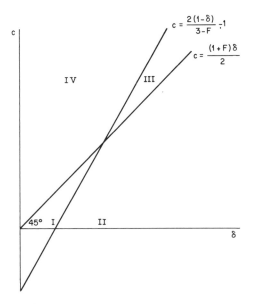

Figure 1 Patterns of equilibrium: I, Unique equilibrium, $0 < \pi^* < 1$; II, unique equilibrium with $\pi^* = 1$; III, equilibrium with $\pi^* = 0$, equilibrium with $\pi^* = 1$; IV, unique equilibrium with $\pi^* = 0$.

postulate is that all low-price stores adjust p^L to $\tilde{p}$. But when $\pi < \pi^*$, $\tilde{p} < p^0$, so profits of low-price stores are less than those of high-price stores. Hence π increases, until π^* is reached. Conversely, if $\pi > \pi^*$.

Some interesting properties immediately emerge from this example. *An increase in the proportion of the population with low search costs*

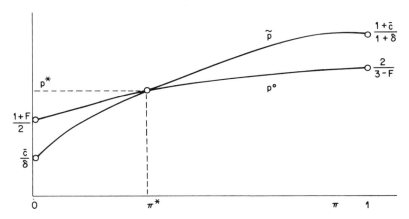

Figure 2 Analysis of equilibrium.

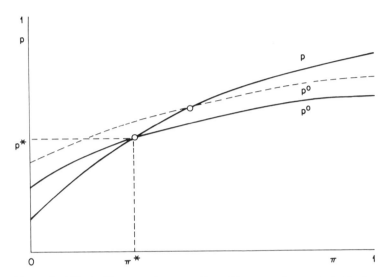

Figure 3   Effect of increase in proportion of low search cost individuals.

increases the proportion of high-price stores, and increases the price charged in the low-price stores. This result may be seen by direct calculation from Eq. (9); alternatively, in Fig. 3 we observe that an increase in F shifts the p^0 locus up, but leaves the $\bar{p}$ locus unchanged. Hence, p^* and π^* both must increase. This appears to be contrary to intuition until it is observed that it does not pay low search cost individuals to store; hence, the larger the proportion of these individuals in the population, the smaller the gain from lowering the price. To compensate, the equilibrium price must be higher. But to induce the high search cost individuals to purchase at the low-price store, they must then be persuaded that they will be more unlikely to find a low-price store next period, i.e., π must be increased.

Similarly, an increase in search costs $\bar{c}$ lowers π and lowers p, and thus, provided π is not too much in excess of 0.5, it increases the variance of price. Again, this result may be seen by direct calculation; alternatively, in Fig. 4 we observe that an increase in c shifts the $\bar{p}$ locus upward but leaves the p^0 locus unchanged. Hence p^* and π^* must both decrease. But although it increases price dispersion, it unambiguously makes consumers better off, since the probability of obtaining a lower price is unambiguously increased.

The analysis remains unaffected if the low search cost individuals have a small but positive search cost.

Notice that we have the seemingly paradoxical result that the high search cost individuals exert a positive externality on the low search cost individuals.

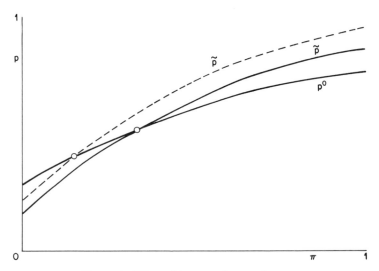

Figure 4 Effect of increase in search costs.

A numerical example may help clarify the analysis. Let $F = \frac{1}{2}$, $\bar{c} = \frac{1}{8}$, $\delta = \frac{1}{4}$, $\pi^* = \frac{2}{7}$, $p^* = \frac{23}{30}$. At $\pi = 1$, $p = 1$, each store sells one unit to each customer: $R = 1$. If p is lowered to 0.9, sales increase by 25%—half of the young customers buy for storage and hence profits are increased by price cutting. But if all firms charged a price low enough to induce the high "transactions cost" individuals to buy in the sale for future needs, the price would have to equal $\bar{c}/\delta = \frac{1}{2}$. But any single store, by raising its price to 1, would lose only 25% of its sales. (Of its customers, $\frac{1}{3}$ are young with $c = 0$, $\frac{1}{3}$ are young with $c = \bar{c}$, and $\frac{1}{3}$ are old with $c = 0$; it sells 1 unit to each except for the young with $c = \bar{c}$, to whom it sells 2 units.) Thus, profits would increase by 50%. The only possible equilibrium is that involving some stores charging a high price, some charging a low price.[3]

---

[3] Actually, the argument for the existence of a price distribution is even stronger than we have made it here. In our example we have implicitly assumed that the first search (store visited) costs nothing the first period, and costs λc the second, with the second search both periods being prohibitively expensive. If $Ep + \lambda c > 1$, the individual will not enter the market the second period. Taking that into account modifies (7) to read (using the fact that $Ep = \pi + (1 - \pi)p^L$)

$$
R = \begin{cases}
p, & \text{if } p > \max\left(\dfrac{1}{1+\delta}, \dfrac{1 - \bar{c} - \pi}{1 - \pi}\right), \\[2ex]
p\left(1 + \dfrac{1 - F}{1 + F}\right), & \text{if } \dfrac{1 - \bar{c} - \pi}{1 - \pi} < p < \dfrac{1}{1+\delta}, \\[2ex]
p\left(1 + \dfrac{1 - F}{1 + F + \pi(1 - F)}\right), & \text{if } p < \dfrac{1 - \bar{c} - \pi}{1 - \pi} \text{ and } p < \dfrac{1}{1+\delta}.
\end{cases}
$$

The analysis of the more general model follows on lines parallel to that of our example.

We let $\bar{p}$ denote the solution to (4a) for various values of π, and p^0 be the solution to (5) for various values of π. The intersection of the two loci at values of (π, p) between zero and unity define an equilibrium with a price dispersion.

We would like to be able to argue that both loci have the same shape as in our example, but it is clear from straightforward differentiation that this may not be the case; the slope of the $\bar{p}$ locus depends on the density f and its derivative f', while p^0 depends on the density f. Since we have imposed no restrictions on f, the loci may take on a variety of shapes.

Normally, we would argue, an increase in π, the percentage of high-price stores, would raise $\bar{p}$, the profit maximizing price, for two reasons: first, the reason for having a low price is to induce young, high transaction cost individuals to buy for future consumption; as π increases, the proportion of this group in one's customers is reduced. Secondly, an increase in the proportion of high-price stores increases the reservation price for any group, thus making it possible to charge a higher price to induce the same percentage of individuals to buy in sales.

Analytically, we obtain

$$\frac{d\bar{p}}{d\pi} = \frac{(1 - F) + [\pi f + f'p(1 + \delta)/c](1 - p)/c}{f(1 + \delta)/c + [\pi f + f'p(1 + \delta)/c](\delta + \pi/c)}.$$

Clearly, a sufficient condition for $d\bar{p}/d\pi > 0$ is that $f' \geq 0$.

Similarly, normally we expect p^0 to be upward sloping; an increase in π increases profits because it induces more customers to buy for future consumption, but lowers profits (per customer) because of the composition effect already noted. Normally the function $R(p, \pi) = 1$ has two solutions for p for any given π; but only the upper one is relevant for our purposes. p^0 is not the value of p which maximizes R, i.e., is not the solution to $R_p(p, \pi) = 0$: the individual competitor ignores the effect of his increasing the price on the composition of individuals arriving at the store. This compositional effect is always negative so that individual competitors overestimate the return to price increases, and thus $R_p(p, \pi) < 0$. Thus, if we assume the compositional effect dominates, $dp^0/d\pi < 0$, while if the direct effect dominates, $dp^0/d\pi > 0$. (In our example there was no compositional effect.) (See Fig. 5.)

Analytically, we obtain from (5)

$$\frac{dp^0}{d\pi} = \frac{[(1 - F) - f(1 - \pi + p\,\pi)/c](1 - p)}{2 + \pi(1 - F) - f(1 - \pi + p\,\pi)(\delta + \pi)/c}.$$

Both the denominator and the numerator may be positive or negative.

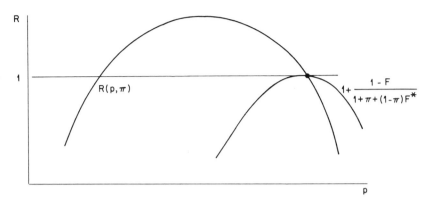

Figure 5   Revenue functions as viewed by firm and industry.

Thus, p^0 and $\bar{p}$ loci may intersect several times—each representing an equilibrium price distribution.

A comparative statics analysis of the effects of a change in the distribution of search costs is considerably more complicated than before; the effect turns out to depend on the effect of the change both on the total number of individuals who find it profitable to store (at the old price distribution), i.e., on the change in the value of F, and on the number of individuals who are on the margin of storing and not storing, i.e., on the change in the value of f. For instance, it is possible that the number of high search cost individuals increases (F decreases) and the number of marginal individuals increases (f increases), so that the $\bar{p}$ locus, in the neighborhood of the old equilibrium, is unaffected (Fig. 6). On the other hand, an increase in F always lowers p^0 (for each value of π). Hence, if $\bar{p}$ is upward sloping, we find that the effect of the increase in the number of high search cost individuals is (as before) to lower the price of low-price stores and to increase the proportion of low-price stores in the population. But clearly, other changes in the distribution F could have quite different effects on the equilibrium price distribution. Notice, however, that what is critical for the analysis of the effects are only the change in F and f at the old equilibrium; a decrease in search costs for very low search cost individuals, i.e., a perturbation in the distribution which leaves F and f unaffected would have no effect on the equilibrium price distribution.

3. Concluding Remarks

We have shown that the market equilibrium may be characterized by price distributions, even though in a socialist economy there would be no

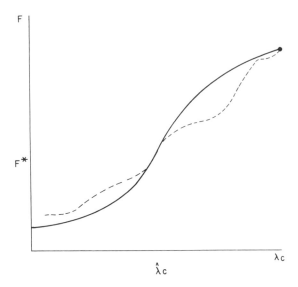

Figure 6 Change in distribution of search costs has no effect on equilibrium.

price distribution. The price distribution in this example, as in the earlier studies of Salop and Stiglitz, originates solely from the attempt to exercise monopoly power. Although there are differences among individuals in the model presented here, there is no difference in consumer surplus enjoyed by different individuals; a monopolist in this market would charge everyone a price of $p = 1$. Thus, monopolistic competition does lead to some individuals receiving a lower price than they would have in pure monopoly. But note that in this example it is the high transaction cost individuals who exert a beneficial externality, as it were, on the low transaction cost individuals, for firms attempt to induce the former to buy for future consumption at their store by lowering their price.

As in our earlier studies, it should be clear that there are a number of alternative interpretations of the model presented: a fraction of the stores could charge the high price, or the stores could all follow a mixed strategy, with the low price being interpreted as a "sale." The distinction between purchase for immediate consumption and purchase for immediate plus future consumption can be interpreted as equivalent to the distinction between purchasing a nondurable or a durable item (to provide the same kind of services). Finally, differences in price may be interpreted as differences in quality. To what extent the apparent product variety is due to the phenomenon described here remains a moot question.

References

Butters, G. (1977). Equilibrium Distributions of Sales and Advertising Prices, *Review of Economic Studies* (October).

Diamond, P. (1971). A Model of Price Adjustment, *Journal of Economic Theory* p. 156.

Grossman, S., and Stiglitz, J. (1975). Impossibility of Informationally Efficient Markets, *American Economic Review* (to be published).

Grossman, S., and Stiglitz, J. (1976). Information and Competitive Price Systems, *American Economic Review* (May).

Mortensen, D. T. (1973). Search Equilibrium in a Simple Multimarket Economy, Center for Mathematical Studies, Discussion Paper No. 54, Northwestern Univ. (October).

Salop, S. (1977). The Noisy Monopolist, *Review of Economic Studies* (October).

Salop, S., and Stiglitz, J. (1977a). Bargains and Ripoffs: A Model of Monopolistically Competitive Price Dispersions, *Review of Economic Studies* (October).

Salop, S., and Stiglitz, J. E. (1977b). Luck of the Draw: A Simple Model of Equilibrium Price Dispersion with Identical Agents, presented to conference at Bell Labs. (February).

Salop, S., and Stiglitz, J. E. (1977c). On the Existence of Equilibrium with Costly Search, presented to conference, Bell Labs. (February).

Salop, S., and Stiglitz, J. E. (1977d). Search Costs, Monopoly Power and Price Distributions (mimeographed), Stanford, California.

Scitovsky, T. (1976). *The Joyless Economy*. London and New York: Oxford Univ. Press.

Shilony, Y. (1976). Mixed Pricing in Locational Oligopoly, *Journal of Economic Theory*.

Stiglitz, J. E. (1973). Equilibrium Wage Distributions (Cowles Foundation Discussion Paper), *Economic Journal* (to be published).

Stiglitz, J. E. (1976a). Utilitarianism and Horizontal Equity: The Case for Random Taxation, IMSSS Tech. Rep. No. 214, Stanford Univ., Stanford, California.

Stiglitz, J. E. (1976b). Prices and Queues as Screening Devices in Competitive Markets, IMSSS Tech. Rep. No. 212 (August) Stanford Univ. Stanford, California.

Department of Economics
Stanford University
Stanford, California

PART II

INTERNATIONAL TRADE AND DEVELOPMENT

The Long-Run Incidence of Government Policies in Open Growing Economies*

Michael J. Boskin

Philippe R. De Ville

1. Introduction

The analysis of the incidence of government policies in open economies typically has been made in a comparative static framework; e.g., McLure (1969) and Krauss (1973). The analysis of incidence in a growth context is quite recent and confined to closed economies (Sato, 1963; Krzyzaniak, 1967; Sato and Hoffman, 1974; Feldstein, 1974; Myers, 1970). The purpose here is to attempt *to begin* to bridge the gap between these two lines of

* We are grateful to the Center for Research in International Studies at Stanford for support of the early stages of this work.

research by examining the impact of government policy on saving and growth, and hence factor returns, in the context of a simple dynamic model of international trade.

Our model is similar to the complete specialization case[1] of the Oniki–Uzawa–Bardhan two-country, two-sector dynamic trade model. However, we relax the assumption of labor immobility and allow labor migration in response to wage differentials.[2] The economic situation we have in mind consists of a country, region, or amalgam of countries producing capital goods, retaining (saving) a fraction of them for domestic use, and exporting the remainder to another country, region, or group of countries in exchange for consumer goods. The essential features of the model are described in detail in Section 2.

We analyze the long-run incidence of a flat rate income tax financing the government budget. Tax receipts are assumed to be redistributed to consumers for consumption expenditures and to firms for expenditures on capital formation. The budget being assumed always balanced, our analysis is thus analogous to the familiar balanced-budget incidence of the comparative static case. In Section 3, we derive the long-run effects of tax rate changes on aggregate saving behavior, steady state equilibrium growth paths, and, hence, factor returns in *each* economy. Indeed, such changes affect saving and capital accumulation in several ways. First, the size of the budget affects aggregate saving and capital accumulation whenever the marginal propensity to save out of disposable income of the private sector differs from the marginal propensity to spend revenues on capital formation by the government.[3] Second, a change in the tax rate by changing directly the net aftertax factor returns also affects the allocation of labor between the two economies. These two combined effects are analyzed in the case of equal, and constant, saving propensities out of income from capital and labor by the private sector. The incidence analysis indicates under what conditions wage and rental rates rise or fall, the tax is exported to "foreign" labor and/or capital, etc.

Under certain conditions, the analysis of Section 3 enables us to predict whether the steady state return to capital and to labor, in each economy, will rise or fall. In order to gain some insight into the potential magnitude of these effects, some numerical examples are presented in Section 4. We

[1] Indeed, in a world with growing factor supplies, trade would tend to induce specialization when the two economies are more or less equal size.

[2] See Oniki and Uzawa (1965) and Bardhan (1965). Our colleague Pentti Kouri points out that labor migration in response to tax incentives is a key feature of the relation between Sweden and Finland.

[3] This differential propensity to save has been important in many discussions in macroeconomics; see the work of Bailey (1973) and David and Scadding (1974).

also explore the sensitivity of the incidence estimates to variations in values of several key parameters: saving rates, elasticities of substitution, etc. These examples make clear the potential importance of the long-run phenomenon described in Section 3.

2. The Basic Model

Consider a simple two-country, complete specialization, dynamic model of trade:

$$c = f(k_c), \tag{1}$$

$$x = g(k_x), \tag{2}$$

where c is capital goods output per capita in economy c and x is consumer goods output in economy x. The production functions f and g are assumed to be linear, homogeneous, and strictly quasi-concave with positive marginal products everywhere; k_i ($i = c, x$), of course, is the capital–labor ratio in economy i.

$$\dot{L} = nL, \tag{3}$$

$$L_i = E_i L \qquad (i = c, x), \tag{4}$$

where L is world population, assumed to grow at constant rate n, and E_i is the proportion of the world population in i. Dots denote time derivatives. E_i, of course, is constant in the steady state, but may vary in the transient phase due to migration.

$$\dot{K}_c = c_d L_c, \tag{5}$$

$$\dot{K}_x = c_e L_c. \tag{6}$$

The increase in the capital stock of c, $\dot{K}_c$, is the proportion of capital goods output used domestically and of x, $\dot{K}_x$, is the share of output exported.

$$c = c_d + c_e, \tag{7}$$

$$x = x_d + x_e. \tag{8}$$

Total output in each economy equals exports (subscripted e) plus domestic use (subscripted d).

$$pc = s_c + pc_d, \tag{9}$$

$$x = s_x + x_d. \tag{10}$$

Total national income, valued in units of consumer goods, equals consumption plus saving. The price of the capital good relative to the consumer good is p.

$$(1 + t_c)r_c = f'(k_c)p, \tag{11}$$

$$(1 + t_x)r_x = g'(k_x), \tag{12}$$

$$(1 + t_c)w_c = [f(k_c) - k_c f'(k_c)]p, \tag{13}$$

$$(1 + t_x)w_x = g(k_x) - k_x g'(k_x). \tag{14}$$

We assume perfect competition in each economy; hence factor rewards equal the value of their marginal product, where r_i and w_i are aftertax rental and wage rates, respectively. Given our assumptions, the income tax levied in each economy is equivalent to an equal rate tax on capital and labor.

$$w_c = w_x. \tag{15}$$

Net after-tax wage rates are equalized by labor migration. The wage equalization process determines [via (13)–(15)] the relative price of capital goods.

$$E_c + E_x = 1. \tag{16}$$

The world population is fully employed and divided in proportion E_c/E_x between c and x.

$$pf(k_c)E_c = s_c E_c + s_x E_x. \tag{17}$$

The supply of machines equals the demand, and, hence, aggregate savings.

$$s_c = \theta_c pf(k_c), \tag{18}$$

$$s_x = \theta_x g(k_x). \tag{19}$$

A constant share of output θ_i is saved in each economy.[4]

Combining equations (7), (9), and (18), we note that the saving of c equals the output of capital goods used internally and that of x equals exports of consumer goods:

$$pc_d = \theta_c pf(k_c), \tag{20}$$

$$x_e = \theta_x g(k_x). \tag{21}$$

---

[4] We use this assumption as a convenient first approximation; see David and Scadding (1974) for empirical support of this proposition, usually termed Denison's law. Boskin (1978) reports nontrivial positive interest elasticities of private saving. We shall deal with more general saving behavior in a sequel.

Combining (20) and (21) with (17) yields the balance of trade equilibrium condition:

or

$$E_c pc_d + E_x x_e = E_c pf(k_c) \qquad (22)$$

$$E_c pc_e = E_x x_e. \qquad (23)$$

The value of c's exports of capital goods equals the value of x's exports of consumer goods. Since p must satisfy the trade balance condition, we may rewrite (23) (using the saving functions) as[5]

$$p = \frac{\theta_x g(k_x)}{(1 - \theta_c)f(k_c)} \frac{E_x}{E_c}. \qquad (24)$$

Substituting (13) and (14) into (15) and inserting p from (24), we obtain

$$\frac{f(k_c) - k_c f'(k_c)}{(1 + t_c)(1 - \theta_c)f(k_c)} \frac{E_x}{E_c} = \frac{g(k_x) - k_x g'(k_x)}{\theta_x g(k_x)(1 + t_x)}. \qquad (25)$$

Solving (25) for E_x/E_c (denoting by F_L and G_L the elasticities of output with respect to labor in c and x, respectively, and F_K and G_K correspondingly) we see that the equilibrium labor allocation depends upon saving behavior and technology in each country:

$$\frac{E_x}{E_c} = \frac{L_x}{L_c} = \frac{(1 - \theta_c)}{\theta_x} \frac{G_L}{F_L} \frac{(1 + t_c)}{(1 + t_x)}. \qquad (26)$$

If both production functions are Cobb–Douglas, the equilibrium allocation of labor is constant and uniquely determined by the two saving rates, the two tax rates, and the capital intensities of the two production processes. In this case, output per capita and wages grow at the same rate. Wage increases in one economy induce a change in p sufficient to preserve the wage equalization without labor migration.[6]

3. Income Taxation

As already noted, the long-run effect of government policy on wage and rental rates in each economy occurs via the effect on saving and capital accumulation. We adopt the comparative dynamic approach of comparing steady state equilibria.[7]

[5] Of course, a bargaining situation would develop in the case of large changes in the supply of exports of capital. We may think of our model as applicable to small changes within a context of agreed upon general orders of magnitude in the terms of trade.

[6] The case of immobile labor is discussed by DeVille (1973). We intend to deal with the case of mobile capital in a sequel to this work.

[7] This is by now well established in economic growth theory. See, of course, Solow (1956). Sato (1963) points out that the speed of convergence to the new steady state equilibrium may be quite slow.

If we assume proportional income taxation at rates t_i ($i = c, x$), the saving functions [(18) and (19)] may be rewritten as

$$s_c = \theta_c pf(k_c) = [s_{pc} + t_c(s_{gc} - s_{pc})]pf(k_c), \tag{18a}$$

$$s_x = \theta_x g(k_x) = [s_{px} + t_x(s_{gx} - s_{px})]g(k_x), \tag{19a}$$

where s_{pi} is the private savings rate in i, t_i the income tax rate, and s_{gi} the rate of "government investment" out of tax proceeds. Note that when the government and private saving rates are *identical* in *each* economy, the scale of public economic activity does not affect aggregate saving.[8]

Letting $\phi_i = \dot{k}_i/k_i$ and $\mu_i = \dot{E}_i/E_i$, the patterns of trade and capital accumulation may be described by the following pair of differential equations:

$$\phi_c(k_c, k_x) = \theta_c f(k_c)/k_c - \mu_c(k_c, k_x) - n \tag{27}$$

and

$$\phi_x(k_c, k_x) = [(1 - \theta_c)f(k_c)/k_x]E_c/E_x - \mu_x(k_c, k_x) - n, \tag{28}$$

where

$$\mu_c(k_c, k_x) = \left(\frac{\sigma_x - 1}{\sigma_x} G_K \frac{\dot{k}_x}{k_x} - \frac{\sigma_c - 1}{\sigma_c} F_K \frac{\dot{k}_c}{k_c} \right) E_x$$

and

$$\mu_x(k_c, k_x) = \left(\frac{\sigma_c - 1}{\sigma_c} F_K \frac{\dot{k}_c}{k_c} - \frac{\sigma_x - 1}{\sigma_x} G_K \frac{\dot{k}_x}{k_x} \right) E_c,$$

where σ_i is the elasticity of substitution in economy i. For analytical convenience in the derivations to follow, we shall assume $\sigma_x = 1$.[9] However, we allow $\sigma_c \gtreqless \sigma_x$.

This system of simultaneous differential equations has the unique stable steady state solution

$$k_c^* = (\theta_c/n)f(k_c^*), \tag{29}$$

$$k_x^* = [(1 - \theta_c)/\theta_c](E_c^*/E_x^*)k_c^*. \tag{30}$$

---

[8] Bailey (1973) conjectures that the private sector sees through the government veil and exactly offsets the effect of fiscal policy. While Bailey's analysis is intriguing, David and Scadding (1974) present results inconsistent with Bailey's conjecture.

[9] A comment on the relative sizes of the two economies is useful at this stage. If the elasticities of per capita output with respect to per capita labor are 0.3 and 0.2 in c and x, the initial shares of labor in national income are 0.7 and 0.8, respectively, the saving rates are 0.2 and 0.15 in c and x, the capital–labor ratio in x is $\frac{2}{3}$ that in c, and over 80% of the world's labor force is in x.

Substituting for E_c^*/E_x^* from (26), we obtain

$$k_x^* = [F_L^*\theta_x(1 + t_x)/G_L\theta_c(1 + t_c)]k_c^*. \tag{31}$$

The two relations between saving and the steady state equilibrium capital–labor ratios given by (29) and (31) may be analyzed to examine the comparative dynamic incidence of budgetary policy. Throughout, we assume the overall saving rates are a decreasing function of the tax rate (i.e., $s_{pi} > s_{gi}$).[10] Differentiating (29) with respect to t_c (recall that θ_c is a function of t_c), we obtain

$$\frac{dk_c^*}{dt_c} = \frac{dk_c^*}{dt_c} + \frac{dk_c^*}{d\theta_c}\frac{d\theta_c}{dt_c} = \frac{k_c^*}{t_c}\left[\frac{1}{F_L}\frac{(s_{gc} - s_{pc})t_c}{\theta_c}\right] < 0. \tag{32}$$

Likewise, differentiating (31) with respect to t_c, we get

$$\frac{dk_x^*}{dt_c} = \frac{dk_x}{d\theta_c}\frac{d\theta}{dt_c} + \frac{d\theta_c}{dt_c} = \frac{k_x^*}{t_c}\left[\frac{F_K^*}{F_L^*}\frac{1}{\sigma_c}\frac{(s_{gc} - s_{pc})t_c}{\theta_c} - \frac{t_c}{1 + t_c}\right] < 0. \tag{33}$$

Hence, we have

PROPOSITION 1   An increase in the income tax rate in c will decrease the steady state capital–labor ratio of both economies.

This result is to some extent counterintuitive. For a *given* level of output, a decrease in θ_c produces an increase in exports of capital to x. Equation (33) assures us that the decrease in the output of capital goods more than offsets the increase in the propensity to export. Hence, actual exports of capital goods decline. Note also that if $F_K^* > \sigma_c$, the capital–labor ratio of x falls proportionately more rapidly than that of c.

Recall that

$$E_c^*/E_x^* = \theta_x F_L^*(1 + t_x)/(1 - \theta_c)G_L(1 + t_c)$$

and let $E_c^*/E_x^* = E$; then

$$\frac{dE^*}{dt_c} = \frac{dE^*}{d\theta_c}\frac{d\theta_c}{dt_c} + \frac{dE^*}{dt_c}$$

$$= \frac{E^*}{t_c}\left[\frac{(s_{gc} - s_{pc})}{\theta_c}\left(\frac{\theta_c}{1 - \theta_c} - \frac{F_K^*}{F_L^*}\frac{\sigma_c - 1}{\sigma_c}\right) - \frac{t_c}{1 + t_c}\right]. \tag{34}$$

Hence, if $\sigma_c \leq 1$, $dE^*/dt_c < 0$. If $\sigma_c > 1$, $dE^*/dt_c < 0$ if $\theta_c > F_K^*$. Equation (34) tells us that if the elasticity of substitution in the capital goods producing economy is smaller than unity, labor migrates from c to x as wages in c decrease more rapidly than output. If $\sigma_c > 1$, the same result obtains if the saving rate in the capital goods economy exceeds the elastic-

---

[10] The results, of course, would be reversed if we assumed that the government savings rate exceeds the private savings rate.

ity of output with respect to capital. Only when $\theta_c < F_k^*$ is the sign of (34) indeterminate. Hence, we have

PROPOSITION 2   An increase in the tax rate in the capital goods producing economy will decrease its share of the "world" population if the elasticity of substitution is less than unity *or* if the saving rate exceeds the elasticity of output with respect to capital.

The equilibrium aggregate capital–labor ratio k^* may be found by solving

$$\dot{k} = f(k_c)E_c - nk$$

when $\dot{k} = 0$. Hence,

$$k^* = f(k_c^*)E_c^*/n. \tag{35}$$

Differentiating (35) with respect to t_c, we obtain

$$\frac{dk^*}{dt_c} = \frac{k^*}{t_c} \left\{ \left[\frac{F_K^*}{F_L^*} \left(1 - E_x^* \frac{\sigma_c - 1}{\sigma_c} \right) + E_x^* \frac{\theta_c}{1 - \theta_c} \right] \right.$$
$$\left. \times \frac{(s_{gc} - s_{pc})t_c}{\theta_c} - \frac{E_x t_c}{1 + t_c} \right\} < 0 \qquad \text{always.} \tag{36}$$

Hence, we have

PROPOSITION 3[11]   An increase in the tax rate in the capital goods producing country will decrease the aggregate capital–labor ratio.

Note from (29) and (30) that

$$\frac{dk_x^*}{dt_x} = \frac{k_x^*}{t_x} \left[\frac{(s_{gx} - s_{px})t_x}{\theta_x} + \frac{t_x}{1 + t_x} \right] \gtreqless 0 \qquad \text{and} \qquad \frac{dk_c^*}{dt_x} = 0.$$

PROPOSITION 4   An increase in the tax rate in the consumer goods economy will decrease its capital–labor ratio if the elasticity of its saving rate with respect to the tax rate is greater than the elasticity of the capital–labor ratio with respect to the tax rate for a given saving rate. It will have no effect on the capital–labor ratio of the capital goods producing economy.

An increase in the tax rate in the consumer goods economy tends to decrease its saving rate and capital–labor ratio; however, the tax increase may induce labor migration; capital exports from c to x will then tend to rise and so will the capital–labor ratio in x. The net effect is indeterminable analytically and depends on the various elasticities involved. However migration flows affect only the speed of adjustment in the transient phase of economy c.

---

[11] Compare with Sato and Hoffman (1974).

Turning now to effects on prices and factor returns, we have

$$\frac{dp^*}{dt_c} = \left\{ (G_k - 1) \left[\frac{F_K^*}{F_L^*} \frac{1}{\sigma_c} \frac{(s_{gc} - s_{pc})t_c}{\theta_c} - \frac{t_c}{1 + t_c} \right] \right\} \frac{p^*}{t_c} > 0$$

and

$$\frac{dp^*}{dt_x} = \frac{p^*}{t_x} \left[G_K \frac{(S_{gx} - S_{px})t_x}{\theta_x} + \frac{(G_K - 1)t_x}{1 + t_x} \right] < 0. \tag{37}$$

PROPOSITION 5 The relative price of capital increases when t_c increases and falls when t_x increases.

Since aftertax wage rates are instantaneously equalized, we have

$$\frac{dw_i^*}{dt_c} = \frac{w_i^*}{t_c} \left\{ G_K \left[\frac{F_K}{F_L} \frac{1}{\sigma_c} \frac{(s_{gc} - s_{pc})t_c}{\theta_c} - \frac{t_c}{1 + t_c} \right] \right\} < 0. \tag{38}$$

Since the capital–labor ratio in economy x decreases as t_c increases, the wage rate will fall and, because of labor migration, so will the wage rate in c.

The interested reader may verify that the gross-of-tax return to labor in c may rise or fall with an increase in the income tax rate in c (obviously, the gross return in x falls).

The gross-of-tax return to capital will rise in both x and c since their respective capital–labor ratios have decreased:

$$\frac{d(r_c(1 + t_c))}{dt_c} = \frac{r_c(1 + t_c)}{t_c} \left[\frac{1}{\sigma_c} \frac{(S_{gc} - S_{pc})t_c}{\theta_c} \left(\frac{F_K G_K - 1}{F_L} \right) \right.$$
$$\left. - (G_K - 1) \frac{t_c}{1 + t_c} \right] > 0 \tag{39}$$

and

$$\frac{d(r_x(1 + t_x))}{dt_c} = - \frac{r_x}{t_c} G_L \left[\left(\frac{F_K}{F_L \sigma_c} \right) \frac{(S_{gc} - S_{pc})t_c}{\theta_c} - \frac{t_c}{1 + t_c} \right] > 0. \tag{40}$$

However, the net return to capital in the capital goods producing economy may increase or decrease:

$$\frac{dr_c}{dt_c} = \frac{r_c}{t_c} \left[\frac{1}{\sigma_c} \frac{(S_{gc} - S_{pc})t_c}{\theta_c} \left(\frac{F_K G_K - 1}{F_L} \right) - G_K \frac{t_c}{1 + t_c} \right] \gtrless 0. \tag{41}$$

Thus, while owners of capital in the consumer goods producing economy invariably gain from a tax increase in the capital goods producing economy, owners of capital in the capital goods producing economy may gain or lose as a result of an increase in t_c. Reasonable estimates of the parameters in Eq. (41), however, imply that capitalists in c are likely to gain absolutely from the increased tax.

Thus, we have

PROPOSITION 6   An increase in income taxation will drive down the net wage rates in both economies and drive up the rental rate on capital in x and (usually) c.

The stake of labor in capital accumulation is obvious; when the private sector has a higher marginal propensity to save than the public sector, increasing the scale of the public sector via income tax finance will drive wage rates down. Since the net return to capital increases (usually), capital gains absolutely and labor bears more than the full tax.

Turning to the tax policy of the consumer goods producing economy, we note that

$$\frac{dw_c}{dt_x} = \frac{w_c}{t_x}\left[(G_K - 1)\frac{t_x}{1 + t_x} + G_K\frac{(S_{gx} - S_{px})t_x}{\theta_x}\right] < 0, \qquad (42)$$

$$\frac{dw_x}{dt_x} = \frac{w_x}{t_x}\left[G_K\frac{(S_{gx} - S_{px})t_x}{\theta_x} + (G_K - 1)\frac{t_x}{1 + t_x}\right] < 0, \qquad (43)$$

$$\frac{dr_c}{dt_x} = \frac{r_c}{t_x}\left[G_K\frac{(S_{gx} - S_{px})t_x}{\theta_x} + (G_K - 1)\frac{t_x}{1 + t_x}\right] < 0, \qquad (44)$$

$$\frac{dr_x}{dt_x} = -\frac{r_x}{t_x}\left[(G_L + 1)\frac{t_x}{1 + t_x} + G_L\frac{(S_{gx} - S_{px})t_x}{\theta_x}\right] \gtreqless 0. \qquad (45)$$

Hence, we have

PROPOSITION 7   An increase in income taxation in the consumer goods producing economy drives down wage rates in both economies as well as the rental rate in c (because of the change in terms of trade); however, owners of capital in x may gain or lose as a result of the tax.

Finally, let us analyze the possible changes in the steady state level of per capita consumption in both countries. For the consumers goods producing country, per capita consumption is equal to that part of the consumers goods output which is domestically used. It follows that

$$\frac{dx_d^*}{dt_c} = \frac{x_d^*}{t_c}\left[G_K\left(\frac{F_K^*}{F_L^*}\frac{1}{\sigma_c}\frac{(s_{gc} - s_{pc})t_c}{\theta_c} - \frac{t_c}{1 + t_c}\right)\right] < 0. \qquad (46)$$

Per capita consumption in country c is equal to the per capita exports of consumer goods times the ratio of the two labor forces $L_x/L_c = 1/E$. Now

$$p^*c_e^* = \theta_{xg}(k_{x^*})/E^*. \qquad (47)$$

Differentiating Eq. (47) with respect to t_c, we have

$$\frac{dpc_e^*}{dt_c} = \frac{pc_e^*}{t_c}\left\{(1 - G_k)\frac{t_c}{1 + t_c} + \left[(1 - G_k)\frac{F_k^*}{F_L^*}\frac{1}{\sigma_c} + \left(\frac{F_k^*}{F_L^*} - \frac{\theta_c}{1 - \theta}\right)\right]\right.$$
$$\left.\times \frac{(s_{gc} - s_{pc})t_c}{\theta_c}\right\}\frac{d(pc_e)}{dt_c} \gtreqless 0. \tag{48}$$

PROPOSITION 8   An increase in income taxation in the capital goods producing economy will always decrease the steady state per capita consumption in the consumer goods producing country. The effect on the steady state consumption per capita in the capital goods producing economy is indeterminate.

We may summarize the incidence analysis by noting that an increase in the size of the public sector (financed by income taxation) in the capital goods producing economy decreases capital accumulation and the steady state capital–labor ratio. This in turn drives up the marginal product of capital. Owners of capital in the consumer goods economy clearly benefit and those in the capital goods producing economy probably also benefit after tax. Thus, the tax on income in the capital goods producing economy is borne in full—or even more than in full—by labor in both economies. Part of the tax is exported to labor in the consumer goods economy, part borne by labor in the capital goods economy.

Increases in income taxation in the consumer goods economy are borne by labor in both economies and capital in c; capital in x may gain or lose. Again, at least part of the tax is exported—this time to both labor and capital in the capital goods producing economy.

We turn now to some numerical examples of the relative importance of these effects.

4. Numerical Examples

A convenient way to summarize the effects of the income-tax financed expansion of government activity is to calculate the elasticities of the relevant variables—wage and rental rates—with respect to tax changes for some reasonable values of the relevant parameters—tax and saving rates, elasticity of substitution, etc. This is easily accomplished by converting the formulas previously derived to elasticities. Table 1 presents the elasticities of the relative price of capital goods, the wage rate (equalized via migration), and the rental rate in each economy with respect to the income tax rate under a variety of assumed values for the elasticity of substitution, the private saving rate, and the tax rate.

A cursory examination of Table 1 reveals some interesting insights into

TABLE 1

Elasticities of Factor Prices with Respect to t_c [a]

		$\sigma_c = \frac{1}{2}$	$\sigma_c = 1$	$\sigma_c = 1\frac{1}{2}$
$t_c = 0.35$	$s_{pc} = 0.2$			
	η_p	0.40	0.29	0.25
	$\eta_{wr} = \eta_{wc}$	−0.17	−0.12	−0.11
	η_{rc}	0.85	0.38	0.23
	η_{rr}	0.40	0.29	0.25
	$s_{pc} = 0.1$			
	η_p	0.31	0.25	0.22
	$\eta_{wr} = \eta_{wc}$	−0.13	−0.11	−0.10
	η_{rc}	0.47	0.20	0.11
	η_{rr}	0.31	0.25	0.22
$t_c = 0.5$	$s_{pc} = 0.2$			
	η_p	0.59	0.41	0.35
	$\eta_{wr} = \eta_{wc}$	−0.25	−0.18	−0.15
	η_{rc}	1.46	0.68	0.42
	η_{rr}	0.59	0.41	0.35
	$s_{pc} = 0.1$			
	η_p	0.43	0.33	0.30
	$\eta_{wc} = \eta_{wr}$	−0.19	−0.14	−0.13
	η_{rc}	0.77	0.33	0.19
	η_{rr}	0.43	0.33	0.30

[a] Based on calculations with $F_L = 0.7$, $G_L = 0.7$, $s_{gc} = 0.05$.

the model presented. It is now confirmed that, for reasonable values of the parameters, the rental rate in the capital goods economy will increase when the tax rate is increased. The rental rate in the consumer goods economy will also increase. The elasticity of the rental rate in the capital goods producing economy, of course, declines as the elasticity of substitution increases; it is nontrivial unless the elasticity of substitution is quite large. Had we modeled capital as the mobile factor, of course, equalization of the aftertax return to capital would imply that capital in both x and c share the gains from the increased marginal product of capital equally.

The decline in the wage rate is quite modest and declines with increases in the elasticity of substitution. While the decline in the wage rate is modest, the total transfer of resources from labor to capital is quite large: the transfer to owners of capital is spread among a large number of workers.

Finally, Table 2 presents corresponding elasticities with respect to t_x. Reasonable parameter estimates imply rather modest elasticities of factor prices with respect to t_x.

TABLE 2

Elasticities of Factor Prices with Respect
to t_x [a]

	$s_{p,x}$	
	0.1	0.2
γ_p	−0.28	−0.33
$\gamma_{wc} = \gamma_{w,x}$	−0.28	−0.33
$\gamma_{t,x}$	−0.31	−0.19
γ_{rc}	−0.28	−0.33

[a] Assumes $G_L = 0.7$, $t_x = 0.4$, $s_{g,x} = 0.05$.

5. Conclusion

We have presented an analytical model and some numerical examples
of a dynamic model of tax incidence in an open economy. The basic result
of the model is the tendency for expansion of public economic activity
financed by income taxation to be borne by labor—both foreign and
domestic. This highlights the vested interest of labor in capital formation.
Are these results robust to generalizations of the model? We are currently
working on a variety of such generalizations: different saving behavior;
payroll and/or profit tax finance; nonspecialization; and capital mobility.
We hope thereby to stimulate interest in the analysis of the effects of
alternative national tax policies on the world economy.

References

Bailey, M. (1972). The Optimal Full Employment Surplus, *Journal of Political Economy*
(July) 649–661.
Bardhan, P. K. (1965). Equilibrium Growth in the International Economy, *Quarterly Journal
of Economics* **79**, 455–464.
Boskin, M., (1978). "Taxation, Saving and the Rate of Interest," *Journal of Political Econ-
omy* **86**, No. 2, Part 2, 53–327.
David, P., and Scadding, J. (1974). Private Saving: Ultrarationality, Aggregation and "Deni-
son's Law," *Journal of Political Economy*.
DeVille, P. (1973). Essays on Taxation in Open Growing Economies, Ph.D. thesis, Stanford
Univ., Stanford, California.
Feldstein, M. (1974). Tax Incidence in a Growing Economy with Variable Factor Supply,
Quarterly Journal of Economics (November), 551–573.
Krauss, M. (1973). International Trade Aspects of the Corporation Income Tax, CREG
Memo No. 168, Stanford Univ., Stanford, California.

Krzyzaniak, M. (1967). The Long-Run Burden of a General Tax on Profits in a Neo-Classical World, *Public Finance* **22** (4), 472–491.

McLure, Ch. E. (1969). The Inter-Regional Incidence of Regional Taxes, *Public Finance* **24** (3), 457–483.

Myers, M. G. (1970). Equilibrium Growth and Capital Movements between Open Economies, *American Economic Review* **60**, 393–397.

Oniki, H., and Uzawa, H. (1965). Patterns of Trade and Investment in a Dynamic Model of International Trade, *Review of Economic Studies* **42**, 15–38.

Sato, R. (1963). Fiscal Policy in a Neo-Classical Growth Model: An Analysis of Time Required for Equilibrating Adjustment, *Review of Economic Studies* **30**, 16–23.

Sato, R., and Hoffman, R. F. (1974). Tax Incidence in a Growing Economy, in *Public Finance and Stabilization Policy* (W. L. Smith and J. M. Culbertson, eds.). Amsterdam: North-Holland Publ.

Solow, R. (1956). A Contribution to the Theory of Economic Growth, *Quarterly Journal of Economics* **70**, 65–94.

Michael J. Boskin
Department of Economics
Stanford University
Stanford, California
and
National Bureau
of Economic Research
Cambridge, Massachussetts

Philippe R. De Ville
Catholic University of Louvain
Louvain, Belgium

Further Evidence on the Relationship Between International Reserves and World Inflation*

H. Robert Heller

1. Introduction

The relationship between changes in international reserves and world-wide inflation was investigated in a recent paper (Heller, 1976). The basic hypothesis presented was that the sharp increase in international reserves in the early 1970s helped to precipitate a world-wide monetary expansion that was an important causal factor in the ensuing global inflation.

* This paper was written while the author was Chief of the Financial Studies Division of the International Monetary Fund. The opinions expressed are those of the author and do not necessarily reflect those of the International Monetary Fund or the Bank of America, where the author is now Vice President for International Economics. Mr. Kellett Hannah was responsible for the computer work.

Several reasons provide the impetus to take another look at the evidence presented in that paper: the availability of a qualitatively improved data base, data covering a more recent time period, and new data allowing us to take explicitly into account the effects of international reserve changes on base money and through it on the money supply and ultimately world inflation. Also, the current paper utilizes path analysis to explore the relationship between the major aggregates in greater detail.

2. The Data

The concept of the world money supply, which is of crucial importance for our purposes, has been the subject of much attention in recent years. Some economists argue that the concept of the world money supply has meaning and relevance only under a fixed exchange rate system, and question its usefulness under a flexible exchange rate system. These economists claim that, under flexible exchange rates, national money supplies are determined exogenously by the monetary authorities of the individual countries and that it makes little sense to add up these independently determined money supplies into a world aggregate.

Under all exchange rate regimes, individual households and firms may have an interest in global aggregates, such as the world rate of inflation, world real income, and world money income. This interest arises from the fact that many decisions in an open economy will be influenced by developments taking place in other parts of the world. It has become recognized that flexible exchange rates provide only a partial insulation from external real and monetary disturbances, and that inflation in other countries may have an impact on economic developments in the country under consideration. The same holds true for changes in income abroad.

Recently, Day and Heller (1977) developed alternative concepts of the world money supply that take account of the various exchange arrangements that might influence the appropriate measurement of the world money supply. Under fixed exchange rates and with endogenous money supplies, the impact of monetary policy changes in one country on world inflation is independent of the velocity of circulation in that country. The appropriate way to measure the world money supply expansion in a given year is therefore to weight each country's monetary expansion rate by the nation's money stock (in the previous period). Under flexible exchange rates, velocity differences do matter, and increases in the world money stock should be calculated by weighting each country's monetary expansion rate by that country's national income.[1]

[1] For a theoretical analysis of these assertions, see Day and Heller (1977).

The data actually used here are annual percentage changes of the various global aggregates, using averages of monthly data to arrive at annual average percentage changes. The period is 1958–1975, and the data pertain to the western world. Both moving gross domestic product (GDP) weights and moving money weights are utilized for base money M_B, the narrow money stock M_1, and the broadly defined money stock M_2. The other variables are the percentage changes in the average annual stock of international reserves R and the rate of increase of the world consumer price index P.

3. Reserve Changes and the Monetary Base

There are three links in the chain that relate changes in international reserves to observed changes in prices:

(1) the effect of reserve changes on the monetary base,

(2) the effect of changes in base money on the quantity of money in existence, and

(3) the effect of changes in the quantity of money on the rate of inflation.

We will examine each of these links in turn and also present evidence on the truncated relationship between reserve changes and world inflation.

Changes in international reserves can be caused by several factors, most of which do have a direct monetary impact. An inflow of reserves that results from a balance of payments transaction will have a direct monetary impact because the purchase of the reserve assets—be they foreign exchange or gold—by the central bank will necessarily involve the payment of a quid pro quo, which, in general, is a liability of the central bank. Increases in central bank liabilities result in an increase of the monetary base. A major exception to this is a special drawing right (SDR) allocation, because an SDR allocation is customarily not monetized, although there is nothing that would prevent a country from doing so. It may be worth noting that an increase in International Monetary Fund (IMF) quotas does not have a direct effect on the unconditional international reserves of a country since only the quota payments made with reserve assets will be reflected in the IMF Reserve Position of the country. Reserve assets as conventionally defined will not change although conditional reserves increase. In addition to the direct monetary consequences of a reserve change, there may be indirect effects in the countries that gain reserves as they may feel less constrained in the design of their economic policies.

Table 1 shows the various source components of reserve changes for the years 1968–1975. The data show clearly the dominant role played by changes in foreign exchange reserves. In every year, changes in foreign exchange were the largest source component, totaling SDR 118.6 billion over the 1968–1975 period on a net annual basis. In contrast, changes in the gold component amounted only to SDR 4.3 billion, changes in SDRs equaled SDR 9.0 billion, and changes in the IMF Reserve Position totaled SDR 9.9 billion. These data clearly establish the dominant role of the foreign exchange component as a source of reserve changes.

Changes in the book value of reserve assets do not have a direct balance of payments or monetary impact as they do not involve international transactions. Of course, these valuation changes can be monetized as well. This practice has been followed by the United States on the occasion of the two dollar devaluations, when the Treasury asked the Federal Reserve to credit its account with an amount equal to the increase in the book value of the United States gold stock. Under these circumstances there will be a monetary impact if the Treasury spends the proceeds. Valuation changes of reserves amounted to a net total of SDR 10.3 billion for the world in the 1968–1975 period. The largest changes were accounted for by the two dollar devaluations in 1971 and 1973. Over the entire period covered by the study (1959–1975) valuation changes played an even less important role, since the value of the United States dollar, as the major reserve currency, did not change prior to 1971. We may therefore be justified in neglecting valuation changes and SDR allocations as a source of reserve changes and will use changes in total reserves as representing balance of payments flows resulting in monetary changes.

An increase in international reserves, that is a purchase of foreign as-

TABLE 1

Sources of Changes in International Reserves, 1968–1975[a,b]

Sources of changes	1968	1969	1970	1971	1972	1973	1974	1975
Gold	−0.6	0.2	−1.9	−1.1	−0.3	—	−0.1	−0.1
SDRs	—	—	3.1	2.8	2.8	0.1	0.1	−0.1
IMF reserve position	0.7	0.2	1.0	−1.3	—	−0.2	2.7	3.8
Foreign exchange	3.0	0.6	12.4	34.1	20.8	14.9	25.9	6.9
Valuation changes	—	−0.1	—	−4.4	—	−8.8	−0.8	3.8
Total	3.2	0.9	14.6	30.0	23.3	6.0	27.8	14.4

[a] In billions of SDRs.
[b] IMF, *Annual Report* (1975, 1976).

sets by the central bank paid for with its own currency, will result in an increase in the liabilities of the central bank. Central bank liabilities are "high powered" base money that can be held either directly by the public in the form of currency or by the commercial banks as a liquid asset.

The following regression equations show the relationship between percentage changes in international reserves R lagged by 1 year, and percentage changes in base money:

$$M_B(M) = 7.39 + 0.36R_{t-1}, \tag{1}$$
$$(8.56)^{**} \quad (4.45)^{**}$$
$$R^2 = 0.57, \quad DW = 1.61,$$

$$M_B(Y) = 7.65 + 0.33R_{t-1}, \tag{2}$$
$$(9.39)^{**} \quad (4.31)^{**}$$
$$R^2 = 0.55, \quad DW = 1.48.$$

The world base money concept utilized, $M_B(M)$, is weighted in Eq. (1) by the national money supplies and, as pointed out earlier, is appropriate for a fixed exchange rate system. The base money concept used in Eq. (2), $M_B(Y)$, utilizes national income weights and is appropriate for a flexible exchange rate system. The equations show that an increase in reserves of one percentage point will result on average in an increase of 0.36 (money weighted) or 0.33 (income weighted) percentage points of the global monetary base in the following period. The coefficient of determination shows that slightly more than half the variance of the dependent variable is explained by the independent variable. The Durbin–Watson (DW) statistics indicate no presence of autocorrelation at the 0.99 level. The numbers in parentheses are the t statistics of the coefficients. Single asterisks indicate a significance at the 0.95 level, while double asterisks indicate significance at the 0.99 level.

The procedure followed in determining the lag structure was to include a reasonable range of lagged independent variables in the regression and to isolate the most significant coefficient by following a stepwise regression routine. In the equations relating changes in base money to changes in international reserves only the reserve coefficient lagged by 1 year was statistically significant at the 0.99 level. No other lagged coefficients were significant at the 0.95 level.

The difference between the regressions using the money weighted [Eq. (1)] and income weighted [Eq. (2)] base money series is very slight. This shows that there is only a negligible divergence between the alternative world base money supply concepts pertaining to fixed and flexible exchange rate systems. Of course, this does not imply that the effects of reserve increase will be identical under fixed and flexible exchange rates—it merely means that the alternative concepts of the world monetary base appropriate for either exchange rate regime do not *in themselves* result in different estimates.

There is also a very real question regarding the extent to which intervention in foreign exchange markets has diminished during the period of floating exchange rates. The vast majority of countries still maintain the value of their currency in terms of an external norm—be it another currency, the SDR, or another currency basket. On 30 June 1976 a total of 93 IMF member countries followed one or the other pegging practice. On that same date, 32 member countries did not maintain the value of their currency within specified margins. It should also be noted that since the advent of generalized floating there has been massive intervention in the foreign exchange markets. It was reported that official foreign exchange market intervention totaled $172 billion in the period March 1973–January 1977 (FRB, 1977). The effects of this large-scale intervention were clearly stated in the *Report for the Year 1976* (Deutsche Bundesbank, 1977):

> During the phases of particular exchange rate unrest, . . . German banks received especially large amounts of short-term funds from abroad; this contributed greatly to the pressure on exchange rates and ultimately, owing to the interventions, to the foreign exchange inflow to the Bundesbank. . . .
>
> In 1976, more than in the preceding years, the Bundesbank was obliged to intervene on the exchange market over prolonged periods. . . . As a result of such transactions the Bundesbank's net external assets grew by DM 8.8 billion in 1976 [p. 35].

The Bundesbank expressed concern over the effects of these foreign exchange inflows in the spring of 1976 on the targeted growth of central bank money and stated that the "serious" overshooting of the monetary growth target in the second half of 1976 was "no doubt partly attributable to the after-effects of the expansionary stimuli received from abroad in the spring [p. 16]."

One may be surprised about the finding of a 1-year lag between an increase in international reserves and increases in base money. Of course, the use of world-wide yearly data is a rather crude yardstick with which to assess these complex relationships. All that is indicated is that the average lag is somewhere between 6 and 18 months. In this connection it is interesting that also the Bundesbank finds a relationship between the external stimuli in the *spring* of 1976 and the expansion of central bank money in the *second* half of the same year [p. 16] which supports our finding of a lagged—rather than instantaneous—relationship between reserves and the monetary base. The existence of a lagged relationship may also reflect the effects of the indirect and policy-related factors rather than the direct mechanical influence of reserve changes on the monetary base.

4. The Monetary Base and the Money Stock

In most countries there is a close correspondence between changes in the monetary base and changes in the money stock. However, it should be noted that this association is not perfect. While the monetary authorities can have a direct impact on the monetary base, other factors—such as commercial bank and nonbank-sector behavior—also have an important bearing on the stock of money in existence at any moment in time.[2] The simple relationships estimated in the following equations show that there is a very close connection between changes in the world monetary base M_B and the world money supply—either narrowly (M_1) or broadly (M_2) defined:

$$M_1(M) = 2.29 + 0.69 M_B(M), \tag{3}$$
$$(2.87)^* \quad (9.13)^{**}$$
$$R^2 = 0.85, \quad DW = 2.34,$$

$$M_1(Y) = 2.87 + 0.69 M_B(Y), \tag{4}$$
$$(3.07)^{**} \quad (7.77)^{**}$$
$$R^2 = 0.80, \quad DW = 2.41,$$

$$M_2(M) = 4.31 + 0.77 M_B(M), \tag{5}$$
$$(3.97)^{**} \quad (7.84)^{**}$$
$$R^2 = 0.80, \quad DW = 2.12,$$

$$M_2(Y) = 3.72 + 0.89 M_B(Y), \tag{6}$$
$$(3.51)^{**} \quad (8.84)^{**}$$
$$R^2 = 0.83, \quad DW = 2.60.$$

Furthermore, the relationships hold both for the money- [Eqs. (3) and (5)] and the income- [Eqs. (4) and (6)] weighted series. The regression coefficients vary between 0.69 and 0.89 depending on the monetary concepts utilized. In all cases the regression coefficients are significant at the 0.01 level, and all coefficients of determination are 0.80 or higher. No significant autocorrelation is present. What may be surprising is that the relationship between changes in the monetary base and changes in the money supply in the hands of the public seems to be "instantaneous" as indicated by the absence of lags in Eqs. (3)–(6). Here again the use of annual data may obscure the existence of a short lag.

[2] See Burger (1971) for a review of the money supply process.

Taken together with the lag of 1 year found in the relationship between changes in international reserves and changes in the monetary base, and the zero lag between changes in the base and changes in the money stock, we find a total lag of 1 year in the relationship between changes in international reserves and changes in the money supply. This is in agreement with the findings of our earlier study (Heller, 1976, p. 73), in which we also determined that there is a 1-year lag between changes in reserves and changes in the money supply when we used annual data and a lag of 3.8 quarters using quarterly data.

5. The Relationship between Money and Prices

The final link in our chain connecting changes in reserves, the monetary base, money, and prices, is the relationship between money and prices. The price concept utilized is the average annual change in world consumer prices as published regularly by *International Financial Statistics*. As independent variable we used the various money supply concepts introduced earlier. The four relevant regressions are given in the following equations and again show very similar results for the different weighting schemes:

$$P = -2.38 + 1.01M_1(M)_{t-2}, \tag{7}$$
$$(1.99) \quad (7.58)^{**}$$
$$R^2 = 0.80, \quad DW = 2.26,$$

$$P = -3.81 + 1.11M_1(Y)_{t-2}, \tag{8}$$
$$(2.42)^* \quad (6.60)^{**}$$
$$R^2 = 0.74, \quad DW = 2.09,$$

$$P = -3.62 + 0.88M_2(M)_{t-2}, \tag{9}$$
$$(2.46)^* \quad (6.94)^{**}$$
$$R^2 = 0.78, \quad DW = 2.05,$$

$$P = -4.05 + 0.86M_2(Y)_{t-2}, \tag{10}$$
$$(2.50)^* \quad (6.53)^{**}$$
$$R^2 = 0.75, \quad DW = 2.01.$$

The regression coefficients are near unity for the narrow money supply and somewhat below unity for the broader money stock concept. The coefficients of determination are all above 0.74, and the regression coefficients are all significant at the 0.99 level. Autocorrelation again presents no problems.

It may be worth emphasizing that both the money weighted money supply concept relevant for fixed exchange rates and the income weighted concept appropriate for flexible exchange rate systems again yielded very similar regression coefficients. The best results were achieved with a 2-year lag between money changes and price changes. These results are consistent with those obtained in the earlier study (Heller, 1976, pp. 77–78), in which we also established a 2-year lag for the annual data and a lag of slightly more than $1\frac{1}{2}$ years using quarterly data.

6. Regression Path Analysis

A check on the internal consistency of our results may be performed by estimating directly the relationship between reserve changes and money supply changes and also the relationship between base money and prices. As a further check on the overall accuracy of the results, we can directly relate the changes in international reserves to the world rate of inflation. Only these latter results are discussed in detail in the main body of the paper, but the relevant regressions on the intermediate links are presented in the Appendix.

The relationship between global international reserve changes and changes in world consumer prices is estimated as

$$P = \underset{(11.22)**}{3.31} + \underset{(2.30)}{0.07R} - \underset{(1.39)}{0.06R_{t-1}} + \underset{(2.88)*}{0.14R_{t-2}}$$
$$+ \underset{(4.67)**}{0.22R_{t-3}} + \underset{(2.56)*}{0.10R_{t-4},} \tag{11}$$
$$R^2 = 0.98, \quad DW = 1.75.$$

In this equation we allow reserve changes of the current year and the previous 4 years to influence changes in world consumer prices. While the coefficients for reserve changes lagged by 2, 3, and 4 years are significant at the 0.95 level, only the 3-year coefficient is significant at the 0.99 level. It may therefore be reasonable to approximate the relationship by a truncated regression using only reserve changes lagged by 3 years as representative of the entire lag structure:

$$P = \underset{(12.13)**}{4.02} + \underset{(12.50)**}{0.37R_{t-3},} \tag{12}$$
$$R^2 = 0.93, \quad DW = 1.53.$$

Also, this coefficient is significant at the 0.99 level. The coefficient of determination in both equations (11) and (12) is very high, and autocorrelation presents no problem. We may conclude that there is a mean lag of approximately 3 years between changes in global international reserves and changes in world consumer prices. This finding is in agreement with our previous study where we found a lag of $2\frac{1}{2}$ to $4\frac{1}{2}$ years to be operative (Heller, 1976, p. 84).

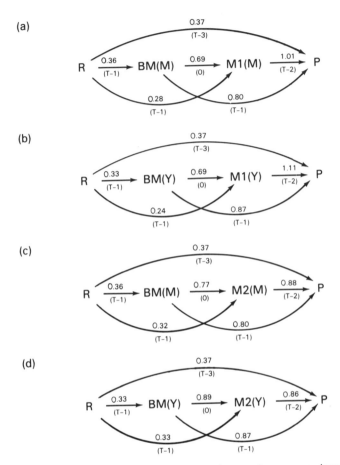

Figure 1 The relationship between percentage changes in reserves, base money, money, and prices.

These regression estimates along with those presented in the Appendix permit us to check on the consistency of the different regression coefficients and to further document the chain of causality by the use of regression path analysis.[3] In Fig. 1 we show the relationship between changes in global international reserves, changes in world base money, changes in the world money supply, and changes in world consumer prices. The four different concepts of the world money supply introduced previously are employed: in Fig. 1a, the narrow money weighted by national money supplies $M_1(M)$, and in Fig. 1b, M_1 weighted by national incomes $M_1(Y)$;

[3] For an introduction to path analysis, see Duncan (1966).

in Fig. 1c, the broadly defined money supply weighted by the national money supply $M_2(M)$, and in Fig. 1d, the broad money supply weighted by national income $M_2(Y)$. There are two concepts of the base money supply: the national-money-weighted series in Figs. 1a and 1c and the national-income-weighted series in Figs. 1b and 1d. The numbers above the arrows in the figure give the coefficients showing the effect of a 1% increase in the independent variable on the dependent variable. The numbers below the arrows represent the estimated number of years intervening in the respective relationships.

A few observations are in order. First, there is a striking similarity among the coefficients in Figs. 1a–1d. This may be taken to imply either that there is not much difference between the alternative money and base money concepts employed or that there are only slight differences between the exchange rate regimes for which the alternative concepts are relevant. It will be recalled that we argued that the money-weighted series depicted in Figs. 1a and 1c are relevant for a fixed exchange rate system, while the income-weighted series utilized in Figs. 1b and 1d are more appropriate for the flexible exchange rate system.

Second, the sizes of the coefficients estimated for the alternative pathways in Figs. 1a–1d are more or less consistent. This robustness of the results could not be achieved with the fixed-weight monetary series utilized in the previous paper. Sweeney and Willett (1977, p. 302) noted that the inconsistent results achieved with the fixed-weight money series did not inspire confidence in the estimates and questioned the validity of the results. An inspection of Figs. 1a–1d shows that the results from the data using annually reweighted money supply series are generally very consistent. For instance, in Fig. 1a the impact coefficient of R on $M_1(M)$ estimated directly is 0.28, while it can be calculated as being equal to 0.25 on the basis of the linkage through $M_B(M)$. Similarly, the impact coefficient of $M_B(M)$ on P is estimated to be equal to 0.80, while the one calculated on the basis of the linkage through $M_1(M)$ is equal to 0.70. Finally, the estimated coefficient for the impact of R on P is equal to 0.37, while the one calculated on the basis of the chain relationship is equal to 0.25. Similar observations pertain to the relationships shown in the other parts of the figure.

7. The Industrial and the Developing Countries Considered Separately

One may argue that it is inappropriate for the purposes of this analysis to include the United States in the aggregates because the United States monetary base is not—or only is minimally—affected by changes in United States international reserves. Furthermore, changes in United States reserves have been minimal in the last few years. A reexamination of the empirical conclusions excluding the United States also gives us an opportunity to study the robustness of the relationships for different country groupings.

Here we present further empirical results on the relationships studied for two country groupings: (1) the industrialized countries, excluding the United States, and (2) all developing countries combined.

Most of the developing countries still adhere to fixed exchange rates, and according to our previous argument, money-weighted data series are more appropriate under fixed exchange rates. A large number of the industrialized countries—especially the larger ones—have adopted flexible exchange rates, and the income-weighted concept is therefore to be preferred for these countries. The estimates for the industrialized countries are

$$M_B(Y) = \begin{matrix} 8.18 \\ (9.63)^{**} \end{matrix} + \begin{matrix} 0.20R_{t-2}, \\ (3.99)^{**} \end{matrix} \tag{13}$$
$$R^2 = 0.50, \qquad DW = 2.12,$$

$$M_1(Y) = \begin{matrix} 9.30 \\ (3.89)^{**} \end{matrix} + \begin{matrix} 0.53M_B(Y), \\ (2.39)^* \end{matrix} \tag{14}$$
$$R^2 = 0.26, \qquad DW = 1.68,$$

$$M_2(Y) = \begin{matrix} 6.68 \\ (4.89)^{**} \end{matrix} + \begin{matrix} 0.58M_B(Y), \\ (4.62)^{**} \end{matrix} \tag{15}$$
$$R^2 = 0.57, \qquad DW = 1.74,$$

$$P = \begin{matrix} -3.46 \\ (1.49) \end{matrix} + \begin{matrix} 0.65M_1(Y)_{t-3}, \\ (4.27)^{**} \end{matrix} \tag{16}$$
$$R^2 = 0.60, \qquad DW = 1.04,$$

$$P = \begin{matrix} -7.52 \\ (4.28)^{**} \end{matrix} + \begin{matrix} 1.04M_2(Y)_{t-2}, \\ (7.93)^{**} \end{matrix} \tag{17}$$
$$R^2 = 0.84, \qquad DW = 2.20,$$

$$P = \begin{matrix} 0.81 \\ (0.81) \end{matrix} + \begin{matrix} 0.06R \\ (1.77) \end{matrix} + \begin{matrix} 0.03R_{t-1} \\ (0.75) \end{matrix} + \begin{matrix} 0.06R_{t-2} \\ (1.57) \end{matrix}$$
$$+ \begin{matrix} 0.13R_{t-3} \\ (3.67)^{**} \end{matrix} + \begin{matrix} 0.16R_{t-4}, \\ (4.43)^{**} \end{matrix} \tag{18}$$
$$R^2 = 0.78, \qquad DW = 0.27,$$

and those for the developing countries are

$$M_B(M) = 14.64 + 0.38R_{t-1}, \tag{19}$$
$$(7.73)^{**} \ (4.51)^{**}$$
$$R^2 = 0.56, \qquad DW = 1.49,$$

$$M_1(M) = 6.21 + 0.67M_B(M), \tag{20}$$
$$(7.27)^{**} \ (16.99)^{**}$$
$$R^2 = 0.95, \qquad DW = 1.21,$$

$$M_2(M) = 4.51 + 0.88M_B(M), \tag{21}$$
$$(3.26)^{**} \ (13.63)^{**}$$
$$R^2 = 0.92, \qquad DW = 1.04,$$

$$P = -6.46 + 1.18M_1(M), \tag{22}$$
$$(2.17)^* \ (8.03)^{**}$$
$$R^2 = 0.80, \qquad DW = 1.03,$$

$$P = -2.49 + 0.87M_2(M), \tag{23}$$
$$(0.89) \ (7.18)^{**}$$
$$R^2 = 0.76, \qquad DW = 0.82,$$

$$P = 10.61 + 0.17R + 0.26R_{t-1}, \tag{24}$$
$$(5.80)^{**} \ (2.13)^* \ (3.38)^{**}$$
$$R^2 = 0.62, \qquad DW = 0.77.$$

Starting with the industrial countries, we find that in Eq. (13) the regression coefficient relating base money changes to reserve changes to be smaller (0.20) than for the world as a whole (0.36). Also, the lag is longer, a finding that is somewhat surprising. The coefficients of the industrial countries relating the money supply to base money are also somewhat smaller than for the world as a whole. For the narrow money supply we have a coefficient of 0.53 instead of 0.69, and for the broader definition of money we find 0.58 instead of 0.89. Turning to the relationship between the money supply and prices, we find that a 1% increase in the narrow money supply will increase prices by 0.65% (as opposed to 1.01% for the world as a whole). The respective coefficients for the broadly defined money supply are 1.04 for the industrial countries (excluding the United States) and 0.86 for the world. It should be noted that all coefficients, save one, are significant at the 0.99 level, with the remaining one significant at the 0.95 level.

Considering the relationship between changes in reserves and consumer prices directly, we find that a 1% increase in reserves will result after 4 years in a cumulative price increase of 0.39% [Eq. (18)]. It is interesting to note that the main impact occurs in the third and fourth years. This is mainly due to the lagged response of prices to monetary changes, which averages 2–3 years according to Eqs. (16) and (17).

Turning to the developing countries, we find rather similar results. The impact of reserve changes on base money [Eq. (19)], however, is stronger than in the industrial countries. A 1% increase results a year later in a 0.32% increase in base money. This is indicative of the fact that reserve changes have a larger influence on monetary developments in the developing countries than in the industrial countries. The relationship between reserve money and the monetary aggregates is very similar to that for the world as a whole. The regression coefficients for the narrow money supply are 0.67 for the developing countries and 0.69 for the world. For the broadly defined money supply they are 0.88 and 0.77, respectively. The relationship between money and prices is also as expected: a 1% increase in the narrow money stock results in a price increase of 1.18% in the developing countries (1.01 for the world as a whole), while a 1% increase in the broadly defined money stock results in a 0.87% increase of consumer prices for the developing countries compared to a 0.86% inflation rate for the world as a whole. Every single regression coefficient for the developing countries is significant at the 1% level.

The reduced-form relationship between reserve changes and prices for the developing countries is shown in Eq. (24). According to this estimate, a 1% increase in reserves results in a cumulative price change of 0.44% within a year. Further lagged coefficients are not significant.

The results for the developing countries and the industrial countries (excluding the United States) are comfortably close to the estimates for the world as a whole, showing that the relationships between reserves, money, and prices are valid globally as well as regionally. However, a noticeable difference is found in the length of the lags, which are estimated to be much shorter in the developing countries than in the industrial countries.

8. Conclusions

Further evidence has been presented on the relationship among increases in global international reserves, changes in world base money, changes in the world money supply, and international inflation. It is argued that changes in international reserves result in significant changes in the monetary base and the money supply. In turn, the money supply— broadly or narrowly defined—has an important lagged effect on consumer prices. Various newly developed concepts of world base money and the world money supply were utilized in the estimates.

We found empirical evidence supporting the existence of a significant lagged relationship between changes in global international reserves and changes in world prices. A 1% increase in reserves is estimated to result in a cumulative price increase of approximately $\frac{1}{2}$% within 4 years. The relationship holds on a world-wide level as well as for the industrial countries and developing countries separately. However, the lag in the relationship appears to be shorter for the developing countries than for the industrial countries.

Appendix

The Relationship between International Reserves and Money

$$M_1(M) = \begin{array}{c} 7.16 \\ (11.70)^{**} \end{array} + \begin{array}{c} 0.28R_{t-1}, \\ (4.86)^{**} \end{array} \tag{A1}$$
$$R^2 = 0.61, \quad DW = 1.69,$$

$$M_1(Y) = \begin{array}{c} 7.97 \\ (12.57)^{**} \end{array} + \begin{array}{c} 0.24R_{t-1}, \\ (4.22)^{**} \end{array} \tag{A2}$$
$$R^2 = 0.54, \quad DW = 1.48,$$

$$M_2(M) = \begin{array}{c} 9.49 \\ (13.70)^{**} \end{array} + \begin{array}{c} 0.32R_{t-1}, \\ (4.97)^{**} \end{array} \tag{A3}$$
$$R^2 = 0.62, \quad DW = 1.69,$$

$$M_2(Y) = \begin{array}{c} 10.23 \\ (13.71)^{**} \end{array} + \begin{array}{c} 0.33R_{t-1}, \\ (4.75)^{**} \end{array} \tag{A4}$$
$$R^2 = 0.60, \quad DW = 1.56.$$

The Relationship between Base Money and Prices

$$P = \begin{array}{c} -1.62 \\ (1.86) \end{array} + \begin{array}{c} 0.80M_B(M)_{t-1}, \\ (9.58)^{**} \end{array} \tag{A5}$$
$$R^2 = 0.87, \quad DW = 1.86,$$

$$P = \begin{array}{c} -2.36 \\ (2.66)^* \end{array} + \begin{array}{c} 0.87M_B(Y)_{t-1}, \\ (10.24)^{**} \end{array} \tag{A6}$$
$$R^2 = 0.88, \quad DW = 1.85.$$

References

Burger, A. E. (1971). *The Money Supply Process.* Belmont, California: Wadsworth.
Day, W. H. L., and Heller, H. R. (1977). The World Money Supply: Concept and Measurement, *Weltwirtschaftliches Archiv,* 113, No. 4, 1977.
Deutsche Bundesbank (1977). *Report for the Year 1976,* Frankfurt.

Duncan, O. D. (1966). Path Analysis: Sociological Examples, *The American Journal of Sociology* **72**, July.

FRB (1977). *International Letter,* Federal Reserve Bank of Chicago (March 11).

Heller, H. R. (1976). International Reserves and World-Wide Inflation, IMF *Staff Papers* **23** No. 1, March.

Sweeney, R. J., and Willett, T. D. (1977). Eurodollars, Petrodollars, and World Liquidity and Inflation, *Journal of Monetary Economics* (Supplement on Stabilization of the Domestic and International Economy).

Bank of America, N.T.&S.A.
San Francisco, California

Commodity Reserve Money, Special Drawing Rights, and the Link to Less-Developed Countries

Ronald I. McKinnon

Newly created reserves should be issued by the International Monetary Fund (IMF) against the security of member countries' currencies.

At first, however, these Fund Obligations would be restricted in use and handed over to the International Development Association. The IDA would use them to finance investment projects of developing countries approved by the World Bank's regular screening machinery as technically feasible and economically sound; but giving priority to projects least likely to generate hard-currency earnings and therefore least suitable for financing by loans.

Once the developing countries spent the Fund Obligations, they would become unrestricted reserves, as good as gold, spendable and acceptable in all member countries.

Tibor Scitovsky (1966)[1]

[1] For other writings with a similar theme, see Scitovsky (1965, 1969).

249

1. Introduction

In the company of other very eminent economists, (Keynes, 1943; Stamp, 1958; Triffin, 1971), Scitovsky has advocated a symmetrically "international" money that would replace the widespread use of national monies such as the United States dollar. The monetary basis for world trade since 1945 has been an evolving dollar standard—complemented by a firm commitment to currency convertibility on the part of noncommunist industrial economies.[2] In displacing the dollar or any key national currency from this international role, Scitovsky (1966) has argued that there is a seigniorage gain to be had—and the resulting availability of real resources to the new issuer of international money should properly be placed at the disposal of less-developed countries.

Since the breakdown of the sterling-gold exchange standard in 1931, dozens of schemes for introducing a more purely international money—with no particular national origin—have been proposed. By and large these proposals tend to be variants on two broad themes:

(1)   an international *commodity-reserve currency,* of which the gold standard is but a special case; and

(2)   an international *fiat money* of which the Special Drawing Rights (SDR) facility of the International Monetary Fund (IMF) is an example.

Informed concern for the welfare of less-developed countries has characterized much of Scitovsky's academic career. His book, *Industry and Trade in Some Developing Countries: A Comparative Study* (see Little *et al.,* 1970) is a classic reference work for anyone wishing to distinguish good from bad economic practices within poor countries.

Here, however, I respectfully disagree with Scitovsky regarding liquidity shortages in the world and the practical feasibility of issuing a "purely" international money under either (1) or (2) above. More fundamentally, perhaps, I deny the existence of a pure seigniorage gain to be had that could be "linked" to significant real income transfers in favor of less-developed countries. Scitovsky has advocated an international fiat money, but not a commodity-reserve currency. However, valuation problems are such that the two are usefully analyzed together.

2. A Commodity-Reserve Currency?

A full-bodied commodity-reserve currency is one in which commodities themselves circulate—such as gold and silver coins; or it consists of

[2] The full workings of the international dollar standard, and the importance of convertibility for other national monies, are explored by McKinnon (1979), from which some material in this essay has been adapted.

warehouse receipts that are a direct claim on a given stock of commodities, measured by their weight and fineness. The volume of such money in circulation cannot exceed the stocks of commodities that are held by a monetary authority—the warehouse custodian.

Under a pure gold standard, coins or receipts issued by a bank (goldsmith)—which actually holds the amount of gold printed on the receipts—can both circulate. The amount of "money" in circulation, therefore, depends on the vagaries of goldmining technology and on new discoveries.[3]

A more general commodity-reserve currency is backed by a wider variety of goods which have direct value in use as well as being less subject to uncertainties in the production of or demand for any one of them. All such goods, however, must be sufficiently *homogeneous* to be assayed to a given physical standard that is commonly accepted: Number 1 Northern Red Winter Wheat, 24 carat gold, refined copper of a given grade, and so on. This rather stringent criterion eliminates manufactured goods that are (slightly) heterogenous with respect to function, size and shape, or brand name. Rather few primary commodities—mainly base metals and the most homogeneous of agricultural produce that does not incur unacceptable deterioration in storage—can feasibly be included. Hart's (1976) listing of possible candidates—including commodities suggested by the United Nations Conference on Trade and Development (UNCTAD, 1974)—is reproduced in Table 1.

Only with such homogeneous commodities can the basic monetary unit be defined unambiguously in physical terms, say

1 ounce of gold + 3 ounces of copper + 20 bushels of wheat
+ 18 cwt of frozen porkbellies + 100 cups of coffee + · · ·
= 1 commodity reserve unit (CRU).

The CRU so defined includes these various commodities in *fixed proportions*—sometimes called "symmetalism." Because only quantities are in fixed proportions, relative prices of the underlying commodities are free to vary—as are their absolute prices in CRUs.

More recently, Luke has proposed allowing commodities to be combined in variable proportions, but with purchase prices varying according to a rule such that an acceptable price index of what 1 CRU will buy (in terms of the included commodities) is exactly stabilized (Luke, 1975). Thus, we retain the big advantage of a commodity reserve money: having

---

[3] Any persistent tendency for "too much" gold to be mined so as to cause general price inflation would eventually be stopped by the relative fall in the price of gold that forces the closure of marginal mines; the reverse would be true in the case of too little gold being mined and general price deflation.

TABLE 1

Potential Reserve Commodities for Commodity-Reserve Currency, UNCTAD, and Other Lists[a]

Commodities apparently well standardized and durable in storage				Suggested commodities that may lack standardization and/or durability
Grains, etc.	Other foods	Fibers, etc.	Minerals	
UNCTAD list of 18 commodities[b]				
Wheat	Sugar	Cotton	Copper	Iron ore
Maize	Coffee	Wool	Zinc	Bauxite, alumina
Rice	Tea	Rubber	Tin	
	Cocoa	Jute	Lead	
		Hard fibers[c]		
Additional items with New York Times futures quotations				
Soybeans	Frozen pork bellies	Plywood	Silver	Eggs (shell)
Oats	Frozen orange juice	Lumber		Live beef cattle
Additional items on older lists in literature[d]				
Linseed	Butter	Silk		Tobacco
	Lard	Newsprint		Coal
	Milk, dried	Wood pulp		
Items under UNCTAD consideration[b]				
Groundnuts				Copra
				Palm oil
				Coconut oil

[a] From Hart (1976, p. 6).
[b] UNCTAD (1974, No. 1), Chapter II.
[c] Sisal, henequen, abaca.
[d] Items not listed elsewhere in this table which appear in E. M. Harmon, *Commodity Reserve Currency, The Graham–Goudriaan Proposal for Stabilizing Incomes of Primary Commodity Producers,* (Columbia Studies in the Social Sciences, No. 599), p. 66. New York: Columbia Univ. Press. This list originates with Merrill K. Bennett and Associates, *International Commodity Stockpiling as an Economic Stabilizer,* Food Research Institute, Commodity Policy Studies, No. 8. Stanford, California: Stanford Univ. Press.

a *unit of account* precisely defined in real terms even as paper notes or depository claims are allowed to circulate.

Although technically sophisticated, the additional advantage of Luke's approach is that CRUs (warehouse receipts) can be issued when any *single* homogeneous commodity is tendered to the monetary authority. (Under the old fixed proportions approach, a whole basket had to be tendered— even when some of the commodities in that basket were in short supply.)

The pricing rule is such that, in the aggregate, if more wheat is tendered than copper at some initial set of value weights, the authorities would lower the price of wheat in CRUs and raise that of copper so that the initial value weights are maintained.

Even this neatly generalized version of a commodity reserve currency, however, requires precise homogeneity in each underlying commodity. (Natural rubber of flexible quality would not do.) Along with the additional need to avoid significant deterioration in storage, the total value of the flow of new output of included commodities can, at best, amount to a very small proportion of the world GNP—say, of the order of 5%. [4]

Unlike a pure gold standard that includes the circulation of gold coins, a commodity-reserve money would circulate only as paper notes or as deposit claims. Otherwise, tolerable homogeneity, divisibility, and portability in the medium of exchange would be absent. Who wants to be paid with 10 bushels of soybeans or 100 cans of frozen orange juice? Banknotes worth 10 CRUs would, however, be perfectly acceptable. Presumably, such notes and checking accounts denominated in CRUs would be the only legal tender in international transactions among enterprises, individuals, and governments apart from the money-issuing authority itself. The commodity-reserve bank, of course, would have to stand ready to accept (buy) the designated commodities and issue CRUs in exchange. Indeed, this would be the sole mechanism for increasing the volume of *full-bodied* commodity-reserve currency in monetary circulation.

Should our monetary warehouse[5]—jam packed with a melange of scarce commodities—provide storage facilities for the ordinary commercial merchandising of these commodities? Suppose the buying price exactly equals the selling price—say 0.05 CRU per ounce of copper, and that the storage facilities for copper were "conveniently" located geographically. Then the unwitting monetary authority would be the principal stock holder and source of supply to users, whereas producers would sell all their newly refined copper to the monetary authority for CRUs. The absence of any spread between buying and selling price would amount to a heavy implicit subsidy to having the monetary authority undertake a dominant merchandising role—and to driving all the commercial traders in (stock holders of) refined copper out of business. Much of the monetary authorities holdings would be "working" or "productive" stocks, and hence CRUs issued by the monetary authority—when copper was sold to it—would at least partly reflect this nonmonetary merchandising aspect. It would be analogous to having money issued according to the old *real*

[4] Friedman (1951) makes this necessarily rough estimate.

[5] Of course, one does not have to think of these commodities as all being stored in one physical location.

bills doctrine[6] based on the extension of short-term bank credits for inventory financing, rather than the modern technique of estimating what the social demand for money might be.

Without rehearsing all the well-known faults of the real bills doctrine, comparative advantage seems to suggest that specialist profit seekers in the copper trade are likely to be more efficient merchants than central bankers. And the commodity-reserve bank should disengage from the multiplicity of problems associated with the marketing of copper, groundnuts, wheat, soybeans, and so on by simply imposing a spread that comfortably exceeds the private merchants' "normal" profit margin between buying and selling prices.

For example, the authority might now offer to buy copper for 0.045 CRU and sell it for 0.055 CRU at any point in time with the parity in the middle varying flexibly through time according to Luke's rules. Now the world's stock of refined copper would be partitioned into

(1) the "idle" hoard of the monetary authority that is the real backing for the issue of CRUs, and
(2) the working inventories of copper merchants.

If the price of copper did not tend to move much one way or another, the monetary authority would be neither buying nor selling. Decentralized merchants would service the huge flow of day-to-day transactions associated with copper production and consumption—and similarly with all the other commodities in the monetary basket. Only when the CRU price of copper (or other commodities) tended to fall substantially would copper be tendered to the monetary authority who would issue CRUs in exchange: the supply of copper (and the other commodities) being simply the obverse of the monetary demand for CRUs. And this increase in the "monetary" stock of commodities would be taken out of commercial circulation.

Although not always very clear about it, the older writers (B. Graham, 1944; F. D. Graham, 1942; Hart 1976) seem to advocate this partitioning between the monetary and commercial stocks of the relevant commodities. Unfortunately, this partitioning makes the *social cost* of any substantial issue of CRUs *unacceptably high*. In order for the world money stock in CRUs to expand, valuable physical commodities would be impounded so that they were no longer be available either for consumption or as an intermediate input in production. Suppose the stocks of CRUs were

---

[6] The doctrine that the banking system as a whole should be allowed to expand the money supply freely as long as loans are made for "productive" purposes—largely the purchase of short-term trade bills from sellers of commodity merchandise.

substantial—say 30% of world trade.[7] Besides the incredible initial social cost of building up the commodity stockpile, as the world economy grows 30% of any increase in international trade would be diverted to this monetary hoard!

This heavy social cost would prevent CRUs from being used *voluntarily* as an international means of payment or as a precautionary store of value. The cost to individual nations or firms of acquiring CRU balances net would be too high, and they would continue to exchange national monies directly unless all were simultaneously ruined by some catastrophe such as hyperinflation.

Suppose, however, a very strong international authority imposed an all-inclusive international clearing union, in which each national central bank kept exact tabulations of its international payments and receipts. Then, monthly settlements in CRUs, where bilateral deficits and surpluses were cleared multilaterally,[8] would be forced through the single world clearing bank. Proposals to introduce a commodity-reserve money have (unsurprisingly) been accompanied by the suggestion that nations and individuals be prevented from holding monetary reserves in the form of gold or the currencies of other countries (Hart, 1976, pp. 9–10)—particularly United States dollars. But this dramatically increased role for national central banks in the clearing process would make the imposition of restrictions on trade or capital flows uncomfortably easy! Even under the old fixed-exchange-rate regime of Bretton Woods, the designers were careful to allow a 1% margin of variation on-either side of parity in order that commercial banks and private firms could make day-to-day foreign payment and receipts without reference to the national central bank. To have central banks become the sole intermediaries in the foreign exchanges, in order to ensure the use of commodity-reserve money, would be socially retrogressive.

While retaining its usefulness as a real unit of account, two financial techniques have been suggested for reducing the overwhelming social costs of commodity-reserve money:

(1)   The commodity backing could be *futures contracts* (taking "long" positions) in the relevant commodities, thus avoiding the physical warehousing of the goods.

(2)   Instead of having full-bodied commodity reserve money, one could have *fractional reserves* against outstanding CRU liabilities.

---

[7] Each country held a monetary reserve equal to three or four months of imports.

[8] Perhaps on the model of the old European Payments Union (EPU) where monthly settlements were made in gold or dollars.

If the CRU system ever got going, one could imagine futures trading in homogeneous primary commodities in which these contracts are denominated in CRU. Then the authority could create CRU by buying commodity futures—purchases that provided financial cover for private merchants who did the physical warehousing. No longer would there be a sharp separation between "idle" monetary commodity reserves and "active" merchandising reserves. The net incremental social cost of the CRU system would be reduced because normal working inventories of the commodities would become part of the monetary reserve.[9] This use of futures markets is clouded, however, by subtle problems of contract enforcement in a world subject to crop failures, famines, embargos, etc. If the goods are not actually in the official warehouse, can one count on forward delivery commitments across very diverse countries in the family of nations? Moreover, existing futures trading is mainly organized in national monies—principally the United States dollar. How would the CRU authority operate in national money markets in its purchases or sales of commodity futures?

The second financial technique for economizing involves moving away from a full-bodied commodity-reserve currency. The CRU authority would be empowered to create money by lending CRUs at interest—while keeping sufficient physical commodities as a fractional reserve. The interest earned could possibly offset storage costs so that the whole system yields a modest deposit rate of interest to the holders of CRUs. Indeed, if full-bodied CRUs ever began to circulate successfully, private banking entrepreneurs would emerge who issued their own CRU notes at more attractive interest rates, and kept only modest commodity reserves (say, 10% of deposits) to guard against a run on the bank. (Fractional reserve money, of course, brings with it this new kind of potential instability.) The consequent reduction in the stock of "idle" commodity hoards would be an important social saving.

But any physical commodities that are held as reserves are still costly. The commodity-reserve currency would continue to depend heavily on political sanctions that "force" all international payments or receipts through a centrally supervised and controlled clearing union. Market pressure by private traders would always exist to exchange one (convertible) national currency for another without going through this rather expensive supernational clearing device.

Does the CRU system have any particular advantages in promoting freer international trade? If a common commodity-reserve money was to replace national fiat monies in domestic circulation in each participating

---

[9] Presuming that the normal stocks of commercial inventories of copper exceeded the normal demand by copper users to buy the product forward.

country, the international means of payment would become the same as that within individual nations. With free trade in the underlying commodity basket, free convertibility and stable exchange rates would automatically ensue just as in the case of the classical gold standard. Unfortunately, there is no reason to believe that introducing a commodity-reserve currency as the basis for world trade would encourage an increase in the number of national currencies that are internationally convertible. Would countries in Latin America, Africa, or Asia be more likely to have an open domestic foreign-exchange market in CRUs than in United States dollars? Less-developed countries retain restrictions on convertibility as an adjunct to practicing covert taxation of their national fiat monetary systems. It seems unlikely that they could be persuaded to give up this degree of national monetary autonomy in return for adopting a (socially costly) commodity-reserve currency for domestic circulation that is controlled by an international institution. For the industrial countries with convertible currencies, the expensive CRU system seems somewhat redundant.

Despite some possible benefit as a world price index or unit of account, I conclude that the on-going social costs and the tremendous wrenching of existing institutions for international exchange hardly warrant a commodity-reserve currency as the principal international means of payments or store of value.

Of course, one might well wish to consider international commodity-price stabilization programs *separately,* and consider the holding of some buffer stocks in common. But purchases and sales of individual commodities would use existing national currencies (singly or in combination) as a unit of account and means of payment. It would merely confuse the operation of these buffer stocks to associate them with some notion of creating a new international money.

3. International Fiat Money and Special Drawing Rights

Suppose commodity-reserve currency is deemed infeasible, but one still wants a purely "international" money that is symmetrical in use with respect to all nations: that is not unduly dependent on any one of them. Is it possible for the International Monetary Fund (or similar agency) to issue a relatively costless fiat money that becomes generally acceptable as an international unit of account, means of payment, and store of value? In particular, what are the prospects for the Special Drawing Rights (SDR) facility of the IMF evolving *independently* into the principal form of international money?

Starting with the old European Unit of Account (EUA) worth exactly 1

United States dollar, associated with the European Payments Union in the 1950s, there is some history of "artificial" units of account being used for international purposes. Ascheim and Park (1976) have collated all of these official and private units of account (Table 2) and all are simply composite bundles of individual national currencies. For units of account only, Ascheim and Park develop the concept of "functional currency areas": how different currency baskets are appropriate for various classes of international transactions in a world of fluctuating exchange rates.

TABLE 2

Summary Classification of Artificial Currency Units[a]

Type of ACU[b]	Year of creation	Value tied to	No. of currencies in basket
Official			
EUA			
Old	1950	Gold	—
New	1975	Currency basket	9
SDR			
Old	1970	Gold	—
New	1974	Currency basket	16
AMU	1974	Currency basket	16
Private			
EUA			
Old	1961	Gold	—
New	1972	Gold	—
ECU or EMU	1970	Immutably fixed exchange rates	—
Eurco	1973	Currency basket	9
Arcru	1974	Current exchange rates	8 out of 12
B-Unit	1974	Currency basket	5
IFU	1975	Currency basket	10

[a] From Ascheim and Park (1976, pp. 7–9, 18).
[b] EUA: European Unit of Account.   Eurco: European Composite Unit.
SDR: Special Drawing Rights.   Arcru: Arab Currency-Related Unit.
AMU: Asian Monetary Unit.   B-Unit: Barclays Unit.
{ECU: European Currency Unit.   IFU: International Financial Unit.
{EMU: European Monetary Unit.

1 EUA = DM 0.828 + F 1.15 + £ 0.0885 + Lit 109 + f 0.286 + BF 3.66 + DKr 0.217
           + £ Ir 0.00759 + Lux F 0.14.
1 SDR = $ 0.40 + DM 0.38 + £ 0.045 + F 0.44 + ¥ 26 + Can$ 0.071 + Lit 47
           + f 0.14 + BF 1.6 + SKr 0.13 + $A 0.012 + DKr 0.11 + NKr 0.099
           + Pta 1.1 + S 0.22 + R 0.0082.
1 Eurco = DM 0.90 + F 1.20 + £ 0.075 + Lit 80 + f 0.35 + BF 4.50 + DKr 0.20
           + £ Ir 0.005 + Lux F 0.50.

From being worth exactly one United States dollar in 1950 (although formally specified in terms of gold content), the official EUA changed to a basket of nine currencies of the members of the European Economic Community in 1975. This new unit of account may well be more appropriate for keeping track of budgetary allocations, taxes, common agricultural prices, and so forth within the Community.

Similarly, the SDR was initially valued at exactly US $1.00 in 1970 (again with the pro forma specification in terms of gold content), and then was changed in 1974 to a basket of 16 of the principal world convertible currencies as shown in Table 2. Given the rather large exchange-rate fluctuations of recent times, this basket may be a more appropriate average for determining the contributions that individual members pay to the IMF in terms of their own currencies and for denominating the outstanding value of IMF loans that must be repaid in convertible currency(ies). The amount of these repayments depends on the exchange rate between that currency(ies) and the composite SDR basket at the time the loan is due (Ascheim and Park, 1976):

> Using the daily market exchange rates of the component currencies against the U.S. dollar, the IMF calculates every day the rate for the new SDR in terms of the U.S. dollar by summing up the dollar value of the currency fractions. It then derives rates for the SDR in terms of other currencies by converting the dollar value of the SDR into other currencies at that day's market exchange rates [p. 10].

The SDR unit of account may come into some limited uses outside of the IMF. The International Air Transport Association once considered fixing air fares in a modified version of the SDR, so that ticket agents must recalculate daily the domestic-currency equivalents of these fares.

In parallel, some private currency baskets or units of account, such as the Eurco (Table 2), have been used by banking houses such as N. M. Rothchild and Sons to denominate a few private bond issues—with the loan proceeds and repayments in any convertible currency in accordance with its exchange rate for the basket as a whole. However, these private transactions involving "currency cocktails" remain very minor in comparison to international bond issues denominated in a single currency such as United States dollars or Deutche marks.

Note that a national convertible currency has always been used as a *means of payment* in transactions with the IMF or in private capital markets—even in those functional currency areas where the unit of account is a currency basket. Does this continuing dependency on national monies reflect an inadequacy in our international institutions that could be overcome by some technically skillful "reform" of the IMF articles defining special drawing rights? My tentative answer is that *no* such reform is possible without impinging in an unacceptable way on the freedom of trading enterprises, individuals, and commercial banks to make and receive international payments without restraint. Why should the prior existence of national fiat monies tend to preempt the emergence of any purely international one as a means of payment?

Each national currency is legal tender—has the full force of state sanction requiring people to use it—for the circular flow of production and consumption within each country. The domain for which the demand exists for a *stock* of domestic money is thus quite well defined. Even here, however, each national central bank only controls the real value of its currency indirectly by financial techniques—rather than operating directly in the market for commodities. The purchase of domestic bonds through open-market operations—or through discounting—is a way of adjusting the supply of national money to the estimated demand for it. In a fixed exchange regime, the purchase or sale of foreign exchange is another financial technique for adjusting the stock of domestic money available for people to hold. Although these financial techniques are imprecise, normally the need for domestic money is sufficiently stable so that a reasonably competent monetary authority can tailor[10] the supply of money to approximate the demand—and thus stabilize the purchasing power of the domestic currency in terms of goods and services.

Unfortunately, a "purely" international fiat money has no natural and uniquely defined monetary domain. The nexus of the international exchange of commodities and services is not the exclusive province of any purely international money, because convertible national monies can always be traded directly. There is no equivalent to a "legal tender" provision for international transactions, and thus a stable—indeed any substantial—private demand for SDR is hard to specify. Even if the supply of international money was not in the hands of a huge bureaucracy representing over 100 countries, the world's leading financial wizard could hardly be expected to use open-market operations or discounting successfully to adjust the supply of international money to the elusive (and possibly nonexistent) private demand for it. In short, such an attempt at monetary independence would likely leave indeterminate the real purchasing power of the international money in question.

Governments could collectively establish a demand to hold a stock of international fiat money—as was seen necessary in the case of a commodity reserve currency. An exclusive international clearing union could be

[10] Unless undermined by fiscal inadequacies—such as uncovered government budgeting deficits.

set up among national central banks. Each national authority would monitor all the external payments and receipts of its country. At the end of each month, bilateral deficits and surpluses would be cleared through the union, and net debtors would have to pay up in the SDR or something like it. Alternatively, to allow more scope for direct private exchange, all exporters or sellers of securities would be required to invoice and receive payment exclusively in the international money. All exchange rates would be established in terms of the official international money. The direct use of national monies as a currency of invoice (unit of account) or a means of payment would be forbidden.

This would indeed be establishing international money by fiat! While politically very difficult to administer, in a technical economic sense a stable demand for the international money might well result. Then through judicious financial procedures for money creation, the international central bank might well have a determinate price level for tradable goods.

However, the coercion involved and the increased surveillance (and possibly exchange controls) by national central banks of private trading enterprises—including commercial banks—would hardly encourage freer trade. What is left, therefore, is what we observe. Because of the difficulties of establishing an independent value for international fiat monies, they see very limited use only as units of account whose real purchasing power is linked to convertible national currencies.

4. The Seigniorage Problem and the Link to Less-Developed Countries

Without coercion, perhaps the door can be left open for a purely international money that is held *voluntarily* by private traders and governments because of its attractive yield and liquidity properties. In the case of the SDR, this latter possibility is closely related to the seigniorage problem.

The *Oxford English Dictionary* (1971) defines "seigniorage" as "A duty levied on the coining of money for the purpose of covering the expenses of minting, and as a source of revenue to the crown, claimed by the sovereign by virtue of his prerogative [p. 2712]."

Although the concept of seigniorage is derived from the circulation of gold and silver coins, it can apply to a more general commodity-reserve currency and to purely fiat monies—including the United States dollar in its role as an international vehicle currency. Moreover, the money issuing institution(s) may assign its revenue to various claimants—as with the oft-discussed "link" proposal to assign the seigniorage from the issue of SDR to less-developed countries.

Before going into these highly relevant institutional details, however, let us formulate the revenue or seigniorage flow from the issue of money in its most general form.[11] Consider first the balance sheet of our money-issuing institution: "deposits" are recognized money for international settlements, "reserves" are the backing for deposits outstanding in the form of some more fundamental asset such as commodity reserves, and "investments" refer to interest-bearing assets purchased on an open capital market such that their yield approximates the opportunity cost of capital in the world economy.

Money-Issuing Institution

Assets		Liabilities	
Reserves	R	Deposits	D
Investments	I		

Total assets = Total liabilities

Seigniorage can be considered a flow per year associated with net money issue, or as the present value of all the present and expected future gains to the money-issuing authority. While remembering that seigniorage may well be assigned to claimants on a flow-per-year basis, let us define algebraically the more inclusive present value concept S over the years $1, 2, \ldots, n$:

$$S = \frac{I_1 r_1 - D_1 i_1 - C}{1 + r_1} + \frac{I_2 r_2 - D_2 i_2 - C_2}{(1 + r_1)(1 + r_2)}$$
$$+ \cdots + \frac{I_n r_n - D_n i_n - C_n}{(1 + r_1)(1 + r_2) \cdots (1 + r_n)}, \tag{1}$$

where r is the open-market rate of interest on investments, i the deposit rate of interest accruing to the holders of international money, and C the costs of servicing the outstanding stock of money including the management of deposits, investment, and reserves. Clearly, seigniorage is only positive when $rI - iD - C > 0$ on average (appropriately discounted) through time.

It is important to distinguish between the *nominal* value of seigniorage S and the *real* value S/P, where P is a price index of what money will buy. Despite its overwhelming social cost, a commodity-reserve currency has one big advantage: the real value of the monetary unit—1 CRU—is precisely established in terms of the underlying commodity bundle. P always

---

[11] My analysis draws heavily on Grubel (1969) and Johnson (1969).

equals one. True, that commodity bundle may not be broadly representative of all goods—particularly manufactures—that enter international trade. But the value in use of the unit of account is itself independent of the amount of nominal money actually issued—which is endogenously determined and outside the control of the monetary authority.

Quite different is a national or purely international fiat money whose real value depends heavily on the amount of nominal money issued relative to the demand for it. For example, suppose the real demand to hold the fiat money in question in any period is

$$D/P = L(\underset{+}{Y}, \underset{-}{r} - i), \tag{2}$$

where Y is the relevant flow of real income within the monetary domain. In the international sphere, Y would have to be interpreted as the flow of world trade.

From Eq. (1) by itself, and if $rI + iD - C > 0$, seigniorage appears to increase when more nominal money is issued: I and D rise proportionately. However, the price level P is now an endogenous variable. Suppose at time zero one exactly *doubled* all nominal money currently in existence, and also doubled expected cash balances and investments in the future; i.e., $D_1, D_2, \ldots, D_n, I_1, \ldots, I_n$, and $C_1, \ldots, C_n$ all are doubled. If this is a once-and-for-all change, then both S and P will also double. The *real* value of seigniorage garnered by the money-issuing institution will remain unchanged. Thus, simply issuing more of a purely *independent* (not based on a basket of national currencies) international money, with a market demand to hold it given by Eq. (2), will not necessarily increase the flow of real seigniorage. The multitude of proposals for arbitrarily increasing the distribution of international fiat money often lose sight of this uncomfortable fact.

If one entertains the notion of continuous inflation in the international money—D and P rise through time—then the seigniorage flow may or may not increase depending on how much D/P contracts as r rises.[12] Indeed, the position of (demand for) any purely international money is likely to be so precarious, for the reasons discussed previously, that any substantial continued depreciation in its real purchasing power would drive it out of existence. People would tend to exchange national currencies directly. Thus, in the analysis to follow, assume that the money-issuing institution is restricted to a level of D in each period that is consistent with no price inflation: P is constant or at least rises no faster than the average of competing national currencies. This is true for the SDR, which is tied to a

---

[12] Since the Fisher effect, incorporating the expected rate of inflation, is built into the open-market rates of interest.

basket of national currencies, and has also been true for the United States dollar.

Using Eq. (1), various candidates for international money can now be classified according to their seigniorage flow.

Case I: A Commodity-Reserve Currency For a full-bodied community-reserve currency, we have $R = D$ and $I = 0$. Income flow from investment is zero, and even if deposit holders are paid nothing, positive storage costs imply that the seigniorage flow to the money-issuing authority is negative. In a formal sense, there would be no seigniorage to dispense—although proponents of a commodity-reserve currency often see it as a vehicle for raising the relative prices of those particular products included in the commodity basket. The storage costs of the commodity stockpile would have to be financed by levying taxes elsewhere.

If only fractional commodity reserves are kept against outstanding deposits, then $R < D$ and $I > 0$. For r sufficiently great and C sufficiently small, S could be positive. Thus, the commodity-reserve scheme could pay for itself. Indeed, the severe pressure for a full-bodied commodity-reserve currency to break down into a fractional one, with either official institutions or wildcat private banks garnering some of the resulting seigniorage, was already analyzed.

Case II: A Fully Competitive Fiat Money Suppose there is no more "fundamental" asset, such as commodity reserves, so that $R \approx 0$ and $I \approx D$. The money-issuing institution uses "virtually" all the proceeds from deposit growth (maintaining our assumption of a stable price level) to purchase interest-bearing investments. The cost C of servicing these investments and the cost of settling international payments—say check clearing on the deposit side—includes both the salaries of bankers and a "normal" yield on the capital put up by banking institutions.[13] Under what circumstances would we expect a "competitive" solution: the deposit rate of interest is bid up so that seigniorage is driven to zero?

Under the world dollar standard, the New York banking community and its unregulated progeny—the Eurodollar market—may approximate this competitive solution at the present time. Suppose $rI - iD - C > 0$ so that seigniorage exists in the collecting of deposits and making loans. Then either new banks will be tempted to enter the world money market or existing banks will try to expand their business. In order to do so, a small increase in i will be necessary to attract the new deposits, and this

---

[13] For private banking systems, the owners' equity should appear above on the right-hand side of the balance sheet of the money-issuing institution. However, this would not influence the seigniorage calculation in Eq. (1).

increase in i will continue until $rI - iD - C \approx 0$. Seigniorage has been eliminated.

If a regulatory agency, such as the United States Federal Reserve Bank, successfully placed a direct ceiling on i—or did so indirectly by imposing heavy official reserve requirements (noninterest bearing) against outstanding deposits—then significant positive seigniorage would potentially exist. This seigniorage could be collected by the United States government or be assigned to a private claimant—e.g., a favored group of borrowers. In the 1960s, however, such regulatory efforts were thoroughly undercut by the development of Eurodollar transacting. (The miniscule voluntary reserves held in New York by Eurobanks are the "working" means of payment—and their effect on i is negligible.) Hence, the world-wide use of the dollar as a vehicle currency in private transacting is not associated with a significant flow of seigniorage to the United States, [14] and approximates a fully competitive international fiat money.

Could a monetary claim, such as SDR, on an official international institution become a competitive form of international money in private capital markets? To be voluntarily held as a store of value and means of payment in private portfolios, its deposit yield, liquidity, and stability as a unit of account must approach that of the fully competitive dollar-based system that now exists. Perhaps such properties could be simulated by the IMF directly, or could be farmed out to private banks who use the SDR as a reserve asset. Even then, there are economies of scale in having a single international vehicle currency—and the dollar certainly has a big head start in familiarity and organization.

Presently, however, the question of an internationally competitive SDR is moot. The deposit rate of interest i has been kept artificially low, necessarily confining the circulation of the SDR to official reserves—as we shall discuss.

Case III: Positive Seigniorage and SDR At least for official reserve assets that are only circulated among central banks, we can safely assume that the cost of administering these transfers is close to zero, i.e., $C \approx 0$. Then, the flow of seigniorage depends on keeping i low relative to r—the relevant yield that measures the opportunity cost of capital. When SDR was first introduced as a reserve asset for national central banks in 1970, the effective rate of interest earned was $1\frac{1}{2}\%$ on any accumulation of SDR beyond the initial tranche assigned to each member country; i.e., if country A acquired 100 SDR as a result of a payments surplus with country B,

[14] More debatable is whether foreign official holders of United States Treasury Bills earn a yield i that is "close to" open-market rates of interest. Among the major industrial economies, central banks have agreed not to hold other kinds of dollar assets, and their demand for reserves may unduly depress the yield on United States Treasury bills and bonds.

A would earn $1\frac{1}{2}$ SDR per year on its new holding, whereas country B would pay $1\frac{1}{2}$ SDR per year. Countries could draw down (spend) up to 100% of their initial allocations providing they reconstituted 70% within a few years. Effectively, users of SDR could borrow at $1\frac{1}{2}\%$, and since this was well below open-market rates of interest, *users* would be collecting the seigniorage S as defined in Eq. (1).

More recently, the IMF has raised the deposit rate of interest to approximate a weighted average of the treasury bill yields of the 16 currencies underlying SDR. From this, however, it subtracts a "liquidity" premium. The result is to leave i in the range 4–5%. This still seems significantly less than the relevant "r"—measured, say, by deposit on lending rates of interest in the Eurocurrency market.

In order to prevent all recipients of SDR from selling them in order to acquire foreign-exchange assets with a higher interest yield (thereby collecting the seigniorage), the IMF strictly limits the situations in which SDR can be spent by any one member and assigned to another. The former can only draw down SDR if it has a "genuine" deficit in foreign payments, and are not simply adjusting their portfolios and acquiring other foreign-exchange assets, whereas the latter are required to accept SDRs if they have a genuine balance of payments surplus, and if their existing holdings of SDR are not more than 200% greater than the cumulative sum of their "free" tranches. The free tranches to individual countries are assigned according to IMF quotas (the importance of countries in world trade) if they choose voluntarily to participate in the SDR system.

Are the surplus countries receiving SDR actually paying seigniorage *net* to the deficit ones? The answer depends on the initial conditions.

Suppose, at the existing price level (determined by the purchasing power of the basket of national currencies underlying the SDR), there was a liquidity "shortage." On balance, reserve holdings were felt to be too "low" and the international capital market was such that governments could not borrow freely to build up their liquidity positions. Then the general distribution of SDR—even with a zero yield on the initial free tranche and only 4–5% on incremental earnings—would be attractive to many countries. The "imperfection" in the international capital market would, by hypothesis, foreclose exchanging the SDR for an equally liquid, but higher yielding, foreign-currency assets.

In Fig. 1, dd' represents the steady state demand for international reserves as a function of the spread between the opportunity cost of capital r and the deposit rate i. C is the percentage cost per year of "servicing" a given level of real reserves (deposits) outstanding—and could be close to zero. Let i_b be the initial deposit rate, which is such that $r - i_b > C$; and let a be the arbitrarily given initial reserve holdings that are posited to be

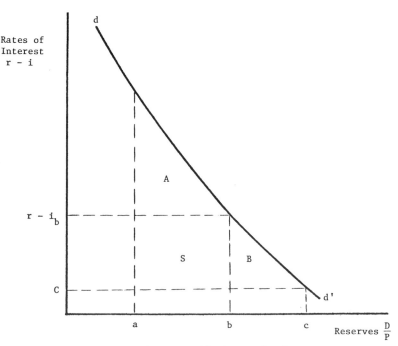

Figure 1   The demand for international reserves.

in short supply. Then, new reserves could be increased from a to b so as to fully satisfy the demand to hold them at the deposit rate of interest i_b. The reserve "shortage" would be eliminated. Insofar as the area under the aggregate demand curve (above the cost of servicing reserves) accurately represents incremental welfare from having international money,[15] the social gain from increasing reserves is simply the triangle A plus the rectangle S.

But who gains and who loses by the increase in reserves? Consider the extreme case in which all the new reserves are given only to those countries with incipient deficits. They are immediately spent and transferred to surplus countries. Then S neatly represents the seigniorage that the monetary authority assigns to the deficit countries—revenue that, in principle, the sovereign monetary authority could have kept for itself. The surplus countries are not effectively taxed because they want the additional reserves to relieve their illiquidity. Indeed, the welfare of the surplus countries rises by the triangle A. Hence everybody is better off as the reserve "shortage" is overcome!

---

[15] An analytical oversimplification that monetary theorists are fond of using.

The foregoing, based on the posited existence of a reserve shortage at the prevailing price level, is the formal analytical argument for the need to introduce the SDR as a reserve asset (store of value). The same argument then justifies the existence of unrequited seigniorage that can be safely assigned to poor (deficit) countries while leaving the wealthy (surplus) countries better off. The argument underlies the famous "link" proposal made by many eminent academic economists such as Stamp, Scitovsky, and Jan Tinbergen on behalf of agencies such as the International Development Association (IDA) and the United National Commission on Trade and Development (UNCTAD). [16] They would link the issue of new international reserve assets such as SDR to development assistance—by giving SDRs directly to poor countries or having the SDR tranches of the wealthy countries assigned to development banks (such as IDA) to increase their capacity to lend on "soft" terms.

What are the counterarguments against this well-intentioned endeavor to improve world welfare and income distribution at the same time? The analytical case for the link rests heavily on the presumption that a reserve shortage now exists at the prevailing world price level: we are at point a in Fig. 1. The international capital market is highly imperfect so that incipient surplus (wealthy) countries cannot borrow at competitive rates of interest—or collectively run trade surpluses—so as to build up their liquidity (official reserve) positions to desired levels. Suppose instead that an open American capital market, together with unregulated Eurocurrency transacting, constitutes a nearly perfect international capital market. The tremendous competitive pressure within this banking system raises deposit rates of interest on highly liquid dollar assets very close to competitive lending rates—save for a small margin that just pays for the bankers' salaries and other costs; i.e., $rl - iD - C \approx 0$. Then we have full liquidity *without* any SDR issue, as represented by point c in Fig. 1. At point c, the international supply of liquidity, D/P is already expanded to its social optimum, given the cost of producing it. World welfare increases by the triangle B in comparison to the suboptimum at b.

This alternative uncomfortable presumption implies that neither seigniorage nor the welfare of the potential surplus countries increase with new tranches of relatively low yield and illiquid SDR. Unexploited social gains as represented by the areas S and A no longer exist. Being fully liquid already, the surplus countries see the SDR system as a potential claim against their real resources—when they have to accept unwanted SDR in return for running a trade surplus with poor countries.

For philanthropic reasons, the wealthy countries may not object to

[16] The contributions of many authors in many international forums over a 20-year period are well summarized by Park (1973).

modest aid giving in this form, but they will want to carefully hedge their liabilities. Hence, the restriction that they need only accept additional SDR up to twice their initial tranche, that any single country can opt out of new tranches, and why the facility itself has not been expanded very far relative to other forms of reserve holding. As a practical matter, we note that SDR remain less than 4% of total holdings of official reserves.

In summary, a direct conflict exists between achieving full liquidity internationally and using the same monetary vehicle as a clandestine credit line to subsidize worthy borrowers—the link to less-developed countries. As long as they are meant to be a subsidy device to users—and in practice less-developed countries tend to spend their SDR allocations rather quickly—then potential private "depositors" for holding SDR voluntarily will be even fewer and farther between than official holders are now. The consequent tax on depositors (reduction in interest rates) probably ensures that the SDR facility will never be able to substantially displace national monies in international exchange.

References

Ascheim, J., and Park, Y. S. (1976). Artificial Currency Units: The Formation of Functional Currency Areas, *Essays in International Finance* No. 114 (April).

Friedman, M. (1951). Commodity-Reserve Currency, *Journal of Political Economy* 203–232 (June).

Graham, B. (1944). *World Commodities and World Currency*. New York: McGraw-Hill.

Graham, F. D. (1942). *Social Goals and Economic Institutions*. Princeton, New Jersey: Princeton Univ. Press.

Grubel, H. (1969). The Distribution of Seigniorage from International Money Creation, in *Monetary Problems of the International Economy* (R. A. Mundell and A. K. Swoboda, eds.). Chicago, Illinois: Univ. of Chicago.

Hart, A. G. (1976). The Case of 1976 for International Commodity-Reserve Currency, *Weltwirtschaftliches Archiv* 112 (No. I), 1–30.

Johnson, H. G. (1969). A Note on Seigniorage and the Social Saving from Substituting Credit for Commodity Money, in *Monetary Problems of the International Economy* (R. A. Mundell and A. K. Swoboda, eds.). Chicago, Illinois: Univ. of Chicago.

Keynes, J. M. (1943). International Clearing Unions, Text of a Paper Containing Proposals by British Experts, London, *The International Monetary Fund 1945–65*, Vol. 3, *Documents*, pp. 19–36. London: International Monetary Fund.

Little, I. A. M., Scitovsky, T., and Scott, M. (1970). *Industry and Trade in Some Developing Countries: A Comparative Study*. London and New York: Oxford Univ. Press.

Luke, J. C. (1975). Inflation-Free Pricing Rules for a Generalized Commodity Reserve Currency, *Journal of Political Economy* 83, No. 4 (August).

McKinnon, R. I. (1979). *Money in International Exchange: The Convertibility-Currency System*. London and New York: Oxford Univ. Press.

Oxford Dictionary (1971). *The Compact Edition of the Oxford English Dictionary*, Vol. II.

Park, Y. S. (1973). The Link between Special Drawing Rights and Development Finance, *Essays in International Finance*, No. 100 (September).

Scitovsky, T. (1965). Requirements of an International Monetary System, *Princeton Essays in International Finance* No. 49 (November).

Scitovsky, T. (1966). A New Approach to International Liquidity, *American Economic Review* (December), 1212–1220.

Scitovsky, T. (1969). *Money and the Balance of Payments*. Chicago, Illinois: Rand McNally.

Stamp, M. (1958). The Fund and the Future, *Lloyd's Bank Review* (October) 1–20.

Triffin, R. (1971). The Use of SDR Finance for a Collectively Agreed Purpose, Banca Nazionale del lavoro *Quarterly Review* (March) 3–12.

UNCTAD (1974). United Nations Conference on Trade and Development (unpublished).

Department of Economics
Stanford University
Stanford, California

PART III

MACROECONOMICS

Equilibrium Theory and Growth Theory*

Nicholas Kaldor

1. Introduction

My purpose is to explain why I regard prevailing economic theory, as taught in the regular textbooks in most of the universities of the Western World, as thoroughly misleading and pretty useless—in terms of the theory's declared objective of explaining how economic processes work in a decentralized market economy. It is useless for formulating nontrivial predictions concerning the effects of policy measures or other changes.

Section 2 is a brief discussion of what I consider to be the basic assumptions of equilibrium theory. Section 3 is a discussion of what is wrong with these assumptions—why these hypotheses are misleading as a starting

* Originally a lecture given in the University of Barcelona, April 1973, and published in Spanish [*Cuadernos de Economia, Barcelona* 2, May–August (1974)].

273

point for making generalizations about the behavior of the economic system. Finally, Section 4 is a brief outline of the postulates needed for an alternative approach—a "nonequilibrium theory"—which I should like to call a "growth theory," because it would be primarily concerned with the manner of operation of the (both exogenous and endogenous) forces in a market economy making for continuous change and development.

2. The Main Characteristics of Equilibrium Theory

The basic characteristics of existing equilibrium theory are:

(1) It is permeated by a basic dichotomy between "wants" and "resources," "tastes" and "obstacles" or "ends" and "means." (One could equally say, with Bentham, between "pleasure" and "pain.")

(2) It follows from the basic assumption that men have given "wants" or "needs," which in a basic, though not precisely definable, sense are given by man's nature, independently of the social environment and of the social institutions created for satisfying them, that the essence of "economic activities" is regarded as that of allocating "scarce means which have alternative uses" (Robbins, 1932). The price system, the market mechanism, and the legal institutions, property rights, contracts, etc., are regarded as social instruments for "resource allocation." Under *ideal* conditions, individuals, whether in their capacity as producers or consumers, by acting rationally but quite independently of each other—that is to say, by acting so as to maximize something—bring about an "optimum" allocation of resources which secures the highest or maximum satisfaction to each member of society in the specific Pareto sense of no one being capable by any change in his *own* arrangements, i.e., in his own set of decisions concerning production or consumption, of making himself *better off* without making some others, or at least one other person, *worse off*. A's pleasure is maximized subject to B's being given. So everyone is as well off as he could be subject to everyone else's satisfaction being given.

(3) "Wants" are satisfied by the consumption (or destruction) of "goods" (including nonmaterial services). Goods are produced out of labor, natural resources, and goods; i.e., to a large extent, goods are produced out of each other, and only a proportion of goods produced in any year are destined to satisfy wants in that year. The goods which are available at any point of time, or over an interval of time (such as a year) for the purposes of producing goods, together with the labor and natural resources so available, are called "resources."

(4)   The essence of equilibrium theory consists of stating, in a comprehensive manner, the properties of such a Pareto equilibrium—having demonstrated that on certain basic "axioms" such an equilibrium can be assumed to exist. The necessary axioms include, first of all, that the supply of resources (the total amount of each kind that is available) is given "exogenously" in some sense—though what the precise meaning of exogeneity is when one tries to clothe the skeleton and think of "resources" as concrete objects as they appear in reality, and not just as mathematical symbols in a system of equations, has never been satisfactorily resolved.

(5)   For the purpose of demonstrating the existence of such an "equilibrium," it is also assumed that the productive relationships—the "transformation functions" or "production functions"—are universally *known* and of a *given* number; equally, there are a *known* and *given* number of different goods.

(6)   Equally, the distribution of the *ownership* of resources among individuals is given exogenously.

(7)   Similarly, the preference functions of each individual are assumed to be given and invariant over time, and invariant also with respect to the preferences of other individuals.

One can draw a distinction between the axioms necessary for a Pareto-optimal resource allocation to exist, and the additional assumptions required for supposing that a *market economy* will tend to function in such a way as to bring about (fully, or with a certain degree of approximation) an equilibrium allocation of resources. In order to show that the market mechanism will function in this way, it is necessary to suppose further that:

(a)   transformation functions must be *linear;* there is an absence of increasing returns (or economies of scale), i.e., production is equally efficient, irrespective of the scale of production;

(b)   competition must be *perfect*—each individual "transactor" can sell anything or buy anything in unlimited amounts without affecting market prices, and therefore prices are the only type of information required for individual decisions; and

(c)   there is *perfect knowledge* of all relevant prices by all "transactors" (or "economic agents");

(d)   there is also "perfect foresight" in the sense that over time the experience of individuals serves to *confirm* (and not to contradict or "disappoint") the expectations in the light of which they made their decisions in the past.

The real purpose of all these assumptions is to show that there is at least one set of prices which, *if established in the markets,* would leave everyone content to go on as they are—that it would not be to anyone's interest to revise their decisions (or "plans") concerning their *own* activities in the sphere of production and consumption. But this in itself is not sufficient to show that markets will operate so as to approach an equilibrium of this description from any arbitrarily given starting point. For, if transactions are conducted at nonequilibrium prices, this in itself will alter the conditions of equilibrium—it will come to the same as a change in the distribution in the ownership of resources between different individuals. (It can also affect conduct by creating false anticipations.) Hence, in the pure Walrasian model, it is assumed that the system of equilibrium or market-clearing prices is established *before* any transactions are made, by a process of *"tatônnement,"* [1] which is the same as assuming that the markets *are* in equilibrium, without showing how they got there. Nor has it been demonstrated that this equilibrium is a stable one; i.e., that it would maintain itself in the face of chance disturbances.

Moreover, the whole approach is necessarily "static" in the sense that it assumes that the forces operating in the economy can be characterized in terms of a *unique* point (or a predetermined point) to which any *changing* system converges and at which all forces making for change are exhausted—in other words, to a state in which the various forces hold each other in balance in such a way as to establish an unchanging routine. Once the system attains equilibrium, it remains in it forever.

Now all human societies are in a process of continual change—a change which differs from the continual biological change of ecological systems in nature only in that it is far speedier and takes more spectacular forms. Within the framework of equilibrium theory, there are two ways in which attempts have been made to introduce change into the system while preserving the notion that it is in continuous equilibrium:

(1)   The first is the assumption that there are "markets" at which purchases and sales can be made not only for the current period but for *all* future periods as well; decisions then depend on prices in both the current and all the "future" markets; the system is in intertemporal equilibrium when, at the ruling prices, both the "spot" and "future" market supplies and demands are in equilibrium for *all* future periods and not only for the current period. The purpose of this approach is to establish that on certain axioms, such an equilibrium price system for all "commodities" (with

---

[1] The meaning of the French word *"tatônnement"* according to *Petit Larousse* is *procéder avec hesitation.* In Walras, it means a cautious approach to business which enables people to discover the right prices *before* transactions are made.

each "commodity" having a time suffix for the date of its availability) exists. The real world admittedly bears only a very limited resemblance to this model, since apart from some specific commodities for specific periods in the near future, such futures markets do *not* exist.[2]

(2) The other approach is to assume that changes are only due to purely exogenous factors which proceed in time wholly independently (or at least *largely* independently) of economic decisions which depend on prices; and the price system operates so efficiently as to produce an optimal allocation of resources for each period taken separately. In other words, the system is in continuous equilibrium, even though the quantity of available resources and technological knowledge is changing over time—for, in each period, the system produces a Pareto-optimal allocation for the quantity of resources and the knowledge of technology *pertaining to that period.*

The trouble with that approach is that there is nothing in the theory to explain how the system gets into equilibrium and what happens when it is out of equilibrium. The "production frontier" which is supposed to shift at some exogenous rate in time is meaningful only if the system is actually *on* the frontier and not *within* it. For any movement of the system *toward* the frontier increases capital as well as output, and therefore changes at least one of the parameters which define the "frontier."[3]

3. Why Equilibrium Theory Is Wrong

The Walrasian equilibrium theory is a highly developed intellectual system, much refined and elaborated by mathematical economists since World War II—an intellectual experiment, as Kornai (1971) called it. But it does not constitute a scientific hypothesis, like Einstein's theory of relativity or Newton's law of gravitation, in that its basic assumptions are axiomatic and not empirical, and no specific methods have been put forward by which the validity or relevance of its results could be tested. The assumptions make assertions about reality in their implications, but these are not founded on direct observation and, in the opinion of practitioners of the theory at any rate, they cannot be contradicted by observation or experiment.

---

[2] Also it would be a mistake to equate the markets in "futures" in the real world to the "dated" markets of equilibrium theory. The "futures" markets of the real world relate to transactions between hedgers and speculators; they do *not* attempt to match supplies and demands accruing at particular future dates.

[3] This point is further considered on pp. 279–281.

3.1   The Effects of Complementarity

My first criticism of this approach is that it concentrates on subsidiary aspects and not the main aspects of market processes. Equilibrium theory elevates the "principle of substitution" (as Marshall called it) to be the "be-all" and "end-all" of all economic activity—the main explanatory principle of the forces which operate on the economy. "Resources" are limited substitutes (or substitutes at margin) both as regards production and consumption, hence profit maximization and utility maximization are essentially substitution problems—a problem of equating prices to marginal rates of substitution in production and consumption. This is misleading because it ignores the essential complementarity between different kinds of products and different kinds of activities, and the nature of the market impulses which result from this complementarity.

Take, for example, capital and labor. These are essentially complementary to each other; this aspect is far more important than the fact that they are also "substitutes" in some respects—i.e., that enterprises can be induced by relative price changes to use more or less mechanized techniques of production involving greater or lesser amounts of "capital" per worker.

The French Physiocrats and English classical economists were of course conscious of this complementarity; they regarded the role of capital accumulation as one of raising production by increasing the level of employment of the economy (so as to increase the amount of labor that is effectively utilized in production) and not for the purpose of substitution of "capital" for "labor" in relation to labor already employed.

Another example is the interdependence of different kinds of economic activities as is shown in the distinction between the primary, secondary, and tertiary sectors. Industrial (or manufacturing) activities—which are "secondary"—consist of the processing or refinement of crude products which are the output of the so-called "primary" sectors, agriculture and mining. They depend on agriculture also for food which is the consumption-good or wage-good par excellence. Hence, an increased availability of primary products is a necessary precondition for increased industrial output; in the same way, an increase in industrial activity necessarily increases the demand for primary products. The same is true of "tertiary" services: the scale on which they can be provided is dependent on the output of both the primary and secondary sectors.

In equilibrium theory, if the economy is assumed to possess two industries such as manufactured goods A and food products B, the available resources are supposed to be divided between them, depending on consumer preference. The nature of neoclassical general equilibrium in the

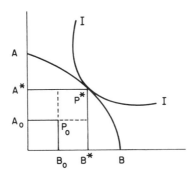

Figure 1

simplest case of two factors and two industries is shown in Fig. 1. The locus of "efficient combinations" is given by the "production frontier" A–B. This assumes that factor supplies X and Y as well as the transformation functions for A and B are given. Ignoring (for the purpose of our argument) the difficulties in the way of representing collective preferences by indifference curves, point P^* can be said to represent the "equilibrium" position at which the two kinds of products are produced in the most preferred ratio, and at which output (A^*, B^*) is at a maximum, given the resource constraints.

But this is a false way of looking at things. The two industries do not make use of the same resources and, insofar as they do, these resources are not, in any meaningful sense, allocated between them.

Labor is common to all activities, but there is always "surplus labor" in agriculture—labor can be withdrawn without any adverse effect on output and normally with a favorable effect. (This can be expressed by saying that normally the marginal product of labor working on the land is zero or negative. The reason is that the density of population living on the land is generally such that output actually produced does not require the *effective* employment of more than a fraction of the labor force available.) There is no such thing as "full employment of labor" except as a short-term phenomenon in a given area (or locality).

Equally, capital cannot be regarded as a *given* quantity which is allocated between the two sectors. On the contrary, each sector generates (or "accumulates") its own capital in the course of its own expansion.

The growth of output and the growth of capital, in the sense of the increase in the stock of goods (or stock of durable goods) serving the purposes of production, are not two different things but merely two different *facets* of the same process; neither is prior to the other nor a precondition of the other. It would be better to say that they are the same thing viewed from two different aspects. Fisher (1906) was the first economist to my knowledge who emphasized this by saying that the stock of goods existing *at a given moment of time* is "capital"; the flow of goods accruing *over a period of time* is "income."

It is true that the competition between the owners of capital to seek the most-profitable activities brings about a certain tendency to equalization in the rate of return; but this is not because capital "flows" between the various sectors in any real sense, but because the rate of accumulation of capital in each particular sector varies positively with the rate of return of that sector, so that sectors with higher rates of profit will expand relatively fast in relation to other sectors and this tends to bring their relative prices, rates of profit, and hence rates of accumulation down, so that the *profile* of the rate of expansion of different sectors tends to approach a structurally determined pattern, determined primarily by technical relationships and also by the income elasticities of demand of consumers. (In reality, at any one time the high rates of profit are made in the so-called "growth industries" resulting from dynamic change.)

But the main point to bear in mind is that under favorable conditions (of which I shall say more later), the expansion of any one sector tends to stimulate (via a demand effect) the expansion of the others; so that production, under favorable conditions, escalates by a kind of chain reaction—each sector receives impulses through market phenomena, and transmits impulses in turn.

The market is thus not primarily an instrument for *allocating* resources. It is primarily an instrument for transmitting impulses to change; it would be truer to say that the market mechanism creates or generates resources than that it allocates them. (There is, of course, also an allocative aspect, but I think this should be regarded as subsidiary and not the primary or most important aspect, and, as Kornai (1971) has recently shown, the markets can perform their allocation functions through a "stock-adjustment" mechanism which is not primarily guided by prices and which is capable of functioning irrespective of prices.)

The implication is that the so-called "equilibrium position" (or the locus of all such positions, such as the "production frontier" shown in Fig. 1) cannot be derived from a study of "data" independently of the actual position in which the economy finds itself at any given time. For, suppose that the initial position of the economy at $t = 0$ is P_0, yielding outputs A_0, B_0. Since these outputs serve as the commodity inputs of the processes of production (and are not use-goods destined for personal consumption), any movement of the system toward optimal allocation necessarily enlarges the quantity of resources available to the economy and therefore changes the position of the production frontier.

Since P_0 was a nonoptimal position by definition (i.e., a position at which the marginal rates of substitution of the factors in the two industries were *not* equal), any movement of the system toward "equilibrium"—i.e., to the northeast of P_0—will increase the amount of resources available to at least one of the two industries, if not both. Hence, if P^* was assumed to be the optimum position of annual output when starting from an initial position P_0, it could no longer be the optimal position if one started from any intermediate point such as P_l, with $A_l > A_0$ and $B_l > B_0$ as outputs. This means that the position of the frontier can be defined only if the state of the economy is actually *on* the frontier to start with. Otherwise, one cannot define the frontier except by reference to some *particular* starting point; and any movement of the system toward the frontier from that starting point will necessarily shift the "frontier" itself outward. The optimal output cannot be defined except by reference to the quantity of capital; but the quantity of capital cannot be defined except by reference to output, since output and capital are fundamentally only different ways of looking at the same thing.[4]

Thus the first thing which is wrong with the paradigm of equilibrium theory is thinking of a "given" quantum of resources which are "scarce" and always fully utilized, and which are effectively allocated between different uses. This view permeated the classical school of Ricardo and his followers as well as the neoclassical economists, and it is at the basis of Say's law, *la théorie des debouchès*. The latter is best expressed in Mill's (1848, p. 95) dictum that "there is no over-production; production is not excessive, but merely ill-assorted." If agriculture can employ only a limited number of men (because of the shortage of land), the rest could be employed only in industry and services. If this meant an "overproduction" of industrial goods and services relative to agricultural goods, industrial prices[5] would fall in terms of agricultural prices (agricultural prices

---

[4] Adherents of the neoclassical theory may object that this is no more than a "complication," since under the assumption of homogeneous and linear functions the increase in output associated with an increase of capital will be less than proportionate to the increase in capital, so that after a certain number of steps (or a certain number of time periods) the actual frontier will eventually be reached even if that frontier will by then have become far removed from what it appeared to be at the starting date. But this proposition critically depends on the assumption of linear homogeneity of the production functions which ensured that any increase in capital per man will increase output per man less than proportionately. If one abandons the assumption of linearity and allows for increasing returns, it is no longer true—in which case one could equally hold *either* that the frontier will forever remain an unattainable goal *or* that the distinction between an actual historical situation and the equilibrium situation ceases to have a definite meaning.

[5] The same holds for the prices of services provided by the tertiary sector, but for simplicity we shall neglect the existence of the tertiary sector in this analysis.

will rise in terms of industrial prices, which is the same thing). This will mean a transfer of "real" purchasing power from industry to agriculture, which will go on until the producers in the agricultural sector are able to buy all the goods which industry is capable of producing in excess of industry's own absorption of such goods, whether for purpose of consumption or capital investment. Hence, the price mechanism of competitive markets, which causes a *fall* in the prices of goods in excess supply and a *rise* in prices of goods in excess demand, will always bring about a set of prices at which *all* markets are cleared—to say that demand can never be sufficient to match the potential supply for any or all commodities is the same as saying (according to the Say–Mill view) that the supply would still exceed the demand if the price of any or all commodities fell to zero.

However, this view ignores the peculiar nature of labor, the price of which can never fall to zero—however much the potential supply exceeds the demand in the labor market. Since industrial activities—the processing of crude products of agriculture and mining—invariably require labor, the value added by manufacturing activities cannot fall below a certain minimum (given the productivity of labor in terms of industrial goods), and this minimum sets a limit to the extent to which agricultural prices can rise in terms of industrial prices. But this is the same as saying that in normal circumstances supply cannot equal demand *simultaneously* in both the market for agricultural goods and the market for industrial goods. If the agricultural market is in equilibrium in the sense that the maximum which the sellers are prepared to sell at the prevailing price equals the maximum which the buyers are willing to buy at that price, the industrial market will *not* be in equilibrium in that sense, since the amount actually produced and supplied may be smaller than the amount that would be supplied at the prevailing price, if sufficient demand existed at that price. It is therefore wrong to suggest that the actual output of the economy is determined by the availabilities of resources—capital, labor, and land—which will then be fully utilized irrespective of the structure of demand. If agricultural output is limited by the scarcity of land and not be the availability of labor, and the price of industrial goods in terms of agricultural products is dependent upon the minimum wage which must be paid to labor, then industrial production will be limited by demand and not by the available resources, while the amount of capital available to industry will necessarily vary *pari passu* with the level of industrial production; in other words, capital will also be limited by demand.

This is the intellectual basis of the doctrine of the "foreign trade multiplier," according to which the production of an (industrial) country will be determined by the *external* demand for its products, and will tend to be that multiple of that demand which is represented by the reciprocal of the proportion of *internal* incomes spent on imports. This doctrine asserts the very opposite of Say's law: the level of production will *not* be confined by the availability of capital and labor; on the contrary, the amount of capital accumulated, and the amount of labor effectively employed at any one time, will be the resultant of the growth of external demand over a long series of past periods which permitted the capital accumulation to take place that was required for enabling the amount of labor to be employed and the level of output to be reached which was (or could be) attained in the current period.

Keynes, writing in the middle of the Great Depression of the 1930s, focused his attention on the consequences of the failure to *invest* (due to unfavorable business expectations) in limiting industrial employment *below* industry's attained capacity to provide such employment; and he attributed this failure to excessive saving (or an insufficient propensity to consume) relative to the opportunities for profitable investment. From this came his concentration on liquidity preference and the rate of interest as the basic cause for the failure of Say's law to operate under conditions of low investment opportunities and/or excessive savings, and the importance he attached to the savings/investment multiplier as a short-period determinant of the level of production and employment.

In retrospect, I believe it to have been unfortunate that the very success of Keynes's ideas in connection with the savings/investment multiplier diverted attention from the "foreign trade multiplier" which, over longer periods, is a far more important and basic factor in explaining the growth and rhythm of industrial development. For, over longer periods, Ricardo's presumption that capitalists save only in order to invest, and hence the proportion of profits saved would adapt to changes in the profitability of investment, seems to me more relevant; the limitation of effective demand due to oversaving is a short-run (or cyclical) phenomenon, whereas the rate of growth of "external" demand is a more basic long-run determinant of both the rate of accumulation and the growth of output and employment in the "capitalist" or "industrial" sectors of the world economy.

3.2 Increasing Returns

The second major objection (which in some ways is connected with the first) concerns the assumption of linear-homogeneous production functions, i.e., the neglect of increasing returns to scale. Here again classical economists show an insight and awareness that is lacking in the neoclassical school. Adam Smith, as is well known, attributed primary importance to the proposition that the efficiency of production—i.e., the productivity of labor—depends on the division of labor, and the division of labor in turn depends on the size of the market. He devoted the first three chapters of the *Wealth of Nations* to an exposition of this basic law, and he regarded the existence of this law the most important reason for the existence of a "social economy"—one in which men devote themselves to producing particular things for the market and obtain the commodities they require largely through exchange. Smith's view was that the degree of specialization in particular processes or in particular portions of processes is constantly enlarged through an increase in the size of the market: the processes of production used when 20,000 pins can be sold daily are very different from the processes used when the daily demand was only for a few hundred pins. Hence productivity expands as the market expands, but the increase in productivity resulting from a larger market in turn enlarges the market for other things and by the same token causes productivity to rise in other industries. As Young (1928) said in a famous article:

> Adam Smith's famous theorem amounts to saying that the division of labour depends in large part upon the division of labour. This is more than mere tautology. It means that the counter forces which are continually defeating the forces which make for economic equilibrium are more pervasive and more deeply rooted than we commonly realize" [p. 533].

Young said that with increasing returns "change becomes progressive and propagates itself in a cumulative way [p. 533]."

Indeed, these cumulative forces—which Myrdal (1957) called "the principle of circular and cumulative causation"—largely explain the polarization of the world between the rich and the poor countries that occurred during the last two centuries. Owing to increasing returns, industries tended to be developed in particular growth centers, and in their development they inhibited the growth of industrialization in other areas. The country which became rich and attained high incomes per head was a country which became "well endowed" with capital and in which therefore the capital/labor ratio became very high. But this capital was largely accumulated out of reinvested profits in consequence of increasing demand, and the ability to use so much capital in relation to labor is very largely a reflection of the scale of activities and not of the relative price of capital and of labor. As Young (1928) emphasized, it would be absurd to suppose that it would "pay" to make a hammer just to drive a single nail, or to furnish a factory "with an elaborate equipment of specially constructed jigs, lathes, drills, presses and conveyors to build a hundred automobiles." It was the increase in the size of the market (not the savings or the rate of interest paid on loans) which made it possible to use so much more capital per worker. The best proof of this resides in the fact that while the capital/labor ratio increases dramatically in the course of progress (and varies dramatically in the same period between rich and poor countries), these enormous differences (of the order of 30 : 1 or 50 : 1) in the capital/labor ratio are quite uncorrelated with differences in the capital/output ratio. If production functions were as neoclassical theory supposes—as is assumed, for example, by Samuelson (1967) who emphasized as the central proposition of neoclassical theory that *"capital/ labor up: interest or profit rate down: wage rate up: capital/output up"*—the capital/output ratio would be all the higher the higher the capital/labor ratio.[6]

In fact, the universal experience has been that whether one takes cross-sectional studies, as between different firms in the same industry or of the same industry in different countries, or takes a time-series analysis of the movement of labor productivity and of the capital/labor ratio over time, there is no evidence at all to show that high labor productivity— which is almost invariably associated with a correspondingly high capital/ labor ratio—is associated with any increase in the amount of capital per unit of output. If anything, the contrary appears to be true. The capital/ output ratio in the more advanced countries, such as the United States which has the highest capital/labor ratio and the highest output per man, is *lower* than in countries at a low level of industrial development, such as India.

Neoclassical economists attempted for a time to reconcile these phenomena by introducing the *deus ex machina* of a "Harrod-neutral" technical progress which proceeds at an exogenous rate in time. Since technical progress is incapable of being independently measured, this of course was equivalent to making the whole theory untestable or vacuous. Moreover, technical progress is supposed to proceed at some exogenous rate in time, whereas the phenomena to be explained—the high correlation between the capital/labor ratio and of output per man, and the absence of any correlation between these two factors and the capital/output ratio— applies equally to cross-sectional comparisons of firms and industries and to time comparisons. The observed phenomena are, of course, capable of a much simpler explanation: the existence of increasing returns to scale, which makes it possible to use more and more capital with an increase in the scale of production, without encountering diminishing returns. If the use of more-specialized machinery is economical only with higher levels

---

[6] In fact, it is easy to calculate on the basis of a Cobb–Douglas-type production function that if the capital coefficient of the function is one-third and the labor coefficient two-thirds, doubling the capital/labor ratio would involve the increase the capital/output ratio by one-half.

of output, there is no reason why a rise in labor productivity should be associated with any fall in capital productivity, but with that explanation, the whole neoclassical value theory clearly goes out of the window.

4. An Alternative Approach to Growth Theory

Most abstract economic models postulate a "closed system," but they apply the conclusions reached to open systems, such as national economies, without being fully aware of the inconsistencies involved in this procedure. "Foreign trade" has always been treated as a special branch of the subject; for the general analysis of prices and markets, it was usual to assume a closed economy, defined by given resources, commodities, markets, etc., which are self-contained.

There is no such really closed system except the world economy as a whole, and, to capture the really important aspects of the economic mechanism, one ought to use a paradigm which embodies the significant features of the world economy as a unit as a starting point in the basic theoretical model before tackling the more complicated models required for particular non-self-sufficient "regions" or "countries."

In a first approximation, one should consider the world economy as consisting of two vital sectors: the production of primary goods (food and raw materials) and the production of "secondary" goods (industry—the processing of crude materials into manufactured goods, whether for industrial use or for final consumption).[7]

Primary production is agriculture (including forestry and fisheries) and mining. These are "land-based" activities in the sense that natural resources play a vital part in the ease or difficulty of their performance—e.g., climate, the nature of the soil, and what is beneath the surface in the form of minerals. In some languages, such as German, such activities are referred to as "archproduction" (*Urproduktion*). This conveys the idea that this is the *fond et origine* of all human activities—everything else comes from there; it also conveys the idea that production at any time is governed by the *productivity of the soil*—which is not just a matter of nature but of the state of technology and the amount of capital expended in the past—and not by the productivity of *labor*. For, however essential labor is in all such activities, there is always more labor (and generally much more labor) available than can be *effectively* used on any given area of land. This is because the density of population in any given area is itself a function of the productivity of the soil—the more food is produced, the

---

[7] The tertiary sector—services of all kinds—could be ignored in a first approximation.

more people there will be. Since the output of the soil is a constraint on the labor force, one cannot, at the same time, assume that the labor force is the effective constraint on production—only one of these constraints is likely to "bite" at any one time. And there can be no doubt that with rare exceptions—such as when a region is invaded by new settlers bringing with them a much superior technology capable of producing very much more food per acre of land, as was the case with the first European settlers in America or Oceania—it is the Malthusian constraint which is the critical one, and not the labor constraint. Hence, there is generally disguised unemployment in the rural areas of the world, and economic development essentially consists of tapping these labor reserves. In the course of development, the proportion of population in agriculture diminishes in a dramatic fashion. (In prewar Bulgaria it was 90%; in present day Britain it is less than 3%.)

Secondary production converts crude materials into finished goods in two ways—through direct inputs, such as raw wool or cotton made into clothes, and through the food consumed by industrial labor, which is an "indirect" input.

It is important to emphasize that the potential supply of labor to industry is *unlimited;* since the transfer of labor from the primary to the secondary sector (allowing for international as well as intranational migration) can be limited only by the rate at which such labor can be absorbed or utilized, it cannot be constrained by the size of potential supply. (This is true even when international migration is inhibited, so long as capital and enterprise can move across political frontiers.)

But while the supply of labor to industry is practically unlimited, the price paid for the use of that labor cannot fall below a certain amount in terms of primary goods. For wages must cover a certain minimum means of subsistence, irrespective of the size of excess of the supply of labor over demand. Moreover, it is the peculiarity of industrial labor, in modern days of high organization and even in the ancient days preceding modern industrial capitalism, that the supply price of labor *in terms of food* contains a strong conventional element; wages tend to have a downward rigidity in terms of food prices, around the "attained" or "customary" level, at any rate in free (nonslave) societies, even when that level bears no recognizable relationship to subsistence needs in some biological or calorific sense.

This makes the prices of industrial goods in terms of agricultural products—the terms of trade between industry and agriculture—virtually independent, except in very short periods, of the supply/demand situation in agriculture. (That is to say, agriculture is not likely to obtain *better* prices in terms of industrial goods in times of scarcity. It is less clear that it does not obtain *worse* terms as a result of superabundance, but I believe that over longer periods the latter proposition is likely to be true as well.) Hence, the level of prices of processed goods in terms of foodstuffs is determined by three factors $\bar{w}$, l, π, and given by the formula

$$p = (1 + \pi)\bar{w}l$$

where p is the price of manufactured goods in terms of food, $\bar{w}$ the wage of labor in terms of food, π the share of profits in terms of food, and l the labor requirements per unit of output = 1/(productivity).

There are important asymmetries in the position of these two sectors:

(1)   Primary output can be assumed to grow at a certain rate owing to technological progress in landsaving inventions (whether in the form of new crops or new means of planting, new fertilizers, cheapening transport, or the discovery of new substitutes, e.g. synthetics, requiring fewer natural resources). All these have in common is the fact that they are land saving—i.e., they allow more to be extracted from a given natural environment. However, the exploitation of new technology requires capital investment; capital investment is a matter partly of the size of the surplus over the consumption needs of the primary sector, and partly of the terms on which industrial goods can be obtained in exchange for primary products—in other words, on the terms of trade p. Hence, the rate of growth of primary output will be all the greater the more favorable are the terms of trade to agriculture. This is projected by the downward-sloping nature of the $\dot{A}/A$ curve in Fig. 2.

(2)   With regard to industry, as was argued earlier, there is a minimum supply price below which no production would be forthcoming; this at the point k where $p = \bar{w}l$. Industrial production can grow only if some part of the output is "ploughed back" in the form of industrial investment. To the

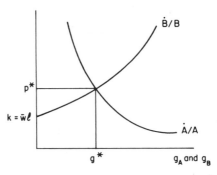

Figure 2 $\dot{A}/A$ is the growth rate of agricultural production, $\dot{B}/B$ the growth rate of industrial production.

extent that this happens, $p > k$, the excess $(p - k)/k$ being equal to the share of output which is "retained" by the sector for the purpose of investment by the sector. In industry, therefore, investment "finances itself" since it generates equivalent profits (excess of p over k) automatically. If, in addition, part of the profits are consumed (profits generate consumption), $p - k$ will be that much larger.

(3)   This means that, in the case of *secondary output*, the *supply price* of industry curve $\dot{B}/B$ starting from $k = wl$ will rise in a functional relation to $g_B \equiv \dot{B}/B$ (Fig. 2).

There should exist at any one time a point at which $g = g_A = g_B$ and (abstracting from consumption out of industrial products) $p = (1 + \pi)\bar{w}l = (1 + gv)\bar{w}l$. Whether this point is reached and, if reached, maintained over time, is a complex problem which I cannot enter into here. But *supposing* the system does have a tendency to settle at p and will grow at the rate g, this itself will vary with time, since, owing to economies of large-scale production and laborsaving (as distinct from land-saving) technical progress, $dl_t/dt < 0$, B/B will shift downward with time, hence p_t will be falling with t, and g_t will be rising. With both labor- and land-saving technical progress and a *given* real wage in terms of food (or primary products), economic growth should not only be continuous but would show a tendency to continual *acceleration* (at any rate when exhaustible resources are ignored).

(4)   However, there is no *need* for this to happen in this way. Real wages need not be constant at $\bar{w}$; $dw_t/dt > 0$ is quite possible, owing to all kinds of things—monopolistic or oligopolistic price policies by industrial firms, or the pressure exerted through trade unions.

A special case is $dw_t/d_t = - dl_t/d_t$, in which p_t will be constant over time and g_t will be constant $(dg_t/d_t = 0)$. But $dw_t/d_t > - dl_t/d_t$ cannot be excluded either, in which case $dg_t/d_t < 0$: with wages rising faster than productivity in industry, the equilibrium growth rate will tend to diminish.

(5)   In any case, we can assume that the rate of expansion of industrial capacity is "induced": the "accelerator principle" governs the rate of capital accumulation in the industrial sector. At any given p_0, the growth of "outside" demand proceeds at the rate g_0 and this induces, by a multiplier/accelerator process, a corresponding rate of capital accumulation and of the growth of output in industry.

(6)   Hence on *this* model, industrial growth is dependent on the exogenous components of demand for industry—that part of the demand which comes from "outside" the industrial sector: the growth of its exports (even though this may only amount to a small fraction of the total output or demand—the rest will tend to be resonant with it). Hence *industry* will determine what the terms of trade will be, since p will depend on factors endogenous to the sector; but the growth of purchasing power of the

primary sector (which is the same as its growth of output $\dot{A}/A$) will determine the growth rates of both; and $\dot{A}/A$ is itself a function of p.

All this, of course, is a tremendous oversimplification, deliberately neglecting numerous complicating elements. But the main message to be drawn is that if one assumes that markets function so as to be consistent with expansion—which means that an increase in supply of A will increase the purchasing power of the A sector for B products and vice versa—the rate of growth will ultimately depend on the growth of foodstuffs and basic materials, which is itself dependent on p as shown by some such relationship as the $\dot{A}/A$ curve in Fig. 2.

So, finally, it is the progress of land-saving inventions—including here the continued invention of new substitutes for existing materials and sources of energy—which not only sets the limit to growth, but in the long run governs the rate of growth.

All this is true if we regard world industrial output as a single entity. To analyze the divergent trends in the growth rate of different regions and countries, we must go further and consider the competition between different industrial areas. Owing to the economies of large-scale production and of spatial (geographical) concentration, industrial growth tends to be concentrated in urban areas: the growth of industry and of urbanization are closely related. But any *particular* region may have a rising, constant, or falling share in the total world market for "industrial goods" (including its own "protected" market). In the course of time, new industrial centers emerge and displace, or narrow, the market for the older centers. The fast-growing countries *gain* in competitiveness, for their "efficiency wages" $w_t l_t$ fall in relation to those of areas which grow more slowly—whose market share is diminishing.

In industrial growth, owing to increasing returns, Myrdal's principle of "cumulative and circular causation" operates. Success breeds success; regions or "countries" whose industrial exports increase faster than world net exports have a faster rate of economic growth; this tends to depress the rate of growth of the regions whose share of world trade is diminishing in consequence.

Industrialization is the key factor in economic development. All rich countries with high incomes per capita are industrialized countries. Myrdal's principle explains why rapid growth tends to be concentrated among a relatively small number of "successful" areas, and also, why, within that fortunate group of areas, the relative wealth and standard of living are subject to continuous change—poorer areas with lower efficiency wages overtake areas which were initially richer, but, owing to higher wages in relation to their productivity, are unable to stand up to the competition of others. Both the growing polarization of the world between developed and underdeveloped, or rich and poor countries, and the remarkable shifts in the relative positions of individual "rich" countries are, in my view, to be explained by the same basic principle.

References

Fisher, I. (1906). *The Nature of Capital and Income.* New York: Macmillan.

Kornai, J. (1971). *Anti-Equilibrium.* Amsterdam: North-Holland Publ.

Mill, J. S. (1848). *Principles of Political Economy,* Vol. II. London: John W. Parker.

Myrdal, G. (1957). *Economic Theory and Underdeveloped Regions.* London: Duckworth.

Robbins, L. C. (1932). *An Essay or the Nature and Significance of Economic Science,* p. 12. London: Macmillan.

Samuelson, P. A. (1967). *Economics—An Introductory Analysis,* 7th ed., p. 715. New York: McGraw-Hill.

Young, A. A. (1928). Increasing Returns and Economic Progress. *Economic Journal* (December).

Kings College
Cambridge University
Cambridge, United Kingdom

Dynamic Competition and Economic Stability

Burton H. Klein

1. Introduction

This article has a twofold objective: first, to show how a predictive theory of dynamic competition can be formulated on the basis of empirical observation; second, to show that in the real world competition plays a more impressive role than it does in the world of classical economic theory.

Dynamic competition can hardly be described as a new form of competition. It was initially discovered by Adam Smith and consists of rivalry between business firms to provide better or cheaper products. I propose to show it is no accident that on the basis of his observations Adam Smith became an ardent champion of competition. Dynamic competition, I shall argue, plays two mutually related roles whose importance far outweigh the achievement of a high degree of static (or allocative) efficiency. First, while it can be debated whether the quantitative significance of monopoly in bringing about a misallocation of resources is equal to a 2 or 5% once-and-for-all increase in the gross national product, I will show that the difference between industries displaying minor or major league behavior in their degree of competitive rivalry can easily amount to a 5% difference in the *annual rate of progress*. Second, while static competition acts as a deterrent on wage and price increases, I will show that dynamic competition performs the role of an economic stabilizer inasmuch as it acts both as a stimulus to productivity gains (to pay for increases in wages without inflation) and as a deterrent on wage and price increases. And if my argument is correct, we should expect an increase in the degree of competitive rivalry to be accompanied by a downward shift in the Phillips curve—a decline to be followed by an upward shift.

2. The Phenomenon to Be Explained

Progress may take the form of either more and more output per unit of input or more or less continuous improvements in quality. And as Kuznets and others have shown, whichever form it does take, when plotted against time the typical picture is that of an S-shaped curve (with large advances followed by smaller and smaller advances.[1]

In addition to the overall shape, there is another noteworthy feature of the curve. Though the advances occur almost like clockwork, viewed as isolated events the individual advances (as shown by the solid lines in Fig. 1) are quite unpredictable. In other words, we are dealing with a phenomenon which exhibits a high degree of predictability when viewed on a macroscale and a high degree of unpredictability when viewed on a microscale.

I do not say, of course, that in all cases the advances come about regularly. Indeed, one of the important characteristics of the process to be explained is why in some instances the advances do come about like clockwork. Examples in the fields of propeller-driven aircraft, jet engines, and computers are to be found in Fig. 2.

Individual advances are quite unpredictable inasmuch as they involve the correction of errors in previous hypotheses and changes in initial conditions the entrepreneur himself cannot predict. In fact, to achieve a satisfactory mutation the entrepreneur typically becomes married to and divorced from a succession of hypotheses. Moreover, the hints for under-

[1] For discussions of the S-shaped curve phenomenon, see Kuznets (1959) and Enos (1962).

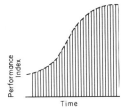

Figure 1   A dynamic process.

standing why a particular prior hypothesis did not work out satisfactorily (which is more than half of the battle in discovering a new hypothesis) ordinarily come from a variety of interactions with other people. Indeed, as will be pointed out, the more unpredictable the interactions, the more likely will be a favorable outcome!

In short, the essential role of the entrepreneur is to generate new ideological mutations. And by performing this role the entrepreneur becomes an engineer of *irreversible* change. After significant discoveries such as the DC-3 or the IBM 360 series computers the probability distributions of the world are no longer the same.

Why, then, are significant advances aimed at improving the efficiency of a technology quite unpredictable? Evidently God planned the world in such a way as to leave something to the imagination of man. The reasons are implicit in the laws of nature: "implicit" in the sense that nature imposes limits beyond which it is impossible to go without making new discoveries. To be more specific, consider Sadi Carnot's theory about the efficiency of machines which in turn paved the way for the ideas contained in the second law of thermodynamics.[2] Carnot's theory tells us that the physical efficiency of a machine—the amount of work the engine can generate in relationship to the heat put into it—is proportional to the temperature difference which can be obtained, or

$$\text{physical efficiency} = W/Q_1 = (T_1 - T_2)/T_1,$$

where W/Q_1 measures output of work per unit of heat, and $(T_1 - T_2)/T_1$ measures the difference in temperatures between which the engine runs divided by the highest temperature.

The temperature difference which can be obtained is in turn limited by the best available fuels, the best available materials, and the engineering know-how to make the machine approximate an ideal reversible machine. To be sure, Carnot's theory applies to the physical efficiency of machines and not necessarily to their economic efficiency. For example, increasing

[2] For further discussion, see Feynman *et al.* (1963).

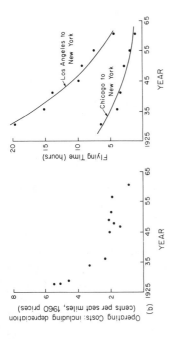

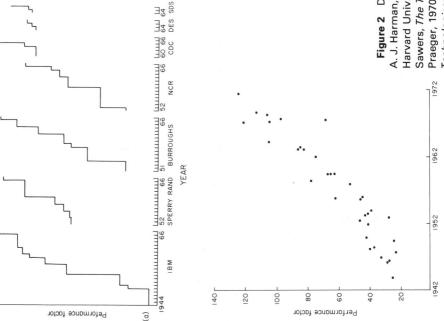

Figure 2 Dynamic processes. (a) Actual computer performance. [Data from A. J. Harman, *The International Computer Industry.* Cambridge, Massachusetts: Harvard Univ. Press, 1971.] (b) Indicators of airline efficiency. [R. Miller and D. Sawers, *The Technical Development of Modern Aviation,* pp. 29–47. New York: Praeger, 1970.] (c) Aircraft turbine engine performance. [Data from R. Shishko, *Technological Change through Product Improvement in Aircraft Turbine En-gines, Santa Monica, California: Rand Corp., No. 1971.]*

the physical efficiency of a machine by using more expensive materials or fuels would not necessarily result in a gain in terms of economic efficiency. However, amending the theory to take into account the cost of achieving a higher degree of efficiency does not change its basic nature. Carnot's theory enables engineers to determine which way is "up"—the measures which, if successful, would result in an increase in efficiency. On the other hand, it does not pretend to predict the success of particular measures.

Technological progress also takes the form of scaling machines so they can be used in new applications. For example, turbine engines were used in Swiss mines before they were developed for use in airplanes. However, because there are constants in the laws of nature and new materials which prevent scaling at will, typically, difficult scaling problems are overcome only by the discovery of new materials. Galileo is usually credited with having discovered that limits exist with respect to scaling. Pondering in his *Two Sciences* the problem of how big a bone would be required to build a dog twice as high, he found it simply could not be done without the invention of a stronger bone. Galileo, it is often said, discovered that engineers are needed to invent new kinds of bones! But it is important to note that progress in scaling does not only result in building bigger plants; it can also result in smaller plants. For example, the new electric process for steel manufacture can achieve the same economies as the oxygen process—but with much smaller plants.

The pioneering of a new technology ordinarily involves overcoming limits set by both scaling and Carnot's theory on the efficiency of machines. The curves relating the rate of progress to time tend to be S shaped because the process of pioneering a new technology is much like that of mining gold. In the initial phase, when the degree of uncertainty is the largest, the potential for making impressive discoveries is also likely to be the greatest. But eventually engineers will become frustrated in their search for significant advances and will turn their attention toward bringing about more predictable and less ambitious advances. However, the cost of bringing about even incremental advances will eventually become so large that other engineers will go in search of new gold mines. For example, although it brought about a smaller advance, the DC-7 commercial airliner cost about ten times as much as the DC-3.

From where do the discoveries come to make new S-shaped curves? Assuming that the industry has already reached the stage of slow history, the advances will seldom come from major firms in the industry in question. In fact, of some 50 inventions—contained mainly in the study by Jewkes *et al.* (1969)—which resulted in new S-shaped curves in relatively static industries—I could find no case in which the advance in question came from a major firm in the industry. In some cases (e.g., Bessemer steel, the electric steel process, jet engines, the Polaroid Land camera), the inventions came from newly established firms. In others (e.g., the diesel locomotive, synthetic fibers, computerized machine tools), the inventions came from firms in other industries or universities. Not only does such evidence sharply contradict the Schumpeter–Galbraith hypothesis on automatic progress, but it brings into question some of the most sacred notions about economic stability. Whereas conventional wisdom holds that a stable economic system is as predictable as the planetary system, an economic system in which progress comes about at a regular rate involves unpredictable microbehavior: the more rapid the rate, the more unpredictable will be the microbehavior. Fast history is more unpredictable than slow history. And when new technologies revive a stagnant industry it can be predicted that the mutations will be brought about by a newcomer to the industry!

In some industries, new S-shaped curves are discovered quite regularly, while in others there is evidence of only one S-shaped curve. But in either event, more or less continuous progress can be looked upon as a "dynamic process." As the term has been used in the past in economics, a "dynamic process" involves the element of time, and its path is important. However, to qualify as a "dynamic process" in modern terms, the process must involve quite unpredictable changes in initial conditions. Another closely associated difference between a static and a dynamic process is that whereas the former only involves reversible change, the latter involves irreversible change. For example, changes in factor prices lead to reversible change. But a dynamic process is irreversible because it changes the knowledge of the world.

Now that a dynamic process has been described, it should be apparent why neither classical microtheory nor Bayesian probability theory can be used to explain it. The use of either would involve what has become known as the fallacy of composition error:

> An error in which what is true or seems to be true of the parts is alleged to be true of the whole—or what is true or seems to be true of the whole is alleged to be true of the parts.

Obviously smooth overall economic performance (the whole) cannot be attributed to entrepreneurs who are engaged in maximizing behavior. In order to maximize it is essential to assume that the alternatives are known. But if entrepreneurs were to restrict their role to only making choices among known alternatives, they never would be able to discover new alternatives! A Bayesian entrepreneur can deal with change—but only very gradual change. By assuming a quite mechanical process for revising prior probability distributions, Bayesian probability theory assumes, in effect, that an entrepreneur has no imagination. And an entrepreneur with no imagination would not be able to generate a significant ideological mutation.

Some economists not only tend to regard individual firms as microcosms of the GNP accounts, but they argue as if smooth microbehavior can be deduced from smooth macroperformance. However, this kind of reasoning also involves the fallacy of composition error. Indeed, I propose to show that in a world in which smooth progress occurs, there must be more than one kind of firm.

Therefore, to avoid the fallacy of composition error it will be necessary to introduce some new concepts. A key concept of dynamic theory is the distinction between micro- and macrostability. Microstability is the stability associated with an unchanging environment; and it implies a world in which only reversible change occurs—a world in which it is always possible to make good predictions on the basis of initial conditions. By contrast, macrostability is the stability associated with bringing about smooth progress; and it implies a world in which new knowledge is generated at a more or less constant rate. When fast history is being made, the degree of macrostability is said to be high; and when the S-shaped curve is rising slowly, the degree of macrostability is said to be low.

It might seem that the degree of macrostability should be measured by the "smoothness" of the curve, that is, by the regularity of the advances. However, as we already have seen, the essence of progress is the ability to adapt to new circumstances. Therefore, when the curve rises steeply and the technological environment changes more rapidly, a higher degree of macrostability is implied.

Economists accustomed to thinking in terms of a static concept of stability will regard a dynamic concept as being very unnatural. However, if the dynamic concept seems somewhat unreal, I suggest that the reason lies in confusing heavenly with earthly stability. In heaven, where there are perpetual truths, the environment is always highly predictable and stable. But on earth, where there are no perpetual truths, a "stable" environment is one in which man is prepared to acknowledge that when examined at close range his sacred theories may not be true.

Granting that earthly stability requires microbehavior which results in quite unpredictable changes in initial conditions, the problem at hand is to explain

(1)   the smoothness of the S-shaped curve and
(2)   the driving mechanism involved in determining whether history is fast or slow, and
(3)   to relate microbehavior and macroperformance by showing the

particular changes in microbehavior that will occur when the rate of progress either speeds up or slows down.

In Section 3 it will be shown how the first two points can be explained in terms of a theory of dynamic competition, and in Section 4 the relationship between macroperformance and microbehavior will be considered.

3. Dynamic Competition

As Stigler (1957) pointed out in one of his brilliant essays on the history of economic thought, from the time of Adam Smith to the time of Alfred Marshall the concept of competition which ruled the minds of economists was one involving rivalry between business firms to introduce better and/or cheaper products. Not until after Marshall's time, with the gradual acceptance of Cournot's concept of perfect competition, was the rivalry finally eliminated from competition.

One of the principal differences between the theory of perfect competition and the theory of dynamic competition is that whereas the former assumes that buyers and sellers have perfect information, the latter assumes that they have imperfect information. In fact, the entrepreneur's role in society is to discover things which seem to meet such an obvious need that people will think the discoveries were invented by themselves. Or to put the point another way, entrepreneurs act as marriage brokers between that which is possible from a scientific and technological point of view and that which is desirable from an economic point of view. And it is imperative that entrepreneurs believe all their recipes are but partial truths, because only if they assume a world of imperfect knowledge can better alternatives be discovered.

Another principal difference between the theory of perfect competition and the theory of dynamic competition is that whereas the effectiveness of the former depends on the number of sellers (with competition becoming perfect when the number of sellers becomes so large that each can have a negligible influence on price), the effectiveness of the latter depends on the degree of *competitive interaction*. The degree of competitive interaction is determined by the degree of advance sought by firms in a particular industry. When firms seek only marginal advances, as, say, in the automobile industry, they demand a low rate of progress from each other. On the other hand, when firms engage in ambitious advances, as, say, in the computer industry, they demand a larger rate of progress from each other; and if a firm sought only relatively trivial advances in a fast-history industry, it simply would not be able to survive. In short, the difference between industries in which the degree of competitive interaction is low and in those in which it is high is the difference between the minor and major athletic leagues.

What type of economic reality corresponds to a competitive interaction of "zero"? On the one hand, the theory of perfect competition can be thought of as a special and limiting case of the theory of dynamic competition: as an imaginary world in which there are no remaining economic potentials to exploit—an economy of pin mills, so to speak. On the other hand, in more earthly terms, there are those industries which engage in consonant behavior with respect to products and prices—industries whose behavior is strikingly similar to that of the nineteenth century trusts.

The essential difference between static and dynamic competition is that, whereas the former occurs under conditions of zero or weak uncertainties, the latter occurs under conditions of *strong* uncertainties. In my terms, a world of "zero" uncertainties would be a completely deterministic world: a world in which there can be neither uncertainty nor risk. A world of "weak" uncertainties would be one whose probability distributions were completely known; one in which it should be possible, therefore, to obtain insurance against all unforeseen events. In terms of the definitions advanced by Knight some years ago (1921), a world of statistical uncertainties would contain no genuine uncertainty, but it would contain an element of risk. However, in my terms, such a world would contain neither uncertainty nor risk. If people could completely insure their homes against fire—if they could count on the fact that a fire would result in no bad surprises—why should they not be completely indifferent if their homes burned down? And if business firms could completely insure themselves against the actions of their competitors, why should they engage in any research and development? If a firm is never able to catch its competition by surprise, why should the firm not be indifferent to its competitors' actions?

By contrast, a world of "strong" uncertainties is one in which it pays to heed feedback because business firms can create more or less serious dilemmas for their competitors. As defined in the dictionary, a "dilemma" is a position of doubt or perplexity in which a choice must be made between two or more equally unfavorable alternatives. And business firms which exist in the real world of strong uncertainties are more or less constantly involved in weighing two equally unfavorable alternatives: the technological risk involved in bringing about an advance and the competitive risk involved in losing a market to a competitor. Contrary to what seems to be a widespread impression, business firms bringing about impressive advances are not necessarily acting as fearless competitors—they may be acting out of desperation. For example, at the time Boeing developed the prototype for the 707 jet airplane, it had lost $50 million on its stratocruiser commercial airplane, and consequently risked being driven out of the commercial market altogether. Likewise, at the time IBM went into the computer business, its prospects were none too promising. At that time, its product lines consisted of butcher scales, meat slicers, coffee grinders, time clocks, and an assortment of punched card and tabulating equipment. In short, whereas classical theory assumes only positive incentives (in the form of a hidden hand), negative incentives (in the form of a hidden foot) can be quite as important in explaining behavior.

What can be said about the difference in incentives between those industries which seek only modest advances and those which seek major advances? Let us assume, first, that in the field in question something like half of the buyers engage in comparison shopping. Obviously, without buyers who search no progress could come about.

Assuming that such buyers exist, it can be stated that the essential difference between the minor leagues in which the degree of competitive interaction is low and the major leagues in which it is high is that in the latter case changes in market shares which result from the introduction of new products is likely to be significantly greater. Why? As the reduction in price or the improvement in quality for a given price is made larger and larger, a state will be reached in which there is a large "income" effect; an effect which will, in turn, cause consumers to make large-scale changes in their affiliations. For example, it has been found that whereas a new airliner which promises a 5% reduction in operating and maintenance costs only has a marginal impact on demand, a 15 or 20% reduction is likely to have a major impact (Phillips, 1971). Though a 5% reduction in costs may not warrant airline companies setting up maintenance and training facilities for the new airplane, a 15 or 20% reduction does have a very significant income effect for them.

How, then, can dynamic theory explain the smoothness of progress and the degree of macrostability?

Under conditions of strong uncertainties, firms cannot take out insurance against the actions of their competitors. So what must they do? They must insure themselves against uncertainty by being prepared to do to their competitors what their competitors can do to them. And since competitors cannot predict others' discoveries, the output of such competition is a diversity of approaches for attaining the same general objective. To be sure, not all approaches will be equally successful. Indeed, it is in providing options that microdiversity is the hidden hand of macrostability.

It is important to note, however, that a diversity of ideas can be generated only as long as competitors cannot predict others' actions. Only because firms must insure themselves against uncertainty can smooth progress be made!

The degree of macrostability depends on whether entrepreneurs aim for modest or ambitious advances. When entrepreneurs aim for only modest advances, they demand in return only a modest rate of progress and history will be slow. On the other hand, when entrepreneurs aim for significant advances, they demand a larger rate of progress from others—which means overcoming larger discontinuities to promote a more steeply rising rate of progress.

Logically speaking, there are, of course, other ways progress might come about. In particular, we can imagine a monopoly headed by Schumpeter's hero entrepreneur who brings about progress quite automatically. The essence of Schumpeter's automatic progress theory as set forth in his *Capitalism, Socialism and Democracy* (1942) is that the rate of progress does not depend on the degree of competitive interaction. I am willing to grant that the rate would never go to zero, because the top leadership of business firms would always have an incentive to swell the ranks of the nobility in order to prevent the middle management from taking over altogether. It is my contention, however, that the rate of progress cannot be predicted independently of the degree of competitive interaction.

How can it be known which theory is more nearly correct? If it is assumed that the test of all knowledge is the ability to predict, then the question is which theory makes better predictions, mine or Schumpeter's? One way to test the two theories is to observe changes in market shares. If my theory is correct, in industries where progress is rapid we should expect to observe quite significant changes in market share, because such changes are associated with a high degree of competitive interaction. On the other hand, if Schumpeter's theory is correct, we should expect to observe rapid progress with relatively constant market shares. And one case which might seem to support his hypothesis is the rapid progress made in reducing the cost of long distance and international phone calls (Fig. 3).

Because telephone companies do not compete with each other for markets, here seems to be a case in which the degree of competitive interaction is close to zero. Nevertheless, other forms of competition did take place. There was competition to provide undersea telephone cables and communications satellites. And to the extent allowed by the Federal Trade Commission, there was competition with private companies to install their own microwave relay systems. Furthermore, progress gener-

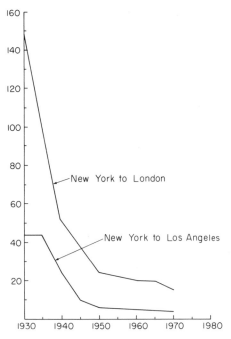

Figure 3   Long-distance telephone rates (5 min, person to person). [AT&T (January 1974).]

ated by AT&T was not as automatic as many people had assumed, because (as Fig. 3 also shows) as far as long distance and international calls are concerned, there has been a definite slackening in the rate of progress.

On the other hand, the chemical industry has sustained progress longer than any other industry. But this is an industry in which there is a high degree of competitive interaction as measured by changes in market shares. And the same has been true in the aircraft engine, commercial aircraft, and semiconductor industries.

Another test of the dynamic theory advanced here concerns the internal characteristics of firms. As will be seen in some detail in Section 4, in the more competitive industries firms must deal with more uncertainty—and the more uncertainty with which they must cope, the greater will be the degree of "openness" demanded. To meet this demand requires quite specific changes in the internal characteristics of firms. And if my argument is correct, we should expect quite significant changes in both the types of people who get ahead most rapidly and in the degree of constraint imposed upon their interactions whenever there is a significant increase or decline in the degree of competitive interaction.

4. The Relationship between Microbehavior and Macroperformance

Suppose that an industry remains in a "dynamic equilibrium" in the sense that during the period under consideration the degree of competitive interaction remains more or less constant. Also suppose that a sufficient period has elapsed for firms to become more or less fully adjusted to this equilibrium. If my argument is correct, there is a unique relationship between the degree of uncertainty with which an organization must deal and its internal characteristics. To be sure, we can expect to observe identical behavior in business firms no more than in criminal-law firms. Nevertheless, it is my contention that, just as large differences can be observed between probate-law firms and criminal-law firms, we should expect to find large differences between business firms engaged in making fast history and those producing slow history.

To make this argument I employ the concept of openness, which plays more or less the same central and unifying role in dynamic theory as does the concept of specialization in static theory, inasmuch as it not only permits us to explain how ideological mutations are generated, but it enables us to relate microbehavior and macroperformance.

An "open system" is one in which there is a two-way interaction between the system and its environment. For example, if an entrepreneur is defined as the "system" and the technology in question as the "environment," then an effective interaction will be one in which the entrepreneur discovers that his previous ideas with respect to the efficiency of that technology were only partial truths, and he is, therefore, able to bring about a significant improvement in the technology. An economic system, therefore, would be defined as "open" when interactions between entrepreneurs and their technological environments are permitted to result in the generation of new knowledge.

By contrast, a closed economic system is a special case of an open economic system in which there is assumed to be no environment. In science, the classical example of a theory based upon a closed-system paradigm is Newtonian celestial mechanics. And in economics the classical example of a theory based upon a closed system paradigm is to be found in Walrasian general equilibrium economics. However, there is a difference between the manners by which Newton and Walras went about establishing their theories. Newton based his theory upon observations made by Tycho Brache which, in turn, had been brilliantly analyzed by Kepler. Newton demonstrated the utility of his theory by showing that it could make fantastically good predictions. By contrast, Walras simply assumed a closed economic system: one in which the alternatives had to be taken as a given. And he never bothered to make any predictions.

Indeed, from Walras's point of view it really was not necessary to make predictions, because by assuming a closed economic system he left entrepreneurs with no choice other than to engage in profit maximization!

On the other hand, a semiclosed system paradigm can be described as a special and limiting case of an open system in which the environment must be taken as a given. The classic examples are Darwinian biology and Marshallian economics. One chief difference between a closed- and a semiclosed-system paradigm is that the latter does permit some degree of uncertainty with respect to the adaptions which may take place. Thus, whereas a closed system model is completely deterministic, the best mathematical representation of a semiclosed system paradigm which has been developed to date uses Bayesian probability theory. When choosing between alternative probability distributions, a Bayesian entrepreneur is in effect making choices in the face of a given environment.

From these descriptions it should be clear that we might consider a semiclosed-system paradigm as one with a lower degree of openness than an open-system paradigm, and a closed-system paradigm as one with a zero degree of openness. Moreover, it also should be apparent that under the general category of an open system, higher and lower degrees of openness can be conceived. Openness is essentially a capability for dealing with uncertainty—the more the uncertainty, the greater the requirement for openness. The ability to detach hints from particular experiences in order to use them to guess at new ideological mutations is a function of openness. Hints may come from either a relatively narrow or wide spectrum of experiences (or experiments). For example, less uncertainty is involved when undertaking to design a new type of spark plug than is involved in "guessing" about or inventing a new type of propulsion designed to do significantly better than any developed to date at minimizing both fuel consumption and emissions. And with more uncertainty involved, making the latter type of discovery will require a greater degree of openness.

What openness buys is a greater freedom of choice in making good use of diversity. Diversity can be defined narrowly or broadly. More specifically, it can be defined as

(1)   making choices between well-known substitutes,

(2)   making choices between alternative probability distributions, and

(3)   as hints to be used for the generation of new alternative probability distributions.

It can be assumed that just as (2) includes (1) as a special case, so does (3) include (1) and (2). And it is easy to show that an entrepreneur's freedom of choice in making good use of diversity to deal with uncertainty will increase if he is willing to define diversity more broadly.

To consider this matter further, let us think of the appropriate strategy for Dennis the Menace to employ when playing Scrabble with his rival, Bruce. Leaving out of account for the moment the manner by which Dennis defines diversity, it should be apparent that, generally speaking, scores in successive games of Scrabble will not only depend upon the diversity of letters picked D, but also upon the freedom of choice which is exercised in making use of diversity (FC), or

$$S = f(D, \text{ FC}).$$

Figures 4a and 4b illustrate the functional relationships for a fairly typical situation. No matter how diversity is defined, as Figs. 4a and 4b show, exercising close to 100% freedom of choice will result in substantially higher scores. For example, if diversity is defined as making choices among known alternatives, then a profit maximizer can do a good deal better than a player who refuses to make substitutions.

How broadly or narrowly should Dennis the Menace define diversity? It all depends upon the type of player his opponent is. If Bruce is a completely predictable profit maximizer who can be counted upon never to speculate on words he thinks he knows—in other words, if Bruce is the type of a person who never makes bets with himself—then it obviously will not pay Dennis to define freedom of choice very broadly. Why take unnecessary risks?

Conversely, assume that Bruce is a highly unpredictable player, who on the basis of his knowledge of the structure of the English language is willing to guess at words he has never before used. For example, if only slightly imaginative, Bruce might be willing to attach "non" or "pre" to known words to form words he has never used. On the other hand, Bruce

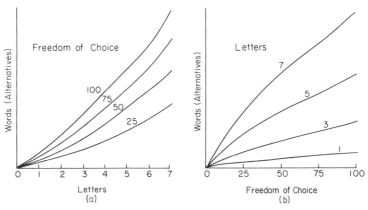

Figure 4   Making words: (a) alternatives versus letters (freedom of choice constant); (b) alternatives versus freedom of choice (number of letters constant).

might be the type of player who is willing to make use of far less obvious hints about the structure of the English language. And as Bruce defines diversity more and more broadly, Dennis will discover he cannot afford to be unimaginative. If Dennis has any hope of winning the game, he obviously must exercise quite as high freedom of choice as Bruce.

In short, more openness buys a greater freedom of choice. And the question of the optimal degree of openness cannot be divorced from uncertainties associated with an external environment. The more uncertainty that is involved the greater will be the demand for openness.

Now it is true, of course, that if the ability to deal with uncertainty were a free good, firms would be able to respond to new circumstances almost routinely. However, people with the combination of personality characteristics required for a high degree of openness do not tend to be in oversupply. Not only does openness require imagination to detach hints from particular experiences to guess at new ideological mutations, but it also requires flexibility. And, most important of all, openness requires people who are not only sensitive to negative feedback, but who are willing to acknowledge that at close range all of their sacred theories may not be true.

Because they employ more imaginative and flexible people, some firms are better able to deal with uncertainty than others. In fact, specialization exists not only in the sense that firms produce different kinds of goods and services, but also in the sense that they engage in more and less predictable activities. For example, in the 1920s some companies operated airlines and also developed and produced airliners. But it was not too long before these multipurpose organizations concluded that though related, a separation from one another would be mutually advantageous. If the airline companies had continued to develop their own airplanes, progress would have had to be sacrificed to obtain a greater degree of dependability. Conversely, if the airplane companies had continued to operate their own airlines, dependability and static efficiency would have had to be sacrificed to obtain progress and dynamic efficiency. For the same reason, the automobile industry relies mainly on subcontractors for its progress, as do the electric utility companies. And within AT&T for many years there has been a division of labor with Bell Telephone Laboratories specializing in "dynamic" and Western Electric in "static" efficiency.

Nevertheless, no firm possesses an unlimited capability to deal with uncertainty. And it can be assumed that as the degree of uncertainty is increased, the ability of firms to deal with dilemmas will not only decline, but a point will be reached at which the organization will be overwhelmed (Fig. 5).

Because the ability to deal with uncertainty is limited, it is impossible in

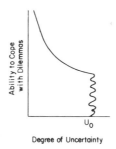

Figure 5 The uncertainty precipice.

a world of progress for individuals or firms to conserve their microstability. For example, a student who tries to get an absolutely perfect answer to the first question on an examination will find that he has made more uncertain his chances of completing the examination. And the same is true of business firms. By making one aspect of a favorable outcome more certain, a firm will find it has made other aspects more uncertain. Suppose, for example, that the top management of a computer or aircraft company insists upon freezing the design very early and lays down a deadline for the completion of the project. If this occurs, the firm must be prepared for a high degree of unpredictability in the cost of the system (Fig. 6).

Therefore, in order to survive, firms must attempt to conserve, not their microstability, but rather their ability to deal with unpredictability. What kind of behavior will be involved in recognizing that there is an uncertainty trade-off? Generally speaking, a sequential decision-making process is involved in which the entrepreneur attempts to preserve his freedom of choice with respect to generating new knowledge. For example, an artist would not begin painting a mural by first making a detailed plan of the final product, because he would recognize that such a procedure is inconsistent with the utilization of knowledge gained during the execution of his project. Rather, he will begin with rough drawings—and only after overcoming crucial uncertainties will he turn to the details. Likewise, firms which are highly skilled in developing new microwave systems or new aircraft engines do not initiate their development work on the basis of detailed plans of the final system. Experience has taught them that they live in a world of strong uncertainties wherein many unexpected events will undoubtedly occur, therefore, to engage in such a restricted procedure would vastly complicate their tasks. So instead they begin with a rough idea of the important constraints which have to be overcome to make significant advances, and then proceed in a manner which does not foreclose the possibility of generating lower-cost solutions to difficult techno-

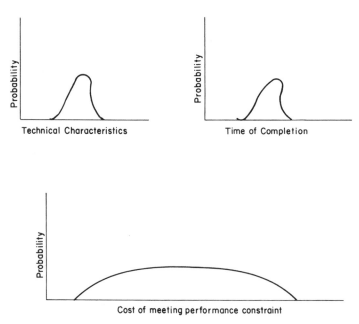

Figure 6 The uncertainty trade-off.

logical problems. What if it proves to be impossible to keep within the cost constraint? The firm can decide on the basis of a relatively inexpensive procedure whether or not it is worthwhile to go ahead with a full-fledged development and production program. In fact, the essential role of exploratory development projects is to ascertain the likelihood of coming within certain cost constraints. Generally speaking, engineers know beforehand whether or not particular approaches will violate physical laws. But what they do not know is how much new alternatives are likely to cost. Therefore, only by establishing a tight cost constraint can it be determined how ingenious they are likely to be.

Now the degree of openness will obviously depend on the degree of uncertainty involved in the activity in question. In general, the tighter the cost constraint, the greater will be the amount of uncertainty involved and the greater the requirement for openness. In fact, it is relatively easy to show that for every degree of uncertainty there is an optimal degree of openness. Let us start by postulating a world of weak uncertainties. In such a world the entrepreneur would know the uncertainty trade-off beforehand—and his problem would be a relatively simple one. Suppose that the uncertainty U associated with a favorable outcome of the dilemma A facing the firm is

$$U(A) = KU(x_1)U(x_2),$$

where K is a constant (which depends on initial conditions) and x_1 and x_2 are the factors upon which A depends. For example, x_1 can represent the initial cost goal and x_2 the initial time goal for building the airplane. On the basis of this assumption, the trade-off between $U(x_1)$ and $U(x_2)$ would be "smooth" (Fig. 7).

The entrepreneur would only have to decide how much a more-definite "time" estimate was worth to him in terms of a less-certain cost estimate. However, while the trade-off shown resembles the one described in the uncertainty principle in physics, once humans are brought into the equation strong uncertainties are introduced, which is to say, life becomes more complicated. An illustration showing that the trade-off cannot be smooth when humans are concerned is that of a contractor who desires to save time during the construction of a building, and thinks he knows the trade-off between his cost and time uncertainties. The contractor believes that with the addition of more and more workers his initial cost estimates will be made more uncertain, because the additional men will impede progress by getting in each other's way. In fact, he understands that if enough workers are added, a point will be reached in which the outcome of their work will be totally unpredictable. He will have people hitting each other with shovels—a situation which can be described as an infinite amount of motion, but no movement. What the contractor does not know is *just when in the course of adding more and more workers the process will become totally unpredictable*. Once human beings are put into the equation, we are forced to acknowledge that the world social scientists observe is a world of *strong uncertainties*.

When the uncertainties are strong, the entrepreneur cannot see the trade-off curve in its entirety. Depending on the degree of uncertainty which is involved, he is in a position to understand the implications of the trade-off between time and cost uncertainty only within rather ill-defined limits (Fig. 8).

Now, the entrepreneur engaged in developing a computer obviously

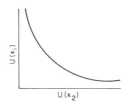

Figure 7 A smooth uncertainty trade-off.

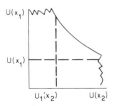

Figure 8   A real-world uncertainty trade-off.

sees a smaller portion of the trade-off curve than the entrepreneur who is trying to save time on a construction project. But regardless of whether the portion is small or large, by placing artificial constraints on his freedom of choice the entrepreneur cannot demand less uncertainty than $U_1(x_2)$ in his initial time goal or less uncertainty than $U_1(x_1)$ in his initial cost target. If it is assumed that $U_0(x_1)$ is the maximum uncertainty in costs, and $U_0(x_2)$ the maximum uncertainty in time with which the entrepreneur can cope (Fig. 9), then it appears that the process of minimizing $U(A)$ defines an upper and lower boundary for the optimal uncertainty in the cost goal and the time target. Hence, a successful optimization process requires that

$$U_1(x_1) < U(x_1) < U_0(x_1) \qquad \text{and} \qquad U_1(x_2) < U(x_2) < U_0(x_2).$$

Another way to describe the optimal degree of openness is as the optimal degree of "constraint." If the firm in question imposes too small a degree of constraint upon itself, it risks being driven out of business by its competitors. But if it imposes too great a degree of constraint, it risks being overwhelmed by uncertainty. Seeking the optimal degree of openness means trying to stay within these limits.

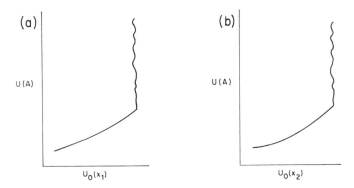

Figure 9   (a) $U(x_1)$, with $U(x_2)$ fixed; (b) $U(x_2)$, with $U(x_1)$ fixed.

How can the concept "the optimal degree of openness" help us establish the relationship between microbehavior and macroperformance? As we already have seen, the greater the rate of progress, the more uncertainty that will be encountered; and the more uncertainty, the greater will be the requirement on openness. The main issue in relating microbehavior to macroperformance is to show how a greater or lesser requirement for openness is reflected in the internal characteristics of firms.

Let us call the rate of progress in improving the performance of a particular technology ΔE. What we would like to know is the difference in microbehavior when the curve is rising rapidly (fast history) and when it is rising slowly (slow history). We should expect to find, in terms of how well they are equipped to deal with uncertainty, two principal differences between organizations engaged in making fast history and those engaged in making slow history. The fast-history organizations will contain a wider diversity of people with respect to their openness and previous experiences, and they will be capable of engaging in a wider diversity of interactions to make good use of human diversity.

4.1 Diversity of People

A fairly good indicator of the openness and hence the creativity of people is to be found in psychological tolerance of ambiguity tests. Psychologists have found that beyond a certain threshold (the threshold depending on the field in question) tolerance of ambiguity tests make better predictions of creativity than do standard intelligence tests (MacKinnon, 1963; Roberts, 1969). Quite consistent with these results, in a large electronics company it was found that the tolerance of ambiguity test predicted better who would make it into the middle management than the standard intelligence test.

It is true, of course, that in fast-history organizations not all will score high in tolerance of ambiguity tests. In such organizations there are many tasks which, as in slow-history organizations, require highly methodical people. What we should expect to find in fast-history organizations, therefore, is a wider diversity of people as measured by tolerance of ambiguity tests.

We should also expect to find in fast-history organizations people who are representative of a much broader background of experiences. Peoples' views of the world are highly colored by their previous experiences. And the more diversity in their experiences, the better able is the organization to cope with uncertainty. Conversely, from the point of view of a firm optimized for slow history, the need for specialists will preclude an organization whose members possess a wide diversity of experiences.

4.2 Diversity of Interactions

A good indicator of the diversity of the interactions in an organization is the diversity of communications. Organizations engaged in making slow history will tend to have a highly developed chain of command, with people becoming more and more specialized in the lower echelons. For example, in the Ford Motor Company there are 13 quite distinct echelons of command, with each lower echelon being more specialized than the one above. Thus, within the engine division there are sections dealing with moving parts and sections which deal with stationary parts. And these sections are further subdivided into individual component groups. In short, such organizations are organized to make good use of human diversity not so much in terms of peoples' openness or their previous experiences as in terms of their particular fields of expertise. And this being the case, the pattern of communications in such organizations tends to be quite predictable—with communications running up and down well-developed hierarchies of command.

By contrast, organizations which are optimized to deal with a greater degree of uncertainty must, if they are to be dynamically efficient, be capable of a greater diversity of interactions, because only by doing so can they make good use of human diversity. Hence, in such organizations there tend to be fewer echelons of command and wider discrepancies between observed behavior and that indicated by the formal organization chart.

It is not only for this reason, however, that organizations optimized for fast history tend to contain a good deal more randomness in their communications. To a much greater extent than slow-history organizations, fast-history organizations thrive on conflict, that is, on impersonalized conflict concerning how best to achieve certain objectives. And because such conflict can only take place in an environment in which there is a good deal of trust, the organization must be relatively unstructured from the point of view of permitting ambiguity in the role relationships—without which trust is likely to be in short supply and conflict is likely to be personalized.

Let us assume that a diversity of people index D_p can be constructed on a scale from zero to one. When the index is zero the people think as one; and when it is one the organization can generate a bewildering assortment of ideas. Likewise, assume that we can postulate a diversity of interactions index D_i measured on a scale from zero to one. When it is zero the interactions are completely prescribed and the organization is quite predictable. When it is one they are completely unprescribed and the organization is in the state of anarchy.

In very general terms we can say that the rate or progress ΔE is a

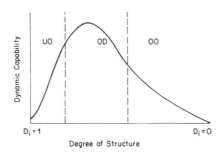

Figure 10 Openness versus the degree of organization.

function of the diversity of people D_p, the diversity of the interactions D_i, and luck L, or

$$\Delta E = f(D_p, D_i; L).$$

What state of organization will maximize the organization's capability for dealing with uncertainty (i.e., its openness)? If the D_i index is zero, the organization is in the state of absolute monarchy and its dynamic capability depends upon luck and luck alone. Conversely, when the D_i index is one, the organization is in the state of anarchy, and luck and luck alone can bring order out of chaos. Therefore, as indicated in Fig. 10, its openness is largest when the organization is in the state of organized disorganization. In this state there is so much randomness in the interactions that luck cannot be distinguished from any other hint, which means that in this state the ability of the organization to deal with uncertainty is maximized.

It is important to keep in mind, however, that, as the degree of uncertainty declines, the optimal organization will contain a greater degree of structure. In fact, if an organization were perfectly optimized for an unchanging environment (i.e., the state of absolute monarchy), it would have no capability whatsoever to engage in dynamic behavior. It is impossible to pursue both the goals of static and dynamic efficiency because an organization cannot be simultaneously optimized for higher and lower degrees of uncertainty. To make good use of existing knowledge (as distinct from generating new knowledge) a firm must be organized to take maximum advantage of the economies of specialization—and this inevitably means paying a price in terms of dynamic efficiency.

5. Diversity and Stability

There are three principal types of diversity. Provided that sufficient competitive pressures exist to induce business firms to exercise a high freedom of choice in making good use of diversity, we will find that associated with each type of diversity is a related type of stability:

(1)   Diversity in the form of well-defined substitutes permits lower variance outcomes, because with a greater availability of substitutes outcomes are less sensitive to luck.

(2)   Diversity in the form of ill-defined substitutes not only permits lower variance outcomes, but as entrepreneurs engage in buying information they will increase the availability of well-defined alternatives and the degree of redundancy in the economy.

(3)   Diversity in the form of new ideological mutations not only increases the degree of redundancy but it enables smooth progress to be made in overcoming discontinuities.

However, dynamic competition provides not only a stimulus to smooth progress (either in the form of improved quality or of reduced costs), but also a constraint on wage and price increases. A firm which attempts to increase its wages more rapidly than its productivity or its prices significantly more rapidly than it improves the quality of its products would defeat its purpose.

Inasmuch as competition acts as both a stimulus to productivity gains and a deterrent on wage and price increases, it can be predicted that in the absence of competition unions will become both more resistant to technological change and less statesmanlike in their demands for higher wages. For example, it is no accident that at a relatively early date restrictive union practices flourished in the railroad industry in the United States. Nor is it any accident that in Britain the absence of competition and the presence of restrictive labor practices have gone hand in hand. A country with little or no competition is one in which microstability is sooner or later destined to become the law of the land.

Can there be a *general decline* in competition in a country—and if there is, how will that country's economic performance be affected? Let us suppose that industrial revolutions tend to come in bunches. Let us further suppose that as industrial revolutions die out there is a significant decline in the average degree of openness in the economy. An economy with a low degree of openness is more vulnerable to both inflation and recession, because in such an economy inflation can be halted only by widespread unemployment. To be more specific, when there is a decline in openness (and a curtailment of the ability to engage in dynamic competition), dynamic theory predicts an upward shift in the Phillips curve, and when the average degree of openness increases, a downward shift. Why? To be sure, competition as an economic stabilizer does involve some frictional unemployment. But, because competition operates on the basis of positive as well as negative incentives and involves an expansion of employment in more-competitive firms as well as a contraction in less-competitive firms, as it dies out of an economy positive incentives will play a smaller role—with the economy acquiring a larger inflationary bias and inflation beginning at higher levels of unemployment.

The primary example of a country which lost her dynamic stability, never to regain it, is, of course, Britain. The British industrial revolutions were almost entirely centered on the application of steam power for transportation and to a variety of industries. And when the industrial revolutions died out, the established firms almost automatically became more structured and lost their ability to engage in dynamic behavior. Because new trees did not become established in the forest at the same rate as the older ones lost their ability to engage in dynamic behavior, Britain's decline in openness proved to be quite irreversible: after the Great Depression of 1875 the British economy never recovered its dynamic vitality. Thus, it is no accident that Britain developed a chronic inflation problem in the late nineteenth century; and that as far as Britain is concerned, the Phillips curve has been remarkably stable.

What about the economic performance of the United States? The post-World War II industrial revolutions which included synthetic fibers, a long list of new pharmaceuticals, television, computers, computerized machine tools, the oxygen and electric processes in steel, jet airliners, underseas telephone cables, and communications satellites were quite as profound as any experienced in its entire history. But since about 1965 the revolutions have been dying out. Evidence of a decline in dynamic behavior in the United States is to be found in the loss of technological leadership: whereas the United States once was a near monopolist in the exploration of technology-intensive commodities (commodities whose development requires a relatively large number of engineers and scientists per unit of output), the United States is now importing about half as many technology-intensive commodities as it is exporting. Evidence of a decline in dynamic behavior is also to be found in a slowdown in productivity in manufacturing relative to other countries and a reduction of the absolute number of scientists and engineers in industry (see Fig. 11).

On the basis of these macroindicators a very significant decline in the degree of openness of United States firms can be predicted with an upward shift in the Phillips curve. And it is apparent such a shift has occurred. In the period 1955–1965, United States unemployment averaged 5.3% of the labor force, and the consumer price index increased less than 2% annually. But as of 1974, the United States experienced an 11% inflation rate with about a 5.5% unemployment rate (ERP, 1975). To be sure, it is fashionable to blame inflation on the energy shortage. But even before

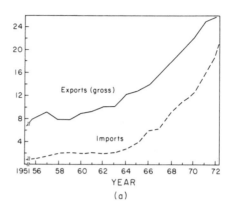

(a)

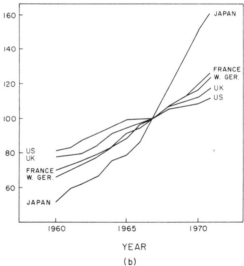

YEAR

(b)

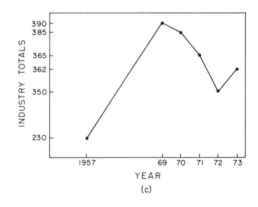

YEAR

(c)

the energy shortage the inflation rate in the United States was about 9% (ERP, 1975).

What, then, must happen if the decline in competition in the United States is not to prove to be quite as irreversible as the decline in Britain? In the past, the dynamism of the United States economy was restored by the appearance of new organizations, whether established by new firms or by existing firms. However, there is a real question as to whether the United States or other countries will be able to maintain their dynamism in the future by establishing new firms. Not only is the United States economy a more integrated economy than it was 25 years ago, so is the world economy. In terms of Marshall's simile, this means that a relatively few older trees in the forest can jeopardize the survival of the entire forest!

I suggest, therefore, that unless new ways can be found to promote competition or to otherwise remedy the shortage of risk-taking in the United States, it is likely to experience quite as irreversible a decline in competition as has Britain.

References

Enos, J. L. (1962). *Petroleum Progress and Profits: A History of Process Innovation*. Cambridge, Massachusetts: MIT Press.

ERP (1975). *Economic Report of the President*, pp. 128–147. Washington, D.C.: U.S. Govt. Printing Office (February).

Feynman, R. P., Leighton, R. B., and Sands, M. (1963). *The Feynman Lectures on Physics*, Vol. 1, pp. 44-2–44-10. Reading, Massachusetts: Addison Wesley.

Jewkes, J., Sawers, D., and Stillerman, R., (1969). *The Sources of Invention*, 2nd ed., pp. 214–215. London: Macmillan.

Knight, F. H. (1921). *Risk, Uncertainty and Profit*, p. 249. Boston: Houghton Mifflin.

Kuznets, S. (1959). *Six Lectures on Economic Growth*. New York: Free Press–Macmillan.

MacKinnon, D. W. (1963). The Characteristics of Creative Architects, AIA–ACSA Teacher Seminar.

Phillips, A. (1971). *Technology and Market Structure*. Lexington, Massachusetts: Heath Lexington.

Roberts, E. B. (1969). Entrepreneurship of Technology, in *Factors in the Transfer of Technology* (W. H. Gruber and D. G. Marquis, eds.). Cambridge, Massachusetts: MIT Press.

Figure 11 Indicators of macroperformance. (a) Decline in technological leadership (technology-intensive manufactured products). [Graphs from M. Boretsky, *Science* **179** (March 2, 1973).] (b) Indexes of output per man hour in manufacturing (1967 = 100). [Data from A. Meef, Unit Labor Costs in Eleven Countries, *Monthly Labor Review*, 1971, United States Department of Labor, Bureau of Labor Statistics.] (c) Full-time-equivalent number of research and development scientists and engineers, by industry, January 1957–1973.

Schumpeter, J. A. (1942). *Capitalism, Socialism and Democracy*, pp. 153–163. New York: Harper.

Stigler, G. (1957). Perfect Competition Historically Contemplated, *Journal of Political Economy* **65** (February).

Division of Humanities and Social Science
California Institute of Technology
Pasadena, California

The Economics of Keynes

John H. Power

1. Introduction

After four decades, the economics profession is still seeking a consensus on the interpretation of Keynes's *The General Theory* (1936). Moreover, we are perhaps further away from such a consensus today than we were 10 years ago when the success of practical Keynesian policies could override doubts about the importance of Keynes's contribution to pure theory. Then the "New Economists" were only too happy to concede theoretical points to neoclassical critics if, in turn, it were agreed that within the institutional constraints of modern, industrialized societies, discretionary monetary–fiscal policies are superior to unaided market forces for the purpose of attaining a high level of employment without serious inflation. If all that was accomplished by flexibility of the general levels of wages and prices was the ultimate creation of the right level of real money balances, then why not do this more expeditiously through control of nominal balances? And if the response of spending to monetary changes might, in some circumstances, be delayed or uncertain, then why not combine fiscal policy with monetary policy to achieve a quicker and surer effect? The debate over macroeconomic equilibrium theory could be conceded so long as Keynesian forecasting and policy-planning models were ascendant.

Thus in the face of what Clower has termed the "Keynesian counter-revolution" a truce emerged, as Leijonhufvud (1968) noted, on the basis of two propositions:

> (1) the model which Keynes had the gall to call his "General Theory" is but a special case of the Classical theory, obtained by imposing certain restrictive assumptions on the latter; and (2) the Keynesian "special case," while theoretically trivial, is nonetheless important because it so happens that it is a better guide in the real world than the general (equilibrium) theory [p. 7].

But the move toward consensus in the 1960s went beyond this, at least in the United States. Leading New Economists, while "Keynesian" in their short-run contracyclical policy prescriptions, tended to be neoclassical in their growth theory.[1] Thus, while the market could not be trusted with the task of short-run stabilization via wage and price flexibility, the "stylized facts" of modern economic growth could best be explained by neoclassical adjustments of relative factor prices and proportions. Indeed, in the neoclassical–Keynesian synthesis (hereafter referred to as the Synthesis), it seemed that there was an important complementarity between Keynesian stabilization and neoclassical growth. If monetary–fiscal policies could counter short-run disturbances, long-run flexibility of relative prices and factor proportions would accommodate changing growth parameters to ensure unimpeded growth at the "natural" rate.[2]

Two events have occurred over the past decade to upset what seemed to be an incipient evolution of a consensus on Keynesian economics. First is the apparent failure of Keynesian policies to provide a reasonable com-

---

[1] Samuelson, Solow, and Tobin, for example, seem to fall in this category.

[2] The synthesists are caught in a cross-fire, of course, between the monetarists, who believe that discretionary policies accentuate disturbances, and the Cambridge (England) "Neo-Keynesians," who deny the legitimacy of the neoclassical growth theory. While these schools have impressive memberships and raise issues of great importance, they will be neglected here because their principal theses appear to me to stand outside of the tradition of Keynes's *The General Theory*. This may raise eyebrows in England, but the view here is that "Neo-Ricardian," rather than "Neo-Keynesian," better describes the Cambridge position.

bination of high employment, price stability, and growth. As Hicks (1974) has put it recently,

> Instead of producing *real* economic progress, or growth, as they had for so long appeared to do, they were just producing inflation. Something, it seemed clear, had gone wrong. . . . So the issue which had seemed closed is reopened. We have to start, in a way, all over again [p. 4].

The other event that has helped to upset the uneasy consensus already described is the forceful attack on the theoretical underpinnings of the neoclassical resurgence which was launched by Clower (1965) about a decade ago, and carried forward by Leijonhufvud (1968), Hines (1971), and others. To this writer the arguments of Clower *et al.* are generally convincing as far as they go, and their effect is to help to reestablish the validity of Keynes's original theoretical position. I think, however, that they do not go nearly far enough. And in one very important respect—namely, the treatment of involuntary unemployment—there remains an ambiguity, perhaps carried over from Keynes, that seriously weakens the argument. We shall see that putting the Keynesian theory in a growth context serves to remedy this defect, and provides us with a much stronger concept of involuntary unemployment.

Despite the efforts of Clower (1965), Leijonhufvud (1968), and others, the majority in the economics profession has been very reluctant to abandon the standard model of the Synthesis; and seems unlikely to respond favorably to Hicks's suggestion to "start all over again." In this writer's view, however, we might indeed benefit by returning to square one—*The General Theory*—to begin again.

Permit me to preface my attempt to contribute to this with a very brief account of how, in my opinion, we got off the path that should have led from *The General Theory*. Because of inconsistencies and ambiguities in that work, it would be easy to lay a part of the blame on Keynes himself. I think, however, that this would be grossly unfair. In the course of his "long struggle of escape" from old ideas, he provided a tremendous push forward into a realm of economic doctrine of which, as Clower has put it, "no authorative account had ever been given." Nor could he have been expected to anticipate all the areas of difficulty and controversy that have emerged in the course of digesting *The General Theory*. The economics of Keynes, as understood here, is that line of development of economic thought that Keynes initiated—not simply *The General Theory* itself.[3]

---

[3] Patinkin (1975) has recently expressed a similar view of the nature of Keynes's contribution to economic theory: "Keynes analytical strength lay in his creative insights about fundamental problems that led him to make major 'breakthroughs'—leaving for those that followed him to formalise and complete his initial achievements [p. 266]."

Nevertheless, *The General Theory* did indeed represent a revolutionary change in thinking about employment, interest, and prices. The nature of this change was not easy to comprehend even for Keynes, who was most familiar with it. For others, the early simplified "Keynes-and-the-Classics" models were an important aid in learning what the revolution was all about. But they represented only a first step in gaining some insight. Standing alone, they were (and are) only caricatures of the general theory. Yet it is these caricatures that we find today in textbooks, represented as Keynesian theory.[4]

The renaissance of Walrasian general equilibrium theory came soon after via Hicks's *Value and Capital* (1939); and thereafter it was modish to set Keynesian theory in the Walrasian framework. For reasons that Clower has ably demonstrated, this was not only inadequate, but highly misleading. Shortly thereafter, the real-balance effect on consumption from movements of the general price level was discovered independently by Haberler (1941, pp. 498–503), Pigou (1941, pp. 127–129), and Scitovsky (1940, pp. 68–88). Unfortunately, the timeless, static versions of Haberler and Pigou received the major share of attention. Scitovsky, in contrast, had laid emphasis on the importance of the time rate of movement of prices, the limitations thereon, and the implications of a regime of limited wage and price flexibility. In so doing he arrived at a reaffirmation of the Keynesian position; but it was the attempted refutation of Keynes by Haberler and Pigou that established the real-balance effect in the Keynesian–neoclassical synthesis. Finally, Patinkin's (1965) marriage of the real-balance effect to the Walrasian system of price adjustment provided the Synthesis with a means of avoiding the logical inconsistencies inherent in the former. For where, outside of a timeless regime of administered equilibrium prices, could one expect transactors to treat each price change as permanent? And yet, without this, we cannot retain the convention—so important in defining absence of money illusion—of measuring the real value of wealth by deflating nominal values by the *current* price level.[5]

Modern "growth theory" also followed shortly after *The General Theory*. Harrod's essay was published in 1939. Earlier, Lundberg (1937) had set out the Harrod condition for growth equilibrium only to dismiss it as trivial and to direct his attention to more interesting cases of

---

[4] Note Hicks's (1974) recent comment: "To many students, I fear, it [the IS/LM diagram] *is* the Keynes theory. But it was never intended as more than a representation of what appeared to be a central part of the Keynes theory [p. 6]."

[5] For a critique of the real-balance effect in a non-Walrasian world, see Power (1969).

growth disequilibrium. But the profession preferred to explore the conditions for equilibrium growth and the characteristics of alternative equilibrium growth paths, with the result that growth theory has become one of the more sterile branches of the discipline.[6] Moreover, growth theory has never successfully linked back to *The General Theory*. Generations of students have been brought up to believe that Keynes confined his analysis to the short run. Both Harrod (1948, pp. 10–11) and Hicks (1950, p. 3; 1965, Chapters 7, 10, 23) unfortunately contributed to this dichotomy by treating the general theory as strictly short-run or static, instead of developing their growth and cycle theories within Keynes's (1936, pp. 204, 219, 307–309, 323–324, 373, 375) clearly indicated growth context. It may not be entirely unfair to suggest that this helps to explain why Hicks's cycle theory became something of a dead end and Harrod's warranted and natural rates of growth have lost their separate identities in the reigning neoclassical growth theory.

This is only a partial list of the misdirections we have taken, but it will serve, perhaps, to indicate a principal thesis of this paper: that the economics profession, in attempting to digest *The General Theory,* took what appeared to be some short cuts to the high road of understanding that turned out, instead, to be stray paths that, in some cases, simply circled back to the pre-Keynesian position.[7] Thus, we ignored the growth context within which Keynes (1936, pp. 293–294) placed his short-run analysis, and ignored also his insistence on a dynamic theory of "shifting equilibrium" in place of the neoclassical theory of static equilibrium. Instead, we took over the "Keynes-and-the-Classics" caricatures, with their static IS/LM curves and special emphasis on elasticities, wage rigidity, and money illusion. Then we found this "Keynesian" theory wanting in a Walrasian general equilibrium framework with its implication of instantaneous, or timeless, adjustments of prices to equilibrium levels. The "Pigou effect" was set in this context, rather than in the more realistic context Scitovsky had employed, wherein restraints were imposed on the time rates of price movements. And finally, we established a dichotomy in macroeconomic theory between the long run and the short run, relegating Keynesian considerations only to the latter while assuming the existence of some mechanism (neoclassical or Kaldorian) for ensuring equilibrium

[6] Neither Harrod (1939) nor Domar (1946) can be blamed for this misdirection. Each strongly emphasized the potential for disequilibrium in their well-known original works on growth theory.

[7] Note Clower's (1967) comment: "Modern attempts to erect a general theory of money and prices on Walrasian foundations have produced a model of economic phenomena that is suspiciously reminiscent of the classical theory of a barter economy [p. 1]."

growth at full employment in the former context. Attempts to integrate growth and cycle theory have all but been abandoned.

Now all this would not matter if macroeconomics had flourished along these lines. I think that I am safe in saying, however, that it has not. True, the forecasting and policy-planning models have fared somewhat better than Keynesian equilibrium theory. But they tell us almost nothing about the deeper issues of macroeconomic theory and policy such as, for example, the unemployment–inflation dilemma. This suggests that it might be valuable to return to *The General Theory* to try to see again where it should have led us.

The first and most important step in this task is, I think, to put the Keynesian theory in its own characteristic growth context. This means setting Keynes's short-run theory of shifting equilibrium in a world of persistent growth disequilibrium of a type to be defined later as the Keynesian case. This will distinguish the Keynesian context not only from the automatic equilibrium of the neoclassical world, but also from the disequilibrium growth context of the nonindustrialized countries—a case that Keynes ignored. Putting Keynes in his own growth context will not only eliminate the dichotomy between the long run and the short, but will also give us a far better explanation of the "stylized facts" of growth history. It will enable us to extend the Clower–Leijonhufvud critique of the Synthesis onto more damaging ground and to give stronger meaning to Keynes's concept of involuntary unemployment. It will give us additional insights into the nature of the unemployment–inflation dilemma. Finally, it will enable us to generalize the general theory beyond Keynes's vision to the case of nonindustrialized countries, and, indeed, beyond that to the question of world employment.

Before proceeding to the main task, I should offer one caveat. I shall shamelessly ignore the serious problems of aggregation in macroeconomics that Robinson and others have raised.[8] My reasons are twofold. First, I have no contribution to make toward their solution. Second, I feel that the retreat into parables that fear of Robinson's wrath has produced is a serious limitation on the relevance of macroeconomic theory. Keynes (1936, p. 39) considered such questions to be "conundrums." This paper follows in that spirit. Whether or not it is justifiable to do so depends ultimately on the extent to which it improves our understanding of macroeconomic relationships in the real world—an empirical question.[9]

---

[8] See, for example, the readings in Harcourt and Laing (1971).

[9] It is remarkable how economists who are ever ready to belittle environmentalists for their inadequate appreciation of the opportunity costs of a purer environment will, themselves, tend to close their eyes to the opportunity costs of a purer theory.

2. Keynesian Growth Theory

Keynes's *The General Theory* can be placed, I think, within the mainstream of economic growth theories—this despite the fact that his formal exposition there was mainly restricted to the short run in which population, stock of capital, and state of technology are given. Even in the summary chapter 18, in which these assumptions are explicitly made at the outset, Keynes (1936, pp. 253–254) ends with a discussion of the effects of rates of investment alternately below and above a certain rate at which, presumably, the marginal efficiency of capital could remain constant. This foreshadows his more explicit discussion in Chapter 22 of the business cycle as characterized by an oscillation of investment around a long-run maintainable rate (at the range of interest rates that the monetary authority and the liquidity preferences of the public permit). Full employment is achieved only when investment exceeds the long-run maintainable rate, and recurrent slumps are periods during which capital must be made scarce again by bringing investment below what today we would call the "natural" rate of capital formation. Keynes (1936, pp. 317–318), indeed, used the term "normal rate of growth in a given epoch," in this connection. He was more explicit in Chapter 21 as to what he meant by this:

> During the nineteenth century, the growth of population and of invention, the opening up of new lands, the state of confidence and the frequency of war over the average of (say) each decade seem to have been sufficient, taken in conjunction with the propensity to consume, to establish a schedule of the marginal efficiency of capital which allowed a reasonably satisfactory average level of employment to be compatible with a rate of interest high enough to be psychologically acceptable to wealth-owners. . . .
>
> Today and presumably for the future the schedule of the marginal efficiency of capital is, for a variety of reasons, much lower than it was in the nineteenth century . . . [pp. 307–308].

Repeatedly in Chapters 16, 22, and 24, Keynes (1936, pp. 219, 317–318, 321–324, 373, 375) indicated his view that full employment saving was in excess of the investment requirements of growth in countries such as Great Britain and the United States, and that only recurrent recessions kept capital scarce enough to maintain the historical rate of return on capital. Thus he clearly had in mind a growth context in which, in post-Keynesian terminology, the warranted rate of growth chronically exceeded the natural rate. And the business cycle was an integral part of the response to this disequilibrium. Indeed, recurrent recessions could serve to permit the disequilibrium to persist indefinitely.

Now one could claim that the passages just referred to were *obiter dicta* and irrelevant to the central argument of *The General Theory*. However, if they are in harmony with the short-run model, and if they enrich our understanding of that model, it would be foolish to treat them as such. One might, indeed, go further to argue that Keynes' short-run theory cannot be fully understood outside of a growth-and-cycle context. This means, however, as we shall see, that the short-run model is that of Keynes's "shifting equilibrium" within the business cycle—not the static "Keynes-and-the-Classics" caricature.

In developing this thesis, it will help to put Keynes in the mainstream of growth theories that began with Adam Smith. The classic growth problem is the relation between saving, as the source of capital accumulation, and the growth of available labor. The connecting link is, of course, the capital–labor ratio; and the classic condition for growth equilibrium can be put simply as

$$S = k(n + \lambda)L, \tag{1}$$

where S is saving, k the capital–labor ratio, L the labor force, n its proportional time rate of growth, and λ the rate of labor saving, defined as the proportional time rate of increase of k. This leaves land and natural resources in the background as is common in simple growth models today.

Since the purpose here is to contrast Keynes's solution of the classic growth problem with that of his predecessors, I will focus on the Keynesian case of growth disequilibrium—a warranted rate in excess of the natural rate of growth. In terms of Eq. (1) this means $S > k(n + \lambda)L$. I shall argue that Keynes did not challenge the "classical" analysis of the opposite case of growth disequilibrium. His specific mission was to generalize the "classical" theory by adding his analysis of the case of deficiency of aggregate demand—saving in excess of the investment requirements of growth.

For the classical economists through Mill, we can simplify by taking k as a constant and saving as identical with investment. S/k, then, represents the growth of "classical" demand for labor (as opposed to "Keynesian" demand for labor, defined later). More saving meant excess demand for labor and higher real wage rates at the expense of profits. Capital accumulation could nevertheless proceed at a higher rate because population growth would respond to the higher wage rate to produce equilibrium wage and profit rates for given propensities to save and procreate. The long run saw a race between diminishing returns and Mill's (1900, pp.

443–451) various offsets that kept the stationary state a "hand's breadth" away: technological progress, export of capital, wasteful government expenditures, and waste of private capital in the "commercial revulsions" of the business cycle.

Marx (1939, p. 645) parted company with the other classical economists in rejecting Malthusian population theory as "a libel on the human race" and substituted his own "law of population peculiar to the capitalist mode of production"—labor saving. He did not clearly differentiate between labor saving that was induced by a rise of wage rates and that which was autonomous, but both were present. Marx further assumed that the combination of the two kept labor chronically in surplus supply—a kind of unemployment that will accordingly be termed "Marxian."

This is an appropriate place to clarify the meaning of labor saving. Let the "natural stock of capital" at any time be defined as

$$K_{n_t} = k_t L_t,$$

where k is determined, at given factor prices, by the state of knowledge and the structure of the economy, both of which are assumed to be functions of time. Differentiating with respect to time yields

$$\dot{K}_n = \dot{L}k + \dot{k}L,$$

where the dot over the variable indicates a time derivative and the t subscripts have been omitted for convenience. This can be rewritten as the "natural rate of investment"

$$I_n = k[\dot{L} + (\dot{k}/k)L].$$

The Marxian autonomous rate of laborsaving is $(\dot{k}/k)L$, and it may be interpreted in the following way: If, as Marx apparently assumed, technical change incorporates a Hicksian laborsaving bias and structural change involves the shifting of employment relatively toward the more-capital-intensive sectors, $(\dot{k}/k)L$ will be positive; and, in the absence of net capital formation, the labor that is thereby "saved," together with the growth of labor supply $\dot{L}$ would simply swell the "reserve army of unemployed." The natural rate of investment then is the rate that (at given factor prices) implies a flow of absorption of labor from the reserve army just equal to the flow into the reserve army from labor saving plus growth of labor supply. Adding induced labor saving, i.e., making k a function of changes in the real wage rate w, transforms the classic condition for growth equilibrium of Eq. (1) into

$$S = k(w)[\dot{L} + (\dot{k}/k)L] \qquad \text{or} \qquad S = k(w)(n + \lambda)L, \qquad (2)$$

where λ is $\dot{k}/k$, the proportional time rate of labor saving. Rewriting (2) as

$$S/k(w) = (n + \lambda)L, \qquad (2a)$$

we have the classical growth of demand for labor on the left and growth of "free labor" supply on the right.[10] As Marx (1939) put it: "The demand for labour is not identical with the increase of capital, nor supply of labour with the increase of the working class [p. 654].'' The reason is, of course, the appearance of induced labor saving on the left and autonomous labor saving on the right of (2a). Marxian unemployment arises, then, as a result of an excess supply of free labor,

$$S/k(w) < (n + \lambda)L, \qquad (2b)$$

which he attributed to a high value for λ and the recurrence of increases of k in response to incipient labor scarcity and rising wages (Marx, 1939, pp. 642–655). For our purposes we can attribute it equally, if we like, to a shortage of saving or an excessive rate of population growth.[11]

Keynesian unemployment arises, of course, from a reversal of the inequality in (2b); thus it is structurally opposite to Marxian unemployment. To see this more clearly, we can rearrange (2b) and spell out in more detail what is on the left-hand side. Thus,

$$syL > k(w)(n + \lambda)L, \qquad (2c)$$

where y is income per worker and s is the ratio of saving to income. Since yL is full-employment output, saving is at the full-employment level. The right-hand side is, as already noted, the natural rate of investment, and we will call the left-hand side the warranted rate of investment. In the classical and Marxian world this inequality indicates labor scarcity, since actual investment is identified with saving. In Keynesian theory, investment is ultimately constrained by the right side, the natural rate; hence, it cannot be maintained at a level that would match full-employment saving. In the Keynesian world, then, this inequality indicates deficiency of aggregate demand and, therefore, a derived Keynesian demand for labor that falls short of labor supply at the given real wage. The condition for growth equilibrium can now be put as

$$syhL = k(i,w)(n + \lambda)L, \qquad (3)$$

[10] I have put Marx together with the classical economists in effect as embracing Say's law, despite the many passages in Marx that indicate such was not his intention. My excuse is that the main purpose here is to define a category of unemployment that arises not from a deficiency of demand for goods, but from a flow of free labor supply that is excessive in relation to the rate of job creation that full utilization of saving would permit.

[11] Marx (1939, pp. 648–649, 643) would not have liked this. He was scathing in his denunciation of those who attributed unemployment and low wages to population growth. Moreover, he treated labor saving as embodied in capital formation; hence, more saving meant more investment and faster labor saving.

where i is the rate of interest and h is the proportion of the labor force employed.[12] Keynesian growth equilibrium requires a value for h sufficiently below unity to yield the equality in (3).

It is important for what follows to emphasize the distinction between the classical and Keynesian demands for labor. In dynamic terms, the (growth of) classical demand for labor is, as already noted, S/k—saving being identified with capital formation. In static terms the classical demand is K/k—the assumption being that, given factor prices, there is some optimal utilization of the capital stock, as well as some optimal factor mix; and these determine the aggregate demand for labor without any constraint from the side of aggregate demand for goods.[13] This classical demand corresponds to Clower's (1965) "notional demand," which depends only on relative prices.

Keynes, by denying Say's law, was able to derive an aggregate demand for labor (and for the services of capital) from the aggregate demand for goods. The Keynesian demand for labor is I_a/sy, where I_a is actual investment, not necessarily equal to either syL or $k(n + \lambda)L$. I_a/s is, of course, effective aggregate demand and this together with a very simple employment function $1/y$ determines the derived demand for labor.[14]

Note that, in the dynamic version of the classical demand, investment (identified with saving) plays a role of job creation in the sense of providing resources complementary to labor (with the implicit assumption that these resources will not be kept idle—hence labor is demanded); while in the Keynesian demand, the role of investment is to create a demand for the output of those jobs, which determines, in turn, to what extent capital resources will in fact be kept idle.

The reader may wish to protest at this point that, following Marx, we now have k as a function of the real wage rate, and, therefore, we cannot speak of an equilibrium with involuntary unemployment. Why cannot the real wage rate fall to cure the unemployment? At the risk of anticipating too early the results of relaxing the assumption of fixed factor prices, my answer is simply that for full-employment growth equilibrium the real wage rate should be higher (to raise k), not lower. And it is not easy to see

---

[12] It will simplify the exposition if we define L, the labor force, as those desiring to work at the going real wage rate less a constant proportion of frictional unemployment. $L(1 - h)$, then, measures involuntary unemployment.

[13] The notion that the aggregate demand for goods should constrain the use of capital is alien to classical (and neoclassical) theory. Adam Smith (1937) put it forcefully: "A man must be perfectly crazy who, where there is tolerable security, does not employ all the stock which he commands [p. 268]."

[14] These demands are simply points, rather than schedules, since at this stage we are still taking factor prices as given. Moreover, this is a highly simplified version of Keynes's employment function.

how a market condition of unemployed labor will, in this case, give rise to the correct market signal. As Clower has taught us, if the auctioneer does not perform his task of equilibrium price administration instantaneously (or in a timeless world), we risk getting false information from income-constrained trading at disequilibrium prices ("false trading").[15]

While this is getting ahead of the story, it should also serve to remind us that we have a neoclassical growth theory which *does* rely on movements of relative prices to ensure growth equilibrium. Indeed, Eq. (3) is the usual simple condition for neoclassical growth equilibrium if we set h equal to unity. In per worker terms it becomes

$$sy = k(i,w)(n + \lambda). \tag{4}$$

If we add the usual Cobb–Douglas production function

$$y = f(k) \tag{5}$$

and set factor prices equal to marginal products

$$i = f'(k), \tag{6}$$

$$w = f(k) - f'(k)k, \tag{7}$$

we have an elementary version of neoclassical growth theory. This is shown in Fig. 1. Typically, neoclassical growth theorists limit themselves to descriptions and comparisons of positions of steady state growth equilibria, which requires the further assumption that λ is a Harrod-neutral rate of technological progress—i.e., $\dot{y}/y = \dot{k}/k$.

What happens in the neoclassical growth model as a result of an increase in "thriftiness" is well known, though exactly *how* it comes about is a bit of a mystery. In the new equilibrium following an upward shift in the sy curve, k and y will have risen, $f'(k)$ and i will be lower, and w will be higher.[16] Some versions arrive at this result by assuming a one-commodity world in which what is not consumed is necessarily accumulated and combined with labor in production. This is a way of retaining the classical assumption of Say's law. It must be assumed also, of course, that capitalists will acquiesce in a squeeze on the rate of profit from higher real wage rates.

There are two other versions, however—one belonging to the true neo-classicists, and the other to the neoclassical–Keynesian synthesists. In the former, disequilibrium automatically leads to the requisite changes in rela-

[15] What is remarkable about this particular piece of false information is the extent to which it can mislead not only transactors in the market, but also economists as analysts of unemployment.

[16] It should be evident that a fall of $n + \lambda$ equally gives rise to the Keynesian case of growth disequilibrium and to the same sort of neoclassical response.

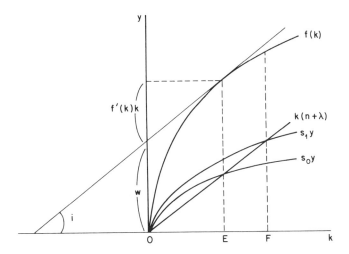

Figure 1 Neoclassical growth equilibrium.

tive factor prices to restore equilibrium. In the Keynesian case of disequilibrium, arising from a rise of s, for example, interest rates would be
expected to fall and real wage rates to rise until k and y had risen to their
new equilibrium values, though it is not easy to construct a scenario for
this "happening" outside of a Walrasian system of administered equilibrium prices.

Recognizing this, the Synthesis invokes "Keynesian" short-run stabilization policies to keep the economy on a steady path while the long-run
neoclassical adjustment can take effect. This, at least, is my interpretation
of their view, and the following passage from Solow (1970) seems to
support it[17]:

> Now I want to conduct an artificial experiment. Suppose the econ-
> omy maintains a constant rate of unemployment; it will sound more
> cheerful if we describe it as maintaining full employment, but any
> constant unemployment rate will do for the purpose of the experi-
> ment. (A centrally planned economy does this by fiat; a mixed econ-
> omy might do it approximately by monetary–fiscal policy, though it
> would take a richer model to describe the process in any detail—it is a
> little tricky because the policy mix has to keep the saving rate con-
> stant, to stay within the parable.) So long as the unemployment rate is
> constant, employment must be growing at the same rate as the labor

[17] Solow employs a somewhat different notation and a diagram that reverses the directions
of Fig. 1. Accordingly, I have altered his text slightly so as to make it understandable in the
present context (alterations in brackets). In addition, technological progress is absent from
Solow's presentation at this point; hence, λ is missing.

force, n. Start this economy outside the steady state and let it continue to play these full-employment rules of the game. If we start it to the [left] of the steady state, its stock of capital is growing at a faster rate than n. The ratio of [capital] to [employment] must be [rising], and the economy is moving to the [right] along the horizontal axis. We started it with $[sy]$ bigger than $[kn]$; if it maintains a constant unemployment rate, $[k]$ must rise. This process must contine so long as $[sy]$ exceeds $[kn]$. Eventually $[sy] = [kn]$. The full employment path for this economy tends to the steady state [pp. 21–22].

Monetary–fiscal policy is introduced here for the mixed economy clearly as a substitute for the back-door version of Say's law that comes with the one-commodity assumption. Though Solow (1970) had made the latter assumption earlier, he was rightly uncomfortable with it in this context, for, as he put it:

> Even a well-told parable has limited applicability. There are always tacit or explicit assumptions underlying a simplified story. They may not matter for the point the parable is trying to make; that is what makes parables possible. When they do matter the parable may mislead [pp. 1–2].

To his credit, Solow was not willing to mislead by invoking the Say's law implication of the one-commodity assumption to ensure that investment matched constant-employment saving.

The introduction of Keynesian stabilization policy as a substitute for Say's law is not as innocent as it may appear, however. Indeed, the policy requirements turn out to be very precise. As Solow noted, we are not permitted to reduce s. In Fig. 1, we see that what is required is that investment (per worker) should immediately rise to the new value of sy at E. This maintains the Keynesian demand for labor at the constant-rate employment level. At the same time, the higher rate of investment cannot be allowed to result in idle capacity. Given n and λ, this requires that the *incremental* capital–labor ratio—call it k'—for this investment should be raised enough to make $k'(n + \lambda) = sy$. We now see that, while in comparisons of steady states it is k that must have the right value, at any moment of time it is k' that counts for full-employment growth. Provided $k'(n + \lambda)$ is kept equal to sy by monetary–fiscal policies at each moment of time in the long process of adjustment from E to F in Fig. 1, Solow's condition is met. This means, then, that k' is the focus of policy, and some combination of lower interest rates and fiscal incentives to higher capital intensity is required. If this policy is implemented consistently, the long process of adjustment from E to F will be a smooth one with k rising gradually to its new equilibrium value as k' exceeds k and old capital is replaced by new at a higher capital intensity.[18] But where is the neoclassical aspect of the adjustment? The whole thing has been accomplished by the consistent application of a Keynesian full-employment policy, constrained by the requirement not to influence s. The neoclassical cat disappears, leaving only a Keynesian grin!

It should be added that this is also the policy prescription of Keynes (1936). He expressed disagreement with the underconsumptionists both on theoretical grounds—a rise in k' can substitute for a fall in s, and on practical grounds: "I am myself impressed by the great social advantages of increasing the stock of capital until it ceases to be scarce [p. 325]." Hence, Keynes's policy-planning model gives the same result as the neoclassical equilibrium model; the difference is that the former requires the right policies, while the latter relies on automatic market forces. In the light of this, it is not clear what the neoclassical–Keynesian synthesis synthesizes that Keynes had not already synthesized.

We can now grasp the essence of Keynesian growth theory. The key assumption is that in the face of Keynesian growth disequilibrium (warranted rate exceeding natural rate), there is no mechanism by which relative prices would adjust quickly and fully to preclude false trading and the false information that follows from it. A rise of the saving propensity, for example, does not produce the neoclassical adjustment, described previously, but results in a deficiency of effective aggregate demand and cumulative quantity adjustments away from full-employment equilibrium. As a result, false information appears. Instead of revealing labor as relatively scarce and saving as relatively abundant, so as to induce the requisite rise in the real wage rate and fall in the interest rate, the adjustment produces, instead, Keynesian unemployment, indicating an apparent surplus of labor, while excess saving disappears with the decline of income (Power, 1958, p. 41).

Recall that Keynesian growth equilibrium is described by

$$syhL = k(i,w)(n + \lambda)L, \tag{3}$$

where h is sufficiently below unity to bring about the equality. Much attention has been focused on the inconsistency of persistent involuntary unemployment with equilibrium (Patinkin, 1965, pp. 313–334), but this misses Keynes's point as we shall see when we put the Keynesian growth equilibrium in a cyclical context as Keynes himself did. Growth will not be "steady state" at the less-than-full-employment equilibrium, but will follow a cyclical path around this equilibrium, reaching full employment

[18] During the process, $n + \lambda$ is supplemented by the *induced* rate of labor saving from a rising k.

only at the peaks of the cycles. Growth cannot be sustained at full employment, however, because of the underlying growth disequilibrium when h is equal to unity, described by

$$syL > k(i,w)(n + \lambda)L. \tag{3a}$$

Note that k is a function of the interest rate and the real wage rate, as in neoclassical theory. It is not the failure of factor proportions to respond to changes in relative prices that is the hallmark of Keynes's theory. It is, rather, the failure of relative prices to respond appropriately to the disequilibrium shown in (3a). We return to this in Section 3 on Keynes's short run. For now, we simply assume that relative prices do not move so quickly to new equilibrium values in the face of a deficiency of aggregate demand as to preclude Keynes's quantity adjustment.

Keynes (1936, Chapter 22) gave us only an outline of his view on the application of his theory to the business cycle; for, as he put it, a full treatment would "occupy a book rather than a chapter [p. 313]." Accordingly, I will not attempt to do more than fit his outline into the context of the growth disequilibrium he postulated. This requires looking rather carefully at his schedule of the marginal efficiency of capital, however, for he viewed the business cycle "as being occasioned by a cyclical change in the marginal efficiency of capital, though complicated and often aggravated by associated changes in the other significant short-period variables of the economic system [p. 313]."

In Chapter 11 of *The General Theory*, in which Keynes introduced the marginal efficiency of capital, he took an essentially static and partial equilibrium view. The marginal efficiency of a particular type of asset would diminish as investment in it increased "during any period of time" because the expected yield would fall and because its supply price would increase. Then, the marginal efficiency schedules of particular assets could be aggregated to get the schedule of marginal efficiency of capital in general. This might be legitimate if we confined ourselves to an equilibrium that is based on the expectations of the moment. When we come to the business cycle, however, we must deal with the interactions of investments in a context of expectations changing in response to surprises and disappointments—i.e., to Keynes's system of shifting equilibrium in which each momentary equilibrium carries within it the seeds of further changes in expectations.

The marginal efficiency of capital (MEK) schedule is based at any moment on expectations, but these expectations are subject to continual revision in the light of actual results (Keynes, 1936):

> it is an essential characteristic of the boom that investments which will in fact yield, say, 2 percent. in conditions of full employment are

made in the expectation of a yield of, say, 6 percent., and are valued accordingly. When the disillusion comes, this expectation is replaced by a contrary "error of pessimism," with the result that investments, which would have yielded 2 percent. in conditions of full employment, in fact yield less than nothing [pp. 321–322].

Keynes clearly had in mind the presence of a "real" schedule in addition to those based on expectations that could be overoptimistic or overpessimistic. The position of the real schedule depends on the rate of growth of investment opportunities—Keynes's "normal rate of growth in a given epoch," based on "the growth of population and of invention"; while its slope depends on the responsiveness of capital intensity to the rate of interest. It is, indeed, none other than the natural rate of investment, written as

$$I_n = k(i)(n + \lambda)L.$$

The relation of this schedule to the expectations-based schedules is shown in Fig. 2, in which the solid-line schedule is I_n and the dashed-line schedules are those based on expectations.

For Keynes, the boom was a period of overoptimism where expectations were doomed to disappointment, while the depression was a period when underinvestment brought a sufficient scarcity of capital to restore its marginal efficiency to previously experienced levels. The length of the depression depended on the "average durability of capital" and the "normal rate of growth" [1936, p. 318]. The cycle, itself, was a fluctuation of the expectations-based schedules around a real schedule that would permit full employment only at a rate of interest lower than expectations (of future interest rates) based on past experience and the boldness and perspicacity of the monetary authorities would permit:

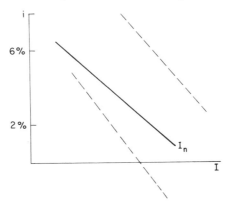

Figure 2 The natural rate of investment and the marginal efficiency of capital.

The rate of interest . . . may fluctuate for decades about a level which is chronically too high for full employment;—particularly if it is the prevailing opinion that the rate of interest is self-adjusting, so that the level established by convention is thought to be rooted in objective grounds much stronger than convention, the failure of employment to attain an optimum level being in no way associated, in the minds either of the public or of authority, with the prevalence of an inappropriate range of rates of interest [p. 204].

There are two important aspects of the interaction between the expectations-based schedules and the real schedule. First, overoptimism and overpessimism cannot go on forever, but must eventually be corrected by the presence of the real forces. Each can last long enough, however, to create a surplus or scarcity of capital at prevailing interest rates. So a correction once started can go on for some time, and the interaction of movements of aggregate demand with long-term expectations (and confidence therein) makes inevitable a cumulative process that overshoots the needed correction.

Thus there are three elements in the cyclical fluctuation of the MEK schedule that Keynes believed dominated the business cycle:

(1)   a cumulative process that caused movements in one direction to continue beyond the natural position of the MEK schedule,

(2)   a position of the natural schedule that was inadequate for full employment at the average level of interest rates that prevailed over the cycle, and

(3)   the constraint of the natural MEK schedule on the cumulative process, causing it to reverse at a certain point.

Keynes's outline did not take him as far as an explanation of the upper and lower turning points, and no attempt will be made here to remedy this deficiency.[19] Rather the principal interest here is what this cyclical adjustment mechanism implies for long-run growth.

For this it will be useful to introduce Fig. 3.[20]

The labor force L, as defined above, is growing at rate n, so that any point on the L axis is increasing in value at that rate, as are values along the gL axis. Both y and k, measured by the *slopes* of the lines so designated, are growing at rate λ, the rate of Harrod-neutral progress. This means that values along the I and Y axes are increasing over time at rate

[19] Hicks's (1950) theory of the trade cycle provides explanations that are compatible with Keynes's view.

[20] This is an adaptation of a diagram from Power (1955, p. 198).

$n + \lambda = g$, the natural rate of growth. The values of g and s, also indicated by the slopes of the designated lines, are constant.

Starting with the labor force at time t—point L_t in Fig. 3—we can find I_n, the natural rate of investment, by moving left along the solid line to g, then up to k, and over to the I axis. Similarly, we can find I_w, the warranted rate of investment, by moving in the opposite direction via y and s.

The situation shown in Fig. 3 is the Keynesian case of growth disequilibrium—$I_w > I_n$. If the actual rate of investment were held at I_n, which of course it cannot in the long run exceed, there would be a deficiency of aggregate demand and the derived Keynesian demand for labor would be $\bar{h}L_t$, as shown by the inner dashed line, from I_n to $\bar{h}L_t$ via s and y.

With a constant s, this cannot be a stable, less-than-full-employment equilibrium, however, even with rigid prices. For in this *noncyclical*, stagnation case we must put h on both sides of Eq. (3), so that we have

$$syhL = k(i,w)(n + \lambda)hL. \tag{3b}$$

The reason is, of course, that in a noncyclical world we cannot count on the existence of the excess capital capacity required to enable the economy recurrently to go beyond its average rate of employment to full employment; that is, we must redefine I_n to include the influence of $h \neq 1$, as we have done in the right-hand side of (3b). Then if, inequality (3a) also holds (as in Fig. 3),

$$syL > k(i,w)(n + \lambda)L, \tag{3a}$$

the only solution is $h = 0$. In Fig. 3, we would move to the left from $\bar{h}L_t$ along the dotted line to a new I_n via g and k. The continuation of this dotted line would, of course, trace a cobweb path converging on the origin.

Keynes (1936, pp. 217–218) dealt with this in his extreme example of the Keynesian case—his stationary state—by assuming that s declined with Y; that is, he gave s a positive intercept on the Y axis, shown as s' in Fig. 3. Thus, he was able to reach the stationary state with a positive value for h. The s' of Fig. 3 was drawn for convenience to yield the same solution as before, at $\bar{h}L_t$.

The cyclical case is more interesting. Here the assumption of a constant s may be compatible with Keynesian equilibrium at a positive h, because h may not appear in the definition of I_n. Suppose that the capital stock tends to be adjusted to the pattern of cyclical growth in such a way that there is excess capacity at all levels except full employment ($h = 1$). Then h also indicates the utilization of capital capacity (Domar, 1946). The

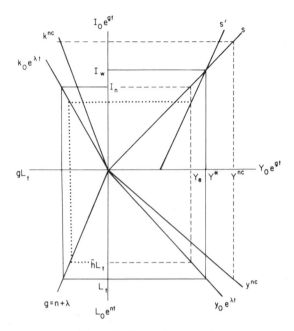

Figure 3 Keynesian growth.

natural rate of investment will continue to provide capital sufficient for the employment of L—not $\bar{h}L$. This means, then, that employment could fluctuate in the cycle around $\bar{h}L$ indefinitely, reaching L only at the peaks and falling below $\bar{h}L$ in the troughs. Note that if we did not make this assumption we could not reach L even at the peaks.

This assumption would appear to be less easy to defend, however, the lower is $\bar{h}$, because of the greater amount of excess capacity required. One can easily imagine a Keynesian case of chronic excess saving (at full employment) in relation to the natural rate of capital formation which would exhibit, as a symptom, a recurrent scarcity of capital stock so that the latter would appear to be the obstacle to full employment. This would be a very striking example of false information arising from false trading.

It is reasonable, however, to assume that s would decline with $\bar{h}$. This is well accepted in the cyclical context. In the long run, too, we should expect a higher average rate of unemployment to depress s, since the unemployed are dependent consumers, just as children and the retired. In our life-cycle theories, then, we should expect s to respond to a higher proportion of unemployed in the population in a way similar to the response to a higher proportion of the other dependent categories. Therefore, if one prefers, one could include h on the right side of (3a) and give s

a positive intercept on the Y axis. This, too would permit Keynes's adjustment to the Keynesian case of growth disequilibrium to be a fluctuation around $\bar{h}L$. Saving would rise more sharply in the upswing, but the gestation period for investment would mean a greater likelihood that the recovery would be impeded by a temporary capital stock shortage and that bottleneck inflation would be a problem (Keynes, 1936, pp. 300–301).

In either case we have, in Keynes's growth theory, an adjustment to the classic growth problem that is strikingly different from classical, Marxian, and neoclassical adjustments. Classical theory (Mill aside) had shifts in income distribution and induced population growth as adjustment mechanisms. Marx had excessive labor saving recurrently creating Marxian unemployment. The neoclassical theory has continuous, smooth adjustments of relative factor prices to keep warranted and natural rates of capital formation equal. With Keynes, an excess of the warranted over the natural rate can, by contrast, persist indefinitely in a cyclical pattern of growth, the burden of adjustment falling on $\bar{h}$, the average proportion of employment over the cycle. And the cyclical aspect of the Keynesian solution to the classic growth problem is of the greatest importance, as we shall note in greater detail. For not only does it build in expectations that are detrimental to the operation of the neoclassical price adjustment mechanism, but it creates false information about equilibrium market relationships as well.

Years ago, Kaldor (1961) set out what he called the "stylized facts" of modern growth history and argued that: "None of these 'facts' can be plausibly 'explained' by the theoretical constructions of neo-classical theory [pp. 178–179]." He underestimated the neoclassical growth theorists. By incorporating Harrod-neutral progress as a key assumption, the neoclassical model of growth equilibrium described previously neatly reproduces the "stylized facts." Kaldor can complain, of course, that introducing a special assumption about the nature of technical progress is not "explaining" anything, but that argument cuts two ways. In any case, as Solow (1970, p. 2) has stated, whether or not these are indeed the facts of modern growth history, their explanation is what modern growth theory is all about. It is pertinent to ask, then, how the Keynesian growth theory, outlined above, fits the "stylized facts."

First, what are the "facts"? There are six, but two of them relate to comparisons of growth performance in different countries and are not directly relevant here. The others can be compressed into the following:

(1) Output per worker y has grown at a roughly constant rate λ.

(2) Capital per worker k has grown at about the same rate as y, so that the capital–output ratio k/y has been approximately constant.

(3)   The rate of return on capital has exhibited no definite long-run tendency to rise or fall.

A corollary of (2) and (3) is, of course, that factor shares have tended also to be approximately constant. Note that *not* included in the "stylized facts" to which both Kaldor and the neoclassical growthmen accommodate their theories are:

(4)   a declining rate of population growth,
(5)   a transformation from an agricultural to an industrial economy, and
(6)   business cycles!

The Keynesian solution of cyclical fluctuation around a less-than-full-employment equilibrium position is contrasted in Fig. 3 with the neoclassical steady state solution. The neoclassical adjustment to the Keynesian case of growth disequilibrium is the upward shift of k to the position indicated by k^{nc}. Along the production function, y will increase also (in lesser proportion) to y^{nc}. In the new steady state, employment will be at L_t ($h = 1$) and income will be at Y^{nc}, which is greater than the Keynesian full-employment level Y^*. In both solutions, Y will grow at rate g, the natural rate, and y will grow at rate λ. The paths over time can be compared in Fig. 4, where Y_a is the actual cyclical path in the Keynesian solution and Y_e the Keynesian equilibrium path. The slopes are the same for the neoclassical and Keynesian paths, of course, but even the Keynesian full-employment path Y^* is below Y^{nc} because of the permanently higher k that the neoclassical solution provides. [Keynes (1963, pp. 220–221, 376–377), of course, in his policy-planning model, urged an even higher k to the point that capital would no longer be scarce—its marginal efficiency would be zero.]

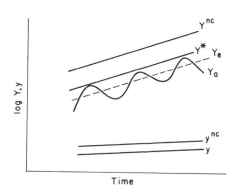

Figure 4   Alternative income growth paths.

Despite their differences, the neoclassical and Keynesian growth theories equally well fit "facts" (1)–(3). The former, however, cannot account for (6)—business cycles are ad hoc in the neoclassical world. In the Keynesian system, by contrast, cycles are an integral part of the solution.

What about (4) and (5)—declining rate of population growth and industrialization? They are neglected by neoclassical growth theorists no doubt because they do not matter. Their theory requires no assumption about a particular sort of disequilibrium to which the economy tends in the course of growth. The neoclassical adjustment mechanism purports to handle equally well any sort of variations in growth parameters that might occur. Keynes's theory, by contrast, was designed specifically to repair a deficiency in the "classical" theory—the neglect of Keynesian unemployment owing to the denial of a Keynesian demand for labor. In pre-Keynesian economics, all unemployment (beyond frictional) was of the Marxian variety—the real wage was too high when the capital stock was fully (or optimally) utilized. And Keynes agreed that Marxian unemployment was voluntary. His mission in introducing Keynesian unemployment was of historical, as well as theoretical, significance, as he well recognized. Keynesian unemployment and the particular constellation of growth parameters that gave rise to it (summed up in $I_w > I_n$) was a problem of the twentieth century, not the nineteenth (Keynes, 1936, pp. 306–309).

Additional "facts" (4) and (5) are of great importance for this assumed constellation of growth parameters. The role of a declining n is obvious. The role of industrialization may be less so, hence, some explanation may be in order (Power, 1962). The natural rate of growth is $n + \lambda$. In a world of structural change, labor saving (λ) can come equally from changing factor proportions within each sector and from changing weights of sectors with different factor proportions. Let $\lambda = \lambda_1 + \lambda_2$ to represent labor saving from the first and second influences, respectively. In the course of a transformation from an agricultural to an industrial society, λ_2 can assume relatively high values. The high rate of growth of Japan in recent years, for example, has been possible partly because of the rapid shift of labor out of agriculture. As the transformation nears an end, however, λ_2 declines rapidly both because the population remaining in agriculture is relatively much smaller and because factor proportions in agriculture are less dissimilar to those in the rest of the economy. Thus, in the course of what Kuznets calls "modern economic growth," n and λ_2 at first rise and then decline as the "mature economy" phase is approached. It is this phase of economic history that Keynes had in mind in assuming what I have called the Keynesian case of growth disequilibrium.

Thus, the Keynesian growth theory also fits neatly Kaldor's "stylized facts'' and accommodates, as well, three other important ''facts'' of modern growth history that are ignored by the neoclassical version. Indeed, the neoclassical theory must add to the special assumption of Harrod-neutral progress the additional assumptions that structural change, too, was Harrod-neutral and that λ_1 rose just rapidly enough to offset the combined fall of n and λ_2. Otherwise, the rate of return on capital should have fallen. We should ask ourselves, then, which is a more plausible explanation of the roughly constant rate of return on capital in our growth experience: the above fortuitous special characteristics of technical progress and structural change that neoclassical theory requires, or the reluctance of capitalists to invest at rates of return below historical levels, a reluctance that gives rise to recurrent recessions that eliminate the surplus saving that could have been invested only at lower rates of return?

3. The Short Run

As noted in Section 1, Keynes's short-run equilibrium theory has typically been judged within the framework of a timeless Walrasian world in which trading occurs only at equilibrium prices. As Clower and Leijonhufvud have argued, this is an inappropriate context for understanding Keynes. Following Marshall, he saw a world of constant change in which time could be divided for convenience of analysis into finite periods of varying length, each with its own *ceteris paribus* conditions, with the results ultimately fitted together to gain a fuller understanding. As Marshall (1948) put it:

> The element of time is a chief cause of those difficulties in economic investigations which make it necessary for man with his limited powers to go step by step; breaking up a complex question, studying one bit at a time, and at last combining his partial solutions into a more or less complete solution of the whole riddle [p. 366]. . . .
> . . . in the world in which we live . . . every economic force is constantly changing its actions, under the influence of other forces which are acting around it. . . . Further all these mutual influences take time to work themselves out, and, as a rule, no two influences move at equal pace. In this world therefore every plain and simple doctrine as to the relations between cost of production, demand and value is necessarily false; and the greater the appearance of lucidity which is given to it by skillful exposition, the more mischievous it is. A man is likely to be a better economist if he trusts to his common sense, and practical instincts, than if he professes to study the theory of value and is resolved to find it easy [p. 368].

This admonition from Marshall is a good one to remember whenever we are tempted in the classroom to shift the LM schedule "instantaneously" to a full-employment intersection with IS, in response to Walrasian rules of price behavior.

For Keynes (1936), then, there was nothing inconsistent about less-than-full-employment equilibrium. All equilibria are transitory when viewed in relation to longer periods of time. In particular, as already noted, he described his short-run solution as a "shifting equilibrium . . . in which changing views about the future are capable of influencing the present [p. 293]." It is not easy, therefore, to compare directly Keynes's short-run theory with a neoclassical version in the standard static IS–LM framework. Nevertheless, it is possible, I think, to gain considerable insight into the differences by starting with such a comparison, provided that we follow Marshall in "trusting our common sense and practical instincts" in interpreting the results.

A common textbook macroeconomic model might look something like the following:

$E(Y, i) = Y$	equilibrium in the goods market,	(4a)
$L(Y, i) = M_0/P$	equilibrium in the money–securities market,	(4b)
$Y = f(N, K_0)$	aggregate production function,	(4c)
$W/P = f_N$	equilibrium in the labor market,	(4d)
$N = j(W/P)$		(4e)

where M_0 is the given money supply, K_0 the given capital stock, W/P the real wage rate, and N employment. This model is essentially neoclassical in that equilibrium in the labor market occurs independently and imposes a full-employment solution on the rest of the system. Thus, one can get Keynesian results only by assuming inconsistencies in the system, such as a fixed money wage rate or an infinitely elastic liquidity preference function (Bailey, 1971, pp. 47–52).

The system of Keynes is somewhat different, however, and does not depend on such oddities as wage rigidity or a liquidity trap. Equations (4a) and (4b) can be retained intact. The others are modified as follows[21]:

$$Y = F(N,K), \qquad (4c')$$
$$P = (W/F_N)(1 + m), \qquad (4d')$$
$$W = W(Y). \qquad (4e')$$

First, note that K is not given at K_0. Keynes (1936, pp. 42 (footnote), 124, 288, 299) made repeated references to underutilization of capital in

---

[21] When aggregate demand reaches the full-employment value, labor is back on its supply curve, and Eq. (4e) is reinstated.

combination with unemployment of labor.[22] Second, prices in general are made dependent on marginal costs of production and the degree of monopoly m—Keynes's given "degree of competition [p. 245]." Third, it is the money wage, not the real wage, that is determined in the labor market; and bargaining conditions are such that W is positively related to Y:

> That the wage unit may tend to rise before full employment has been reached, requires little comment or explanation. Since each group of workers will gain, *cet. par.*, by a rise in its own wages, there is naturally for all groups a pressure in this direction, which entrepreneurs will be more ready to meet when they are doing better business. For this reason a proportion of any increase in effective demand is likely to be absorbed in satisfying the upward tendency of the wage unit [p. 301].

We have, of course, six unknowns for the five equations, since K is not fixed. We will test our common sense and practical instincts on the behavior of K in a moment. First, however, it will be convenient to look at the solution for any reasonable assumption about K, and compare it with the neoclassical model. Given such an assumption, we have from (4d') and (4e') the general price level P as a function of real output Y. Then (4a) and (4b) determine i and Y. Putting this in terms of IS–LM, we have in the Keynesian system a single LM schedule rather than a family of schedules for alternative values of P. And this is not because P is fixed, but because, as in the theory of the firm, it is governed by short-run marginal cost and is, therefore, a function of Y. Then Eq. (4c') determines the level of employment rather than the level of income (Wells, 1974). We have a Keynesian demand for labor derived from the demand for goods. Only in the limiting case would this be a full-employment demand. In contrast, the neoclassical version has a governing classical demand for labor in Eq. (4d), on the assumption of a constant, optimal utilization of capital.[23]

When, however, the Keynesian equilibrium is at less than full employment, we have not only a derived Keynesian demand for labor short of the classical demand, but also a derived Keynesian demand for the services of capital short of the neoclassical optimal level of utilization. If capital were perfectly malleable in the short run, this would not be the case, since capital could be substituted for labor even as output is reduced and work-

---

[22] He was not consistent, however (Keynes, 1936, p. 17).

[23] This is oversimplified, of course. The utilization of capital will respond to changes in factor prices. Nevertheless, we can distinguish between such changes and Keynesian changes in utilization owing to variations in aggregate demand (Winston, 1974).

ers are laid off. We know, however, that in fact capital utilization and employment of labor are strongly correlated in the business cycle.

I will make a very simple assumption about how K varies with Y in the cycle and try to defend it on three grounds: first, that it is not unrealistic, second that any reasonable modification will not affect the rest of the argument, and third, and most important, that it will help to avoid a confusion that has plagued discussions of the Keynesian short run since 1936.

My simplifying assumption requires that capital is "putty-clay" and that the production process is perfectly divisible; that is, while there is wide range for factor substitution at the time investments are made, once capital is in place factor proportions are fixed. But we can vary employment of both labor and capital continuously at constant returns to scale.

This effectively quashes the debate over whether or not labor must suffer a decline in the real wage rate when we move from a Keynesian less-than-full-employment position to full employment. Moreover, it simplifies the description of the Keynesian demand for labor; it is simply a point, horizontally to the left of the intersection of supply and (classical) demand in the labor market.[24] These assumptions are not essential to what follows, while they simplify the argument. In particular, the assumption that the real wage rate is unaffected by the level of employment in the short run helps us to focus on what happens to the full-employment equilibrium real wage rate. And that *is* important for what follows.

To give a hint as to why, consider the following situation: We start with a rise of s, the saving propensity. This raises the rate of growth of classical (full-employment) demand for labor vis à vis the rate of growth of labor supply. The full-employment equilibrium real wage rate is higher, as shown in Fig. 1. But in the Keynesian system, the rise of s creates a deficiency of aggregate demand and Keynesian unemployment. Now suppose that Keynes's original assumption holds—that the real wage rate must fall to permit the unemployed labor to be reabsorbed with the given stock of capital.[25] It appears that there are two conflicting rules as to the required movement of real wage rates in this case. One relates to the shape of the short-run production function with a given stock of capital and variable utilization of capital and labor. The other is more important since it relates to the long-run production function in neoclassical growth theory. The fundamental solution to the problem of Keynesian unemployment requires a movement along the latter function to a higher k, if we

[24] Patinkin (1965, pp. 316–324) uses such a point to describe involuntary unemployment.

[25] In fairness to Keynes we should note that he stressed nonhomogeneity of factor inputs (both labor and capital) rather than variable proportions as responsible for short-run rising supply price [Keynes, 1936, pp. 42 (footnote), 299–300].

follow the neoclassical equilibrium model or the Keynesian policy-planning model.[26] Yet all of the attention has been focused on the short-run function, the tacit assumption being that an inability of the real wage rate to decline rapidly enough has something to do with the persistence of Keynesian unemployment. As we shall see shortly, it would be more to the point to say that it is an *upward* "stickiness" of the real wage rate that is associated with the persistence of Keynesian unemployment. In any case, this is a more interesting question and we will be able to pursue it more directly if we follow the simplifying assumption I have already made about the shape of the short-run production function.

Suppose for a moment that we have a Walrasian system with an auctioneer who, at any sign of disequilibrium, stops all trading until he is able to announce the new equilibrium set of prices. In this world, following Clower, notional demands and effective demands would be identical; that is, each transactor would decide what he wanted to buy and sell on the basis of given prices, and, by virtue of what Clower calls "Say's principle," each would plan to earn from his sales enough to finance his purchases. If these prices were, indeed, the equilibrium market-clearing set, then each would be able to make effective his notional demands. If, however, the auctioneer should fail to perform this function in the face of market disequilibrium, some would find that actual sales fell below planned and, as a result, effective demands would be constrained below notional demands. Trading would be going on at disequilibrium prices (false trading); quantity adjustments in response to income constraints would have intruded on the pure price system; and, as we have already noted, false information might appear.

Let us apply this to a Keynesian case of growth disequilibrium. Again let s rise. Immediately there would be an excess flow of funds to the money–securities market and a deficiency of demand in the goods market. The auctioneer stops all trading until he finds the reduction of the interest rate and increase of wage rates that would raise k' (or k, depending on how timeless we want to be) just enough to allow $k'(n + \lambda)$ to match the new, higher sy. Equilibrium, then, would be restored in all markets.

Now suppose that the auctioneer instead dozes off, permitting the disequilibrium to persist. Transactors would be on their own. In the money–securities market, the presence of large stocks of securities in relation to the current flows of supply and demand plus some elasticity of stock demand from relatively inelastic expectations would prevent the interest

---

[26] We need not follow either of these, of course, since there are other solutions. See Section 4.

rate from moving quickly to the new equilibrium level.[27] As a result, deficiency of demand would persist in the goods market. Entrepreneurs there, not knowing what the new equilibrium prices are, and faced with reduced revenues, would now have income-constrained effective demands below their notional demands for labor (and capital services). Finally, then, the disequilibrium would reach the labor market in the form of Keynesian unemployment. Should the auctioneer suddenly awaken, notice the unemployment of labor, and follow his Walrasian instinct by ordering a cut in wage rates, he would be no more misled than the conventional wisdom which purports to explain the persistence of Keynesian unemployment by the reluctance of labor to accept a lower wage.

The Clower argument is perfectly general, however, and applies also to Marxian unemployment, as well as to a case I shall label ''monetary unemployment.'' For the Marxian case, suppose that it is n that rises instead of s. The auctioneer should reduce the real wage rate and raise the interest rate to induce a lower k' and, ultimately, a lower k. In the real world, however, the real wage rate might not easily decline. In less-developed countries, for example, it is common to assume that there is an institutional floor to the real wage rate, determined by the average product of labor in communal agriculture or, perhaps, by government policies. The modern ''search theory'' also purports to explain why workers may refuse to accept a lower wage, and this is often put in a context where the existing real wage is above the equilibrium level. In both cases, then, the resulting unemployment is of the Marxian variety and, therefore, voluntary in Keynes's sense.

Monetary unemployment differs from both Keynesian and Marxian unemployment in that the natural and warranted rates of growth are equal. Unemployment arises simply because the actual rate of investment is below both I_w and I_n owing to a deficiency of real money balances. This might seem to be a trivial case, since there is no structural problem at all and the matter of providing the right money supply ought to encounter no serious obstacles. Yet this seems to be the kind of unemployment that is in the minds of Patinkin and Friedman, for example, and perhaps also in those of the synthesists. It is not easy to be certain of this because of the almost universal tendency to abstract from long-run growth problems while treating short-run stabilization questions. This suggests that there is commonly an implicit assumption that some transcendental forces are continuously at work to keep the economy at or very near neoclassical

---

[27] See Scitovsky (1940) for an early and still-classic analysis of the downward stickiness of interest rates. See also his more recent analysis (1969).

growth equilibrium so that short-run fluctuations are simply deviations from the "golden-age" path. This is very different, of course, from the Keynesian view set out above.

The idea of monetary unemployment comes through most clearly in Patinkin's work (1965). Unemployment there can always be cured by a sufficient proportionately equal decline of money wage rates and prices. Since the cure is simply a rise in the value of real money balances with real wage rates and interest rates unchanged, the label, monetary unemployment, seems appropriate.

We get into difficulty, however, when we try to apply Patinkin's analysis to the Keynesian case—$I_w > I_n$. Again, consider a rise of s. The new Patinkin equilibrium, arrived at via the real-balance effect, will in this case include a lower interest rate. But in a well-behaved neoclassical world this implies also a higher real wage rate! Somehow prices must fall more than in proportion to money wage rates in the Patinkin process if we are to reach a true equilibrium. It is not easy to imagine how unemployment in the labor market would lead to that result in Patinkin's system.[28]

Where does all of this leave Keynes's concept of involuntary unemployment? Keynes (1936), himself, contributed greatly, I think, to the confusion that has surrounded this subject because of his initial definition that appeared in Chapter 2 of *The General Theory:*

> Men are involuntarily unemployed if, in the event of a small rise in the price of wage-goods relatively to the money wage, both the aggregate supply of labour willing to work for the current money-wage and the aggregate demand for it at that wage would be greater than the existing volume of employment [p. 15].

This definition was given *before* he developed the concept of effective demand in Chapter 3; and he provided an "alternative, equivalent definition" (in Chapter 3), which made involuntary unemployment depend on inadequate effective demand. Thus, the essence of involuntary unemployment is a situation where the Keynesian demand for labor is to the left of the classical demand and the real wage rate is above the corresponding point on labor's supply curve. The question of prices having to rise relatively to money wage rates is a red herring. It involves only the shape of the short-run production function, and whatever its shape—whether the real wage rate must rise, fall, or remain constant—the Keynesian definition of involuntary unemployment is the same. In Chapter 2, before his

---

[28] Indeed, in his second edition of *Money, Interest and Prices,* Patinkin (1965, pp. 359–365) conceded that the process might not reach an equilibrium in the case of Keynesian growth disequilibrium. For the full argument, see Power (1959).

explanation of effective demand, Keynes had simply described a special case of involuntary unemployment.

This special case has received most of the attention, however. Typically, discussions of the persistence of Keynesian unemployment have focused on questions of money wage stickiness, money illusion in the supply curve of labor, and so forth, completely neglecting the fact that a persistent excess of the warranted rate of growth over the natural rate, which alone can account for Keynesian unemployment, implies that the real wage rate is too low for long-run equilibrium.

It is because of his assumption of this special case, of course, that Keynes felt compelled to explain why labor would be willing to return to its supply curve via a rise in prices, but not via a fall in money wages. This, too, has produced confusion, though Keynes must have thought it to be too obvious to require much explanation. Alchian (1970) has recently rationalized Keynes's view in terms of search theory:

> When one employer cuts wages, this does not signify cuts elsewhere. His employees rightly think wages are not reduced elsewhere. On the other hand, with a rise in the price level, employees have less reason to think their current real wages are lower than they are elsewhere. So they do not immediately refuse a lower real wage induced by a higher price level, whereas they would refuse an equal money wage cut in their present job. It is the revelation of information about prospects elsewhere that makes the difference [p. 44].

I will not suggest, however, that Keynes was the pioneer search theorist. He probably had a simpler, though very compatible, explanation in mind. We need only to remind ourselves of the difference between the supply curve of labor to a firm or industry and the supply curve of labor in general to understand it. The former is likely to be highly elastic, while the latter will have a very low elasticity (both with respect to the real wage). If one wants to dramatize the point in starkest fashion, he need only to make the former infinitely elastic and the latter inelastic. Then we must follow Keynes (1936) in assuming resistance to "reductions in money-wages applying to particular industries" and acquiescence in "a change in the purchasing-power of money which affects all workers alike" [p. 14]." There is no question whatsoever of money illusion.

We still face a dilemma, however, in that the real wage rate that would enable the unemployed to be reabsorbed with the existing stock of capital need not be the same as the real wage rate that would accompany the k' that equates sy to $k'(n + \lambda)$—i.e., the rate that would permit full employment to be *maintained*. Considering whether or how this dilemma might be resolved finally brings us to the question of the unemployment–inflation trade-off in Keynesian theory. First, recall that Keynes (1936) gave two reasons for his special assumption that the real wage rate must fall in the short run as the economy moves toward full employment. One was the relative scarcity of resources complementary to labor, especially equipment. But this would be a factor influencing mainly the time rate at which we could approach full employment:

> If we assume a sufficient interval for the quantity of equipment itself to change, the elasticities of supply will be greater eventually. Thus a moderate change in effective demand, coming on a situation where there is widespread unemployment, may spend itself very little in raising prices and mainly in increasing employment; whilst a larger change, which, being unforeseen, causes some temporary "bottle-necks" to be reached, will spend itself in raising prices, as distinct from employment, to a greater extent at first than subsequently [pp. 300–301].

Keynes seemed to give more attention to the second reason, which is the nonhomogeneity of both labor and equipment, when inputs of both are variable in the short run:

> But if the wage of a given grade of labourers is uniform irrespective of the efficiency of the individuals, we shall have rising labour costs, irrespective of the efficiency of the equipment. Moreover, if equipment is non-homogeneous and some part of it involves a greater prime cost per unit of output, we shall have increasing marginal prime costs over and above any increase due to increasing labour costs [pp. 299–300].

At least with respect to the labor cost component this would imply that a once-over rise of prices relative to money wage rates would be required to reach a given high level of employment. But, while this could give rise to continuing inflation as the previously employed labor sought to prevent its real wage from falling, this may not be the most serious aspect of the unemployment–inflation dilemma.

Suppose that labor and equipment were homogeneous, so that the preceding problem could not arise. Suppose also that equipment is adequate to accommodate full employment of labor—point L_t in Fig. 3, where $h = 1$—without any rise in prices if the wage unit does not rise.[29] Then a policy that could bring actual investment I_a to the level of the warranted rate I_w would mean investment in excess of the natural rate I_n if we are in the context of a long-run Keynesian disequilibrium (see Fig. 3). This,

---

[29] I am also holding the degree of monopoly constant.

however, is an unstable position. Capital formation is proceeding faster than labor supply. Either excess capacity will arise and I_a will decline, bringing Keynesian unemployment, or the policy-makers will attempt to avoid this by increasing effective demand beyond Y^* (corresponding to L_t), thus precipitating a wage–price spiral—Keynes' "true inflation."

Because, as Keynes argued, the wage unit begins to rise before that point is reached we have a rising price level before we reach full employment and "true inflation." Note that in this interval the labor market, even without the auctioneer, is trying to give the right signal. As the economy goes from 7% unemployment to 6% to 5% the wage unit is rising—perhaps at an accelerating rate. This signals imminent labor scarcity, the true underlying situation. The real wage rate should be allowed to rise to begin to effect the rise in k' necessary to cure the disequilibrium and permit sustained growth at full employment instead of recurring business cycles. But if prices are governed, as in Keynes's system, by marginal prime cost and the degree of monopoly, the requisite rise in real wage rates will not occur. Wage–price inflation will preclude it even before full employment is reached. So Keynes had wage–price inflation occurring as output and employment approached full employment, at which point output and employment cease to grow and "true inflation" ensues. There is a vertical Phillips curve at full employment.

Typically, at some point before "true inflation" is reached, of course, the monetary authority moves to bring the expansion to a halt by retarding the growth of money supply and permitting interest rates to rise. So the response to an impending scarcity of labor (and underlying surplus of saving) is to raise the supply price of the relatively abundant factor. False information respects no one—not even the Fed! We should, however, note Keynes's (1936) strictures on this point:

> Thus the remedy for the boom is not a higher rate of interest but a lower rate of interest! For that may enable the so-called boom to last. The right remedy for the trade cycle is not to be found in abolishing booms and thus keeping us permanently in a semi-slump; but in abolishing slumps and thus keeping us permanently in a quasi-boom [p. 322].

Just to imagine what would happen today if our policy-makers attempted to implement such a Keynesian policy with the limited instruments at their disposal should warn us that the unemployment–inflation dilemma is even more serious than the conventional view of it admits. Keynes (1936, p. 327) himself made a similar qualification to the statement just quoted a few pages later.

Finally, we must note the important role that the cyclical adjustment process plays in keeping expectations within the bounds of Keynes's assumptions. Given the relatively passive role of the monetary authorities, each boom brings rates of interest considerably above the levels at which steady state, full-employment equilibrium would be possible. This recurrent renewal of experience of unmaintainably high interest rates makes difficult in each ensuing recession the needed downward revision of expectations that would permit interest rates to decline in pace with the marginal efficiency of capital. The slow response of the liquidity preference schedule, together with "a fickle and highly unstable marginal efficiency of capital," is what describes the "Keynesian case" rather than the static elasticity properties of the textbook IS–LM model. Moreover, it was timid or misguided monetary policy that Keynes (1936) blamed, rather than a "liquidity trap," for the persistence of unemployment:

> There is the possibility . . . that, after the rate of interest has fallen to a certain level, liquidity-preference may become virtually absolute in the sense that almost everyone prefers cash to holding a debt which yields so low a rate of interest. . . . But whilst this limiting case might become practically important in future, I know of no example of it hitherto. Indeed, owing to the unwillingness of most monetary authorities to deal boldly in debts of long term, there has not been much opportunity for a test [p. 207].

The role of the cycle in influencing wage and price expectations has been given less attention, but may be equally important. While Keynes (1936, pp. 236–239, 270) did not assume rigid wage rates, nor did he believe that wage inflexibility had anything to do with involuntary unemployment, he nevertheless welcomed money wage "stickiness" as important in contributing to stability in the value of money. At the same time he seemed remarkably unconcerned, in the light of what we view today, about the inflationary potential of continuous "full employment" engineered by Keynesian policies (Keynes, 1936): "No one has a legitimate vested interest in being able to buy at prices which are only low because output is low [p. 328]." Keynes no doubt was simply reflecting his view of the history of inflation since the early nineteenth century in Great Britain and the United States, in which, wars aside, upward price movements never proceeded for very long without a reversal from a business cycle downturn. The long, sustained upswing of the 1960s, however, may give us a foretaste of what we might expect under continuous full-employment aggregate demand without wage and price restraints. We must ask whether the neoclassical–Keynesian synthesis will, by the application of short-run Keynesian policies, give us the long-run neoclassical adjustment to steady state growth or simply wage–price inflation.

4. Generalizing the General Theory: Full Employment in the World Economy

It might be argued that the scope of the economics of Keynes is more general than what I have called the Keynesian case. The failure of the neoclassical adjustment mechanism would imply Marxian unemployment if the growth disequilibrium were of the opposite sort. And the failure of the real wage to fall to the equilibrium level might be explained in the manner that the search theorists or development economists have suggested. But I think that it would be difficult to argue that Keynes had the Marxian unemployment case in mind. There is one passage in *The General Theory* where Keynes (1936) alluded to the situation of a poor economy with little saving: "For a poor community will be prone to consume by far the greater part of its output, so that a very modest measure of investment will be sufficient to provide full employment . . . [p. 31]." Here Keynes clearly has in mind Keynesian unemployment and the Keynesian demand for labor. The role of investment in creating jobs—as opposed to contributing to the demand for the products of those jobs—is ignored. Was this an oversight? Perhaps not. We must keep in mind Keynes's claim that he was generalizing the orthodox theory—not replacing it. It is entirely possible that Keynes considered the problem of Marxian unemployment, where the real wage rate is too high, to be handled adequately by the "classical" theory. Institutional restraints on the real wage rate would come under the heading of voluntary unemployment, as would "search unemployment." Indeed, Keynes (1936) was explicit on this[30]:

> In addition to "frictional" unemployment, the [classical] postulate is also compatible with "voluntary" unemployment due to the refusal or inability of a unit of labour, as a result of legislation or social practices or of combination for collective bargaining or of slow response to change or of mere human obstinacy, to accept a reward corresponding to the value of the product attributable to its marginal productivity [p. 6].

Moreover, it is the long-term interest rate—not the real wage rate—whose downward stickiness explains involuntary unemployment. A case of disequilibrium which required for its cure a rise in the interest rate and a fall in the real wage rate would encounter no peculiarly Keynesian problems and, therefore, was satisfactorily explained by pre-Keynesian theory. Either labor is on its supply curve, in which case the unemployment is voluntary, or the real wage rate is above labor's supply price, in which case labor would accept a reduction—provided, of course, that it is

[30] See also Leijonhufvud (1968, pp. 92–93).

a reduction along the aggregate supply curve of labor via a *general* administered wage cut or a general rise in prices. And, of course, we need have no fear that owners of wealth would resist a rise in interest rates! So it seems that the case of Marxian unemployment does not fall within the scope of Keynes's mission in *The General Theory,* which was to generalize the classical doctrine by adding his concept of involuntary unemployment that is due to deficiency of aggregate demand.

Of course, one might have other concepts of involuntary unemployment. Imagine, for example, that in a less-developed country the equilibrium wage rate might fall below a subsistence level. Or, more simply, consider the case of the unemployed and underemployed poor who are shut off from productive jobs because an elite minority of the labor force has the power to establish real wage rates above the equilibrium level. The unemployed might be willing to work at substantially less real renumeration, yet this would fall in Keynes's category of voluntary unemployment. It is the inadequacy of the classical demand for labor K/k, owing to an excessively high k induced by the high real wage rates, that explains this unemployment—not lack of effective demand. Still, we might want to call this "involuntary Marxian unemployment."

I propose to do just that, and to generalize Keynes's theory by extending it to the case of Marxian unemployment. In so doing, I will make the simplifying assumption that the world is divided into two groups of countries: the more-developed countries (MDCs) which are characterized by Keynesian growth disequilibrium, and the less-developed countries (LDCs) which are characterized by Marxian growth disequilibrium.[31]

We have already distinguished Marxian from Keynesian unemployment. And we have seen that the attempt to prevent unemployment in the Keynesian case leads to wage–price inflation. Similarly, an attempt to eliminate (the growth of) Marxian unemployment by raising I_a to the level of I_n, would mean excess demand inflation as investment would exceed full employment, or full capacity, saving. (If I_a had fallen short of I_n in the past, because of the limitation of I_w, there would exist a "reserve army" of Marxian unemployed and the limitation on output would be full capacity of the capital stock, rather than full employment of labor.) To avoid the inflation, I_a must be held to I_w, but then capital formation runs behind growth of free labor supply and the reserve army grows.

---

[31] I will make no attempt to defend this assumption here, though I believe that, with important exceptions, it is close to the truth. It is particularly difficult to diagnose the case of the United States, which apparently has a relatively low saving ratio s. Moreover, the capital costs of projected environmental and energy programs may involve considerable labor saving. It is certainly not impossible for a rich country, therefore, to fall in the Marxian category. Germany and Japan, on the other hand, appear to be clear examples of the Keynesian case.

Both cases, Keynesian and Marxian, then, are characterized by an unemployment–inflation dilemma, but they are opposite cases of growth disequilibria. Accordingly, opposite remedies are required. In the Marxian case, what is needed is some combination of higher saving and less rapid population growth and labor saving as alternatives to a lower k. In the Keynesian case, lower saving or more rapid labor saving would represent alternatives to a higher k.

Up to now, we have tacitly assumed closed economies. Once we open them to international trade and capital flows, other solutions appear. If, for example, trade developed along Hecksher–Ohlin lines, the MDCs would expand their capital-intensive sectors for export, raising k; and the LDCs would expand their labor-intensive sectors for export, lowering k.

Given the evidence we have on trade patterns, reliance on Hecksher–Ohlin influences might not seem too promising, though trade barriers may help to explain the evidence. Capital flows might offer greater promise, but it is, of course, not the financial flow but the flow of real resources that counts. An import surplus for LDCs represents a flow of real saving from the world which supplements domestic saving to reduce the incidence of Marxian unemployment and excess demand inflation. An export surplus for MDCs, in symmetrical fashion, represents a use of domestic saving to invest in capital (claims against foreigners) that requires no labor complement. We could view the latter as a form of investment with an infinitely high k, whose increased weight in total investment raises the average k—without, it is important to note—reducing the rate of return on capital or raising the real wage rate. For Germany, it is an alternative to importing foreign labor. For Japan, it is an alternative to pulling labor out of agriculture. In a broader sense, however, it is an alternative to reducing the saving propensity or somehow forcing down the rate of return on capital.

In the narrow world of Keynes's *The General Theory* where all countries fall in the Keynesian case, an export surplus means "exporting unemployment." And we have seen in recent years a recurrence of neomercantilism among the MDCs, with each most concerned, in the jockeying of exchange rates, lest it be caught with an overvalued currency. The LDCs, most of whom shamelessly overvalue their currencies, have looked on in wonder at this preference of the rich countries for undervaluation.

In the wider world of generalized Keynes, of course, an export surplus means exporting unemployment only to the extent that MDCs attempt to export capital to each other, rather than to the LDCs. The only way that MDCs in the aggregate can have export surpluses is if, in the aggregate, they export capital to the LDCs. And a surplus of exports from MDCs to LDCs means a mitigation simultaneously of the problems of Keynesian unemployment in the former and Marxian unemployment in the latter.

World employment would be greater with such a pattern of trade and capital flow.

Scitovsky (1966) proposed an ingenious scheme for accomplishing just this a few years back. He explicitly recognized the complementary character of the unemployment problem in the two sets of countries and suggested that his proposal "may be regarded as an extension of Keynesian policy into the international sphere." His scheme, which links world monetary reform with a capital flow from rich countries to poor, is so sane and radical (in the sense of getting to the heart of the problem) that it cannot, of course, compete with the patch-on and patch-up approach that we are currently following. Yet I, for one, cannot see how world monetary reform can succeed in the absence of a clear recognition of the world employment problem and its links to the trade and capital flow relationships between rich and poor. Why not extend the Keynesian idea of a full employment policy-planning model to the world?

5. Conclusion

One way of summarizing this view of the economics of Keynes is to pose the question: was there a Keynesian Revolution? My answer is that, by following Keynes's lead, we have been able to learn, among other things, the following:

(1)   that there is a kind of unemployment that is associated with too low, rather than too high, real wage rates;

(2)   that there is a kind of inflation that is associated with too much, rather than too little, saving;

(3)   that in our macroeconomic theory we must assume that false trading is a common and serious problem, and that it may give rise to false information that thwarts equilibrating adjustments of relative prices;

(4)   that growth disequilibrium of the Keynesian variety could persist indefinitely with the business cycle substituting for adjustments of relative prices to produce a cyclical growth path;

(5)   that the Keynesian cyclical growth path is around the natural rate with even the full-employment peaks falling below the neoclassical growth path (for a given s);

(6)   that this growth trend, around which the economy fluctuates, represents a level of unemployment just high enough to reduce saving to the natural rate of capital formation[32];

---

[32] I leave aside the question whether or not this growth trend is an "equilibrium" path— whether or not the economics of Keynes incorporates a long-run, less-than-full employment growth equilibrium.

(7)   that in this Keynesian case the natural rate of capital formation is inhibited from rising as it should according to neoclassical tenets by the upward stickiness of the real wage rate and the downward stickiness of the rate of return on capital—a stickiness that is recurrently reinforced by expectations derived from the working of the cyclical adjustment mechanism, as well as by perverse monetary policies;

(8)   that this growth theory, based on persistent Keynesian disequilibrium, better explains the "stylized facts" of modern economic growth than do the neoclassical or "neo-Keynesian" theories;

(9)   and, finally, that the symmetry and complementarity between the Keynesian and Marxian cases of unemployment have important implications for policies relating to trade and capital flows between rich and poor countries, as well as for world employment.

Now none of the above could be understood within the limited framework of neoclassical theory; all of the above stems directly from Keynes's attack on that theory. This suggests to me, at least, that Keynes initiated a revolution—one that is not yet widely or fully understood and is still going on.

References

Alchian, A. (1970). Information Costs, Pricing and Resource Unemployment, in *Microeconomic Foundations of Employment and Inflation Theory*. New York: Norton.

Bailey, M. (1971). *National Income and the Price Level,* 2d ed. New York: McGraw-Hill.

Clower, R. (1965). The Keynesian Counter-Revolution: a Theoretical Appraisal, in *The Theory of Interest Rates* (F. Hahn and F. Brechling, eds.). London: Macmillan. (Reprinted in *Monetary Theory* (R. Clower, ed.). Baltimore: Penguin, 1969.)

Clower, R. (1967). A Reconsideration of the Microfoundations of Monetary Theory, *Western Economic Journal* **6**, 1–8.

Domar, E. (1946). Capital Expansion and Growth, *Econometrica* **14**, 137–147.

Haberler, G. (1941). *Prosperity and Depression,* 3rd ed. Geneva: League of Nations.

Harcourt, G., and Laing, N. (1971). *Capital and Growth.* London and New York: Oxford Univ. Press.

Harrod, R. (1939). An Essay in Dynamic Theory, *Economic Journal* **49**, 14–33.

Harrod, R. (1948). *Towards a Dynamic Economics.* London: Macmillan.

Hicks, J. (1939). *Value and Capital.* London and New York: Oxford Univ. Press.

Hicks, J. (1950). *A Contribution to the Theory of the Trade Cycle.* London and New York: Oxford Univ. Press.

Hicks, J. (1965). *Capital and Growth.* London and New York: Oxford Univ. Press.

Hicks, J. (1974). *The Crisis in Keynesian Economics.* New York: Basic Books.

Hines, A. (1971). *On the Reappraisal of Keynesian Economics.* London: Martin Robertson.

Kaldor, N. (1961). Capital Accumulation and Economic Growth, in *The Theory of Capital* (F. Lutz, ed.). London: Macmillan.

Keynes, J. M. (1936). *The General Theory of Employment, Interest and Money.* New York: Harcourt.

Leijonhufvud, A. (1968). *On Keynesian Economics and the Economics of Keynes*. London and New York: Oxford Univ. Press.

Lundberg, E. (1937). *Studies in the Theory of Economic Expansion*. London: P. S. King.

Marshall, A. (1948). *Principles of Economics*, 8th ed. New York: Macmillan.

Marx, K. (1939). *Capital*, Vol. I (from the 1889 ed.). New York: International.

Mill, J. S. (1900). *Principles of Political Economy* (from the 6th ed.). London: Longmans, Green.

Patinkin, D. (1965). *Money, Interest and Prices*, 2nd ed. New York: Harper and Row.

Patinkin, D. (1975). John Maynard Keynes: From the *Tract* to the *General Theory*, *Economic Journal* **85,** 249–271.

Pigou, A. (1941). *Employment and Equilibrium*. London: Macmillan.

Power, J. (1955). Capital Intensity and Economic Growth, *American Economic Review* (Proceedings) **45,** 197–207.

Power, J. (1958). The Economic Framework of a Theory of Growth, *Economic Journal* **48,** 34–50.

Power, J. (1959). Price Expectations, Money Illusion and the Real Balance Effect, *Journal of Political Economy* **47,** 131–143.

Power, J. (1962). Laborsaving in Economic Growth, *American Economic Review* (Proceedings) **52,** 39–45.

Scitovsky, T. (1940). Capital Accumulation, Employment and Price Rigidity, *Review of Economic Studies*. (Reprinted in Scitovsky, *Papers on Welfare and Growth*. Stanford, California: Stanford Univ. Press, 1964.)

Scitovsky, T. (1964). A Study of Interest and Capital, *Economica*. (Reprinted in Scitovsky, *Papers on Welfare and Growth*. Stanford, California: Stanford Univ. Press, 1964.)

Scitovsky, T. (1966). A New Approach to International Liquidity, *American Economic Review* **56,** 1212–1220.

Scitovsky, T. (1969). *Money and the Balance of Payments*. Chicago, Illinois: Rand-McNally.

Smith, A. (1937). *The Wealth of Nations* (Modern Library ed.). New York: Random House.

Solow, R. (1970). *Growth Theory: an Exposition*. London and New York: Oxford Univ. Press.

Wells, P., Keynes Employment Function, *History of Political Economy* **6,** 158–162.

Winston, G. (1974). The Theory of Capital Utilization and Idleness, *Journal of Economic Literature*. **12,** 1301–1320.

Department of Economics
University of Hawaii at Manoa
Honulu, Hawaii

The Aggregate Supply Function
in Keynes's General Theory

Lorie Tarshis

1. Introduction

Opinions clearly differ as to those features of Keynes's *General Theory* that gave it its special novelty—and indeed that made it a revolutionary document. Johnson (1975) stresses that its importance "lies not in its refutation of a classical 'orthodoxy' but in its application of capital theory to the theory of demand for money and the stimulus it provides to study of the dynamics of price and quantity adjustment to changes in aggregate demand [p. 116]." For Robinson (1975), "the revolution lay in the change from the conception of equilibrium to the conception of history: from the principles of rational choice to the problems of decisions based on guess work or on convention [p. 125]." For Meade (1975), "Keynes's

361

intellectual revolution was to shift economists from thinking normally in terms of a model of reality in which a dog called *savings* wagged his tail labelled *investment* to thinking in terms of a model in which a dog called *investment* wagged his tail labelled *savings* [p. 82]." And Moggridge (1975) defines the essence of the change as "an attempt to take monetary economics into the short period, into the real world when markets adjust to changes at widely different speeds under the influence of uncertainty [p. 78]."

My own preference, while it admittedly incorporates elements of at least some of the characterizations set out above, is rather different. Keynes had, in the *Treatise on Money* (Keynes, 1930), at least sketched in the beginnings of his analysis of the role of what he later called the *aggregate demand function* and showed how it was determined. What he had *not* done at that time, and indeed what he only began to achieve at all successfully about midway through 1934, (Moggridge, 1973; Patinkin, 1976) was to *integrate* "the theory of money" and the "theory of value," to use the titles that were then current for these two branches of economics. Putting this differently, the essence of his achievement was to create a *theory of output as a whole; a theory of employment;* or a *theory of the national income.* This shift was signaled in many ways. For one thing, he changed the title he used for his course of lectures. Before 1932, it had been the "Pure Theory of Money." By the autumn of 1932, it became the *"Monetary Theory of Production."* (In my own notes for these lectures, dated 10 October, 1932, I had written, "The change in title is significant. The influence of monetary manipulation on production rather than on prices. . . .") It was this feature of his new work that Keynes most strongly stressed. In the Preface to *The General Theory,* Keynes (1936) points out that:

> When I began to write my Treatise on Money, I was still moving along the traditional lines of regarding the influence of money as something so to speak separate from the general theory of supply and demand. . . . But my lack of emancipation from preconceived ideas showed itself in what now seems to me to be the outstanding fault of the theoretical part of that work . . . that I failed to deal thoroughly with the effects of *changes* in the level of output. . . . This book, on the other hand has evolved into what is primarily a study of the forces which determine changes in the scale of output and employment as a whole. . . . But our method . . . is one which depends on the "interaction of supply and demand, and is in this way linked up with our fundamental theory of value [p. xxii].

The instrument he chose to embody this "interaction of supply and demand," was, of course, the concept of *effective demand*—which he distinguished from the aggregate demand function. In a letter to R. F. Kahn (13 April 1934) [Moggridge, 1973, pp. 422–423] Keynes wrote:

> I have been making rather extensive changes in the early chapters of my book, to a considerable extent consequential on a simple and obvious, but beautiful and important (I think) precise definition of what is meant by effective demand:—
>
> Let W be the marginal prime cost of production when output is O. Let P be the expected selling price of this output. Then OP is effective demand.
>
> The fundamental assumption of the classical theory, "supply creates its own demand" is that $OW = OP$ whatever the level of O, so that effective demand is incapable of setting a limit to employment. . . . On my theory $OW \neq OP$ for *all* values of O, *and entrepreneurs have to choose a value of O for which it is equal;—otherwise the equality of price and marginal prime cost is infringed. This is the real starting point of everything* [my italics].

In fact, it should be obvious, it is also the starting point for the aggregate supply function.

"Monetary theory" provided many of the elements for his analysis of aggregate demand; "value theory" provided the elements for his analysis of the supply counterpart. The aggregate supply function (ASF) was the embodiment or manifestation of the bridge that linked up these two branches of economics.

Keynes (1936) himself, although he devoted little attention to the aggregate supply function in *The General Theory* was nevertheless keenly aware of its importance. Thus he writes in that book: "Hence the volume of employment in equilibrium depends on (i) the aggregate supply function ϕ, (ii) the propensity to consume X, and (iii) the volume of investment D_2. This is the essence of the General Theory of Employment [p. 29]."

Yet the aggregate supply function, for all its importance to Keynes, received relatively little space in *The General Theory*. It is introduced in Chapter 3, receives a few paragraphs of attention in Chapters 4 and 6—and a mention in the Appendix to the latter chapter—and that is it; although Keynes does direct the whole of Chapter 20, entitled "The Employment Function," to what he described as its inverse function. The explanation for his failure to devote much attention to the aggregate supply function is given in *The General Theory*, and also in a letter he wrote to D. H. Robertson a year before the publication of *The General Theory*. Keynes (1936) wrote, e.g., in Chapter 8 ("The Propensity to Consume: 1. The Objective Factors"):

> So far we have established the preliminary conclusion that the volume of employment is determined by the point of intersection of

the Aggregate Supply Function with the Aggregate Demand Function. *The Aggregate Supply Function,* however, which depends in the main on the physical conditions of supply, *involves few considerations which are not already familiar* [my italics] . . . in the main, it is the part played by the Aggregate Demand Function which has been overlooked . . . [p. 89].

In his letter to D. H. Robertson, dated 20 February 1935, he wrote: *"D'"*—later, changed to Z in the General Theory—"is the sales proceeds the expectation of which will cause the output from employing N men to be *produced.* It is simply the age-old supply function" [Moggridge, 1973, p. 513]. And, later in the same letter, (Idem, p. 513.) "Nor do I spend much time on D' except for some embroideries at a later stage, *since it is only a re-concoction of our old friend the supply function*" [my italics]. It is by now all too obvious that Keynes had been mistaken in his view that this part of his work needed little attention. Even so careful an examination of Volumes 13 and 14 of *The Collected Writings* as that undertaken by Patinkin (1976) suggests that Keynes failed seriously in his attempt to clarify the concept. The bridge he regarded as so important in establishing his claim to have effected an integration of monetary theory and value theory was for some of his critics invisible; and for most of the rest it was poorly constructed. The inadequacy of his treatment of this part of his work not only called into question the validity of his analysis in general; it also meant that understanding of the working of the economy was hampered, and as a result policy makers were deprived of a tool which could have been useful—for example, for dealing with stagflation. Our goal here is to clarify this important concept and to show how it may be used.

2. The Meaning

We shall begin our treatment by first considering the meaning to be attached to the aggregate supply function concept. It makes its initial appearance on page 24 of *The General Theory,* where Keynes defines the notion of "the aggregate supply price[1] of the output of a given amount of employment," as "the expectation of proceeds which will just[2] make it worth the while of the entrepreneurs to give that employment."

Reference to letters and memoranda in Volume 13 of *The Collected*

---

[1] Keynes's use of the term supply price differs from the usual one. The difference will be discussed later. This and the following footnote are not, of course, in Keynes's text.

[2] The word "just" should be noted. It has led to serious misunderstanding. We return later to this matter.

Writings (Moggridge, 1973) makes it abundantly clear that Keynes had in mind a short-period supply function in which each entrepreneur was assumed to act so as to establish his output at whatever level would maximize his profit, or at least the profit he expected.

Thus, in an early draft of *The General Theory* dated, as Moggridge (1973) writes, "from well before the first proof version of 11 October, 1934," we have:

> Now a firm's capital equipment being given, there is each day, the question of the train of employment to be set going which will maximize the firm's quasi-rent. Under normal assumptions of competition, etc. the condition of maximizing quasi-rent will be satisfied by a volume of employment such that the prime cost of the *marginal* employment will be equal to the expected sales proceeds of the resulting *increment* of product . . . [my italics].

> Thus the innovation of the present theory, is, at that stage, purely negative. Its significance will depend on our establishing our contention that there is, in general, only one level of output at which equality holds between marginal prime cost and the anticipated price, so that under competition the aim of maximizing profit will cause entrepreneurs to choose that level of employment for which this equality holds [pp. 426–427].

It is clear, incidentally, at least from the second paragraph, that when Keynes refers to "under competition," he means in conditions of perfect—as opposed to imperfect—competition. But it is also clear that he had no real reason for assuming perfect competition. By 1932, at least, the Cambridge group with whom he worked most carefully in getting *The General Theory* ready—R. F. Kahn and Joan Robinson particularly, but also E. A. G. Robinson, G. F. Shove, Piero Sraffa, and others—had completed their analysis of imperfect competition and the short period.

It is worth reading again, too, his letter to R. K. Kahn dated 13 April 1934, which was quoted previously: with W the *marginal* [my italics] prime cost of production where output is O, and P, its expected selling price, "entrepreneurs have to choose a value of O for which $OW = OP$;— otherwise the equality of *price* and *marginal prime cost* is infringed' " [my italics]. And note that if the marginal prime cost of an output differed from its price, assuming perfect competition, or in the more general case that it differed from the marginal revenue, it would mean that the chosen output did *not* promise maximum profits; presumably, such an output would not then be freely chosen, and it would not be an equilibrium output since entrepreneurs would have strong motives for changing it.

We shall have to return later to this point, because although Keynes, it seems to me, is quite clear in holding that a certain output will be in equilibrium only if entrepreneurs believe it to be more profitable than any other, the aggregate supply function has been understood in a quite different sense by at least a few commentators. But first we must look at the function itself, as Keynes sets it out.

The aggregate supply price for any output, we have seen, is that expectation of "proceeds" which will lead entrepreneurs to produce that output—*in preference to any other*. The aggregate supply *function* is then the relationship between, on the one hand, various levels of output and, on the other, those expectations of proceeds that would induce entrepreneurs to make them available. Two points of explanation should be made at this point. First, Keynes here uses the notion of "supply price" *not* as the price per unit, but instead as the total amount of sellers' receipts (net of user cost).[3] Second, Keynes prefers to measure the level of activity of the economy *not* in terms of its aggregate output but in terms of the amount of employment offered. He may have been correct in holding that the difficulties of adding the amounts of employment in the various firms of the economy—when allowance must be made for the differences in skill, etc., among employees—are fewer than those to be faced when their widely varied outputs are to be added. But the world has simply bypassed his objections and every self-respecting country nowadays computes its GNP not only in current prices but also in constant prices; of course, it also provides the implicit GNP price deflators, etc. Hence, we shall, from time to time, use as the independent variable, the total level of output for the economy; at other times, we shall follow his suggestion and use total employment; and, occasionally, we shall use a third variable, the total value of output.

Suppose, to begin our treatment, we are to determine "that expectation of proceeds" that would lead an individual firm to produce a certain output—say, O_1. We assume, as noted before, that the production decision is made with the motive of maximizing the profit of the firm. We assume, too, that the decision-maker is aware of the costs (average, average variable, and marginal) of producing such an output. Finally, we assume that the decision-maker is aware of the character of the market in which he is selling, and in particular of the elasticity of the demand for his product.[4] Since maximum profits are his goal, he will produce that output O_1 *only when the marginal cost corresponding to it is equal to its marginal*

---

[3] This concept (user cost) will be examined later.

[4] Admittedly, management is unlikely even to think in terms of the elasticity of demand or a marginal cost function. But, if the decision about price and output is made with a view to maximizing profits, the materials from which the economist formulates these two concepts must be considered, and that is sufficient.

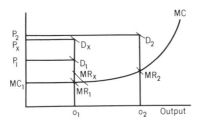

Figure 1 Derivation of price and total receipts required, given MC and K = 2.

revenue (Fig. 1). We realize, of course, that the condition just stated is *not* sufficient. In addition, the price at which he can sell must be at least as high as the variable cost per unit; otherwise, he would earn more (or, in this instance, lose less) by producing nothing at all.

For maximum profit, the marginal revenue (MR) must be equal to the marginal cost (MC) of O_1 or MC_1. Moreover, once we have the value of the elasticity of demand for this product as judged by the firm, we can determine the point above O_1 through which the demand D_1 must pass. It will be given by the formula[5]

$$D_1{}^H = \left(\frac{K}{K-1} \right) MC_1$$

where $D_1{}^H$ is the height of the demand curve above O_1. Thus if K, the elasticity of demand, is 2, the height of D_1 above O_1 or $D_1{}^H$ would be $2MC_1$; if $K = 3$, it would be $\frac{3}{2}MC_1$; etc. In the limiting case which Keynes took for his model with competition perfect and in which, accordingly, the elasticity of demand is infinite, $D_1{}^H = MC_1$. If, in Fig. 1, we assume that the value of K is 2, the height of the demand above O_1 or $D_1{}^H$ that would generate a marginal revenue function that intersected the marginal cost curve vertically above O_1 must be $2MC_1$. If the demand goes through that point, it is clear that the price to be charged would be P_1, where $P_1 = 2MC_1$.[6]

[5] I have recently found the notes I took at a series of lectures entitled "The Short Period" presented by R. F. Kahn in the Michaelmas term of 1932, which ran from October to December 1932. The substance of this paragraph was conveyed in these lectures. While I understand that Keynes had little interest in these developments in value theory, he had surely been made aware of them by Kahn and the Robinsons, among others. It is difficult for me to believe that we should not interpret Keynes's supply concept in this way on the grounds that at the time he was setting it out, 1934 and 1935, he could not have been aware of these matters. But see Patinkin (1976).

[6] If the firm were to charge less than that, it would forego profits; if it were to charge more it could not sell O_1 units; with the MR of the smaller output in excess of the MC, it would again earn less than it could have done.

Since we now have the supply price (in Marshall's sense) P_1, at which O_1 would be made available, we can also readily determine the total receipts, or supply price in Keynes's sense which would persuade the firm to produce O_1. It would be $[K/(K-1)MC]O_1$. Moreover, with the marginal cost function given, and the entrepreneur's estimate of the value of K, *no other level of total receipts from the sale of that output would induce the entrepreneur to make available the target output O_1.*

Of course, if O_1 could be sold at a higher price per unit, say P_x (Fig. 1), it would imply that the demand for the product went through a point vertically P_x above O_1 rather than through a point P_1 above O_1. But with the elasticity of that demand, in accordance with our assumption, still equal to K, the height of the marginal revenue above O_1, would then be also above MC_1. Presumably, then, the marginal revenue function would intersect the marginal cost curve to the right of O_1, and a producer who sought *maximum profit* would have no interest in producing O_1; instead, he would choose to produce something greater than O_1. Hence, it should be clear that when the producer knows the marginal cost of O_1 units of output MC_1, and estimates that the elasticity of the demand for his product when his sales are O_1 is K, *he would choose the output O_1 if and only if he could expect to sell that output at $[K/(K-1)MC_1]O_1$.*

We may now repeat the exercise for a different output, say O_2. Again, assuming that the producer estimates the elasticity of the demand for his product as K (here again equal to 2), he would be willing to produce O_2 if and only if he could expect to realize from its sale a level of receipts equal to $[K/(K-1)]MC_2O_2$ or $2MC_2O_2$.

In short, once we assume that the producer seeks to maximize his profits, we can see that he need only estimate his marginal cost for any particular output and the elasticity of the demand for his product at that output in order to determine the expectation of sales receipts that will induce him to produce that precise output, bearing in mind, of course, the second condition too. In the general case, when the output in which we are interested is O_n, with the marginal cost of that output being MC_n, and with the elasticity of the demand for the that output O_n, being equal to K_n; the necessary condition to induce him to produce O_n, *and neither more nor less*, would be that he must expect to realize receipts from the sale of that output "precisely" equal to

$$[K_n/K_n - 1]MC_nO_n.$$

We should notice, in passing, that if the MC of any output is greater than that for a smaller one and assuming K is a constant (or at least that it does not rise at greater and greater outputs), then $d[K/(K-1)]MCO/dO$ is positive and $d^2[K/(K-1)]MCO/dO^2$ is also positive. This means that the

TABLE 1

Character of ASF When Marginal Costs Are Constant over a Range of Outputs
$(K = 2)$

Output	MC	Supply price (in Keynes' sense)	Difference in supply prices
10	5	$2 \times 5 \times 10 = 100$	—
11	5	$2 \times 5 \times 11 = 110$	10
12	5	$2 \times 5 \times 12 = 120$	10
13	5	$2 \times 5 \times 13 = 130$	10
14	5	$2 \times 5 \times 14 = 140$	10

Conclusion: ASF is linear with an elasticity of 1.[a]

[a] It is possible to get a linear function in other ways too, although its elasticity will be greater than unity if marginal costs rise, but at an appropriately diminishing rate. But this, while correct arithmetically, lacks any significance as a picture of the economy.

"expectations of sales receipts required" must rise for each rise in output and that the rate of rise must increase. That is to say, the function must be convex to the horizontal axis. If it required an increase in the expected sales receipts of, say, 2000 to persuade an entrepreneur to raise his output from 20 to 21, it would require an increase of, say, 3000 in expected sales receipts to persuade him to raise his output from 25 to 26. It will be convex, even if the MC function is linear, so long as it rises to the right and more strikingly convex as the MC function is itself convex. Tables 1–3 illustrate these rules. It will be more strikingly convex, if the MC function itself is convex too, as it is very likely to be once output has reached the level at which the firm encounters increases in marginal costs for each expansion in output.

Figures 2–4 illustrate these results. We assume that K is held constant at 3 throughout.[7]

Now, we must shift the focus of our interest from the output of an individual firm to the output of the whole economy. In principal, no serious problems need be faced—largely because the convention is to sweep them under the rug.

We first have to deal with—or rather to raise—the question what is implied with respect to the outputs of each individual firm when the

[7] It will be noticed that if K changes whenever output changes, the results will be different from those reached here and in Tables 2 and 3 and may well contradict them. Again, these points were set out in Kahn's lectures.

TABLE 2

Character of ASF When Marginal Cost Function Is Linear, but Has a Positive Slope
($K = 2$)

Output	MC	Supply Price (in Keynes's sense)	Differences in supply prices
10	5	$2 \times 5 \times 10 = 100$	—
11	5.5	$2 \times 5.5 \times 11 = 121$	21
12	6	$2 \times 6 \times 12 = 144$	23
13	6.5	$2 \times 6.5 \times 13 = 169$	25
14	7	$2 \times 7 \times 14 = 196$	27

Conclusion: ASF is convex to the horizontal axis.

aggregate output of the economy is to stand at any particular figure. Obviously, this is a matter which falls squarely into the province of the microeconomist; and we shall simply assume that, in principal at least, we can know the composition of a particular output Q_n as the sum of the outputs of each of the many firms that make up the economy; viz., $O_n = {}_1O_n + {}_2O_n + {}_3O_n + \cdots + {}_MO_n$, where there are M firms, each producing its appropriate share of the total. (We use the symbols O_1, O_2, etc., to represent levels of output of a single firm, and $\underline{Q}_1, \underline{Q}_2$, etc., to stand for levels of output for the whole economy.)

Next, we have the problem of aggregating the amounts "required" for each firm taken individually in order to persuade it to produce its appro-

TABLE 3

Character of ASF When Marginal Cost Function Is Itself Convex to Horizontal Axis
($K = 2$)

Output	MC	Supply price (in Keynes's sense)	Difference in supply prices
10	5	$2 \times 5 \times 10 = 100$	—
11	5.5	$2 \times 5.5 \times 11 = 121$	21
12	6.25	$2 \times 6.25 \times 12 = 150$	29
13	7.25	$2 \times 7.25 \times 13 = 188.5$	38.5
14	8.5	$2 \times 8.5 \times 14 = 238$	49.5

Conclusion: ASF is convex (more strongly so than in Table 2) to the horizontal axis.

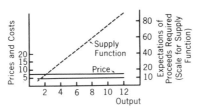

Figure 2 Relation between marginal costs and supply function when MC is horizontal.

priate contribution to the total output. If we were to add the *required* sales receipts—the counterparts of $[K_n/(K_n - 1)]MC_nO_n$—for each firm, our answer would involve a good deal of "double counting" for we would be adding the sales receipts needed by the firm that produces the leather to the corresponding amount for the firm that uses the leather as an input in producing shoes. Of course we may, if we wish, settle for the sum which is gross of this double counting. But, as we shall see, if we are to use this function in conjunction with the aggregate demand function, it will be much easier to net out the double counting; in other words, to measure each firm's output as well as the sales receipts required to induce it to produce such an output on a "value-added basis." And that was Keynes's intention when instead of defining the aggregate supply function in terms of the expectation of sales receipts needed to persuade entrepreneurs to hire any particular number of employees, he defined it in terms of the expectations of "proceeds" required to provide such an inducement. In fact, his concept of "user cost" was designed to permit the conversion of "sales receipts" to "values added."[8]

To get the total expectation of *net* sales receipts (or proceeds) required in order to induce entrepreneurs to make available any particular *output*—or, as Keynes would have it, to induce entrepreneurs to provide the appropriate number of *jobs*—it is necessary to subtract the total of what Keynes called user costs (user cost per unit of output multiplied by the level of output) from the expected (and required) sales receipts. In principal, this is no different from subtracting for any firm those puchases from other suppliers *that constitute costs for the purchasing firm*, in order to measure the "value added" by that firm.

We have seen that so long as the marginal cost function of the firm is

[8] Actually, Keynes's notion of "proceeds" took the process further than the modern national income statistician is prepared to go, because Keynes, unlike the modern statistician, saw no reason to distinguish between the costs of raw materials and components that are used up in the production process and that part of the cost that corresponded to the using-up of tools, equipment, and plant directly resulting from their use in production. The national income statistician today makes no such allowance. Thus, there is an element of double counting in his estimates.

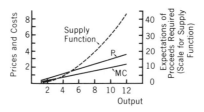

Figure 3 Same as Figure 2. MC is linear and rising. Supply function is convex.

"normal"—by which I mean that once output has reached a certain level, the marginal cost of any output will be higher, the higher is that output—the level of sales receipts (and presumably then of proceeds) required to induce the firm to produce any output will be higher the higher is the output, and moreover that the function which embodies this relationship is very likely to become less and less elastic as output is raised. Putting this differently, it will require larger and larger increments of bait to persuade producers to expand their combined output by any set amount.

We had, when considering the individual firm, noted that if the expectation of receipts from (or proceeds from the sale of) a certain output O_1 exceeded the supply price for that output $[K/(K - 1)]MC_1O_1$, the firm would find it profitable to produce a larger output. What is true for the individual firm is equally applicable to the collectivity. If the proceeds expected from the sale of $\underline{O}_1$ units of output (X in Fig. 5) exceed the aggregate supply price of that output,

$$\sum_{N=1}^{N=M} \frac{{}_NK_1}{{}_nK_1 - 1} {}_NMC_1 \,{}_NO_1,$$

or Y in Fig. 5, where the number of firms in the economy is M, then firms generally would judge it to be even more profitable to raise their total output than simply to go on producing O_1 and charge the higher prices they could get for that unchanged aggregate output. If, in Fig. 5, the line ADF shows the levels of proceeds the firms could expect to realize from the sale of their various outputs, and if ASF is the aggregate supply function, then the total output O_1 does *not* represent an equilibrium situation.[9] Firms would enjoy still larger profits by raising their combined output to O_N, the point of intersection of the ADF and ASF curves.

It is very important that this point be clearly understood. With regard to the output O_1, at which proceeds expected from the production and sale of

---

[9] Or at least it is not if we grant the assumption that the goal of each firm is to earn the highest possible level of profit; nor is it if the motives of the firms—whatever they may be—are properly reflected in the ASF.

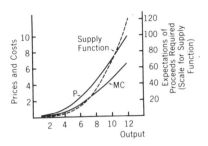

Figure 4 Same as Figure 2. MC is convex to horizontal axis. Supply function is more-strongly convex.

that output exceed the proceeds required to induce producers to make such an output available, refer again to the situation of any one of the firms whose appropriate target output is O_1. (See Fig. 6. Since we have already used much of the notation, we shall not repeat all identification. Assume that demand elasticity is 2.)

Now, in the situation represented in Fig. 5, it is clear that a typical firm—say, the one represented in Fig. 6—will be able to sell its output O_1 at a price well above P_1, about 60% higher if we can judge from the ratio X/Y in Fig. 5. Since the costs of producing O_1 are not altered, it follows that this would represent a far more profitable situation than the one in which ADF intersected ASF at O_1. We shall represent the demand that would confront our firm in such a situation by D_{x-1}. If the firm were to continue to produce O_1, its profits would be *higher* than those it would earn if D_1 were in fact ruling, by an amount equal to $(P_{x-1} - P_1)O_1$. This would, of course, represent a very attractive situation. But with the actual demand for its products at D_{x-1}, the corresponding marginal revenue function would be MR_{x-1} rather than MR_1. And MR_{x-1} would intersect the MC function to the right of O_1, say, at O_2. If the firm were to respond by raising its output to O_2, its profits would be still further increased by the shaded triangular area bound on the left by the vertical line from O_1, from above by MR_{x-1}, and from below by the MC curve up to the point at

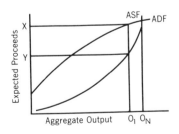

Figure 5 Equilibrium output (aggregate).

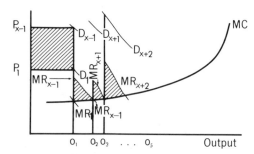

Figure 6 Disequilibrium in firm corresponding to aggregate output disequilibrium.

which MR_{x-1} intersected MC. But even that is not the end of the story, for if firms in general were to respond as this firm does, it would mean an increase in the total output of the economy. But, referring to ADF in Fig. 5, we can see that as a result there would be a secondary increase in the demand for the products of our "typical" firm—say, to D_{x+1} vertically above O_2. And D_{x+1} would generate MR_{x+1} which would intersect MC still further to the right and lead the firm to produce O_3, adding the shaded area bounded by the vertical above O_2, MR_{x+1}, and the MC to its profit. The process would presumably be continued until, referring to Fig. 5, aggregate output reached $\underline{Q}_N$. But the total addition to the profit over and above what could have been earned with output remaining at $\underline{Q}_1$ and the price at P_{x-1} would have been the sum of all such triangular areas as those already indicated.

Some have argued that profits would be maximized at an output that maximized the distance between the ADF curve and the ASF curves. But that would be true only if the ASF curve represented the aggregate variable costs for every output; and while aggregate expected receipts must as a necessary condition be at least as high as aggregate expected variable costs, for otherwise firms would decide to produce nothing at all, the aggregate supply function is, as we have shown, based on a quite different notion.

The reader will surely have noticed that we have introduced the aggregate demand function—the function that relates the total proceeds that entrepreneurs expect to realize from the sale of their outputs to various aggregate outputs. We must emphasize that both functions relate to "those expectations of proceeds," and therefore we are not here alluding to the possibility that what entrepreneurs *actually* receive may turn out to be different from what they *expect* to receive. However, when we are dealing with the aggregate supply function, we are concerned with the producers as *suppliers,* while when we are dealing with the aggregate demand function, we ask *not* how *high must be their* expectations of proceeds in order

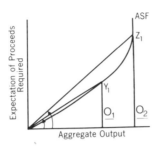

Figure 7 Change in slope of lines from points on ASF to origin indicates changes in prices.

to *induce* them to produce any particular output, but instead, how *high will their expectations of proceeds be* from the production and sale of that particular output.[10]

Returning to the aggregate supply function, we should note that the "price level" may also be identified in Fig. 7. Once again taking O_1 as the aggregate output, its "price level" is merely the ratio of proceeds required to the level of output. In other words, referring to Fig. 7, the price level is shown by the slope of the straight line joining Y_1, on the aggregate supply function, to the origin. For a higher output O_2, the new price is shown by the slope of the line from Z_1 to the origin. Since output must be measured as an index rather than as an aggregate—for instance, as so many tons—average price is also measured as an index.

If the position (and shape) of the aggregate supply function is determined by the marginal costs of the various firms that make up the economy and the elasticities of the demands for the products of these various firms, any significant change in either of these determinants should lead to a change in the aggregate supply function.

Thus, if money wage rates were to increase generally, we should expect the aggregate supply function to be shifted upward and to the left. Beginning, as before, with the individual firm, the increase in wage rates will of course mean an increase in its marginal costs. Assuming no change in K—the elasticity of the demand for its product—the supply price (in Keynes's sense) of any output O_1 will be raised from $[K/(K-1)]_2 MC_1 O_1$ to $[K/(K-1)]_2 MC_1 O_1$, where $_2 MC_1$ is the marginal cost of the output O_1 *after* the increase in wage rates; and, of course, $_1 MC_1$ is the corresponding figure at the original wage rate. If the increase in wage rates is general and marginal costs for the corresponding outputs for each of the other firms are consequently increased, then the aggregate supply price for a given

[10] Later, we shall have a few additional points to make about the aggregate demand function, but these points are not essential for an understanding of the implications for equilibrium of any difference in the heights of the aggregate supply and aggregate demand functions at any particular output.

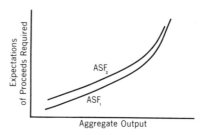

Figure 8 Change in aggregate supply function caused by general rise in money wage rates.

aggregate output will be higher than it was before. Thus, if ASF_1 is the aggregate supply function at the original wage rate, ASF_2 would be the aggregate supply function at the higher wage rate (Fig. 8).

In the same way, increases in certain tax rates—and, in particular, in the rates of those taxes that enter into variable costs—or in the prices of imported raw materials would lead to a similar shift in the position of the aggregate supply function.[11]

3. The ASF against Employment

The aggregate supply function against output, as we have described it, is not the one set out by Keynes. As already noted, he decided to measure the activity of the economy either in terms of employment or in terms of the level (in money) of the national income, deflated by the wage unit. But neither of these alternatives raises any new point of difficulty. Our task now is to show how either of these concepts may be derived from the one already described, and also to point out how much of the information conveyed in the aggregate supply function against output (already described) and in the aggregate supply function against employment (to be described in this section) is simply calculated out of existence when the aggregate supply function against national income (the most familiar form) is derived. For convenience, we label the aggregate supply function against total output ASF-O; we label the aggregate supply function against employment ASF-N; and we label the aggregate supply function against national income ASF-Y.

First, let us look into the relation between ASF-O and ASF-N. We begin, as before, with an account of the factors that determine the supply

---

[11] Later, we shall look at another development which seems to have been an important factor during the period of ''stagflation'' characteristic of the 1970s.

price, in Keynes's sense, of the output of a particular firm, but this time we must take note of the employment level associated with that output. Let us suppose that n_1 employees are needed in order to produce O_1 units of output. Then the supply price of the output corresponding to n_1 employees is, as before, $[K/(K - 1)]MC_1O_1$. The corresponding supply price of the output of n_2 employees is $[K/(K - 1)]MC_2O_2$; and so on for n_3, n_4, etc.

If but only if, average labor costs are constant or do not change with output will the two supply functions have the same characteristics. (Incidentally, we must also assume that marginal labor costs make up the whole, or at least a constant fraction, of marginal costs.) Our first assumption implies constant (average) returns to labor inputs and, hence, a linear relationship, with unit elasticity, between output and employment; it also implies constant marginal costs. But we have already seen that with marginal costs constant, the "contribution" of the firm to ASF-O is linear with an elasticity of 1. It follows that the "contribution" of the firm to ASF-N will also be linear with an elasticity of 1.

It is possible, of course for dO/dn to be constant while at the same time average returns to labor are increasing or diminishing. In these circumstances, with, say, increasing average labor costs and constant marginal costs—the latter following from our assumption that dO/dn is constant— the firm's "contribution" to ASF-N would continue to be linear although its elasticity would be less than 1.[12]

More generally, dO/dn could change with changing output and average labor costs could change too, though at a quite different rate. Such a situation is far more likely to exist in "the real world." In these circumstances, the "contribution" of the firm to ASF-N would no longer be linear; whether it would be more elastic than the corresponding component of ASF-O would depend upon whether average labor costs in the range were falling; it would be less elastic when average labor costs were rising.

A short numerical illustration will help to clarify these matters. Figure 9 illustrates the firm for which we describe these possibilities. In the range A–B, the firm experiences decreasing labor costs or increasing average returns to labor; but marginal costs are rising. We have already seen that when the MC curve is rising to the right, the "contribution" of the firm to ASF-O is convex to the horizontal axis. With increasing average returns to labor, it follows that while ASF-N will continue to be convex, its elasticity will be greater than the elasticity for the corresponding compo-

---

[12] The rate of change in average labor costs is here constrained by our assumption of a constant value for dO/dn.

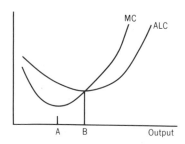

Figure 9 Possible relation: average labor cost function of marginal costs.

nent of ASF-O. The numerical examples given in Table 4 will be suggestive. Note that:

(1) The contribution of the firm to ASF-O is convex.

(2) The contribution of the firm to ASF-N is also convex.

(3) The elasticities of the contribution of the firm to ASF-O are successively 1.51, 1.53, and 1.55.

(4) The elasticities of the contribution of the firm to ASF-N are successively 2.13, 2.01, and 1.92, and they are higher than those given in (3).

(5) It might be noted in passing that the two elasticities are less far apart between 12 and 13 units than between 10 and 11 units. This follows from the fact that the rate at which labor costs per unit are falling declines with increases in output.

Beyond *B*, in the range in which average returns to labor are falling, or average labor costs are rising, the elasticity of the firm's contribution to ASF-N will be smaller than that of its contribution to ASF-O. Again, a numerical example (Table 5) will prove suggestive. Note that:

TABLE 4

Output	MC	Required proceeds when $E_D = 2$	Total labor costs[a]	Employment (assuming wage rate of 1)	Average labor costs
10	2	40	30	30	3
11	2.1	46.2	32.1	32.1	2.918
12	2.2	52.8	34.3	34.3	2.858
13	2.3	59.8	36.6	36.6	2.815

[a] Total labor costs are bound to increase, of course, as output is raised from, say, *x* to *x* + 1 units by the amount of the marginal cost corresponding to *x* + 1 units.

TABLE 5

Output	MC	Required proceeds assuming $E_D = 2$	Total labor costs = N if wage rate is 1	Average labor costs
10	2	40	15	1.5
11	2.2	48.4	17.2	1.563
12	2.5	60	19.7	1.642
13	2.9	75.4	22.6	1.74

(1)   The contributions of the firm to ASF-O is convex.

(2)   The contributions of the firm to ASF-N is also convex.

(3)   The elasticities of the contribution of the firm to ASF-O are successively 2.0, 2.45, and 2.84.

(4)   The elasticities of the contribution of the firm to ASF-N are successively 1.39, 1.58, and 1.66, and they are lower than those given in (3).

In *The General Theory*, Keynes (1936) states that "since the proceeds of the marginal product is equal to the marginal factor cost at every point on the aggregate supply curve we have $\Delta N = \cdots = \Delta Z_w = \Delta\phi(N)$, that is to say that $\phi^1(N) = 1$; provided that factor cost bears a constant ratio to wage cost and. . . . This means that if wages are constant and other factor costs are a constant proportion of the wages-bill, the aggregate supply function is linear with a slope given by the reciprocal of the money-wage [pp. 55–56, footnote 2]." He is here referring to what we have identified as ASF-N. Patinkin (1976, p. 87) endorses this conclusion at least with respect to ASF-N, although the rather different proof he supplies for its linearity seems to me to be just as unpersuasive as that of Keynes.

The simplest counterargument to that presented by Keynes is that the ordinary short-run industry supply functions would only be linear (and horizontal) if the marginal cost curves in the component firms were also horizontal. If the marginal cost functions were linear but sloped, say, up to the right, then the ordinary supply function for the industry would also slope up to the right. Even that would be enough to render the supply function in Keynes's sense, with total sales receipts or proceeds substituted for the price per unit, convex. If the slopes of the marginal cost curves in the component firms increased with increases in output, the ordinary supply function for the industry would be convex, while Keynes's industry supply function would be even more convex. Yet at every point on any of these supply functions, the proceeds of the marginal product is equal to the the marginal factor cost—assuming perfect competition.[13] The situation is not altered in its essentials if the base of the aggregate supply function is taken to be employment rather than output. A linear aggregate supply function would arise only, as we have seen, if dO/dn were constant.

The problems of aggregating across the economy for this function are no different from those that arise in deriving ASF-O.

Two more points should be noted about ASF-N. First, like ASF-O it will change whenever there are changes in marginal costs or in the elasticities of the demand for the products of the various firms; in addition, it will change whenever there are changes in average costs. Second, the slope of the line from any point on ASF-N to the origin no longer represents "the price level" but instead the ratio of values added to the level of employment. It will thus depend not only upon output per unit of labor but also upon the prices at which any level of output will be sold in equilibrium. Then, even with diminishing (average) returns to labor, the ratio could be expected to rise if marginal costs were to rise more sharply than average labor costs. It might be noted, referring to the numerical sample given (Table 5), that the ratio shows the following values for 10, 11, 12, and 13 units, respectively: 2.67, 2.81, 3.05, and 3.34, and this increase occurs despite the fact that output is in the range in which the average product per unit of labor diminishes with increasing output.

4. The 45° Average Supply Function (ASF-Y)

Whatever may be the merits of ASF-O and ASF-N, they have, as noted earlier, almost disappeared from the literature of macroeconomics. In their place, we find a third concept—ASF-Y—in which aggregate output or total employment as one of the variables is replaced by "income in terms of wage units Y_w corresponding to a level of employment N." Keynes (1936, p. 90) actually suggests such a substitution when he first introduces the propensity to consume; by implication, since he does not later withdraw his suggested substitution, he must presumably also endorse it for the aggregate demand function. But the point of intersection of what we might by analogy call ADF-Y and ASF-N lacks meaning.[14] Thus we must either make use of such concepts as ADF-N or ADF-O or instead

[13] If competition is not perfect, marginal factor cost of any output represented by a point on the supply function equals the marginal revenue; but that modification changes nothing.

[14] It lacks meaning because the horizontal axis would be labeled money income deflated by wage units for the ADF; while it would have a different label—aggregate employment—for the ASF. And there is no reason to expect a one-to-one correspondence in the scales appropriate to each of these variables.

convert ASF-N or ASF-O into ASF-Y. If we adopt this last procedure, and Keynes does not really deal with the issue in *The General Theory*, we can detect at least an implicit endorsement by Keynes of ASF-Y. In any event, it has become the accepted concept. But as I shall try to show, it is a much less useful concept than either ASF-O or ASF-N.

Its derivation is straightforward. We begin as before with the supply price, in Keynes's sense, required to induce a firm to produce a certain physical output, say O_1. It is $[K/(K - 1)]MC_1O_1$. Let us now express the output O_1 in value terms rather than as physical output. In order to do that, we must multiply O_1 by P_1. But P_1, the price that would rule in equilibrium is simply $[K/(K - 1)]MC_1$. Hence, we find that in order to induce a firm to produce an output worth $[K/(K -)]MC_1O_1$, the firm must be able to expect to sell it for the total sum of $[K/(K - 1)]MC_1O_1$: the same amount. Such an equality would presumably hold for any output valued in money, and for any firm. Aggregating these, we learn that the aggregate supply price of an output valued at X is X, of an output valued at Y is Y, and so on. For the whole economy, the expectation of proceeds required to induce its firms to produce an output worth, say, $200 billion, would be $200 billion; to produce an output worth $1.8 trillion, the expectation of proceeds required as an inducement would be $1.8 trillion; and so on.

Such an aggregate supply function would be illustrated diagrammatically, assuming vertical and horizontal axis had identical scales, by a straight line extending out at an angle of 45° from the origin (Fig. 10).

Keynes never illustrated ASF-Y or any other for that matter, diagrammatically, but the 45° straight line from the origin—sometimes labeled ASF and sometimes labeled output equals income—is by now a commonplace. There are two points to be made in connection with it, assuming that we can accept is as useful.

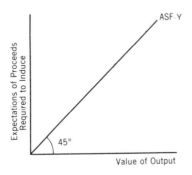

Figure 10 The ASF-Y.

In some treatments, the diagonal line extends out a certain distance and then it breaks suddenly to the north, the point of discontinuity generally being described as at the capacity level of the economy. But, actually, while it may be useful to identify capacity (at present prices), there does not seem to be any justification for making ASF-Y turn to the vertical at that point. It is as though the diagonal part of the line identifies ASF-Y, while the vertical part has to do with the shape of ASF-O or ASF-N at the capacity of the economy.

Patinkin (1976) sought to justify the 45° radius-vector as representing the aggregate supply price (function?) in Keynes's sense of the term. While I believe him to be in error in regarding the 45° straight line as Keynes's "aggregate supply prices of that '(any)' level of employment," it seems to me that he is correct in using it to represent what we have called ASF-Y—except for the discontinuity at capacity. However, in his note (Patinkin, 1977) he argues that the aggregate supply curve as a function of Y_w (or ASF-Y in our nomenclature "must lie below the 45° line with a less-than-unitary slope. . . . On the other hand nothing can be specified *a priori* about the convexity or concavity of this curve."

His argument is worth presenting because it seems to me to bring out clearly the precise difference between his and my understanding of the aggregate supply function. He says "if we continue to define" aggregate supply price "as *total variable costs* [my italics] then. . . ." But while the aggregate supply price of a certain output must be at least as great as its total variable costs, for otherwise the firms would decide to produce nothing at all, this is merely a *necessary* condition, it is not a sufficient condition.

If the marginal cost curve for a firm and the elasticity of its demand are set, the condition, subject of course to the proviso set out above, which would lead the firm to produce a certain output is that the supply price, in Keynes' sense of the term, must equal $[K/(K - 1)]MC_1O_1$. For, if it is below this figure (but nonetheless higher than total variable costs), the firm could earn *higher* profits by reducing its output.

Figure 11 will help in illustrating this point. The elasticity of demand is 3. If O_1 is to be produced, the demand must be D_1, for no other demand function with this elasticity would generate MR_1 which intersects the marginal cost curve vertically above O_1. The required expectation of proceeds is then P_1O_1. If the proceeds are only P_2O_1, where P_2 is the height of the average variable costs function, and total proceeds are then equal to total variable costs, the demand curve D_2, which interesects the average variable cost curve (AVC) vertically about O_1 would generate a marginal revenue function MR_2 which lies below MR_1. But this would intersect the MC curve at an output less than O_1: at O_2 in Fig. 11. Thus, the aggregate

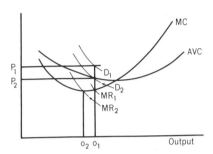

Figure 11   The typical firm's situation if Patinkin's interpretation is valid.

supply price of O_1 units of output in this instance, and indeed in all but a limiting case in which the demand curve is tangent to the average variable cost curve—and when, therefore, the marginal revenue and marginal cost curves intersect vertically below that point of tangency—will be higher than the total variable costs. In that one special case, when the price and average variable costs are equal and the supply price would be equal to total variable costs, the firm of course experiences losses just equal to the amount of its fixed costs.

All ASF-Y really says is that the macroeconomy is in equilibrium when its firms expect their proceeds from a certain output measured in dollars to equal the amount they would *require*, as expected proceeds, in order that they be induced to produce that output. Or again, if in their judgment a certain physical output must be sold for say, $2 trillion, in order to persuade them to produce precisely that output, then that output would be in equilibrium if they, in fact, did expect it to yield proceeds of $2 trillion when it was marketed. But does this really say anything very startling? Or is it not true that anything so valid—and valid no matter what are the circumstances—is unlikely to say anything at all useful. What, for example, happens when equilibrium is not attained?

There are more serious objections than those to the ASF-Y. Unlike ASF-O or ASF-N, it can convey no information about prices, output, or employment. Moreover, it provides no hint as to the character of the adjustment they would make in price, in output or in the two combined, if expected proceeds differ from the sum required.[15] Both ASF-O and ASF-N as we conceive them are "behavior functions," reflecting management's goal of maximizing profit. But ASF-Y has no such content. All its content has been drained from it in the process of deriving it from one of the other two.

[15] Obviously, if we are dealing with a capitalistic economy, we may be able to make a very good guess as to the adjustment it would make, but then we are adding more information to ASF-Y than it itself contains.

Unlike ASF-O and ASF-N, which change whenever either marginal costs alter or the demand elasticities are modified, ASF-Y is unaffected by such changes. This feature may seem to some to be an advantage. But it means that if we are to handle the macroeconomic consequences of such developments, we must provide as a supplement to the ordinary analysis the information that the other two functions contain. Obviously to do this is not impossible, but it is troublesome.

We have claimed that ASF-Y contains less useful information than either ASF-N or ASF-O. The difference can be brought out clearly by developing supply (and demand) functions corresponding to ASF-Y for an industry which is normally analyzed in quite a different way. Suppose we set out the ordinary demand and supply functions for wheat. We assume them to be as shown in Table 6. Inspection of these data will establish the fact that the equilibrium levels of output and price are, respectively, 15 and 5. Moreover, if the price should initially be different from 5, we can identify the forces that would press it toward the equilibrium level. If, for instance, the supply should increase so that the supply price required in order to induce producers to make available each of the amounts listed in Table 6 is reduced by 0.95, the new equilibrium output and price will be 17 and 4.8, respectively. This is of course familiar territory, and its value is clear to see.

Now let us "convert" this information into functions corresponding to ADF-Y and ASF-Y. We would then have the situation shown in Table 7. Inspection of these two functions discloses that "equilibrium" is established when the dollar level of transactions stands at 75.0. But we cannot infer from these data anything about the price or the physical amount of wheat traded.

TABLE 6

Amount	Supply price[a]	Demand price[b]	Amount	Supply price[a]	Demand price[b]
10	4.0	5.5	16	5.35	4.9
11	4.10	5.4	17	5.75	4.8
12	4.25	5.3	18	6.20	4.7
13	4.45	5.2	19	6.70	4.6
14	4.7	5.1	20	7.25	4.5
15	5.0	5.0			

[a] Price required to induce producers to make the amounts in column 1 available.

[b] Price at which buyers would be willing to purchase the amounts in column 1.

TABLE 7

The Aggregate Supply Function and the Aggregate Demand Function

Value of wheat	Expecta-tion of proceeds required	Proceeds actually expected	Value of wheat	Expecta-tion of proceeds required	Proceeds actually expected
40 ($=4 \times 10$)	40	55 ($=5.5 \times 10$)	85.60	85.60	78.40
45.1 ($=4.1 \times 11$)	45.1	59.4 ($=5.4 \times 11$)	97.75	97.75	81.60
51.0 ($=4.25 \times 12$)	51.0	63.60	111.60	111.60	84.60
57.85	57.85	67.60	127.30	127.30	87.40
65.80	65.80	71.40	145.00	145.00	90.00
75.0	75.0	75.00			

In Fig. 12 we set out the two functions. Again it is clear that the equilibrium level of output stands at 75.0.

Now suppose that the supply of wheat increases in the normal sense with the price required to induce producers to make any specific amount of wheat available being reduced by 0.95. Obviously ASF-Y is not altered; given the equivalence of scales on the two axes, the 45° straight-line ASF is invariant.

However, we must now take into account a change in the ADF—a paradoxical development because this is required even though nothing happens to the demand itself, in the ordinary sense of the term. Yet with the changed "supply," in Table 7 the first entry in the first column is altered from 40 to 30.5; the next entry is 34.65. . . . The new ADF is now as shown in Table 8.

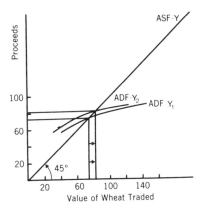

Figure 12 Effect of change in supply of wheat on aggregate demand function wheat.

TABLE 8

The Revised Aggregate Demand Function after "Supply" Raised

Value of wheat	Proceeds actually expected	Value of wheat	Proceeds actually expected
30.5	55	70.40	78.40
34.65	59.4	81.60	81.60
39.60	63.60	94.50	84.60
45.50	67.60	109.25	87.40
52.50	71.40	126.00	90.00
60.75	75.00		

Again, inspection will establish that the dollar value of transactions will now be set at 81.60. But there is no way of determining, without going back to the raw data, whether this increase in dollar value is made up of higher prices and a greater level of output, or lower prices and a still larger increase in the level of output, or anything else.

Diagrammatically, while ASF-Y does not shift, the position of the ADF does change from ADF-Y_1 to ADF-Y_2. But we are still unable, by referring to Fig. 12, to make any determination as to how price and output (taken separately) would be altered by reason of the *increase* in supply. If we wish to be strict in our interpretation, we are likewise unable, without referring back to the more basic data which was the source of our aggregate functions, to state how the process of moving toward a new equilibrium is set in motion.[16] And we must still grapple with the additional paradox that a rise in the supply (in the Marshallian sense) has to be converted into a rise in the ADF, if our analysis is to be couched in terms of the now-conventional ASF function, i.e., ASF-Y.

Recalling Keynes's own judgment as to the nature of his contribution— that he had succeeded in forging a link between value theory and monetary theory and that his analysis was, on this account, capable of dealing with such aggregates as total output, or total employment—it is ironic that the form in which the aggregate supply function is usually presented

[16] To assume that the ordinary aggregate demand function would be uninfluenced by any revaluing of output, such as would be caused by, say, a drop in productivity, and that as a result, the only adjustment need be to apply the unchanged consumption function to the new money values does not seem reasonable. But this seems to me to raise some basic questions about the aggregate demand function that require careful attention. For one thing, an effort should be made to clarify the consumption function to discover, e.g., whether, and if the answer is yes, how its form changes when the base is altered from employment to aggregate output (in fixed dollars) to aggregate output (in current dollars, but deflated by wage units).

(ASF-Y) provides no information at all about these aggregates. The charge that Keynesian economics can really offer little help for an analysis of inflation—and especially of inflation in any economy in which unemployment is appreciable—appears to be valid. But perhaps that is because, as Leijonhufvud (1968) has reminded us in a different connection, there is a world of difference between "Keynesian economics" and "the economics of Keynes."

A short summary will be in order before we provide examples of how ASF-O or ASF-N can be used.

The intersection of ASF-O or ASF-N and the appropriate aggregate demand function does represent a position of equilibrium in this sense; that given the marginal costs of the various firms and the elasticity of demand for the product of each of them (as seen by the firm in question), firms in the aggregate have no incentive to alter their prices or output from that indicated by the intersection, because, on average, at that aggregate output and level of employment each is maximizing its profit.[17]

Neither ASF-O or ASF-N is at all likely to be linear. The former would be linear only if marginal costs were constant over a range of output; the latter only if average labor costs were constant. Keynes (1936, p. 55, footnote 2), who argued that ASF-N would be linear with a slope of unity, or later in the same footnote that it would be linear with a slope given by the reciprocal of the money wage was implicitly assuming the constancy of marginal costs.

We have up to this point tried to make a case for the view that Keynes's concept of the aggregate supply function has a very important role in his analysis; that without it, we should find at least some difficulty in seeing clearly that his macroequilibrium—assuming that it embodies profit-maximizing behavior on the part of the firm—is stable. But we noted at the beginning that it can also help us to deal with some of the problems of the day. We shall now provide a sketch of the kind of analysis that makes use of his concept.

First, let us compare briefly two policies for dampening inflation: an increase in income taxes and an increase in sales taxes or other indirect business taxes. Since our concern here has to do with "prices," we are bound to employ ASF-O.[18] An increase in personal income tax rates does not, at least directly, bring about an increase in costs in the typical busi-

---

[17] Equality of the aggregate of course does not guarantee that each firm is in equilibrium. One may want to expand its output, but if so this would be offset by the desire of another to contract its output.

[18] Naturally, we could make use of either of the others, but if we were to do so, we should have to supplement the basic analysis with another that concerned itself directly with prices.

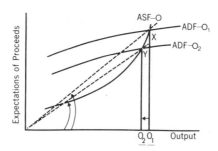

Figure 13 Direct effect of increase in personal income taxes on aggregate output and prices.

ness firm.[19] Nor does it affect the "degree of monopoly" or the elasticity of the demand for the products of the typical firm. Consequently, we may conclude that ASF-O would not be changed.

The primary effect of the increase in income tax rates would be to lower the aggregate demand function. Corresponding to any level of GNP in constant prices, the level of disposable personal income would be lower than before and consequently the consumption function (with GNP as base) would be reduced.

The effects of such a change can then be summarized as shown in Fig. 13. It can be seen that the level of output, or the GNP in constant prices, would fall, although as shown in Fig. 13, the decline would be relatively small. The original price level—represented by the slope of the straight line from X to the origin—would be lowered to correspond to the reduced slope of the straight line from Y to the origin.[20]

By contrast, an increase in the rate of indirect business taxes brings about an increase in the variable costs of doing business, and consequently in the marginal costs of any output. Apart again from consid-

---

[19] There may be indirect effects stemming from such a rise in personal income tax rates as, for example, if labor unions press for higher wage rates to compensate their members for the higher income tax rates to which they are exposed. If so, it is not difficult to allow, separately, for the increased wage rates. For the present, we shall assume that no indirect effects are likely.

[20] The ASF-O was drawn on the assumption that the marginal cost function for the various firms were applicable whether the direction of movement of output was upward or downward; that is perhaps an unwarranted assumption. In addition, it was assumed that the elasticity of the demand for the typical firm's product was independent of the direction of change in the demand for that product; and that too should perhaps be questioned. Certainly when oligopolistic considerations generate "the kinked demand function," it seems to me that the direction of movement in the demand may be a very important factor in determining whether the kink becomes more or less pronounced, and, hence, in determining whether the effective elasticity becomes smaller or greater. These considerations may yield a rather smaller decline in price than we show here, and a rather larger decline in the level of output.

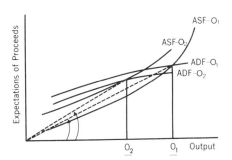

Figure 14 Direct effect of increase in sales taxes on aggregate output and prices.

erations having to do with oligopoly, we may reasonably assume that the elasticity of demand for the product of the firm would remain unchanged. As a result, we may conclude that ASF-O_1 would fall to ASF-O_2 (in Fig. 14). The aggregate demand function could also be expected to show a decline simply because an increase in sales taxes would, other things being equal, widen the gap between the GNP and the amount of disposable personal income corresponding to any level of the GNP. The effect here, however, is likely to be smaller, simply becomes some of it will leak away in the form of reduced corporate profit taxes, reduced undistributed corporate profits, and reduced personal taxes, as well as a reduction in personal savings—which would, of course, also be a leavening force when personal income tax rates are raised.

This implies that though output—the GNP in constant prices—falls as a result, the price level is increased or at least it may be increased. It is not at all impossible, then, that increasing sales tax rates will deflate output and employment, but actually raise prices.[21]

Finally, we shall examine the consequences for prices and employment of a tight money policy and especially of one that raises the costs of borrowing to the highly unusual levels seen in Canada, and to a lesser degree in the United States, in recent years.

The analysis that follows is intended to deal not with an increase in interest rates from a moderate level to a high level, but instead to consider the effects of an increase to an *unusually* high level. Firms exposed to such unprecedented interest rates would, if they were able, want to adjust their assets and liabilities: reducing their liabilities sharply, and matching these reductions if possible with a *balanced* reduction of their assets. But to a marked degree they are, in the short period at least, locked in with respect to most of their assets. They would probably suffer an unacceptably large

[21] All of the considerations noted in footnote 20 are relevant here too, and of course they may modify the results.

capital loss from putting some of their machinery and other equipment up for sale, and the argument would be even stronger against a plant liquidation. They might have some opportunities to reduce their holdings of financial assets—of accounts receivable, for instance—but any success they might enjoy in this direction would be at the expense of other firms, and in particular of their customers who probably face the same pressures. Their best hope at such a time would be to attempt to operate with smaller inventories—inventories of raw materials, components, goods in process, and finished output. And judging at least on a qualitative basis, this is precisely what firms have done in recent years.[22] At retailers, stocks are typically low, and some of the variety formerly available is likely to be missing. Deliveries from manufacturers are often held up, and that despite the apparent availability (in Canada) of large numbers of unemployed and of equipment operating at less than its rated capacity. In short, with respect to short-period adjustments at least, the economy seems to be operating close to its capacity. Yet, in many lines, production has not gone much above the levels attained in 1972 or 1973.[23] Capacity, in respect to the ability of firms to adjust their output to short-period shifts in demand, has been curtailed at least in part because interest rates are at levels so high that firms have been severely pressed to make the only economies they can.[24]

A reduction in ''capacity,'' under existing circumstances, is likely to affect the aggregate supply function in two ways. First, it means that the marginal cost of an output that is close to the shrunken capacity of the firms will be higher than the marginal cost of the same output when that output was lower in relation to capacity.[25] Second, when each firm finds

[22] Published ratios of inventories to sales are not likely to be very informative in periods of inflation because of problems connected with the valuation of inventories.

[23] Many will undoubtedly interpret this as the result of labor's present unreadiness to work—the same interpretation that their elders advanced in the early 1930s to account for another group of unemployed. I find such an explanation unpersuasive simply because I can remember how ready the unemployed labor of, say, 1936, was to work when jobs become available 3 or 4 years later.

[24] Against this argument, it may be claimed that while nominal interest rates are admittedly very high, ''real'' interest rates are extraordinarily low. Well, if they are as low as it is claimed they are—perhaps minus 2% or so—one must then explain why firms are not showing an unprecedented eagerness to borrow in order to finance inventory accumulation and expenditures on plant and equipment. One must also explain why shortages at the retail and manufacturing levels persist.

[25] Certainly, there are also other factors that should have a prominent part in accounting for the increases in marginal costs that can be observed, such as the large increases in wage rates and in the prices of such imported raw materials as crude petroleum in recent years. I emphasize here the results of the pressures to economize on inventories, because they seem to have received too little attention.

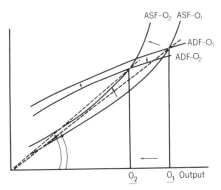

Figure 15 Possible effects on prices and aggregate output of increase in interest rates from very high level.

itself operating close to capacity and, more important, when it finds that its competitors in the industry are confronted by the same strains, that situation is likely to bring about a significant reduction in the elasticity of the demand for a firm's product as it judges the situation. At such a time the ordinary penalty of raising price is suspended or at least weakened, simply because each firm knows that even if it does raise its price, its customers have no other suppliers to whom to turn.

These considerations—increases in marginal costs, and reductions in the elasticity of the demands for many of the various products of the economy—are bound to bring about a sharp movement to the left in ASF-O.

The rise in interest rates naturally also has effects on the aggregate demand function, and it is for this reason that the policy of very tight credit commends itself to so many. But it is not unlikely that the reductions in the two functions will only exacerbate the situation, as is suggested by Fig. 15.

Obviously, I do not put this hypothesis forward as a "full explanation" for stagflation or as implying a prescription for ending it. Insofar as it makes sense, it seems to me to call for a sharp reduction in interest rates with an increase in taxes selected so that marginal costs in the typical firm are *not* raised. There would, of course, remain the problem of dealing with the effects of the price rises of imported raw materials and rapidly advancing wage rates, but even these increases might be reduced if firms were able to operate at the rated capacity of their fixed assets and did not have to face unnatural constraints which are likely to foster monopoly power.

Keynes, in his latter to D. H. Robertson of 20 February 1935 from which we have quoted earlier (Moggridge, 1973) writes:

The Employment Function [which Keynes describes as the inverse of the aggregate supply function] is *frequently* heard of again. It runs through the whole book, though it is true that its theoretical side is only developed in detail in a later chapter. For I make the volume of output depend on the conditions of demand and supply. The notion that supply is never heard of again suggests that you think that I, like yourself, throw over all my fundamental economic principles when I come and study fluctuations [p. 514].

Now, whether Keynes was fully justified in claiming so much for himself is perhaps open to question; whether his indictment of Robertson was valid is still more doubtful; but I believe that if he could make a judgment of contemporary economics, he would have very strong grounds for condemning us for throwing over "all (our) fundamental economic principles when (we) come to study fluctuations."

References

Johnson, H. (1975). "Keynes & British Economics." In *Essays on John Maynard Keynes* (M. Keynes, ed.). Toronto: Macmillan, 1975.

Keynes, J. M. (1930). A Treatise on Money. In 2 vol. Macmillan & Company, London, 1930.

Keynes, J. M. (1936). *The General Theory of Employment, Interest and Money.* New York: Harcourt.

Keynes, Milo (ed.) (1975). Essays on John Maynard Keynes. Cambridge Univ. Press. Cambridge, 1975.

Leijonhufvud, A. (1968). On Keynesian Economics and The Economics of Keynes. Oxford, 1968. New York.

Meade, J. (1975). The Keynesian Revolution. in Milo Keynes (1975).

Moggridge, D. (1975). The influence of Keynes on the Economics of his Time (in Milo Keynes).

Moggridge, D., ed. (1973). *The Collected Writings of John Maynard Keynes,* Vol. 13, The General Theory and After, Part 1, Preparation. London–Edinburgh: Macmillan–St. Martin's Press.

Patinkin, D. (1976). *History of Political Economy* **8,** No. 1 (Spring, 1976).

Patinkin, D. (1977). The Aggregate Supply Function: A Correction, *History of Political Economy* **8,** No. 1 (Spring).

Robinson, J. (1975). What has become of the Keynesian Revolution? In Milo Keynes (1975).

Scarborough College
West Hill, Ontario, Canada

Money and the Money Wage Rate

Paul Wells

1. Introduction

In Chapter 17 of *The General Theory,* Keynes advanced the wholly new and difficult to accept proposition that *sticky money wages are an essential property of money.* In spite of the profound and far-reaching implications Keynes's hypothesis would have for both economic theory and public policy if true, few economists have taken much interest in this question.[1] As a result, this potentially powerful contribution to economic theory has been wasting away in limbo for 38 years, not sufficiently alive to threaten the accepted view regarding the theoretical and practical desirability of freely flexible money wages and prices, but not sufficiently moribund to

[1] Aside from Lerner (1953), Davidson (1969), Robinson (1961), Kaldor (1960), and Weintraub (1978), few economists have allowed themselves to be troubled by Keynes's insight.

be of no concern whatsoever to some economists. To help repair this regrettable lack of interest, and to call attention to the need for more research on the subject of sticky versus freely flexible money wages, this paper will render a brief analysis in support of Keynes's contention. My aim in doing so is not to settle this issue once and for all, for the question being examined is far too complex and too important to be left to one paper or one writer. Rather, my purpose is to provide a preliminary analysis of Keynes's argument in the hope that more work will follow.

The support for Keynes's remarkable assertion rests largely on the contentions that (a) the money wage rate is the *numéraire* of the monetary system, and (b) a flexible *numéraire* would cause the value of money to flex randomly, which, in turn, would destroy the usefulness of money both as a store of value and as a medium of exchange.

2.   The Money Wage Rate as the *Numéraire*

The argument in support of the money wage rate being the *numéraire* of the monetary system begins with the observation that not only are labor services used in the production of every single good and service the economy provides, but that these services are the only currently paid-for input common to the production of all goods. In view of the universal use of labor, it follows that the cost of labor plays a dominant role in determining the overall level of costs of production and hence prices of any modern money using production–exchange economy. Other things being equal, every rise or fall in the money wage rate will produce a responding rise or fall in all costs and in all prices. From this perspective, it can be seen that the money wage rate is not simply one price embedded in a system of many prices. It is not just another price of another good; a price coequal with all other prices, not just another price for another auctioneer to call out. The money wage rate is the anchor price of the economy. It is the price which positions the economy-wide level of costs, prices, incomes, and expenditures. In brief, the money wage rate is the *numéraire* of the economic system simply because it is the predominant determinant of the value of money.

The broad overall impact on the cost–price structure produced by a change in the money wage rate may be contrasted with the strictly local effects produced by, say, a rise in the price of artichokes. Here, the prices of some small number of substitutes may rise and the prices of some complements may fall. In any event, no change in the value of money will take place. No all-pervasive change in the level of costs, prices, incomes, and expenditures will follow a change in the price of artichokes. To take another example, suppose now the price of a more generally utilized factor, say steel, were to rise for some reason not connected with a change in the money wage rate. Here, the costs and prices of many products would rise, and perhaps the value of money would fall. But in comparing labor services with steel, the *numéraire* property of the money wage rate emerges when it is recognized that because of the more universal use of labor, a given percentage rise in the wage rate will produce a more universal rise in costs and prices and, hence, a greater percentage fall in the value of money than would an equal percentage rise in the price of steel.

3. Money and Sticky Prices

Having established the *numéraire* property of the money wage rate, Keynes went on to argue that money could not function either as a medium of exchange or a store of value if wage rates, costs of production, prices, incomes, and expenditures were to rise and fall—frequently and unpredictably—in response to the randomly intermittent appearances and disappearances of excess supplies of labor, commodities, and finance that characterize modern economic systems. Since the utility of money "is solely derived from its exchange value" (Keynes, 1959, p. 231), the services money provide can be rendered "only if there is sufficient stability in its purchasing power in buying the goods that it represents" (Lerner, 1953, p. 383). Accordingly, thoroughgoing wage and price flexibility of the type envisaged by many present-day economists would destroy a money's purchasing power, and so render it useless both to the buyers and sellers of goods and services and to the lenders and borrowers of finance. In Lerner's words, "Any money which was completely cured of wage and price rigidity would not be able to survive as money [p. 385]."

The reason a money cannot long survive if its value is subject to frequent random variations is that such fluctuations would destroy its general acceptability. Why this is so can be seen if we remember that in order for an object to function as money, it must, at base, be capable of discharging claims on demand without imposing a capital loss on either party to a transaction. Thus, sellers will accept money in return for the goods they supply only if the dollars they receive have approximately the same value as the dollars they spent producing output; only if the value of the dollars they earn match the value of the dollars which were used to denominate their liabilities. Viewed this way, the probability of unpredictable upward movements in the value of money would erode its acceptability simply because such downward turns in prices would make it nigh impossible for even the best managed of firms to cover their recently incurred operating costs out of current receipts. Production, buying, selling, using, indeed all activity, require time: Time to plan, time to initiate, and time to carry out. The planning, carrying out, and realization of economic activity would be greatly disrupted by random upward flexes in the value of money.

A fall in the general price level, no matter when or how frequently it occurred, would always occur between the time expectations were formed, plans made, resources contracted for, production carried out, and costs recovered. A downward flex in the price level would make it near impossible for businesses to relate or establish a correspondence between the money value of even just-suffered operating costs and the money value of current receipts. In general, because of the time dimension inherent in all economic activity, a flex up or down in the value of money would expose buyers and sellers to random capital losses. The possibility of suffering random capital losses which a system of flexible prices entails would therefore make it extremely hazardous for the public to conduct their economic activities in terms of money; in terms of a money that is unstable at any price level. Rather than tolerate such a dangerously vagarious money, the public would search for and find, or if necessary invent, a less speculative, surer standard of value and medium of exchange. Slowly or quickly, a stable money would be found that would enable the public to conduct their economic affairs in some more rational fashion in the face of the ordinary day-to-day risks and uncertainties inherent in life.

The possibility of sudden upward movements in the price level would have an equally destructive effect on the acceptability of money. The contract practice of specifying in money terms the prices of goods and services in advance of their delivery, and in advance of their payment, would expose sellers to the possibility of capital losses. For example, a fall in the purchasing power of money between the time wage rates are agreed upon and labor services delivered, and the time wages are received and income spent, would break the link between the value the market places on labor services at the time wages are determined and the value labor actually receives for its services. In these circumstances, the practice of quoting wage rates in straight money terms would soon be abandoned. More generally, suppliers of goods and services will quote prices, accept payment, and incur obligations in terms of money only if there is some close correspondence between the value of money at the time obligations are made and the time they are satisfied—between the time income is earned and income is received and spent, or between the time debts are run up and debts are repaid.

In addition, a money whose value could fall by several percent in the course of a week, and then could fall again, or perhaps rise, depending on the current balance between aggregate supply and demand, would be of little use to borrowers and lenders alike. Businesses would cease borrowing money to finance capital spending simply because in such circumstances they would not be able to calculate either the direct money costs of their prospective capital projects or the expected yield their spending might return. The link between current capital outlays and prospective yields is highly tenuous under the best of conditions, but if the value of money were subject to erratic change, this already fragile nexus would disappear altogether. Furthermore, few businesses would be willing to issue debt and commit themselves to making fixed money payments whose real value would be a random variable. As for lenders, they would find that stocks, bonds, savings accounts, pension funds, and just plain cash balances would no longer be satisfactory stores of value. In a world in which the value of money could flex up and down, money would not be borrowed, lent, or stored—it would not be used. Instead of promoting full employment, overall wage and price flexibility would simply destroy the utility of money.

It has been argued, however, that a flexible price system in which all money wages and all prices rise and fall by equal percentage amounts would not impair the utility of money. But, surely, no economist who has studied the behavior of individual prices could accept this contention for the obvious reason that it is not possible for all prices to flex simultaneously by equal percentage amounts in any real economy. Lerner (1953) saw this clearly when he wrote,

> Unless we are to suppose away the whole universe, we will have different arrangements in different cases for making the appropriate abrogations of contracts. We will have different degrees of the influence of custom in different parts of the economy. Some prices will therefore fall much more than others. There will be injustice and chaos. . . . Everything will be in disorder and nothing predictable—except perhaps one thing: that the public will not stand for a continuation of such disturbance and injustice. No matter what else they retain in their social order they certainly will not retain the monetary unit. It will have been rendered quite unfit to do its main job [p. 384].

4. Sticky Money Wages

What has been argued is that in order for money to function as a standard of value and a medium of exchange, the value of output as a whole must be sticky in terms of money. But for the value of output to be more or less stable in terms of money, sticky money wage rates are essential. This is because (Davidson, 1969) the "money wage-rate is a ubiquitous component of the flow–supply prices of commodities and that labor costs are uniquely related to short-run market prices [p. 319]," so that, "If wages are sticky in terms of money, then the short-run supply price . . . of output will . . . vary only with the law of diminishing returns in the short run, and changes in productivity in the long run [p. 316]." The money wage rate, then, is the *numéraire* of the monetary system, and to have a stable *numéraire*, sticky money wages are essential. Sticky wage rates imply sticky costs of production and a relatively stable value of money. With these conditions holding, economic plans can be drawn up, wage and other contracts specified in money terms, costs calculated, and prices determined all on the assumption that a generally acceptable stable money obtains.

We can now better understand Keynes's (1959) observation that, "To suppose a flexible wage policy is a right and proper adjunct of a system which on the whole is one of *laissez-faire*, is the opposite of the truth [p. 269]." For some decades our monetary system has been secure from the threat of downward wage and price flexibility, and this has been all to the good. What is not all to the good is the fact that society still remains exposed to the danger of rapid upward movements in money wages and prices.

References

Davidson, P. (1969). A Keynesian View of the Relationship between Accumulation, Money, and the Money Wage Rate, *Economic Journal* **79**, 300–323.

Kaldor, N., ed. (1960). Keynes' Theory of the Own Rates of Interest, *Essays on Economic Stability and Growth*, Chapter 2. London: Duckworth.

Keynes, J. M. (1959). *The General Theory of Employment, Interest, and Money*. London: Macmillan.

Lerner, A. P. (1953). *Essays in Economic Analysis*. London: Macmillan.

Robinson, J. (1961). Own Rates of Interest, *Economic Journal* **71**, 596–600.

Weintraub, S. (1978). *Capitalism's Inflation and Unemployment Crisis*. Reading, Massachusetts: Addison-Wesley.

Department of Economics
University of Illinois
Urbana, Illinois

ECONOMIC THEORY, ECONOMETRICS, AND MATHEMATICAL ECONOMICS

Consulting Editor: Karl Shell

UNIVERSITY OF PENNSYLVANIA
PHILADELPHIA, PENNSYLVANIA

DATE DUE

GAYLORD

PRINTED IN U.S.A.